THE TEACHING OF GEOGRAPHY IN SECONDARY SCHOOLS

(ISSUED BY THE)
INCORPORATED ASSOCIATION OF
ASSISTANT MASTERS IN
SECONDARY SCHOOLS

FIFTH EDITION

CAMBRIDGE
AT THE UNIVERSITY PRESS
1967

Published by the Syndics of the Cambridge University Press
Bentley House, 200 Euston Road, London, N.W. 1
American Branch: 32 East 57th Street, New York, N.Y. 10022

This edition © Cambridge University Press 1967

Library of Congress Catalogue Card Number: 67-12846

Memorandum on the Teaching of Geography

First Edition January 1935
Second Edition May 1939
Reprinted December 1946

The Teaching of Geography in Secondary Schools

Third Edition September 1952
Reprinted February 1954
Fourth (Interim) Edition March 1956
Reprinted April 1958
Fifth Edition 1967

Printed in Great Britain
at the University Printing House, Cambridge
(Brooke Crutchley, University Printer)

CONTENTS

iii

CONTENTS

LIST OF ILLUSTRATIONS

PLATES

FOREWORD

The Teaching of Geography was first published in 1935 and since then there have been three new editions and five reprints of existing editions.

A new committee has now carried out a complete revision of the whole work, taking into account recent developments in Secondary education and new techniques in teaching the subject. It is hoped that this fifth edition also will achieve a wide circulation and exert an important influence on the theory and practice of the teaching of Geography in Secondary schools of all types.

In the preparation of this book the Association has again had the good fortune to be able to draw on the devotion, knowledge and experience of many members and friends to all of whom it expresses its grateful thanks.

A.W.S.HUTCHINGS

May 1967

Secretary, Incorporated
Association of Assistant
Masters in Secondary Schools

THE CENTRAL COMMITTEE

D. J. Cadman
Stratton School, Biggleswade, Bedfordshire

R. Cole
Formerly of T. P. Riley School, Bloxwich, Walsall

L. H. Elliott
Latymer Upper School, Hammersmith, London, W. 6

W. C. Middlebrook, *Editor*
Nottingham College of Education, formerly of Bancroft's School, Woodford Green, Essex

J. C. Parrack, *Chairman*
Leek High School, Leek, Staffordshire

T. W. Randle, *Secretary*
Penistone Grammar School, near Sheffield, Yorkshire

R. A. Ransome
The Grammar School, Chipping Norton, Oxfordshire

W. N. Teale
Nantwich and Acton Grammar School, Cheshire

A. Walker
The Padgate College of Education, Fearnhead, near Warrington, Lancashire, formerly of Ashburton Secondary Boys' School, Croydon, Surrey

R. G. Willetts
Whitchurch Grammar School, Cardiff, Glamorgan

LIST OF CORRESPONDING MEMBERS

J. Ashton
Formerly of Wirral Grammar School for Boys, Bebbington, Cheshire

G. F. Baker
Huish's Grammar School, Taunton, Somerset

J. R. Bartlett
St Julian's High School for Boys, Newport, Monmouthshire

D. C. Berresford-Williams
Exmouth Grammar School, Devonshire

P. Bryan
Cambridgeshire High School for Boys, Cambridge

D. D. Brumhead
College of Adult Education, Manchester 2

D. J. Butterworth
Woking County Grammar School for Boys, Surrey

B. Carlson
Bilborough Grammar School, Nottingham

J. H. Chapman
Leek High School, Leek, Staffordshire

R. P. K. Clark
Ford Castle, Berwick-on-Tweed, Northumberland

D. W. Cloke
Crownhill School, Plymouth

J. R. Cooper
Formerly at Howardian High School, Cardiff

J. Corley
Braintree County High School, Essex

C. E. Crawford
Crewkerne School, Crewkerne, Somerset

S. St Clair B. Crawford
Grammar School, Ripon, Yorkshire

J. A. Dawson
Quarry Bank High School, Liverpool

A. L. Dennison
Kingston High School, Hull

G. A. Dunn
Truro County Grammar School for Girls, Cornwall

G. S. Easton
Dinnington Secondary School, near Sheffield

B. J. Edwards
Queen Mary's Grammar School, Walsall

J. I. V. Ennis
Epsom College, Surrey

J. A. Evans
Ilford County High School for Boys, Essex

G. V. Fancourt
Royal Grammar School, Colchester, Essex

D. G. Ferguson
Leyton County High School for Boys, London, E. 10

M. Gray
Formerly at Brookfield Comprehensive School, Kirkby, Liverpool

L. H. Hadlow
Burnage Grammar School, Manchester

A. D. Hammersley
Formerly at Barrow-in-Furness Grammar School for Boys, Lancashire

P. J. Hart
Formerly at Ifield Grammar School, Crawley, Sussex

T. Hodgson
Formerly at King James I School for Boys, Bishop Auckland, Co. Durham

D. Holly
Croesyceiliog Grammar School, Monmouthshire

G. H. Hones
Harvey Grammar School, Folkestone, Kent

R. W. A. Hope
Beaufort School, Bournemouth, Hampshire

E. A. Hutchinson
Henry Mellish School, Bulwell, Nottingham

J. Inch
Wufrun College of Further Education, Wolverhampton

R. W. Jackson
Ysgol Dyffryn Nantlle, Penygroes, Caernarvonshire

L. V. Kelly
Grammar-Technical School, Barry, Glamorgan

H. Mountford
Simon Langton Boys' School, Canterbury

W. A. Moyes
A. J. Dawson Grammar School, Wingate SO. Co. Durham

D. Ord
Pelham County Secondary School, Wimbledon, London, S.W. 19

W. A. G. Pace
City of Leicester Boys' School, Leicester

R. E. Parkinson
White House Grammar School, Brampton, Cumberland

R. Parsons
Grammar-Technical School, Caerphilly, Glamorgan

R. G. P. Perry
Friends School, Saffron Walden, Essex

T. Procter
Bushey Grammar School, Hertfordshire

W. D. C. Rees
The Grammar School, Rhyl, Flintshire

D. Riley
Thornbridge School, Sheffield 12

J. I. Robinson
Hamond's Grammar School, Swaffham, Norfolk

T. S. Rowland
High School for Girls, Douglas, I.O.M.

R. M. Sheldon
Formerly Worsley Wardley Grammar School, Swinton, Lancashire

R. E. H. Smith
Coloma Teachers' Training College, West Wickham, Kent

P. S. Southern
Nelson Tomlinson Grammar School, Wigton, Cumberland

J. Spurway
The Grammar School for Boys, Falmouth, Cornwall

L. M. Stamp
Strodes School, Egham, Surrey

P. W. E. Stowe
Rickmansworth Grammar School, Hertfordshire

E. J. Tatford
Portsmouth Technical High School, Hampshire

A. J. Thomas
Barry Grammar–Technical School, Glamorgan

I. F. Tilbrook
The Grammar School, Chipping Campden, Gloucestershire

G. A. Vincent
Trinity School of John Whitgift, Croydon, Surrey

R. A. L. Whitaker
Salford Grammar School, Lancashire

H. C. Wilks
George Green's School, London, E. 14

NON-MEMBERS WHO HAVE CONTRIBUTED

R. Allison
College of St Mark and St John, London

Miss M. Bates
Rockingham Road Secondary School for Girls, Kettering, Northamptonshire

T. W. Brown
Headmaster, King's School, Gloucester

Miss M. Crawford
Rutherford High School, Newcastle upon Tyne

F. F. Cunningham
The Simon Frazer University, British Columbia

E. Evans
Department of Geology, National Museum of Wales, Cardiff

C. E. Fitchett
College of St Mark and St John, London

L. J. C. Hodge
Formerly Sheffield City Grammar School

J. James
The Principal, College of Further Education, Barry, Glamorgan

P. Johnson,
National Audio-Visual Aids Centre, London, S.E. 27

Mrs D. Martin
Copnor Modern Girls' School, Portsmouth

R. W. Pepper
Eltham Green School, London

Dr H. Robinson
Regional College of Technology, Huddersfield, Yorkshire

A. G. Terry
Latymer Upper School, London, W. 6

D. B. Walshaw
Northgate Grammar School for Boys, Ipswich, Suffolk

PREFACE

Many of the changes in the structure of Secondary education in Britain provided for in the Education Act of 1944 have now become a reality. The freedom which our education authorities enjoy to place their own interpretation on the various clauses of the Act has led to considerable diversity among the Secondary schools in different areas of the country. In whatever ways local schemes differ from one another in detail, however, the accepted and inescapable fact is that Secondary education now means the education of virtually all children between the ages of 11 and 15 years and of smaller though increasing numbers up to the ages of 16, 18 or 19 years.

The present committee was therefore confronted with a situation radically different from that in which the pre-war editions of this book were prepared and also different in many ways from that during the period when work was proceeding on the preparation of the third edition. Up to the time of publication of that edition in 1952 most education authorities had adopted the 'tripartite' system of Secondary education recommended in the Spens Report of 1939. Before 1952 the amount of specialist teaching of Geography in Secondary Modern schools was much more limited than it has since become, while in the few Secondary Technical schools the position of Geography did not differ markedly from that in the Grammar schools. Comprehensive schools had been started by some authorities but were in their infancy, and there was little experience of their problems of teaching organisation or syllabus construction on which to draw. The committee of that time therefore adopted the wise course of bringing the material of the second edition thoroughly up to date and of adding currently relevant matter, including a chapter on the teaching of Geography in the Secondary Modern school.

Circumstances have now changed greatly, and as a result a more drastic revision than any previously carried out has clearly become imperative. The present committee, appointed for this purpose and representative of Comprehensive, Modern, Bilateral, Grammar and Independent Secondary schools scattered about the country, has received much indispensable information and advice from many other members of the Association who volunteered to act as corresponding members. In addition, several non-members of the Association have given most valuable assistance. In accordance with the collective views of both Central Committee and correspondents, modifications have been made in the arrangement of the chapters and, to a greater extent, in their content. The purpose of the book is unchanged; it seeks to put the combined wisdom of many experienced and successful Geography masters at the service of all who have any kind of interest in the teaching of Geography in Secondary schools. The methods and the apparatus described are well tried and it should be readily practicable to make use of them in any properly designed and equipped Secondary school. The committee realises that many Secondary schools do not fall within this category and that in these cases teachers may, in attempting to follow the advice given, be compelled to improvise. While it is not claimed that improvisation is always or necessarily a bad thing, it is to be hoped that sufficient pressure can be brought to bear on the authorities concerned to eliminate the necessity for it so far at least as the essential elements of the subject are involved. In the Preface to the second edition it was stated that: 'In official circles the value of Geography is being increasingly recognised, and the Board of Education has officially sanctioned the construction of rooms specially designed and equipped for the study of Geography.' Unfortunately many education authorities did not at that time take advantage of this sanction, and even today, although officially approved plans for both the design and the equipping of Geography rooms are available, there are many Secondary schools without this provision, and many others in which the provision is inadequate.

The basic plan used in previous editions of the book is largely retained, but the greater part of the text has been entirely rewritten. Among the changes to which attention may be drawn are the inclusion of a number of syllabuses actually in successful use, illustrating several ways in which the requirements of Secondary school courses may be met; an extended section on the use of radio and television broadcasts; an introduction to the methods of programmed learning; and an entire chapter on field-work. Now that the General Certificate of Education has achieved a position of relative stability, in contrast to the speculation and controversy which surrounded its introduction in 1951, the whole subject of examinations has been restored to the main part of the book with a chapter to itself. There are still many uncertainties, of course, in the external examination field; the high hopes held out of beneficial effects from the Certificate of Secondary Education have not been unmingled with misgivings. Two other former appendix sections have been included as chapters in the new edition. That on the Training of Teachers has been enlarged and re-entitled 'The Geography Teacher', whilst that on 'Geography in After-School Life' has been completely recast as 'Geography and Careers'. Lastly it has been found possible to include once again a chapter on Geography Teaching in Overseas Schools.

Today the rapid and accelerating change so often spoken and written about is having and will continue to have a profound bearing on our subject. Many facets of this change are discussed in the book, but two perhaps call for mention here.

Almost every aspect of education has been the subject of recent enquiry and report. Perhaps the most noteworthy fact which emerges is that the two reports of the Central Advisory Council for Education (Crowther, 1959, and Newsom, 1963) both recommend strongly that the clause in the 1944 Act providing for the raising of the school-leaving age to 16 should be implemented not later than 1969 or 1970. Now that this recommendation has been accepted by the government, and assuming the age of commencement of the Secondary stage to remain as at present, all Secondary schools other than some Independent schools must devise five-year courses for the bulk of their pupils, starting in 1966. On the one hand, the uncertainties which at present bedevil the work of Geography teachers in Secondary Modern schools will very much reduced, and they will be able to plan their courses on a much sounder basis than at present. On the other hand, the fact must be faced that new problems and a new challenge have arisen. The universal five-year course cannot be successful if the fifth year is thought of by the pupils concerned as just an extra year's schooling to be endured. The building up of the curriculum as a whole, and the detailed planning and co-ordination of the various subjects within it, must be carried out with the world outside the school constantly in mind. Pupils must be helped to become citizens not merely of the world as it is but of an improved world which they themselves can make, if enough of them possess the knowledge, the desire and the will to bring this about. Properly presented, Geography has a big part to play in the achievement of such an outcome.

The other, and very different, facet of change on which comment is appropriate is the virtual disappearance of colonial empires and the concomitant rise of independent states, particularly in Africa and South-east Asia. From the geographical point of view it is clear that political and social factors are going to come more and more into the foreground as influences on the ways of life of these people. Geographical determinism, in so far as the controlling factor is physical environment, will, even in the less developed parts of the world, come to have less and less validity. We can still paint a broad and simple picture of the major natural regions of Africa; but within each region the contrasts are growing with variations in the development of political institutions and alignments, and with differences in the technical achievements of the inhabitants of the independent states which make up the region. The patterns and commodities of trade may also be caused to deviate from what may seem to be their natural forms in the same way as is already the case in Europe. These changes have begun inevitably to affect the approach to the teaching of the Geography of many parts of the world.

The committee is deeply indebted to Mr J. A. Morris, who read through the manuscript and offered much valuable advice. Whilst this has resulted in many improvements, the committee of course, bears full responsibility for any defects the book may still possess.

The grateful thanks of the Committee are also accorded to Mr T. W. Randle, who has carried out the arduous and exacting duties of honorary secretary with unfailing enthusiasm and judgement; and to Mr W. C. Middlebrook, who, as editor, has given ungrudgingly a great deal of his time to this responsible task, made no easier by the verbal idiosyncracies of the other nine co-authors.

J. C. PARRACK
Chairman

ACKNOWLEDGEMENTS

Among many individuals and organisations whose help has been invaluable, particular reference must be made to Dr T. W. Freeman of Manchester University and officials of the Durham and Birmingham University Appointment Boards for information in connection with the chapter on careers; to the B.B.C. and Associated Rediffusion for help with television and sound broadcasting topics; to the Secondary Schools Section Committee of the Geographical Association for access to its portfolio of Geographical Room plans, and also to the Principal of Nottingham College of Education for allowing the Central Committee to hold some of its meetings there.

For permission to reproduce photographic material we should like to thank the Council of Industrial Design; George Hunter, Toronto; the Lockwood Survey Corporation Ltd. (Toronto); the National Film Board of Canada and Photographic Surveys (Quebec) Ltd.

1

THE PLACE OF GEOGRAPHY;
HISTORICAL DEVELOPMENT
AND TRENDS

Geography now holds an undisputed place in the curriculum of virtually every Secondary school in Britain. This was not the case in the early decades of the present century, and the status which the subject now enjoys is a measure of the widespread recognition of its unique contribution to a complete education. Until a large measure of agreement had been reached on the content of the subject, and until it had been demonstrated that its study imposed an intellectual discipline comparable to those of the classics and the physical sciences, Geography was ignored by the universities. It is no matter for surprise, therefore, that it failed to appear in the time-tables of the older Public and Grammar schools. By 1900, however, two steps had been taken which paved the way for advance. First, a great deal had been done by enlightened pioneers to rid the subject of the vast unco-ordinated array of facts and place-names with which it had earlier been encumbered. Secondly, the facts and names retained were selected for the significance of their interrelationships. Thus Geography developed into a systematic school subject with a philosophy of its own. The progressive recognition of the subject during the earlier years of the present century as a subject suitable for the award of University degrees led not only to its becoming respectable in the eyes of the schools, but also to a steady increase in the number of qualified teachers capable of presenting the subject in an enlightened and inspiring way.

Apart from its establishment in a secure position in the academic world, however, Geography has come to play an increasing part in the thinking of people in general. Accounts of the great explorations of the nineteenth century no doubt led many people in all walks of life to become interested in distant lands. Participation in the world wars of the present century gave rise to a wider first-hand acquaintance with geographical facts and ideas, whilst the current great expansion in facilities for travel has occasioned even greater public interest in many aspects of Geography. This interest has been greatly stimulated by television, with its news items, documentaries and travelogues. Moreover, there is an ever-increasing recognition of the value of geographical training in promoting understanding of the modern world, in facilitating the vital tasks of planning and in affording guidance in relevant cases where governmental decisions have to be made.

The advances which have occurred in geographical thought and geographical teaching since the beginning of the nineteenth century have been associated with, and have to a great extent depended on, three main trends:

(i) the continued increase in factual knowledge of the earth's surface and of the widely varying stages of development reached by human communities in their differing environments;

(ii) the development of a scientific approach to the study of natural phenomena and their interrelationships, accompanied by the evolution of genuine geographical techniques, especially mapping and the use of statistical methods;

(iii) technical advances which, so far as the more developed countries were concerned, increased man's power to transform his natural environment, enabled him to live longer and more healthily and to travel farther and faster than ever before. More recent developments in geophysical techniques helped him to discover important resources in inaccessible parts of the earth's crust. Man's ability to exploit these advances depended on improvements in his recording techniques, the perfection of optical and photographical devices and most recently the application of electronics.

Bound up with the material benefits which follow from technical advance is man's vastly increased power to destroy. The Geographer cannot ignore the deep social and moral issues involved.

DEVELOPMENT IN THE NINETEENTH CENTURY

Throughout the nineteenth century there was a wide gap between geographical thought as expressed by explorers, scientists and philosophers, and the Geography which found its way into the vast majority of schools. Before 1870 elementary education was provided by the 'National' and the 'British and Foreign' schools and by a number of 'Dame' schools. Secondary education was in private schools, some of them endowed Grammar schools, others run on an entirely commercial basis. The Grammar schools in particular were concerned almost exclusively with the teaching of Classics whilst in the Elementary schools the geographical knowledge possessed by the majority of teachers was negligible. Thus, during a period when Humboldt, Ritter and Lavallee abroad and William Hughes and Mary Somerville in England were seeking and proclaiming the inter-relationships between the distribution and character of natural phenomena and those of man and his activities, such school Geography as there was consisted largely of learning by rote long lists of facts and generalisations having scant connection with any sort of reality or reasoning.

The following examples are quoted from Major's *Notes of Lessons*, published in 1875 and intended mainly for the use of teachers in elementary schools. The book consists of over two hundred 'object' lessons sometimes in strange haphazard sequence; e.g. in part of the Geography section: New Zealand, the Mauritius, Races of the North American Continent, Races of the Asiatic Continent, The Euphrates, The Mississippi, The Ganges, Ceylon, Belgium and so on.

EXAMPLE I. MOUNTAIN SYSTEM OF ENGLAND

Subject-matter

I. Different systems. (*a*) The northern, consisting of the Cheviot Hills, and Pennine Chain. The Cumbrian Group, running through Cumberland and Westmoreland. The mountains of Wales, or Cambrian Mountains. The Devonian range, in the county of the same name. The chief ranges of hills are: York Moors and Wolds; Essex and Middlesex Heights; East Anglian and Chiltern Hills; Cotswolds; North and South Downs; Dorset Heights, running through Dorsetshire. Cornish Heights. Clee Hills in Shropshire. Clent Hills, in Worcestershire. Mendip Hills, in Somersetshire, and Quantock Hills, also in the same county. Blackdown Hills on the borders of Devon and Somerset.

II. Description of each. (*b*) Cheviot Hills, highest Cheviot Hill, 2,670 ft, used for feeding sheep. Pennine Chain, begins near Cheviots, and ends at the Peak, in Derbyshire; chief heights, Cross Fell, 2,901 ft; Whernside, 2,284 ft; Ingleborough, 2,361 ft; and Penygant, 2,270 ft. Cumbrian Group, highest Sca Fell, 3,166 ft and Helvellyn 3,055 ft. The Cambrian Group, highest Snowdon, 3,571 ft. Devonian system, Cawsand Beacon, 1,792 ft. The Pennine Chain is intersected by deep valleys. The York Moors are bleak. The Wolds of York and Lincoln are high tracts of chalk, covered with beautiful grass, used as pasture-land for sheep.

III. Mineral wealth. (*c*) Present annual produce of coal in England is 120,000,000 tons; iron, 11,000,000 tons; clays, 1,020,000 tons (fine and fire); tin, 14,000 tons; lead, 100,000 tons; zinc ore, 13,000 tons; arsenic, 3,300 tons; ochres, 7,000 tons; copper ore, 160,000 tons, etc. Total value, £35,000,000.

IV. Drainage of: (d). In the north of England the waterhead is formed between the river basins of the opposite sides of the Pennine Chain. The sources of the rivers of the central, southern and eastern parts nearly meet, and are of trifling elevation. The rivers of Wales run south-east and north-east by the valleys of the Severn and Dee (e).

Method

(a) Point out different systems.

(b) Give descriptions.

(c) Show how important minerals are, and that they are mostly found in mountainous districts.

(d) Point out drainage and value.

(e) Question and summarise.

EXAMPLE II. NEW ZEALAND

Subject-matter

I. Situation. (a). South-east of Australia. Breadth varies, average 150 miles, length 1,100 miles, area 99,500 square miles, or one-fifth more than Great Britain. Population in 1871, whites 256,393, natives (Maories) 38,540, total 294,933. Discovered by Tasman, a Dutchman, in 1642 and in 1777 by Captain Cook. Colonised in 1839 by England. Coast line 3,000 miles long.

II. Mountains. (b). Mount Egmont, 8,270 feet high, North Island. Tongariro, an active volcano. Mount Cook, highest in New Zealand, 13,200 ft high. Mount Edgecumbe near Bay of Plenty. These islands are mountainous, with long valleys running between the mountains, which rise in terraces above each other.

III. Rivers. (c). In the North Island, Waikato, Wanganui, and the Mana-watu upon the western coast. Hutt, flows into Port Nicholson; Wai-ho or Thames, on the east. In the South Island, Wairau, Molyneux, Buller, and Grey. Rivers are numerous, and are fed by the snows of the mountains, they are rapid, and only fit for navigation for a few miles from their mouths.

IV. Productions. (d). Climate resembles England. Vegetables mostly introduced from Europe—ferns, trees (pines), flax, sweet potato, wheat, etc. Animals: marsupials, and rat, mice, hog, dog. People: British, and natives, the latter are the most intelligent of coloured races. Minerals: gold in abundance, coal, lead, sulphur, alum, arsenic, etc. There are numerous hot springs. The northern island seems to be of volcanic origin. Large quantities of wool sent to England.

V. Towns. (e). Wellington, capital. Auckland, the largest. Otago, famous for gold. Nelson, good farming district. Canterbury, one of the finest grazing districts in the world. Lyttleton, a port. Dunedin, peopled by Scotch. (f).

Method

(*a*) Show its excellent situation.
(*b*) Point out mountains.
(*c*) Describe the rivers.
(*d*) Give a brief sketch.
(*e*) Describe the towns.
(*f*) Question and summarise.

The recognition, during the greater part of the nineteenth century, of Physical Geography as a separate science allied to Geology but divorced from the human aspects (e.g. political and historical) of Geography, whilst it undoubtedly encouraged a more scientific approach to the physical aspects, nevertheless hindered the development of Geography as a unified subject. Thus the British Association in 1839 included Physical Geography with Geology in Section C, whilst the Universities of Cambridge (1848) and Oxford (1850) recognised Physical Geography as a separate discipline in its own right, a status withheld from Political (or 'Descriptive') Geography. A marked change of attitude late in the century roughly coincided with the ascent to prominence of Commercial Geography (associated with the names of C. G. Chisholm, L. W. Lyde, H. R. Mill, and A. J. Herbertson), which, as a result of its connections with both the physical basis and the grouping and activities of mankind, played an important part in welding the different aspects of the subject into a recognisable and acceptable unity.

By the time this unity was achieved the slow advance of the subject in the schools was at last showing signs of acceleration. This was due to a number of influences amongst which the most important were:

(i) The later developments of the 'Code'. (This consisted of regulations setting the standard for elementary instruction in various subjects, and was first imposed by the Committee of Council for Education in 1860.) Its effects on Geography teaching began to be felt in 1871, and from then until 1897 its syllabuses underwent frequent revision.

(ii) The interest in Geography teaching shown by Geographical Societies, especially the Royal Geographical Society (founded in 1830 to encourage exploration and discovery), the Manchester Geographical Society and the Royal Scottish Geographical Society (both founded in 1884).

(iii) The teachings of eminent scholars, in particular Sir A. Geikie, H. J. Mackinder, H. R. Mill and A. J. Herbertson.

(iv) The foundation in 1893 of the Geographical Association as a result of a meeting of Public school masters called by B. B. Dickinson of Rugby and presided over by Mackinder.

The association of the 'Code' with the notorious system of 'payment by results' led to widespread cramming and to the publication of many course books in the same vein as Major's, quoted above. Geography syllabuses, however, especially in the 1880s, were relatively enlightened and foreshadowed the modern approach, though their effects were felt only in the Elementary schools and even there did not quickly result in the introduction of enlightened methods. The Public and Grammar schools were completely untouched by the 'Code' and it was not until the early years of the twentieth century that the few prophets of the subject within these schools began to see some reward for their labours.

The efforts of the Royal Geographical Society to improve the teaching of Geography began in 1869 with a scheme for the award of prizes to be competed for by pupils at selected Public schools. This scheme continued for 15 years but did not achieve the hoped-for results and was abandoned in 1884. Of much greater importance was the enquiry carried out for the Society by J. Scott Keltie, into the teaching of Geography in England, in European countries and in the U.S.A. His report, published in 1886 and illustrated by a travelling exhibition of books, maps and apparatus, aroused wide interest and certainly demonstrated the woeful neglect of the subject in most Secondary schools and universities in this country. Though many effects of the enquiry were not immediately felt, an important one was the encouragement given to a small body of schoolmasters who shared the conviction that Geography was important and that, for it to be taught effectively, realism and coherence were essential.

The Royal Geographical Society, through its Honorary Secretary Douglas Freshfield, played a part also in the foundation of the Geographical Association, whose first Chairman was H. R. Mill, the Society's Librarian, and whose first President, four years later, was Douglas Freshfield himself. Mill, as well as Mackinder and Herbertson, played a very active part in the early work of the Geographical Association. In addition, by their writings and lectures on the philosophy and organisation of Geography as well as on methods of teaching it, they contributed greatly towards consolidating its reputation as a valuable educational instrument. In this connection a most important paper described as '...a classic document in the history of the development of British Geography', was that by Mackinder

'On the scope and methods of Geography', read to the Royal Geographical Society in 1887. Thus by the time the 1902 Education Act was passed a great deal of preparatory work had been accomplished, paving the way for the outlook and methods of Geography teaching of the mid-twentieth century. There were still, however, very few University schools of Geography, and only a tiny minority of schools had teachers with the new outlook and with a proper background of geographical knowledge.

TWENTIETH-CENTURY PROGRESS

Although not intended to indicate a teaching approach, Herbertson's paper 'The major natural regions; an essay in Systematic Geography', read to the Royal Geographical Society in 1904, is generally regarded as a landmark in geographical method. It was received with hostility at the time; yet his synthesis of climate, vegetation, animal and human life to produce a unified picture of each of his regional types has had a profound and enduring influence on the outlook of many geographers and on the approach to their subject in the schools. Before his death in 1915 Herbertson had modified details of his original scheme, whilst considerable research and a continuous accumulation of new knowledge have enabled workers to introduce further improvements. The principle remains, however, and although not unchallenged it still provides the basis for a great deal of geographical teaching.

In 1905 the Board of Education published new regulations and recommendations regarding the ground to be covered in a Secondary school Geography course, with valuable suggestions as to methods and apparatus. At the same time university and other examining boards issued new Geography syllabuses. Herbertson himself, writing in the Geographical Journal in 1906, warmly commended the Board of Education requirements for a four-year Secondary school course as 'a substantial mark of progress', though he criticised the absence of reference to human conditions—'people, their plants and animals, their industries and modes of life'—in the early stages. He expressed his view that 'the geographical teaching in early years should be concerned much more with human beings and their surroundings than with a logical presentment of so-called mathematical, physical and biological geography on the lines of the text-book of physiography. The best logical order is not necessarily the best pedagogical order.' In the same article we also find this small paragraph: 'That the Board should recommend field-work and excursions is a great matter, for many teachers who have not tried them declare that it is impossible either to find the time for them or to carry them out with profit. Competent teachers who have tried them tell different stories.' That was in 1906, and much more of the article could well be mistaken for a contribution to a mid-twentieth-century issue of *Geography*.

Yet on the whole in Secondary schools, Public and Local Education Authority alike, Geography was not at that time held in much esteem and was badly taught, largely by verbal methods. Little progress had been made in the universities, amongst which the only established Chair of Geography was that held by Lyde at University College London.[1] There was (in 1906) a School of Geography at Oxford and Lecturers or Readers in the subject at the London School of Economics and in the Universities of Cambridge, Manchester and Liverpool. Even, therefore, in schools where the desire for the enlightened teaching of Geography existed, it was difficult to find teachers sufficiently well trained in the subject to satisfy that desire. There were few, if any, headmasters and no inspectors with a geographical training; Geography did not figure amongst the subjects qualifying for the award of university scholarships; and Geography rooms with satisfactory equipment were virtually unknown.

That there were progressive and forceful personalities at work in the schools is evident, however, from writings and lectures published by the Geographical Association before and during the First World War. The universities were also stirring and it would seem that the tremendous burst of activity which awakened them in 1917 in spite of—or perhaps because of—the war, could no longer be restrained. From then until 1933 there was scarcely a year in which new University Geography courses, departments or professorships were not established. After a lull the process was resumed with full vigour in 1943, in the midst of the Second World War, and has now reached a stage where it is exceptional for a university in the United Kingdom not to possess at least one Professor of Geography. This tremendous expansion in the provision of university Geography courses has had several important effects on the Secondary schools:

(*a*) a rapid increase in the number of schools in which Geography is well taught, and in the number of pupils who are entered for it in external examinations;

[1] The Professorship which had existed since 1863 at King's College, London, lapsed in 1909.

(*b*) the recognition of Geography as an optional subject amongst those qualifying for University entrance, thus supplying heads of schools with an inducement to include it in their sixth-form curriculum. Moreover, although even now there are few entrance scholarships offered specifically in Geography, it is accepted as an optional subject for the purpose of Scholarship awards by most Universities;

(*c*) the increasing recognition by Local Education Authorities that the efficient teaching of Geography demands the provision of properly designed and equipped Geography rooms.

DEVELOPMENTS SINCE 1944

By the 1944 Act the term 'secondary' was redefined to apply to a stage of education and not to a type of school. In the re-organisation which followed the passing of the Act most Education Authorities developed their secondary schools on 'tripartite' lines; up to the middle sixties the greater part of secondary education was carried on in separate Secondary Modern and Secondary Grammar schools. These were often sharply differentiated in their attitude to Geography and in the accommodation, staffing and facilities for teaching it. During the past twenty years, however, it has become increasingly usual for graduate geographers to take up specialist posts in Secondary Modern schools, and at least in newly built schools Geography room facilities are now equal to the best in Grammar schools. In both types 'streaming' has up to the present been the rule rather than the exception, though the development of individual and team work and, in the larger schools, of 'setting', have reduced the disadvantages of streaming.

Comprehensive secondary education in one form or another was begun by some Authorities within a few years of the coming into force of the Act, and in many areas it may become the only kind available in the late sixties and the seventies. This development, together with the intended raising of the minimum school-leaving age to 16, confronts teachers in general and Geography teachers in particular with a challenge. Immediate steps must be taken to devise integrated five-year courses for pupils of all levels of ability; courses having close relationships, at all stages, with the world outside the school. In some well-established Comprehensive schools providing education for children between the ages of 11 and 18 streaming has been largely abandoned for teaching purposes except, perhaps, for the least able pupils. Children take their places in sets which vary in personnel

9

from subject to subject. Movement from one Geography set to another is made possible by using closely related syllabuses all possessing a common basis of essential material. Schemes of Comprehensive education are far from uniform, however; a great deal of experiment will undoubtedly take place for many years to come. Perhaps the most realistic impression of the present position in schools may be obtained from an examination of the amount of time allocated to Geography in the time-table and of the extent to which it is recognised as a subject for which special accommodation and equipment must be provided.

In the first place it is quite clear that in all types of Secondary school where pupils enter at the age of 11 Geography is taught to all pupils, usually for two or three periods a week, for the first two years—in the great majority of such schools for the first three years —of the course. In most Secondary Modern schools all pupils take Geography for the whole of the four- or five-year course. Most Grammar schools, however, have schemes designed to enable their G.C.E. candidates to concentrate in their fourth and fifth years on fewer than the full number of subjects of the curriculum. In a small proportion of these schools Geography is one of the G.C.E. subjects taken by all pupils; but even where it is not, judging by reports from schools and by the number of 'Ordinary' level entries, a high proportion of pupils do in fact study Geography for the whole of the five-year course. So far as the pupils who enter for the G.C.E. 'O' level examinations are concerned this problem of choice of subjects is the same whatever kind of school they attend; and the introduction of the Certificate of Secondary Education has extended the problem over an even wider range of pupils. There still remain, however, a considerable number of pupils in Secondary Modern schools, in Bi-lateral schools with 'Modern' streams and in Comprehensive schools, who do not sit any external examination. Not all of these study Geography but for the large number who do it must be presented as a fascinating practical subject designed to play a vital part in their education for citizenship.

The Independent schools call, perhaps, for separate mention. So far as educational problems are concerned their tradition of recruiting pupils at the age of 13 instead of 11, and of taking a very high proportion of them from Preparatory schools, differentiates them from the Maintained and Aided schools. The boys have only three years (often less if they are gifted) in which to attain the 'O' level standard. Unless Geography holds a strong position in the Preparatory school—and this is by no means the rule—there is little encouragement for them to take it as an 'O' level subject and, paradoxically, it is frequently the dullest pupils who do so. Thus, up to 'O' level, Geography still tends to be a 'Cinderella' subject in these schools, though there are brilliant exceptions.

In all types of Secondary school where education is pursued up to the age of 18 or 19 Geography is to be found amongst the subjects taken at 'Advanced' level, though the importance attached to it varies more widely in the Independent schools and in the Secondary Technical schools than in the Grammar and Comprehensive schools.[1] Whether it is included in an Arts or a Science course depends on the individual school; there are some schools where a pupil can take it in either. From the sixth form there is a regular flow of students to the Geography Departments of the universities, in most of which an Honours degree in the subject may be taken in either of the Faculties of Arts or Science. Many others enter specialist Geography courses at Colleges of Education.

It is inevitable in our present stage of development that the numbers of sixth-form pupils, particularly boys, studying Geography should be much smaller than that of those studying the standard sciences, and it should not be considered a matter for regret that this is so. It is somewhat disturbing, however, that in many schools (though by no means in all) the pupils of the highest all-round intellectual ability go almost automatically into the Science Sixth leaving the second and third best to be shared out amongst the several departments—frequently including that of Geography—on the Arts side. There is little justification for this bias, and those who share the responsibility for advising on the choice of sixth-form

[1] These are the most recent statistics submitted by the G.C.E. Boards:

Columns numbered I: Total number of candidates in all subjects
Columns numbered II: Total number of candidates in Geography
Columns numbered III: II expressed as percentage of I

Board	Ordinary level			Advanced level		
	I	II	III	I	II	III
Oxford and Cambridge	31,860	7,352	22·9	17,703	2,274	12·8
Welsh	25,167	8,306	32·9	6,619	1,160	17·6
Oxford	83,319	27,829	33·9	20,954	3,656	17·5
Southern Universities	8,786	2,480	27·4	1,750	301	17·2
J.M.B.	125,438	45,932	39·4	24,770	7,303	29·4
London	127,177	31,006	24·4	50,661	5,518	10·9
Total	401,747	122,905	30·5	122,457	20,212	16·5

subjects should aim to bring about some reduction in the proportion of really able students specialising in the Natural Sciences.

Two other matters give rise to some disquiet. First, the recognition of Geography as a practical subject requiring properly equipped laboratories and a great deal of storage space, has not proceeded as far as it should have done. When new buildings are erected a Geography room is nowadays almost invariably provided, but in large schools this provision and the equipment that goes with it are often inadequate. Although in a relatively few older buildings satisfactory conversions have been carried out there remain a large number with nothing better than an ordinary classroom reserved—though not equipped—for Geography teaching; and even this facility is not infrequently lacking. The position is in great danger of becoming more and more serious with the increasing tendency for pupils to stay longer at school and will, unless drastic action is taken by Boards of Governors and L.E.A.s, become catastrophic when the minimum leaving age is officially raised to 16. As it is, many teachers in all types of Secondary schools are prevented from giving their pupils opportunities of learning and practising essential techniques and of carrying out individual practical work. Moreover, where space and facilities are lacking, all but the really enlightened and enthusiastic teachers are encouraged to persist in laborious chalk and talk methods which rarely permit pupils to acquire any love for the subject.

The second matter, related to the first, concerns the position of field-work. Up to the Second World War it was exceptional for co-ordinated field-work to be carried out as an integral part of a school Geography course. Since that war more and more teachers have become convinced that field-work is the real foundation of geographical studies. This belief now finds expression in the syllabuses of even the more conservative G.C.E. examining boards, whilst all the C.S.E. Boards insist on the submission of course work based on first-hand practical studies. Yet many Education Authorities and some headmasters are reluctant to recognise that field-work is an educational necessity and is not just window dressing. Even among Geography teachers themselves there are many who, though paying lip-service to the importance of field-work, remain inactive in the face of the practical difficulties involved in carrying it out.

THE FUTURE

It is evident that, although Geography is firmly established in the Secondary school curriculum, the struggle must go on to secure conditions which will enable it to have its maximum educational effect. Success will depend on many factors apart from success in persuading the various authorities of its desirability. On the one hand there is the continuous development of more realistic ways of approaching the subject coupled with the rapid improvement which is taking place in teaching aids of all kinds. On the other, the school population will continue to increase for many years to come, and this increase may well prevent any improvement in the average teacher/pupil ratio. Some economies may be effected in the teaching of basic facts by programming, with or without the use of 'teaching machines'. Geographical education will in future be more concerned, however, with the development of methods of investigation which can be put into practice by pupils and from the results of which a number of important principles can be established. In this connection a great deal of thought will have to be given to the kinds of textbooks that will be needed, and the functions we shall require them to perform. The majority of school Geography books at present are primarily purveyors of facts. They vary in lucidity, in selection of facts, in suitability of illustrative material and in other ways. Some use ingenious devices to help pupils to remember facts. Most include exercises, usually designed to elicit facts, though in some cases requiring reasons for, or discussion of, facts which are given. These last surely point the way to the future pattern of textbooks, in which facts will be presented not as something with which to load the memory, but as material for scientific treatment and as starting-points for further investigation.

Reorganisation into larger Comprehensive units may perhaps facilitate arrangements for the use of films and of broadcast lessons, and may give scope for the use of closed-circuit television. Some proposed schemes of reorganisation, however, do not appear in themselves to alter the present position materially.

Basically, in the future as in the past, the quality of the Geography which is taught will depend on the devotion, skill and foresight of masters. Those responsible for planning the future pattern of secondary education must see to it that the conditions they provide are such that these qualities can be employed to the best possible effect.

2

THE AIMS AND SCOPE OF
SECONDARY SCHOOL GEOGRAPHY

The methods adopted by a Geography teacher will depend on his view of the scope and content of the subject and on his conception of the place it should occupy in a general scheme of education at the secondary stage. The wide range of ability of his pupils will also call for many variations of approach and technique.

THE MODERN CONCEPT OF GEOGRAPHY

It is not possible to define Geography in terms of a body of facts and ideas with which it is exclusively concerned. To a greater extent than most other subjects it draws on the results of widely ranging branches of learning. Where it is unique is in the manner in which it welds such results into an organised philosophy, seeing man in his true relationship with the landscape—partly natural, partly of his own creation—by which he is surrounded. Geography is essentially a dynamic subject, responding to the constant changes which occur in the world largely as a result of man's own continuous, restless search for more knowledge and more power, whilst at the same time relating these changes to the comparatively unchanging physical world.

The very vitality of Geography has led, however, to its somewhat erratic development, to recurrent controversy as to where the main emphasis in teaching it should lie, and even to disagreement concerning the nature of the heart and core of the subject. One difficulty has been that, whereas the facts of mathematical and physical Geography could readily be systematised, those concerned with the various aspects of human Geography have appeared to provide mere memory exercises. This divided concept of the subject, which powerfully influenced the manner in which it developed during the nineteenth century, is even now not completely dead. From time to time attempts have been made to base the syllabus on social or economic groupings of mankind, with little or no reference to those basic physical facts without which human societies and their industrial and trading activities cannot be fully comprehended. Today it is

14

widely accepted that Geography includes all these aspects but that it is particularly concerned with the different regional patterns to which, in various combinations, they give rise. The idea that man's distribution and activities should be regarded as his response to the physical (or perhaps the whole natural) environment tends to become increasingly irrelevant. The main argument against 'environmentalism', with which are bound up such abstractions as 'determinism' and 'possibilism', is, according to Hartshorne, that it is impossible to separate man from non-human nature; that man himself is a most important factor in the production of the characteristics which give personality to an area and differentiate it from other parts of the earth's surface. Although there are great differences of degree, there is no inhabited part of the world where the environment of present-day man is not to some extent man-made.

Division of the land surface of the earth into major natural regions can be effected in terms of only a very few variable factors, such as climate, natural vegetation, surface features, or combinations of these. Within each region so defined there is approximate homogeneity in terms of the factors used, though the lines of separation between regions are for the most part zones of transition. The main justification for basing major regions on climate is that it provides a broadly recurrent pattern consistently related to latitude and to situation with regard to a continental mass and its adjacent seas. Though no two regions in the world are climatically identical it is possible to recognise types within which the climatic elements are similarly interrelated.

Such regional divisions as these are generic types based on the integration, so far as this is possible, of a few universal criteria; between them they cover the whole land surface of the world. To most people, however, they are mere abstractions, having little reality and no personality. The majority of them are in any case too large to possess the latter quality. Subdivision into smaller, specific regions entails the introduction of many additional, often incompatible factors, notably man himself. We are helped to get this problem into perspective by Hartshorne's empirical definition of a region—'an area of specific location which is in some way distinctive from other areas and which extends as far as that distinction extends'. In other words we should study all the factors which give character to an area, be they geomorphological, climatic, pedological, agricultural, industrial, social, etc.—largely an analytical process—and try to discover relationships between them so that the personality of

3-2

the area may be built up. The distinction from an adjacent area will be found where changes in one or more factors produce a significantly different personality. Such a division of a country into smaller regions is bound to be subjective, depending on what factors are given most emphasis by a particular investigator; but so long as the bases of classification are made clear and the observations are sound this need not be a matter of great importance. What is clear is that this method of investigation gives us the best chance of understanding the similarities and differences between different parts of the world, the homes of different human communities.

The regional concept of Geography now commands wide acceptance, though agreement is not unanimous. No one would deny that imperfections and inadequacies exist in any regional system so far devised, but this does not invalidate the claim that the true aims of Geography can most nearly be attained by regional studies. Geography can of course be divided up into a number of branches, each of which is an appropriate subject for specialist study and research. Many important papers on narrowly based studies of, for example, Physical, Economic or Historical Geography have come from the universities or have been read before learned societies, and their conclusions are essential for up-to-date geographical work in schools. The extent to which a systematic approach of this kind, based, that is, on successive isolated aspects of Geography rather than on regions, is suitable for pupils at school will be discussed later. So far as research workers in one or other of the systematic branches of Geography are concerned, the chief danger to which they are exposed is, as W. Kirk has pointed out, that of being led to pursue the particular discipline so deeply that the study of its material becomes an end in itself. Such study may well contribute to our knowledge of some aspect of Physics or Biology or Economics without being of value to Geography. This problem was discussed very fully by Kirk

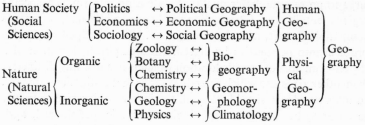

N.B. Historical Geography is the study of one or more of these aspects, at some date in the past.

16

in his article 'Problems of Geography' (*Geography*, Vol. 48, pp. 357–71). The table on p. 16 showing the relationships between disciplines is slightly modified from that given in Kirk's article.

SECONDARY SCHOOL GEOGRAPHY

Although environmentalism has been dismissed by many university geographers as irrelevant, it does not follow that it must be abandoned as a method of approach in schools. School pupils are not mature geographers and, as in other subjects, the vision of the subject presented to them must be in terms which not only excite their interest and stimulate their imagination, but right from the beginning enable them to see that definite relationships exist between the various facts which are established. In this light it may be stated that, for school purposes, Geography is concerned with the form of the earth's surface, with the distribution of various physical and organic phenomena over that surface, with the correlation of these phenomena and their effects on the distribution and character of human communities and their settlements. It deals with the opportunities offered by varied environments for exploitation by men, the ways in which these opportunities have been seized, and the resulting activities—the great variety of land uses, the development of mineral and power resources, the growth of manufacturing industries, the trade which has grown up between different communities and the means by which it is carried on. It aims at presenting a synthesis of all these factors for any recognisable region of the world and for the world as a whole. This synthesis is indeed the very heart of Geography.

The subject's essential tool is the map, an instrument unequalled by even the most graphic and erudite verbal description. For the presentation of such things as locations, distributions and correlations maps constitute by far the most important form of geographical shorthand. Training in both their construction and their interpretation is therefore an essential part of a geographical education.

The contribution of Geography to general education

The pursuit of the objects of geographical study mentioned above must be carried out in such a way as to benefit the pupils themselves by increasing their areas of knowledge and interest; and in such a way also as to help to equip them to form sound judgements concerning peoples and events in any part of the world. As important as the content and order of the syllabus are the outlook developed by a pupil and the methods by which he learns to carry out his own enquiries. The mere acquisition of facts for their own sake has little educational value. On the other hand facts which can be seen to have a place in a familiar pattern, especially if they have some relation to personal experiences, will be remembered without conscious effort.

We may consider the educational contributions of Geography under several headings:

(1) *The scientific treatment of observations.* Reference has already been made to the importance now being attached to field-work. Its special value lies in its introduction into geographical studies of a practical scientific approach by means of which the habit of acute and accurate observation can be stimulated with regard to the interrelated phenomena of the landscape, and the results subjected to the same processes as are accorded to other scientific observations. Field observations are recorded, a process in which the map plays a conspicuous part; different sets of observations can then be correlated and a conception of systematic relationships arrived at.

For practical reasons the amount of field work which can be carried out by any one pupil during his school course is very restricted, and for most of the time the material for observation must be supplied in other ways. Nevertheless, though it reaches the pupil in the form of pictures, statistics or verbal descriptions, these can still be subjected to the same kind of scientific treatment. Provided sufficient examples of a given relationship are encountered it will be possible for pupils to arrive at important generalisations, so much more valuable and meaningful when reached in this way than when provided ready-made as a first, rather than a last, step.

Since many of the observed facts are relevant to other subjects besides Geography, particularly the physical and social sciences, it will be possible to see relationships and to draw conclusions which are non-geographical. These may be perfectly valid, but there is no time to spend on them in a Geography lesson.

(2) *Historical perspective.* A fundamental lesson learnt from the study of Geomorphology is that the land forms of the present result from processes which have been going on for a very long time. Their existing shapes and positions are products of their histories, and they will continue to undergo change in the future. Though the time-scale is very different, the principle is equally fundamental when applied to such aspects of Human Geography as the sites of present-day towns, agricultural and industrial distributions, communication

systems and patterns of trade. Examples given in chapter 3 make it clear that the influence of the immediate physical environment in a given region may vary considerably from one period of time to another, depending very much on the course of history—itself bound up with changing economic conditions—in the region. Clearly, much Human Geography is deprived of its full meaning if historical factors are ignored; it is equally true that historical events and trends owe a great deal to their geographical settings.

(3) *Citizenship and international understanding.* Apart from the close academic links which give Geography its character as a 'bridge' subject between the Sciences and the Humanities, it has a most important part to play in education for citizenship. Geography is very much concerned with the factors which influence the outlook of different human communities. Biased attitudes to communities other than one's own can be, and frequently are, induced by un-scrupulous, tendentious or merely ignorant speech or writing. Those ignorant of the geographical conditions of other people's lives have little logical defence against specious claims made by plausible politicians, and little basis for thinking out sane and positive lines of action for improving their own lot or that of their fellow-country-men. Most of the important political questions of our day are world questions, and the narrow unreasoning patriotisms of the past pro-vide no answer to most of them and may well lead to international disasters. Effective citizenship demands vision which extends beyond local and immediate conditions and which can see that changes in those conditions may very well be associated with changes, perhaps in a distant country, in man's exploitation of his environment, result-ing in changed economic balance. Whether or not we believe that the political unity of the world can ever materialise, geographical knowledge and a geographical approach will make a most important contribution to understanding the development of our own and other nations.

(4) *Careers.* One of the purposes of education is to equip children to make their way in the world after they have left school. In this regard Geography can provide qualifications which will assist their holders to enter rewarding careers both in the public service and in private commerce and industry. The many openings for both graduate geographers and non-graduates with geographical training are sur-veyed in chapter 11. There it will be seen that there is a wide range of careers in which a knowledge of Geography is of value, though hitherto it has been a compulsory subject for only a few of them.

19

(5) *Enjoyment of leisure.* Even those who do not use Geography in the vocational sense gain the added purpose and interest which geographical knowledge can give to holiday travel, now within the reach of a higher proportion of the population than ever before. The significance of a great deal that is seen is much more readily appreciated if the geographical setting is understood. Even the simple ability to read a reasonably detailed map can add much pleasure to, for example, a motor tour by making it possible, first, to identify at least some of the features seen and, secondly, to get off the beaten track instead of being hemmed in by crowds.

In all these aspects Geography contributes to the general education of the future citizen. Probably its greatest value to the child, however, is that, drawing upon most of the other subjects studied in school, it integrates them, showing that they are not unrelated, but all play their part in an overall regional and national pattern. The ability to carry out this kind of integration will be of value throughout life.

SCHOOL GEOGRAPHY COURSES

In order to achieve the purposes for which Geography is taught the syllabus may be arranged on either a 'regional' or a 'systematic' basis. The advantages and disadvantages of these two patterns are fully discussed in chapter 3 and examples of syllabuses actually in use are given in appendix A.

From information supplied to the Committee it is evident that in the majority of schools the course is formulated on a regional basis. Where this is the case it is coming to be more and more realised that in order to arrive at a real understanding of geographical principles the number of regions accorded detailed study must be limited, and each one chosen must be studied more intensively and intimately than was customary in the thirties. This more intensive study does not necessarily entail the cramming of a lot more facts about the region as a whole though clearly all details which give it its distinctive character need to be understood. To help in achieving this understanding 'Sample Studies' are now widely employed (see chapter 4, p. 92).

In the Home Area a wide range of details in confusing abundance confronts the pupil. These details can be studied at first hand, but since many of them are trivial or irrelevant much guidance is needed in the early stages of the course to avoid waste of effort and to ensure a proper perspective. Such local studies are often used as the foundation on which to build up a geographical vocabulary as well as to establish the particular relationships which are encountered, though often not at first recognised, in this Home Area.

It should perhaps be mentioned here that the term 'Local Studies' as used above has a different meaning from that of 'Local Surveys'. The latter expression is generally understood to imply something in the nature of a large-scale project, frequently organised by more than one school department; and although geographical aspects are included others, such as historical, archaeological, civic or architectural, may well occupy a more important place.

Social Studies. Quite apart from survey work these latter aspects of human life are, in many countries abroad and in a few schools in this country, combined with Geography to form a subject known as Social Studies. This can provide a framework for building up a balanced view of mankind. Unfortunately there is no agreement on the content of a school course in Social Studies, and there is a danger that justice will be done to none of the aspects considered. In particular, as has already been pointed out, the social content of Geography has little meaning when divorced from the fundamental physical basis without which the geographical content of Social Studies will be incomplete and distorted. The Committee is not opposed in principle to a combined Social Studies course. It would emphasise, however, that if it is adopted sufficient time must be given to it to enable its component parts to be satisfactorily developed; it must not be used to economise on the time which would otherwise be spent on Geography, History and whatever other aspects of learning are included. The Committee also believes that real understanding of social problems demands maturer minds than those of pupils in the lower forms of Secondary schools. It is sounder to give a grounding in the separate subjects, leading to genuine social studies in the upper part of the school.

Pupils and courses

The pupils with whom we are concerned range from potential honours graduates to those who will always have grave difficulty in learning. Even if we exclude these extremes (both small minorities) the range of mental ability is very wide, and correspondingly different teaching techniques need to be employed. It should be said at once, however, that some direct observation of geographical facts is essential, whatever the capacity of the pupil. So far as the more gifted are concerned the words, maps and diagrams of textbooks and other publications enable them to form their own mental pictures of what is described, whereas the less able find it difficult so to convert these symbols even though the photographs included in most of these books may help in the process. But the limitations inherent in this kind of approach are evident if the impressions created by such a description of an accessible area are compared with those which are formed as a result of an actual study visit to the area. There is a world of difference between looking at a picture, even a large coloured picture projected on to a screen, and being able to move about amongst the objects which the picture portrays, to examine details at close quarters, to see things which are hidden in the picture and to experience the 'feel' of the place. Ability to benefit from field work and the necessary follow-up in the Geography room need not be correlated with i.q. however. The most intelligent pupils are not necessarily the only accurate observers, and good and valuable work may be expected from boys quite a long way down the intelligence scale. For many of these less able pupils, indeed, the field-work approach has proved to be the only one by which the subject can be effectively taught. In view of their natural handicaps the progress which they make as a result of this kind of work shows that the benefit to them is even greater than to their better endowed colleagues. It is necessary, of course, to ensure that the tasks set are not beyond the capacity of the pupils and that what they record is relevant to the purpose of the work. On the other hand, it is desirable that all pupils should be intellectually extended whatever their natural gifts, and that they should take pride in the work they have done.

Turning now to the Geography course as a whole, we observe that the differences for which provision needs to be made arise from two main factors to which attention has already been drawn. First, more ground can be covered and more complex relationships and principles can be grasped by the more intelligent pupils. Secondly, the length of the Secondary school course varies considerably. At the present time in Britain it may may be anything from approximately $3\frac{1}{2}$ years to 8 years; comparative conditions in selected overseas countries are given in chapter 12. The problems to which this variation gives rise are widespread, and, although there are no doubt differences of degree between one country and another, fundamentally all have the same difficulties to overcome. One of these is that generally speaking the less gifted children are the ones who pursue the shortest school courses. This problem of a shortened course arises, however, with another group consisting of pupils who will eventually sit external examinations in schools where some reduction in the number of subjects is imposed, usually at the beginning of the fourth year. Many quite gifted pupils may thus be limited to a three-year Geography course. Taking these into account, typical courses for which provision must be made, in one kind of Secondary school or another, will be:

(1) A 3½- to 4-year course for the bulk of the less intelligent pupils.

(2) A 3- or 4-year course for those pupils who drop Geography after this period of time.

(3) A 5-year course for pupils of moderate ability (e.g. preparing for C.S.E.)

(4) A 4- or 5-year course for brighter pupils preparing for G.C.E. 'O' level.

(5) Sixth-form courses (post 'O' level).

Non-selective schools of Comprehensive type need to provide all these courses; the larger ones, because of their size and the flexibility of their internal organisation, should find that the difficulties, though demanding some ingenuity, are by no means insuperable. Selective schools, on the other hand, have hitherto normally made provision for 'O' level and sixth-form courses only, though it is certain that in future the C.S.E will play an increasingly important part. For reasons mentioned above many pupils, in Secondary schools of all types, study Geography for only three years. If the subject is to play its proper part in their education the course must be constructed in such a manner that by the end of those three years they have acquired at least some integrated view of the world and some ability to apply geographical reasoning in situations where it is relevant.

Sixth-form studies, whether in Comprehensive or in Grammar schools, also present a number of problems. Ideally such studies should form an integral part of a seven-year course, but for mainly practical reasons they tend to be thought of, and arranged, as a separate two-year course in preparation for more advanced examinations. This is difficult to avoid since the main five-year course must be self-contained for the sake of the majority of the pupils, who will not make any further formal study of the subject. Such self-contained courses can nevertheless form a sound basis for the more specialised work of the sixth form. The geographical principles already learnt are still needed though they are subjected to greater scrutiny through the introduction of more difficult concepts. The developing maturity of the pupils and the greater amount of time available also permit the inclusion, in both systematic and regional work, of many details the relevance of which would not be easily grasped at an earlier stage.

23

Practical reasons, this time in the form of shortages of staff, accommodation and equipment, and time-table difficulties sometimes arising from the small number of pupils involved, also frequently prevent the organisation of more than one sixth-form Geography course —that for the specialists who are taking Geography as one of their 'A' level subjects. The interests of these pupils cannot be sacrificed; but as a result those of the non-specialists frequently are. Problems of sixth-form syllabus and teaching methods are fully discussed in Chapter 5.

Schools of Secondary Modern type, so long as they continue to exist, will also have many problems to contend with. Two-thirds of their pupils will not normally sit any external examination. On the one hand there are the G.C.E. and C.S.E. candidates who will take five-year courses in preparation for these examinations. On the other there are the backward pupils, for whom, in the larger schools, special facilities and specialist staff are sometimes made available. These groups have at least an obvious and well-defined aim in the courses they pursue. But the majority of the pupils, likely to leave school soon after the age of 15, not suited to take written examinations, sometimes finding difficulty in absorbing or fully comprehending what they read yet often surprisingly gifted over narrow fields, are entitled to an equal share of teaching time and use of facilities which the school possesses. Geography may well be among the subjects which can capture their interest and imagination. Syllabuses prepared for them must be flexible enough to provide for their varying abilities, and, in teaching, actual experiences combined with visual or audio-visual aids have a big part to play. Among the many aims for which Geography teachers are striving, one which has real relevance for these pupils is the inculcation of a sympathetic view of their neighbours, near and distant. This may be achieved in many ways, some of them far removed from orthodox classroom teaching; it may frequently demand that an unexpected opportunity, occurring as a result of some quite fortuitous happening, must be unhesitatingly seized.

Having indicated the aims and ideals towards which Geography teachers are working and drawn attention to some of the problems to be solved, we are now in a position to discuss the considerations which enter into their detailed application.

3

SCHEMES OF WORK

The syllabus must occupy a central position in the organisation of any Geography department. It is the pivot around which the work of the department revolves, translating educational aims into lessons in which the teacher and the pupil are brought into contact, and giving purpose and continuity to the course.

Some educational systems, such as those of France and the Soviet Union, provide schemes of work for the schools to follow; in a more loosely organised system such as that of England and Wales, the responsibility for devising a course of study falls upon individual teachers. Each syllabus must be developed from general principles and be so devised that it meets the needs of a particular school. In so far as each school is unique and situated in a unique environment, so must each syllabus be unique. With this in mind, this chapter is intended to provide a guide, though not necessarily a pattern to be copied in detail.

SOME FUNDAMENTAL CONSIDERATIONS

1. *The aims of the teacher*

The purposes which Geography masters strive to achieve have been discussed in chapter 2. Beside keeping these purposes in mind the master, in constructing his syllabus, is bound to be influenced by his own philosophy of life. A syllabus unilluminated by a point of view is likely to be little more than an arid list of topics or a scheme of mechanical exercises in teaching methods. On the other hand the master's own outlook should not be presented so dogmatically or inflexibly as to be liable to give offence to the parents of some of his pupils. He must always be prepared to state viewpoints which differ from his own, and to enable each pupil to develop his own honest attitude of mind. The only indoctrination which is permissible is that which inculcates a belief in the personal freedom of the individual to make up his own mind on controversial issues. The detailed syllabus can show the way towards this end though it is mainly in his actual contacts with the pupils that the master can ensure that it is fully attained.

2. *Essentials of the syllabus*

Many masters would now dispute the validity of the assumption that the syllabus should attempt to cover the whole world. The limiting factor of time allowed to the subject, the minor importance of some areas and the fact that several regions are similar in many respects are given as reasons for omissions. Whilst the Committee agrees that certain omissions are necessary and can give greater flexibility to the syllabus, it nevertheless feels that the practice of omitting whole continents is to be deprecated. Each of these large land masses has a unique contribution to make to the pupil's geographical education.[1]

It is perhaps better to look at the problem as one of greater or lesser emphasis than as one of inclusion or omission. Thus, if an area is thought to be worthy of but little stress, it might be relegated to forming a link between two more important regions. Alternatively, when a neighbouring or similar area is being studied, a wall display of photographs and maps might be arranged to highlight the main points of the less important area.

As a guide to the amount of emphasis required the following criteria might be found useful:

(*a*) The suitability of the area for illustrating geographical principles. An example of an area which may well receive more attention than would be warranted if it were not for this criterion is Chile. Here three major climatic types of western littorals are clearly shown;

---

[1] It is interesting to compare the minimum suggested by the Ministry of Education's *Geography and Education.*

'Pupils who are not unduly retarded should have studied at least:

1. Some geography in the field, locally and if possible elsewhere.
2. Some systematic geography, including the distribution over the world of land and sea, major elements of relief, climate and vegetation.
3. The geography of the United Kingdom.
4. The geography of certain regions outside Britain. It is desirable that the areas be chosen sometimes (*a*) in view of their current importance in the world; and it should be remembered that countries in the Commonwealth are always of importance to British pupils; (*b*) as examples of diversity of economic development; (*c*) as examples of past civilisations; and (*d*) simply because good reference literature is available or because the teacher himself is familiar with the area.

'And one would expect them to know also at least the position on the globe of those features which will enable them to take an intelligent interest in the world around them...even within this framework ruthless selection will have to be exercised if the syllabus is not to be overcrowded, so that schools working in the same areas under different conditions may still sometimes have differing syllabuses.'

the reasons behind the differences are such that they can be comprehended by boys; and the human responses are not obscured by too complicated a development of industry.

(b) The political, economic or social importance of the area in the modern world. There can be, for example, no excuse for the neglect of the Soviet Union which occurs in some syllabuses.[1]

(c) Previous knowledge of similar areas. Emphasis can often be lessened where similar areas have been previously studied. If, for example, the Sahara has been studied in detail there will be little need for more than a cursory revision of climate and landforms when other hot deserts are dealt with. When making a choice as to which of similar regions should be chosen for detailed treatment the teacher should take into account such matters as the availability of visual and other aids, his own special knowledge and the interests of his pupils.

Another solution to the problem of insufficient time, practised by some teachers, is to include all the major regions of the world, but from each region to choose only one or two vital topics. In the case of South-west Asia, for example, the whole of the work done might be centred on the oil industry.

[1] See 'The Regional Content of Secondary School Geography' by J. H. Jennings in *Geography*, XLVI (1960), part 4, dealing with the amount of time spent, in Yorkshire schools, on the major regions. The following table is taken from this article:

Time spent in studying the major world divisions, expressed as a percentage of the grand total of time

	All schools	Grammar	Modern
British Isles	28·4	25·8	30·5
Europe without Russia	15·5	15·8	16·3
U.S.S.R.	1·7	0·9	2·1
Rest of Asia	10·1	10·5	10·3
Africa	10·0	11·0	8·4
Australasia	10·1	10·2	9·6
North America	16·3	16·4	16·5
South America	7·9	9·3	6·2
Antarctica	—	—	0·1

A second table, showing the time spent on the different regions within these major world divisions, confirms the view that '...it is difficult to avoid the conclusion that the accepted priorities were quite inappropriate to 1960, even if justifiable a quarter of a century ago. The regional balance pertains to an era when the British Commonwealth meant primarily the white Dominions, before the power of the Soviet Union had been felt, or the people of China been counted and organised. Meanwhile the world changes, and at a rapidly accelerating pace; surely the question of what to teach needs a careful answer if geography is not to join history as a study set in the past.'

27

ORGANISATION OF MATERIAL

Introductory course

When pupils arrive at a Secondary school the level of their geographical knowledge may show some variation. In many Primary schools the children will have followed an imaginative and well-organised course; but because complete uniformity is neither possible nor desirable it may be necessary as a first step to bring them to a more or less common level of attainment, care being taken, however, not to destroy their enthusiasm. Though new techniques will be added and old ones practised throughout the Secondary school course, a particular characteristic of the first year will be the initiation of pupils into many of the basic skills of Geography. Much will be made of the understanding of maps, the recording of observed data and even such simple processes as colouring and printing neatly. Many of the commoner words and phrases of the geographical vocabulary will also be explained at this stage.

Unless this preliminary work is based upon the pupil's own experience and observation in the home district which he knows well, later lessons on places further afield will have only a vague and incoherent meaning for him. The ideas they pass on to him will be inert; lessons will be mere verbalism unrelated in the pupil's mind to real life. Climatic data, for example, will remain only series of figures until he has come to realise their meaning through his own experiences. He must record temperatures which he himself has felt; he must measure the amount of rain which has fallen in a storm which he has seen; he must feel the wind on his face before recording its strength in terms of the Beaufort scale. Similarly the pupil must, through his own observations, come to recognise the main rock types in his neighbourhood and to realise the intricacy of the work performed in the nearby factories and farms.

Since maps are such a distinctive and important feature of geographical studies it is essential that the pupil be led to understand them from the very beginning. In this, perhaps even more than in other aspects, a proper understanding can come only from work based on the home district. Here the pupil can refer from the map to reality and from reality to the map. Maps come to have an intimate connection with his knowledge of the area and thus with real life; they are no longer something to be thought of only as school equipment. As the result of simple experiment and practical work around the school the pupil will learn to state accurately the positions of features identified on the map; to orientate the map correctly, and to develop understanding of scale and relief. The syllabus should make provision for the drawing of maps to scale from the pupil's own measurements, and this kind of activity may well be combined with work using the Ordnance Survey maps of the home district. The 50 in., 25 in., 6 in., 2½ in. and 1 in. maps can each, in appropriate circumstances, be used to considerable advantage; the use of more than one of them for the same well-known area will make easier an appreciation of the meaning of scale. For giving locations, brighter pupils at least should be able to cope with the National Grid in their first year. The concept of the representation of relief on a plane surface is more difficult, but some understanding of the methods used is vital. Layer-colouring must be explained to all pupils, though so far as the Ordnance Survey is concerned only maps on the ¼ in. and smaller scales make use of this system over the whole country. It is, however, the method still used by most atlases and wall-maps. Contour lines will be dealt with at this stage by the brighter pupils, but for many it may well prove advantageous to leave the topic until a later year. Section drawing and the construction of simple relief models can help to avoid a good deal of confusion in the pupil's mind, though it may not be possible to spare class time for the latter activity.

The combination of local observation with written descriptions and map work will provide more help to the pupil in building up his geographical vocabulary and in giving realism to the words he uses. He will begin to learn the correct usage of words describing landscape—'undulating', 'gap', 'dip slope and scarp slope', 'rugged', 'rounded', etc.; and he will get to know by experience how long it takes him to walk a mile and how steep is a slope of one in seven—these concepts cannot be learned from books.

The local area studied will naturally vary in extent from school to school. The unit of study may be a natural one or an administrative one—a river valley, a parish or city. The selection will depend upon whether there are marked natural boundaries or a feeling of local unity.

Many syllabuses aim at extending the experiences of the pupils from the school locality to other parts of the homeland—in our case the British Isles. This extension of the area of study will again broaden the geographical vocabulary, giving real meaning to frequently used terms such as 'mixed farming', 'textile industry', 'steel making' and so on; terms which the pupil will meet many times in the ensuing years.

The treatment of the British Isles cannot, and need not, be comprehensive at this stage. It will consist rather of selected topics: a hill sheep farm in the Highlands, an arable farm in East Anglia, a mining village in South Wales, and so on. It will be largely descriptive, considering effects rather than causes, leaving more difficult analytical work to later stages. The amount of interpretation attempted will of course depend largely on the ability of the pupils.

Ideally, no doubt, the pupils would spend a week or a fortnight in another district offering marked contrasts with the home area as regards both physical conditions and human activities. Children living in an agricultural lowland would benefit greatly from a visit to a hilly industrial area. For most pupils, however, such visits will for long remain an unattainable ideal, and they and their masters must be content with short visits to areas within easy reach of the school. In spite of this restriction, the extension of the home district must not be neglected. Use can be made of contacts which many pupils may have with other parts of the country, though some will have little experience of travel even within Britain. A liberal use of visual aids can help to prevent misunderstandings which might otherwise last for many years; the larger-scale Ordnance Survey maps also will help to show the great differences between areas, for even at this early stage a pupil who lives in South-east England will find many contrasts between maps of his home district and those of the mountains of Wales or Scotland. Differences such as the large areas of rough pasture replacing the close pattern of field boundaries, the packing of contour lines and the many rock outcrops, the sparse population and a variety of other facts can be discovered. Many of them can be garnered even by less able pupils.

The descriptive treatment of the chosen topics has already been mentioned; the teacher must also be quite precise in giving details of the activities he is dealing with. It is not sufficient to refer to an industry in general terms; the pupils must, for example, come to realise the almost claustrophobic sensation of entering a coal mine, the dirt and grime, the boon of pit-head baths. All these are as much a part of the coal industry as the latest production figures. If such lessons are given at this stage they will lend reality to many lessons in the following years—whether the coal industry involved is in the United States or China or anywhere else. If his words are learnt by the pupil with no comprehension of their true meaning, the teacher would be as usefully employed standing in front of a class of parrots. Many teachers may feel that they ought to be making rapid progress at this stage, but they will find that time taken to ensure an understanding of terms which will later be in frequent use is far from wasted; blurred impressions instead of clear mental pictures result from a lack of this preparation.

The introductory course may be completed by the study of selected topics from regions overseas. There is a great variety of possible approaches—adventure and exploration, the pupils' food and clothing, the selection of contrasting regions and many others. As in the earlier treatment of the British Isles the centre of interest should be human activities; exhaustive study is unnecessary. The topics may be so chosen that their study serves as a background to any subsequent regional treatment of the continents. The positions of the selected areas in their respective continents are seen to be related to their general characteristics and 'personalities'. A knowledge of their relative positions on the globe and of the times taken on journeys from one to another can lead to an appreciation of world scales. A very important function of this part of the course must be to inculcate the habit of frequent reference to atlases. Geography teaching has moved very far from the 'gazetteer' or 'capes and bays' Geography of the nineteenth century, but it must not be forgotten that the subject deals largely with spatial relationships; it is essential that pupils really learn where places are.

An introductory course on the lines suggested above seems to be used in a majority of schools. In many cases it occupies the whole of the first year; in other cases only part of the year is taken, the main syllabus being started about half-way through the year. Below are two examples. The first was designed for the 'A' stream in a suburban Secondary Modern school; the second for a class of barely literate boys in the lowest ability group of the same school. The first syllabus occupies slightly less than a term and a half; the second, since the boys' background is so very much weaker, occupies the whole of the first school year. Each class has three periods of Geography a week—one double period and one single—and the 'A' stream has one homework period. The school works on an eight-period day.

'A' stream

Orientation and scales. Maps of desk top; the form room; part of the school locality. Study of the local 6 in. and 2½ in. maps. Orientation exercises on atlas scale maps of the British Isles and the World.

Representation of relief. Relief in atlas maps—layer colours; explanation of contour lines using sand pit and local O.S. maps, field exercises close by school where terrain shows clearly small valleys, spurs and breaks of slope. Exercises on duplicated contour maps; drawing contour maps from simple instructions.

In both the above it will be noted that the stress is on examples from the home district, and various aspects of the area can be discussed as they arise—Why is there a tunnel here? What does the factory make?

A Highland croft. The journey to Scotland—does the atlas tell us anything about what we shall see on the journey? What do the contours and conventional signs of the 1 in. O.S. sheet tell us about the region? The life of the farmer.

An East Anglian farm. Differences of farm locality from that of farm previously studied—use of O.S. maps for comparison. The farmer's year.

A Prairie farm. General map of Canada to show Provinces, main towns and the position of the Prairies. The work on the farm—contrast with the work on the farm in East Anglia.

A Saharan oasis. This offers a complete change of climate from the areas previously studied. The problem of water shortage—irrigation and how people live. Positions of the world's deserts.

A Malayan rubber plantation. Another striking change of climate. How the climate affects the people and their work. Uses of rubber in manufacturing countries.

A South Wales mining village. One-inch maps to show valleys, mines, iron and steel works; effect of relief on town sites and communications. Description of a visit to a coal mine; how iron and steel are made.

The basis of the choice of region here has been contrasts of environment. Relief, climate and mineral resources are all introduced as parts of the environment, in a sufficiently simplified form to be accepted by boys of this age. As stated above the main emphasis is on description.

After a brief period of revision the remainder of the year's work under this syllabus is developed along regional lines, beginning with Australia.

Backward stream

Direction and scale as indicated in the previous syllabus, though a greater allowance of time has to be made.

Representation of relief. This is confined to layer-colouring as used in the pupils' atlases, though when dealing with local O.S. maps spot heights and trigonometrical points will be indicated and correlated with the boys' local knowledge. Only if the subject arises spontaneously will contour lines be discussed, and then not to any depth.

Local Studies. Considerable time should be spent on the local district to ensure that the pupils are thoroughly familiar with it. There should be ample discussion of local factories, products and amenities, as well as of local relief and drainage features.

The remainder of the year's work is closely bound up with the work of the English Department. Since a large proportion of the form are barely literate, the work is based on easily read textbooks which describe journeys about the world. Reading and comprehension exercises largely follow the dictates of the English Department, though atlases are also in constant use in order that the pupils may attain a fair idea of the shapes and relative sizes of the continents and major countries. Though this work could degenerate into merely 'reading round the class' there is no reason why it should not be useful from the point of view of both the English and the Geography Department. The main aim is to assist the boys towards literacy; the subsidiary geographical aim is to give the pupils a sound idea of place, with perhaps some understanding of the people who live in the places about which they read.

Main course

Before considering more fully the order in which the bulk of the material to be used is best presented, certain definitions must be given.

Syllabuses are of two main types, Regional and Systematic. The former divides the world into regions (see chapter 2, p. 15), in each of which the various geographic aspects are studied as parts of the whole, and are integrated one with another. In a Systematic syllabus a single aspect of Geography is examined in a variety of regions. Thus a unit of study in a Regional syllabus might be the Prairies or China; in a Systematic syllabus it might be wheat growing. In schools where the Geography syllabus is of a Systematic type the approach most frequently used is that known as 'Concentric'. In this the aspect of the subject under discussion is dealt with in its closest relation to the pupil before being shown in its national and then in its world setting.

Sample studies, e.g. a detailed study of a single farm or factory, may be used with either of these types of syllabus.

The major portions of most syllabuses appear to be organised on a Regional basis, but there is frequently Systematic treatment of physical and economic factors in the last year, during revision. A small minority of teachers, however, use a completely Systematic syllabus, usually arranged concentrically.

Concentric and Regional syllabuses—rival claims. Advocates of the Concentric approach stress what we must all accept as a premiss— that the child is a person in his own right at every age, and that therefore we cannot maintain that the only value of a particular stage of development is as a preparation for a later stage. With this in mind the Regional approach is criticised as not giving a complete picture of any aspect of the world until the end of the fourth or fifth year, when the pupil leaves school. A Concentric syllabus, on the other hand, repeatedly encircles the globe through different topics of increasing complexity. The world is thus constantly being viewed as a whole, and the interrelationships of its various parts are therefore more easily followed. It is further claimed that when the framework is a Regional one a large region will all too often be taught in isolation, to be linked to the rest of the world for only a short period when its trade with other areas is dealt with. Supporters of the Concentric approach among the Committee's correspondents have made other criticisms which reflect upon the suitability of the region-based syllabus for use in schools. According to one correspondent 'regionalism is a very mature idea—I suppose one could say, the zenith of geographical thinking'. He therefore holds that pupils of school age are too immature to grasp the subtle differences which pervade regions and give them their distinctive atmospheres. As a further criticism of the Regional method of organising material it is suggested that in many cases it becomes rigid and stereotyped, forming an unchanging sequence: position, structure and relief, climate, natural and cultivated vegetation, mineral resources and industry, cities, communications and trade. Another correspondent condemned it as 'this stale, academic regional approach. It kills interest, stuns intellectual stimuli and shakes the foundations of geographical understanding.' Users of Concentric-type syllabuses also claim that, because by their method the world as a whole is constantly under revision, there is no chance that a continent such as Australia or South America can be studied in the first or second year and then be completely ignored for the remainder of the course. A further important point in favour of the method is that the connection between the home district of which the pupil has direct experience, and those parts of the world of which his experience can only be indirect, is closely maintained throughout the course.

As against these claims, many masters point out that some of the criticisms can be made of any type of syllabus. Any syllabus can become stereotyped; this criticism is not so much of the syllabus as of the master. It is the misuse of the method, not the method itself, which should be called into question. Advocates of the Regional approach say that, when properly used, it makes frequent references both to the home district and to other regions of the world, thus retaining some of the most valuable contributions of a Concentric-type syllabus whilst retaining its own greater simplicity of approach. They add that, since the most frequently adopted regional course begins with aspects of Britain and general world topics, followed by the southern continents, a world outlook has been established at least by the end of the second year. One correspondent writes that very often a so-called Concentric syllabus is merely the study of regions which are linked by a common product or field of interest rather than by proximity. The great advantage of a Regional syllabus is that it allows all the factors of relief, climate, human activity and so on to be seen in their true relationships to one another. It is argued that the pupil is more likely to gain a complete picture of, for example, Canada, if he meets the different parts consecutively rather than separately over a period of 4 or 5 years, as he will if following a Concentric type of syllabus. More prosaic arguments used in favour of the Regional syllabus are that most teachers have themselves been taught through it and are therefore more familiar with it; and that the great majority of textbooks are at present based on this method.

Sample studies and reality. The stress put on reality in the first year must be continued throughout the remainder of the course. Many teachers promote this feeling of reality through the use of Sample Studies. These may consist of detailed studies of a single farm or factory, of a village or a town. Some textbooks provide a series of such studies on localities from every continent, though they are sometimes less generous in their treatment of industrial as compared with agricultural areas. A valuable series of Sample Studies has been issued by the Geographical Association, whilst the selected farm studies of the Association of Agriculture, both in Britain and in the Commonwealth, provide a wealth of information and are well worth consideration. For some of the farms studied under this scheme related film strips are available.

Such studies are of greatest value if they can be put into their regional perspective, even in a Concentric syllabus; they then inject realism into the wider studies. Some schools may be able to add to the reality of their work by the introduction into the classroom of overseas visitors. The syllabus must also allow time for all available aids; films can, for example, be used both as background material and as direct teaching aids.

Concentric syllabus. Within a Concentric syllabus the simpler topics, such as the primary industries, should be dealt with first, leaving more complex matters until the senior classes are reached. Of one textbook series arranged in this fashion[1] the publishers write, 'Each of the books contains six topics or themes, and it is suggested that by studying two per term pupils will still have sufficient time

---

[1] *Concentric World Geography*, edited by R. C. Kiloh (Cassell).

for individual work and revision. Book I deals with foods; Book II with timber, minerals and hydroelectricity; Book III with the chief manufacturing industries; and Book IV with transport and what are generally referred to as tertiary industries.'

Though each theme can have a time allocation according to its needs it appears that two or three per term is most usual in English schools. Each theme begins with the home district and then the study is carried to the homeland and the rest of the world. In junior forms the following example might be found:

Theme: Wheat.
1. A local bakery or flour mill, identified on local O.S. maps. Its raw materials, processes and products. It is most desirable that a visit should be made.
2. A British wheat-growing farm. For some rural schools a local farm could be studied; for urban schools a Sample Study could be made.
3. British ports which handle grain. How the grain is handled, and the sources of imports.
4. Wheat growing in Canada; comparison between an English farm and a Canadian one.
5. Other wheat-growing countries.

Later in the course would perhaps come:

Theme: Sea routes.
1. Types of ships and their cargoes.
2. The main shipping routes.
3. Major ports of the world. Descriptions of the work of ports, with more detailed studies of London, New York and Rotterdam to show how it is that certain places become so important in world trade.

Regional syllabus. The main interpretations of the term 'region' have already been considered in chapter 2. In many parts of the world, however, there is much to be said for using political units as the basis for study. Certainly outside school the pupil will more frequently meet references to national states than to natural or geographical regions; but concentration on political units alone may lead to the impression that physical conditions change at each political frontier. The usual course in schools is to arrive at a compromise, the more useful type of boundary in any given case being the one adopted. Thus Africa and South America are usually divided into climatic or vegetation regions, whilst in dealing with Europe political divisions are much more realistic.

The order in which the different aspects of a region may be studied can obviously vary. After locating the region some teachers start with human activities and seek to relate these to the physical and other environmental influences; more, however, begin with the physical basis. In the latter case the logical order is that stated previously (p. 34), concluding as a rule with a study of the region's relations with other parts of the globe through commercial and political ties. Many teachers find this to be the most useful of all approaches;[1] but it is clearly desirable to vary the emphasis given to different aspects if only to avoid the monotony which would result from following the same pattern rigidly for every region. The leading characteristics of each area will in fact dictate where the main emphasis should lie; whether, for example, on relief or climate or industrial development. Still other variations are possible. Some teachers, for instance, begin the work of as many regions as possible with a Sample Study. Not only does this give added reality, but it can be used to show pupils the dangers of 'determinism'. Others prefer, within the regional framework, to present the pupil with a problem concerning the area under discussion. The lessons are then used to help in finding a solution to the problem and to give practice in distinguishing geographical facts which are relevant from those which are not. Examples of such problems quoted by correspondents are: 'How do the Netherlands manage to support such a high density of population?'; 'Why is Lancashire so important as a textile area?'; 'Account for the variety of relief and agriculture in the Paris Basin.'

There appear to be two widely used ways of ordering the continents for study. Of the two Course A seems to be more commonly used.

Course A	Course B
The southern continents	The Americas
North America and Asia	Asia and Australasia
Europe	Africa and Europe
British Isles	British Isles
World revision	World revision

In Course A the choice of the three southern continents for study in the lower forms is consonant with the stage of development of the pupils. These three continents are of relatively simple structure and divide fairly readily into climatic provinces, while their social and economic development is at present less complicated than that of the remaining continents. At this stage the syllabus will not provide overmuch in the way of general physical principles. The emphasis

[1] See 'Regional Geography in the Grammar School' by G. S. Hall, *Geography*, XLIII, part 4 (Nov. 1958).

will be on the effect of differences of relief and climate on human activities. Natural interest among the pupils should result in a certain amount of explanation of, for example, the monotonously high temperatures of equatorial areas, but the syllabus should not be overloaded in this direction. The labouring of aspects of the subject which are too difficult will kill interest; nor need there be any attempt to cover every region of the southern continents in detail. Course A deals with Europe and the British Isles last since it is in the fourth and fifth years that the pupil is best able to appreciate the complex nature of their geography.

The north–south zones of Course B have the advantage of enabling most of the major climatic regions to be covered in each year of the school course, with increasing attention to the underlying principles which control them. The work on North and South America may be planned to bring out the simpler structural features of the earth's surface and to show their influence on human activities. The work on Asia and Australasia, with their sharp contrasts between deserts and well-watered lands, may stress the importance of climate. Europe and Africa may be used to recapitulate the major regions as well as to introduce the more involved economic, social and political relationships of the old-established as compared with the newly emergent countries.

Other types of syllabus. Many teachers, as we have stated, conclude their Regional course with revision on Systematic lines. Some, however, make use of syllabuses in which Systematic studies play an important part earlier in the course. Studies of this kind are usually followed in the junior forms to provide a world view, whilst regional studies make their appearance in the senior forms. One example of such a syllabus submitted to the Committee was organised as follows:

Course C

Year 1. Map work and Physical Geography on a local basis.
The major world regions—tundra, deserts, forests etc.

Year 2. Further map work and Physical Geography.
The main sources and methods of production of some important commodities.

Year 3. The southern continents.

Year 4. Either North America or Europe.

Year 5. The British Isles.

This syllabus makes no attempt to cover the whole world regionally. To compensate for their omission in the regional section, Asia and either Europe or North America (whichever is not included) receives emphasis in the work of the first two years. Despite this, and the fact that the syllabus has other commendable aspects, a majority of the Committee regard unfavourably the omission of such large and important areas. A minority, however, are of the opinion that the time allowed to Geography is insufficient to enable all the continents to be treated regionally. In these circumstances it is felt to be preferable that the regions of some parts of the world should be given detailed study, the remainder receiving outline coverage in the course of general work. The minority of the Committee would therefore be favourably disposed towards this syllabus as it stands.

Another variation is to work according to a Systematic scheme within a specified Regional outline. This type of syllabus will follow an orthodox Regional sequence for each year's work, but within that year will organise the material in the style suggested by the following example.

Year 2. Southern continents.
Lowlands—Amazon and Congo Basins.
Highlands—Northern Andes and East Africa.
Tropical Regions—Queensland and Brazil.
Deserts—The Nile Valley and the Atacama.
Subtropical regions—North-west Africa, Central Chile,
South-west and South-east Australia.

Though not possessing all the advantages of the Concentric scheme this method does appear to have several of them, together with some of its own. It can, for example, be worked in conjunction with the Regional type of textbook possessed by most schools. A disadvantage is that countries, e.g. Australia, are not seen as a whole, but rather as a number of separate parts.

Systematic treatment during revision in the last year of an otherwise regionally based syllabus has already been mentioned. This change of approach has much to commend it, quite apart from the way in which it often helps to meet the requirements of external examining boards. By this method strands of thought which have been followed over the world can be brought together and presented from a fresh viewpoint. The greater maturity of the pupils will enable them to perceive relationships which they could not appreciate when they studied the areas in their earlier years in the school. The various parts of the world are brought into perspective one with another and any branch of the subject, such as Physical Geography, can be seen as a whole rather than as a number of fragments.

GEOGRAPHY OR GEOGRAPHIES?

Many masters, even among those who employ a Regional type of syllabus, find it desirable to concentrate for certain periods of time on one or other of the Systematic aspects of Geography—Physical, Mathematical, Economic and so on. They do so because, in their opinion, a pupil cannot gain a clear picture of a particular aspect if it is presented solely in fragmentary form, incidentally taught at different stages of the Regional course. They maintain that purely incidental treatment tends to prevent the acquisition of a world view of, for example, Physical or Economic Geography; and that, at least in some cases, Regional study presupposes some knowledge of such aspects as Geomorphology, Climatology and Bio-geography. The difficulty can obviously be overcome by adopting a syllabus of the type represented by Course C (p. 38). On the other hand, there is no reason why a teacher who believes in the incidental introduction of Systematic aspects should not generalise in connection with phenomena similar to ones which have been encountered in earlier Regional studies; such generalisations are indeed necessary. He can with equal validity devote several lessons, for example, to the formation of mountains of all types when the topic under consideration is the Andes and their people.

The place of Physical Geography

The advocates of Physical Geography as a study in its own right are perhaps the most numerous among those who support the separate study of the different aspects of Geography. Even the thesis that Physical Geography is not central to the subject in schools, that it is studied not for its own sake but in order to provide data for another and wider theme, cannot detract from its great importance. In terms of man's environment it holds a vital position.

The main elements of Physical Geography in the present context are Geomorphology, Climatology and Bio-geography. Though man is affected by the oceans in his fishing and trading, Oceanography has usually but a small place in the school course.

The topics which are to be specially considered may be studied as they arise naturally in the Geography course, or each one may be deliberately introduced before embarking on a section of a Regional syllabus in which it is especially important. We will consider such a syllabus (e.g. Course A on p. 37) to see where particular items of Physical Geography may best be fitted in.

The introductory course will, as had already been shown, start to build up the vocabulary which the pupil will need to know in order to describe unambiguously the fundamental forms which make up the physical landscape. Some of these he will meet in the course of local studies, and they may suggest the processes which have given rise to them, e.g. a stream, especially when in flood, can be seen to have eroded the valley in which it flows. Soils may be brought to the pupil's notice through an examination of a local brick-pit; and there will be problems to solve such as the occurrence of coal at great depths. The climatological aspect of Physical Geography will be introduced through the school weather station, giving precision of thought to such expressions as 'hot', 'wet', '20 degrees centigrade', '25 inches of rain', and so on.

Studies of the southern continents will suggest the need for the discussion of several aspects of climatology. The influence of wind direction and relief on rainfall are important in Australia, serving to explain relief rain and rain shadow areas. In the Equatorial regions of Africa and South America it is the constantly high temperature and rainfall figures which call for explanation. The swing of the wind belts with the seasons is perhaps more happily dealt with later in the syllabus, but the correlation of seasonal rainfall with the distribution of savanna or Mediterranean vegetation can be shown quite simply. Interrelated factors of climate and elevation need to be considered in order to explain the high proportion of the people of Kenya or of the northern Andean states who live at over 3,000 ft. As suggested in an earlier paragraph, the study of the Andes can be linked to the general question of mountain formation and perhaps to that of earthquake belts.

In the second or third year (depending on the time devoted to the Introductory Course), when North America and Asia are the continents being studied, the effects of erosion can be vividly portrayed by examples from Kansas and Tennessee, whilst the transportation of the soils of those states down the Mississippi can be shown to provide the material for extensive fluvial deposition. The great concentrations of population on the alluvial plains of India and China will stress the importance of such deposits. Both North America and Asia afford examples of all the major landforms, enabling a simple classification to be made. In many cases, such as the Prairies and the Canadian Shield, the Northern Plain of China and the Deccan of India, the unit of study will be a physiographic one. This will remain true even if the syllabus is organised on a Concentric basis. North America also provides the opportunity to extend lines of study begun in the southern continents concerning the variation of climate and vegetation. This is perhaps clearest along western coasts, where it can be used to illustrate the swing of the wind belts, and also the influence of ocean currents on climate. In connection with India and China it will be necessary to study the monsoons, their seasonal and variable nature and the relation between winds and atmospheric pressure. The opportunity will arise here to revise the connections between wind direction, relief and rainfall. The pupils should now be able to identify the approximate positions of stations from their climatic data, and should be familiar with such devices as isotherms and isohyets. They should know the importance of diurnal maximum and minimum temperatures as well as mean temperatures; and they should understand such related facts as the period free from frost. All these topics arise naturally from the study of North America and Asia as such, or from topics of the Concentric syllabus which are based on these areas.

By the time the pupil comes to study Europe and the British Isles he will have encountered a wide range of physical phenomena, the study of which can now be extended and consolidated. The main features associated with, for example, glaciation and river action, already met with in land-form studies in other continents, will be further examined in relation to the Alps and the Lake District, the Thames and the Rhine. Such investigations are much more fruitful when closely linked with the use of Ordnance Survey maps and of similar maps of other countries. More attention can be given to physical structure; pupils should now be able to appreciate its importance and its bearing, direct or indirect, on mining, farming and population distribution.

There is plenty of scope for differences of approach and emphasis. When Geomorphology is being studied for its own sake there will be more stress on the evolution of features, and examples will be chosen which illustrate the processes which have been at work. Gaps, for instance, will be selected as examples of overflow channels or river capture. When, however, it is being taught merely as an aid to the understanding of Human studies, the chosen examples will show gaps primarily as natural routeways which men have utilised for railways, roads or canals. Similarly, in dealing with the glacial deposits of lowlands, a teacher might in one context treat them as the results of ice-sheet advance and decay; in another context primarily as a part of the explanation of the Human Geography of, for example, the plain of North Germany or that of Cheshire and North Shropshire.

Throughout their course pupils will have studied many different types of climate. In the later stages the strands which have been followed in successive years must be brought together in a general classification to give a world view of similarities and differences. By this time also pupils will almost certainly have become familiar with the Weather Map, though its understanding may be too difficult for the less able amongst them.

Whichever type of syllabus is decided upon it is desirable that physical principles should be represented by the best illustrative examples which the teacher can find. The table on pp. 44–5 suggests where many aspects of Physical Geography may be fitted into a Regional scheme. (The topics included in the first-year general course would need to be varied for schools in different parts of the country.) If such a policy is adopted part of the final year may well need to be spent in summarising the aspects of Physical Geography and bringing them together.

The place of Mathematical Geography

Some elementary Mathematical Geography will have to be taught in the first few weeks of the Secondary school course. This will include the concept of scales, and perhaps some simple surveying preparatory to drawing a map of the school. Either in the Introductory course or in connection with one of the southern continents will come a study of latitude and longitude as a means of determining position, though the explanation of these concepts will probably be more easily grasped at a later stage. Australia will give an opportunity for illustrating the differences in time and seasons between that country and Britain. At a later stage a revision journey along the Canadian Pacific or the Trans-Siberian Railway can be made the occasion for a study of the time zones; by the time these are reached in most syllabuses the pupils will be sufficiently mature to understand the relationship between time and longitude. With many pupils, however, the problem of the varying length of day and night is best left until even later. The explanation of such topics as the International Date Line and twilight are also better left until the later stages of the course; with the least able pupils it will probably be unwise to attempt such explanations at all. Map projections will hardly enter the five-year course, though at an early stage most pupils should be made aware that their atlas and wall maps contain distortions.

Relation of Physical Geography to a Regional Course

Syllabus	First form General Course	Second form Southern continents	Third form North America Asia	Fourth form North-west Europe	Fifth form British Isles
Fold Mountains	Oil anticline	New Zealand Andes	Western Cordillera Himalayas	Alps Jura	—
Block Mountains	—	—	—	Ardennes Rhine Highlands	North Pennines
Volcanoes	—	Andes	Japan	Auvergne	—
Lava plateaux	—	—	Washington and Oregon North-west Deccan	Auvergne	Antrim
Limestone scenery	—	—	—	The 'Causses' (Massif central)	Yorkshire Pennines
Escarpments	Box Hill Field-work	—	—	Paris Basin Neckar Basin	The Weald Cotswolds
Artesian Basins	—	Great Australian Basin	—	—	London Basin
Sedimentary rocks	Box Hill Formation of coal	—	—	Paris Basin Aquitaine	London Basin
Granite moors	—	—	—	Brittany	South-west England
Metamorphic rocks	—	—	Canadian Shield	Brittany	Scottish Highlands North Wales Lake District
Faults	Coal mining	—	—	—	North Pennines
Rift valleys	—	East Africa	—	Rhine	Central Lowlands, Scotland
Waterfalls	—	Central Africa	Niagara	Rhine Scandinavia	—
Gorges	—	—	Grand Canyon	Rhine	—
River terraces	Thames—local study	—	—	South-west France	London Basin
River deposition	Thames—local study Chinese farm s.s.	Canterbury Plains	Mississippi Hwang-ho Indo-Gangetic Plain	Rhine Aquitaine	London Basin
Deltas	—	Nile	Mississippi Ganges	Rhone Rhine	Lake District
Valley glaciation	—	New Zealand	Western Cordillera	Alps	Scottish Highlands Lake District North Wales
Continental glaciation	—	—	Canadian Shield	Baltic Shield	—
Glacial lakes	—	—	Canada	Switzerland	Lake District
Glacial deposition	East Anglian farm s.s.	—	Corn Belt	North German Plain Denmark	East Anglia Holderness Cheshire
Marine erosion	—	—	—	—	Cromer South-west England
Sandspits	Fishing—Great Yarmouth	—	Florida	South coast of Baltic	East Anglia
Lagoons	—	—	—	Languedoc The Landes	South Devon
Rias	Cornwall s.s.	Sydney Harbour	Chesapeake Bay	Brittany	South-west England
Fiords	Crofter Farm s.s.	South-west New Zealand South Chile	British Columbia	Norway	West coast of Scottish Highlands
Continental shelf	Fishing	—	Newfoundland	—	Fishing

44

Relation of Physical Geography to a Regional Course (cont.)

Syllabus	First form	Second form	Third form	Fourth form	Fifth form
Raised beaches	—	—	—	Sweden Brittany	West Scotland South-west England
Coral reefs	—	Queensland	Florida	—	—
Sand dunes	—	Sahara	—	Landes	Moray coast
Loess	—	—	Hwang-ho Basin	Paris Basin Belgium Central Germany	—
Temperature— effect of:					
(a) Latitude	Crop, e.g. rubber	Queensland Tasmania North, Central and South Chile	British Columbia California North China Malaya	South Portugal Coast of Norway	—
(b) Relief	Ascent of Everest	Andes Kenya	Rockies Japan Tibet	Alps Norway	North Wales Scottish Highlands
(c) Continental interior	—	—	Prairies Steppes of Asia	Central Germany	—
(d) Warm ocean current	Farm in Cornwall	—	British Columbia	Brittany Norway	South-west England South-west Ireland
(e) Cold ocean current	—	Coast of South-west Africa	San Francisco North Japan	—	—
(f) Frost drainage	—	—	Central valley of California	Champagne Rhine Valley	Vale of Evesham
Rainfall—effect of:					
(a) Relief	Crofter Farm s.s.	Great Dividing Range New Zealand Andes	British Columbia California Japan Himalayas	Massif Central Norway	Wales Dartmoor Lake District West Highlands of Scotland
(b) Convection	—	Congo Basin Amazon Basin	Prairies	Steppes of U.S.S.R.	East Anglia
(c) Rain shadow	—	Murray Basin Canterbury Plains Patagonia	Alberta Interior British Columbia Valley of California	Sweden Rhine Rift	Moray Firth Eden Vale

s.s., Sample Study.

The place of Local Geography

Local Geography, the study of the area in which the school is situated, has already been fully discussed as the basis of the early stages of the Secondary school course (see also chapter 8). The Concentric style of syllabus automatically refers to the local area at the beginning of each new topic; but there is a danger that, in schools where work is based on a Regional syllabus, there may be little reference to the local area after the first year. This must be guarded against, for, as has already been stressed, knowledge of the geographical phenomena of the area which can be studied at first hand is basic to the understanding of regions further afield. Analogies with the home district should be made as frequently as possible throughout the whole of the course.

The place of Historical Geography

That aspect of Historical Geography which studies the Geography of a past era will usually find but a small place in the Secondary school course. More important for our purpose is the aspect which considers the contributions of past generations to the present landscape. The danger of over-generalisation and over-stress on the importance of environmental control, if such influences as these are not taken into account, has already been mentioned. The early evolution of human societies was perhaps largely controlled by the physical environment, but as time passed man's progress became more and more subject to his own will. There will be many opportunities for illustrating this: the exploration and settlement of new continents, the history of which often provides the best introduction to them; the effect of trans-continental railways and trans-Atlantic steamships on wheat growing in the Prairie region and in Denmark; the building of St Petersburg (Leningrad) at the marshy confluence of the Neva and the Okhta; the transplanting of *Hevea brasiliensis* from the Amazon Basin to Ceylon and Malaya; the cutting of the Suez and Panama Canals; the growth of Berlin with the spread of Hohenzollern authority. A last example may be taken from the cotton industry of Lancashire, which cannot be understood without historical as well as geographical knowledge. Here the influence of the opening of the Levantine and East Indian trade routes; the relaxation of Puritan rule with the restoration of the monarchy in 1660; the persecutions of Protestants in Flanders; the inventions of the eighteenth century and the political control by Britain over lucrative markets abroad are as important as the proximity of the coalfield.

The place of Economic Geography

Broadly speaking, Economic Geography may be said to be the study of man's economic activities in relation to his environment. It endeavours to show the conditions which mainly affect the processes of production and distribution of commodities, and the manner in which the influence of these conditions is exercised. It has already been pointed out that man's environment has become something much more complex than can be comprised in an account of his surroundings in terms of relief, climate, vegetation and mineral resources. Very often, therefore, the location of industry is now much more susceptible to economic and social pressures through government action than to either physical influences or the free exercise of economic laws. An example of this is to be found in South Wales. Instead of regarding its industrial complex as being due solely to the presence of the coalfield we must now take into account the fact that many new industries have been established there as a result of governmental policies towards such 'development' areas. Thus help has been given to a wide range of light industries producing such things as plastics, radios and refrigerators. Since, however, in many regions industries have become established and have remained prosperous without any government direction it is important, in order to understand their location, to understand aspects of Economics which impinge on Geography, especially, perhaps, the laws regulating the relationship between supply and demand.

The extent to which, in the main school Geography course, Economic Geography as such should be given a place in the syllabus is by no means agreed. Most, if not all, of the facts which need to be considered are probably best dealt with as they arise in a Regional course; but if time allows there is something to be said for including some Economic Geography in general revision at the end of the course.

The place of Social and Political Geography

In so far as it bears upon the life of mankind, it may be claimed that all Geography is Social Geography. In many respects, however, geographers tend to treat people as anonymous and characterless—devoid of most of the characteristics which in fact make people human. It is the task of Social Geography to restore this reality and to remind us that we deal with real people and real communities. Pupils must also be made aware of the geographical aspects of community life and of man as a citizen of a locality or settlement, of a country and of the world. It should be possible to show that as the first two of this trinity have been reconciled so may the latter two become compatible. The problems of frontiers, race, religion, national customs and standards of living have to be faced. Many customs found in other people will appear strange to pupils of Secondary school age. They must be made aware of the fact that strangeness to them is not necessarily a sign of intrinsic inferiority. There are few things more disturbing than teenage sniggers at things which are alien to their own way of life. Ideological differences, such as those between Communist and Socialist–Capitalist countries, though in themselves outside the scope of school Geography, will have effects which are well within that scope, as in the case of Soviet agricultural organisation.

The amount of Social Geography as such which can be taught will obviously be limited, but, generally speaking, it will increase both quantitatively and in complexity as the course progresses. There will be Social Geography studies in the preliminary stage when time is devoted to the home district; there will be some treatment of the simple social organisation of primitive peoples in the following year, dealing with the responses to such needs as food, shelter and security. Later will come the study of more complex industrial societies and the difficulties met by the newly independent countries in their struggle to raise standards of living. These studies should help to stress the interdependence of communities and the moral obligations which groups, as well as individuals, owe to one another. In all these studies there is sufficient material to show that the colour of a man's skin is of no importance in the judgement of his worth as a man.

Obviously the whole of Social Geography can come to have political significance, but for the most part, in a school course, the political content will be concerned with frontiers and capitals, national aspirations, state organisations and attitudes towards the development of national resources.

The place of map work

All too frequently in schools large scale map work is a feature of the Introductory course, but is then forgotten until several consecutive weeks are allocated to the topic in the fourth or fifth year. This is to be deprecated, for the geographer does not treat maps as an end in themselves but as aids to the understanding of the landscape and the people who live in it. If the pupil gains a sound understanding of maps at an early stage in his Secondary school career the Ordnance Survey and similar foreign maps can become just as much aids as are photographs. It cannot be too strongly emphasised that maps related to the topic under discussion should be found in use at every stage of the course.

Map studies in the Introductory course have already been considered (pp. 28, 29). At this early stage the pupil is mastering the meaning of individual symbols, and for the first two or three years his main problem is to increase his ability to visualise the things which the symbols represent. The transition from this map reading to map interpretation—the drawing of correct conclusions concerning the physical and cultural landscape portrayed by the map—is gradual and not always easy. It should be achieved by the fourth or fifth year, and it is at this stage that the map makes its most useful contribution.

Suitable foreign maps are becoming increasingly available and a few textbooks now incorporate such maps at relevant points. Many teachers, however, find their selection restricted, for one reason or another, to British sheets. It is fortunate that Britain has a wide diversity of landscape, and Ordnance Survey maps can be used to illustrate features of the same types, though not always on the same scale, as many which are found in overseas areas. The following suggestions are only a few of the many possible correlations: western Scotland and the fiords of Norway, British Columbia, South Chile and South-west New Zealand; the Fens and the Polders of the Netherlands or the Marschen of Germany; glacial features found in many mountain ranges from Nepal to Switzerland can also be found in Snowdonia; rias in Devon and Cornwall are comparable to those of Brittany or North-west Spain; flood-plain features can be found as readily along many British rivers as along rivers in other countries. Used in this way the large-scale map becomes not a time-consuming 'extra' but something which cannot be improved upon for giving reality and character to far-away regions. The appreciation of these qualities is required whether the area is one of undulating plains in Australia, a delta in Nigeria or rounded chalk hills in England.

THE IMPORTANCE OF THE TYPE OF PUPIL

In this chapter it has been the intention not to differentiate between the various types of school. There are, however, such wide differences of ability among pupils that it is necessary to refer to a few of the syllabus problems to which they give rise. Some general problems resulting from this wide range have been discussed in chapter 2. Here we are concerned specifically with its effect on syllabus construction.

Abler pupils

The Grammar[1] school master may appear in many respects to have a simpler task in constructing a syllabus than his colleague in a

---

[1] In this section terms such as 'stream', 'Grammar', 'Modern' are used because they are convenient and are understood. In the present partially re-organised state of Secondary education it is not possible to say for how long they will have relevance to the actual state of affairs.

Secondary Modern school because, on the whole, he has to cater for a narrower spread of ability. In some schools, however, he will meet the problem of brighter pupils who are to take a G.C.E. Ordinary level paper after only four years. In such conditions some material must be pruned from the normal five-year course. It is important, however, that the teacher faced with this problem should resist the temptation merely to drop a continent or two from his scheme of work. With brighter boys one should naturally be able to work more quickly, and though this may not be an ideal solution it is at least part of a practical one. Where there are greater powers of retention, references to regions or circumstances similar to ones previously encountered can be made more briefly, and one can expect a larger amount of homework in which pupils can deal individually with topics after some small guidance has been given in class. Reference was made in chapter 2 to pupils who, because of specialisation for examination purposes, have only a three-year course in Geography. The problem here is to devise a course which will serve as a foundation for G.C.E. and C.S.E. work and will at the same time be sufficiently complete in itself to be of educational benefit to these three-year pupils. This is clearly difficult. Thorough grounding provided by the Introductory course is vital. Subsequently, whichever type of main course is followed, the emphasis should be on geographical principles derived from the facts which are studied. Since the British Isles will not be covered in detail in all aspects, British examples of phenomena and principles encountered in other countries should be given wherever possible.

Although the Secondary Modern school master may find himself preparing some able pupils who may later make their way to a university, he will also certainly be faced with pupils who are barely literate—or even completely illiterate. His brightest boys will often be able to follow the same type of course as their contemporaries in Grammar schools. In general, the chief difference between these boys' needs and those of Grammar school pupils will lie in the timing of certain topics. Though both groups may be aiming at the same external examination it will often be found an advantage in the Secondary Modern school to delay the introduction of topics which require interpretation or complex explanation rather than mere description, e.g. the weather map. Grammar school pupils show, on the whole, a greater facility for acquiring information from sources such as newspapers or television programmes, though, even in their case, the master must not assume that his boys know facts he has not himself referred to in class. Secondary Modern pupils probably need more frequent opportunities for revision.

Less able pupils

The remaining groups of pupils are the concern only of those who teach in Secondary Modern schools or in schools with an intake of similar pupils. The majority of these make up what we may perhaps call the 'B' stream. According to the Crowther report, *15 to 18* (H.M.S.O. 1959), these are the pupils who suffer the greatest neglect in our schools, and certainly, for their geographical education, the syllabus presents many problems. Some of these pupils stay at school until the age of 16 years with the object of taking C.S.E.; others take an examination of lower standard (such as the 'County Certificate' awarded by some Local Education Authorities) before leaving at 15 years; still others leave without taking any examination at all.

The replacement of completely external examinations, conducted by a variety of private bodies, by that for the Certificate of Secondary Education is a step of the greatest importance. The most valuable characteristic of this examination is that, in intention at least, it examines the pupils on the course they have actually followed. It is in fact within the power of teachers, with the approval of their Regional Boards, to set their own examinations on their own syllabuses. Preparation for such examinations, in which obligatory practical work performed during the course is recognised by the award of a certain percentage of the marks, can and should provide a valuable stimulus to the pupils concerned.

The syllabus which is prepared for the less able pupils should not be merely a diluted version of that used by those who are better endowed. Such a course, with difficult pieces removed, and others curtailed to make it fit into four years will provide but a weak basis for the work of these pupils. The raising of the school-leaving age to 16 will in any case necessitate the provision of five-year syllabuses for all pupils; but whatever the length of the course it needs to be constructed so that it meets the needs and abilities of the pupils for whom it is intended. The syllabus may be more successful if it has a practical bias, though we must beware of the fallacy that because a boy is not particularly good at academic subjects he will automatically possess practical talents. Frequently the boy who is best in one is also best in the other. Be that as it may, the syllabus must deal with realities which can be brought within the experience of the pupils, and the topics introduced must be carefully selected as having interest and

51

relevance. Not only must a topic be pertinent to the pupil, but he must realise that it is so if he is to accept it as worthy of his concentration and effort.

Either the Regional or the Concentric type of syllabus can be used with success, though it should be remembered that, particularly with the former, the need for frequent revision and reference to areas previously discussed will be even more important than in the case already mentioned. A period of world revision at the end of the course will also be just as vital for these pupils as for the brighter boys who are taking external examinations. Such revision should approach the material of study from a new point of view, and not be merely a recapitulation of what has gone before. The temptation to overload the syllabus with complicated detail must be resisted. Most masters will make the human aspects of Geography the main theme, the work being rather more descriptive and attempting less analysis than would be the case with the types of pupil previously discussed. Some, however, put forward a case for a greater emphasis on Physical Geography on the grounds that the facts and relationships considered are governed by more definite laws than are those of Human Geography. The pupils under consideration, however, have great difficulty in drawing accurate generalisations, and it is on the whole preferable that their grounding in Geography should be carefully carried out with the aid of Sample Studies of farms, villages, factories and so on. In addition, the syllabus should allow time for the generous use of films and other visual aids. Unless this kind of allowance is made there is a great danger of the lessons lacking essential realism and becoming merely a succession of meaningless words.

Backward pupils

With those children who have difficulty in reading and writing all the problems of the 'B' stream are accentuated, and several quite new ones are added. A suggestion for the first year's work with such pupils, in which the Geography course becomes an aid to literacy, has already been made (pp. 32, 33).

We must remember that, even when substantial progress has been made in reading and writing, the reasoning powers and retentivity of these boys are limited. The syllabus must be truly child-centred and the master must never forget that he is a teacher first and a geographer a long way second.

Apart from, though to some extent because of, their lesser mental ability these pupils have, outside school, fewer incentives to learn and often much less encouragement. It is vital that their interest, once captured, should be carefully tended; it is a precarious thing and if it is lost most of what is taught is wasted, boring the boys and frustrating the master. Even before they have left school these pupils will have forgotten much of what they have 'learnt' in the previous years. They will retain permanently that which they believe has a direct relevance for themselves, either as schoolboys or as future workers. As they pass through the school, boys naturally begin to think more about the world outside its gates, and often this leads to apathy towards what goes on inside. This need not be so. Even at this stage the pupil can accept that there are certain things which he should know, and these he will be prepared to learn if they are suitably presented. On the other hand, he cannot assimilate all that one would offer to a brighter boy. Many of the facts and principles which would come alive in the mind of the abler pupil are useless to him because he cannot perceive their relevance, nor can he in any way use them by fitting them into previous experiences, thus extending those experiences.

We should perhaps here be reminded of the maxim from the Consultative Committee's Report on the Primary School in 1931 that 'the curriculum is to be thought of in terms of activity and experience rather than of knowledge to be acquired and facts to be stored'. This applies with as much force to the 'C' stream of a Secondary Modern school as it does to the Primary school. This is not to say that all facts should be abandoned, for many of them are essential. The teacher must determine those facts which he believes to be of the greatest importance to his pupils and must turn them into reality so that they become live experiences, part of a pupil's character and of his permanent store of knowledge.

Since first-hand experience of visiting the country under discussion is only rarely feasible, second-hand experiences must be made as realistic as possible. The allowances of time made in the syllabus for such aids as films must be extremely generous; vivid passages from tales of adventure and exploration are also a great help. It matters little that the pupils may consider that they are merely listening to an exciting story if at the same time they are obtaining that feeling for the character of a region which will produce a realistic reaction when in future they hear its name mentioned. Such a reaction cannot come from lists of names to be learnt by heart. Schools which can find suitable Commonwealth and foreign visitors to come and talk with (not to) their pupils have an extremely valuable aid, of which the syllabus would do well to take account. They cure the syllabus of any tendency towards a narrow, nationalistic outlook, and provide the pupil with a basis on which to build his own value judgements. If he has met people from other countries he will think back to them when he sees those countries harangued in his newspaper. Simple field-work (including visits to factories and farms) can also be of great help, as can work at such places as the Commonwealth Institute. All these devices are means for providing the necessary precision to knowledge without losing the interest of the pupil.

To a large extent, this sort of approach to the teaching of backward boys means that the syllabus is controlled by teaching methods and the availability of material. If one particular part of the world is very much in the news one uses it as a basis for lessons. Similarly, if one finds a visitor from a country one had not thought of discussing, or a film which will not be available later, then the opportunity is taken and the aids used. To one accustomed to the neat appearance of a conventional syllabus, this will seem an untidy approach, lacking in method or discipline. But though chaos can be envisaged in its use, this is not a necessary corollary. The need is for a teacher who will be remaining in the school for at least several years to give coherence to the course. The pupils will not feel conscious, as brighter boys might, of a lack of continuity, of not following a line of thought through several weeks or even lessons.

AVAILABILITY OF TEACHING AIDS

Mention has already been made of this aspect of the problem of constructing a syllabus. With backward pupils it hardly arises for there is not the pressure of an examination syllabus to be taken into account. Even, however, where there is a complete and formal syllabus of work laid down, the scheme must be made sufficiently flexible to allow for certain material to be used, not when it is wanted but when it is available. This applies to television programmes in particular, though, since details of these are published in advance it should be possible to rearrange the order in which certain regions are studied so that advantage may be taken of a television series in a particular year. The use of a tape recorder will avoid this necessity in the case of radio broadcasts. Films present another problem. Those which are in great demand must be ordered eight or nine months ahead of the date when they are needed and it is lamentable that in such cases many Local Authorities do not yet make it possible to obtain them readily. Sometimes a film that has been ordered does not arrive on time, or another one has been substituted; the syllabus obviously needs to be flexible in order to allow for such occurrences. The availability of material may also affect the actual content of the syllabus. For example, if a teacher has decided that time allows only one Sample Study of peasant agriculture in South-east Asia he may do well to choose India, not only because of its Commonwealth links but because he can obtain the Petroleum Film Bureau's film on the subject. Similarly, West Africa may be given greater emphasis in the course than the Congo because of the availability of Unilever's films on the former region.

That universal aid the textbook is, of course, always available, and if allowed to do so could easily come to dominate the syllabus. It is not unknown for a 'syllabus' to consist merely of the chapter headings of such a book; such a list is surely not worthy to be called a syllabus. There are, however, teachers who maintain, with considerable justification, that there should be links between a textbook and the sequence of the course; this at least makes life less confusing for the pupils.

THE INFLUENCE OF EXTERNAL EXAMINATIONS

It is clear that the demands of external examinations now exert a considerable influence on Geography syllabuses in all types of Secondary schools. It must be remembered, however, that to a great extent G.C.E. examination syllabuses represent a consensus of opinion in which teachers can have an effective voice, and that pressure from teachers has brought about many modifications in recent years. Teachers wield even more power in the case of the C.S.E. Finally, a teacher who strongly disagrees with the published syllabuses can submit his own to the Examining Board with which he is concerned.

CORRELATION WITH OTHER SUBJECTS

We are not here concerned with the question of merging Geography with certain other subjects under the title of 'Social Studies'; this has been discussed in chapter 2. Where common ground exists between Geography and another subject there is obviously a possibility of considering it from the two points of view during the same period of the school course. It is the purpose of this section to enquire into the extent to which this is likely to be profitable.

The Norwood Report (*Curriculum and Examinations in Secondary*

Schools, H.M.S.O.) of 1943 points out that the ease with which Geography makes contact with other 'environmental' subjects gives it an advantage, which is '...that Geography at many points invites other subjects to join with it in a concerted attack on the same topic from various points of departure, and in so doing calls attention to the common purposes and utilities of these subjects'. The paragraph goes on to warn: 'On the other hand, enthusiasts for Geography may be inclined sometimes to extend their range so widely as to swallow up other subjects; in so doing they widen their boundaries so vaguely that definition of purpose is lost, and the distinctive virtues inherent in other studies closely pursued are ignored in a general survey of wide horizons. Such virtues cannot be ignored without loss.'

The extent to which different subjects can be linked up varies greatly, and in certain circumstances the idea of correlation can be carried too far. It is only when the study of the border zone between two subjects can be shown to sustain and develop interest in both that there is any likelihood of successful co-operation between the teachers of such related subjects. Effective co-operation depends on the personal relationships which exist between the Geography teacher and his colleagues; those concerned must share the conviction that joint action is desirable in the interests of the pupils. Where initial difficulties have been overcome it is found that broad views are established and school studies can be brought together into the unity which is found in the world outside the school.

In the lower forms questions involved in the reading of maps, particularly those of scale and direction, may receive attention in the Mathematics course, where they will be considered from a different point of view. The principle of the magnetic compass may be explained in the Science laboratory, where lessons will also be given on the measurement of temperature and atmospheric pressure. Geographical work in these forms may include some consideration of the facts concerning night and day, longitude and time; and the Geometry necessary to supply the mathematical explanation of these phenomena, as well as some elementary information about the propagation of light may well be covered during this period. If it can be arranged that the early stages of the History course cover aspects of World History, some of the areas selected for study in the first year of the Geography course may also be chosen to form a background to the History lessons.

Where the geographical study of America takes place in the forms which are also studying the Age of Discovery and the transfer of trade from the Narrow Seas to the oceans, correlation is easy. The work in History can be extended to include the establishment of European colonies and trading settlements on the coasts of America and Africa, the geographical influences involved being dealt with in the Geography lessons. The History course may deal with the results of the wars of independence, the establishment of the United States and the Latin American republics and the Monroe Doctrine, all of which have had important geographical repercussions. The American–Canadian boundary lines will be taken as examples of undefended frontiers established by arbitration.

In the fourth and fifth years of the Geography course, many schools pay special attention to the British Isles and Europe, questions of climate, vegetation and agriculture, fisheries, minerals, industries, population, communications and trade being reviewed. The History course may at the same time be dealing with the period of the Industrial Revolution and with recent years. In this case close co-operation between the teachers of History and Geography should be profitable. The Chemistry course may include consideration of the chemistry of iron, non-ferrous metals, fertilisers, and foods; whilst Physics lessons may have some reference to the generation of electricity. The elements of statistical methods and of diagrammatic illustration afford some contact with the Mathematics course. Where Economics is taken below the sixth form the pupils will often discover that they are dealing with the same human experiences from different points of view.

The importance of correlation in sixth-form work is examined in chapter 5.

From all of the foregoing it is clear that syllabus construction demands attention to a variety of factors influencing both the teacher and his pupils. In appendix A will be found examples of different types of syllabus actually in use in various secondary schools, showing how the principles enunciated in this chapter may be applied in practice.

4

TEACHING METHODS

It is doubtful if any subject lends itself to a greater variety of treatment than Geography. Properly taught its subject-matter becomes exciting and stimulating, but masters should have the honesty to recognise that uninspired presentation is dull and soon produces boredom.

The preparation of lessons

At the outset it would be as well to consider the whole approach to class work. Some masters commit very little to paper beforehand, and rely on their memory for the necessary facts. They depend on intuition and the inspiration of the moment to decide on the way in which a topic should be taught. Typical of this approach is the following comment by a correspondent: 'I might keep a few statistics, but lesson notes, if ever I had any of them, have long since been memorized. I would never use the same material for two successive lessons, let alone in successive years.' Such views, however, are not those of the vast majority of our members, and many masters commit notes, sketch maps, diagrams and ideas of presentation to paper, amending them from time to time by additions or deletions. Since their basic sets of notes are continually being revised, teaching material is always fresh and relevant. New ideas are recorded in permanent form before they are lost for ever. The Committee regard this as normal procedure, and they cannot commend consistent reliance on inspiration. Nor do they regard as practicable the detailed preparation of each individual lesson. Apart from other considerations, the Geography master, a busy man, just has not the time for it.

Keeping up to date

An essential element in the master's notes will consist of statistics and facts, which must always be the most recent available. The absolute necessity of keeping abreast of developments cannot be overstressed, though this task is made no easier by the fact that the statistics provided by different authorities frequently disagree. Valuable sources, apart from reports in reliable newspapers, and the current editions of *Whittaker's Almanac, The Statesman's Year Book,* and *Philip's Geographical Digest*; and articles in the *Geographical Journal*, the *Geographical Magazine*, and *Geography*.

CLASS TEACHING

The size of teaching groups. Teaching methods open to the master depend, to some extent, on the number of pupils in the class. Individual studies are considered later in this chapter, but our correspondents freely admit that most of their time is given to class teaching. Many of them argue that, though this is not the ideal, practical considerations make it inevitable. The large number of pupils in some classes, the lack of suitable equipment, and the necessity of using ordinary classrooms for lessons are reasons advanced to explain the prominence of class teaching. Since this is the classroom situation, its inherent possibilities of method must be explored in detail.

The pupils' effort. Class teaching must start from the principle of pupil involvement. Only in the sixth form, if anywhere in the school, should the master resort to lecturing. Passive pupils are a negation of that principle, and the master must always strive to create purposeful activity in the classroom.

The blackboard

This was a necessary accompaniment of the 'chalk and talk' era of teaching, and as such it was by today's standards very much overused. Nevertheless, it is still one of our most essential aids and holds a rightful place in any discussion of method.

Few masters would now advocate the tedious reproduction by pupils of blackboard notes, but there are those who find some merit in completion exercises. As the name suggests, the master leaves gaps in the sentences which he writes on the board, so that the pupils have to insert the correct words. For this purpose he may rely on their existing knowledge, or ask them to search through their textbooks and atlases.

Although completion exercises are prefererable to the full-scale reproduction of notes the method is not very popular, and its use is probably best restricted to lessons with younger and slower pupils. The majority of masters rightly insist that pupils should compose their own notes, guided wherever necessary by points written on the blackboard. Such points emerge as a consequence of preliminary oral discussion, and will subsequently serve to remind pupils of the main aspects which they should mention. When colour slides or filmstrips have been used to introduce a new topic masters often vary the approach by writing a set of questions on the blackboard. These are carefully arranged, and designed to remind pupils of what they have just seen. By working progressively through the questions, a logical sequence of ideas and points will emerge.

Although the overhead projector has come to stay, the blackboard is still the main item of equipment on which to draw maps. The latter should be simple, bold and clear. The wise choice of colours will contribute to such objectives; orange and yellow lines show up better on the blackboard than blue and mauve. Some masters, however, restrict the use of yellow chalk to the depiction of broad areas such as hills or deserts, arguing that pupils are only too ready to copy the colours used in blackboard diagrams. Yellow lines set against the white background of an exercise book are very difficult to see.

The simple copying of maps or diagrams, as of blackboard notes, invites severe criticism, unless there are safeguards. One possibility is to construct a map in stages, points being added as a result of oral questions. Some masters maintain that the annotated blackboard version should be complete before pupils are allowed to put pen and pencil to paper, thus avoiding divided attention (see Fig. 1, p. 61). If this practice is adopted some of the information can be erased before the pupils make their copies, so that completion demands the exercise of reasoning power on their part.

The application of these techniques in map and diagram construction is well-established practice. An attractive though less commonly used approach, making use of pictures, has been described by P. J. M. Bailey, who calls it the Synthetic Landscape Method (See *Geography*, XLVIII, part 3 (1963)). Its main use is for teaching Regional Geography by selecting the important physical and cultural components of an area, and working them up into a composite blackboard drawing. Pictorial matter of this nature has much more appeal than mapping where average pupils are concerned, and it will also hold the attention of many abler children. Simple panoramic views can be built up through the co-operation of master and class, but in the case of more complicated synthetic views the finished drawing is presented to the pupils at the outset of

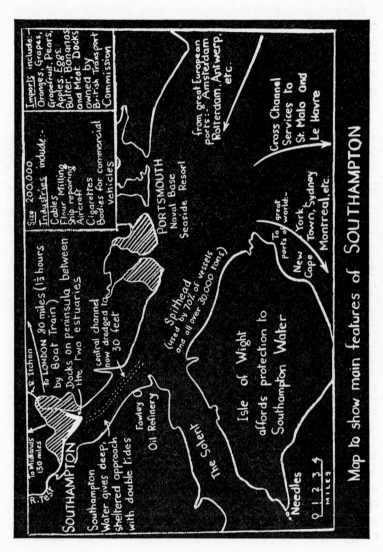

The following text appears within the map illustration:

SOUTHAMPTON

To Midlands 130 miles

R. Test

R. Itchen

To LONDON 80 miles (1½ hours by Boat Train)

Docks on peninsula between the two estuaries

Size 200,000.
Industries include:-
Cables
Flour Milling
Ship repairing
Aircraft
Cigarettes
Bodies for commercial vehicles

Imports include:-
Oranges, Grapes,
Grapefruit, Pears,
Apples, Eggs,
Butter, Bananas
and Meat. Docks
owned by
British Transport
Commission

Southampton Water gives deep, sheltered approach with double tides

Fawley Oil Refinery

central channel now dredged to 30 feet

PORTSMOUTH
Naval Base
Seaside Resort

from great European Ports:- Amsterdam Rotterdam, Antwerp, etc.

Spithead
(used by 70% of vessels and all over 30,000 tons)

The Solent

Isle of Wight
affords protection to Southampton Water

Needles

0 1 2 3 4 MILES

To great ports of world:-
New York
Cape Town, Sydney
Montreal. etc.

Cross Channel Services to St. Malo and Le Havre

Map to show main features of SOUTHAMPTON

Fig. 1. Example of a completed blackboard map.

the lesson, and they proceed to analyse it geographically (see Fig. 2, this page).

Inexperienced masters sometimes have difficulty in drawing complicated outlines on the blackboard, but they should not be deterred on this score. *Blackboard Drawing for Geography* by Crichton and Raw (Nelson) is a very useful book on the subject, while E. G. R. Taylor's *Sketch Map Geography* (Methuen) is full of suggestions for simplifying maps.

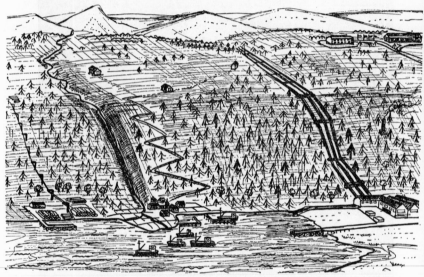

Fig. 2. Looking across a Norwegian Fiord. An example of the Synthetic regional method. A simplified coloured chalk version of this drawing is reproduced on the blackboard and used as source material for class discussion.

Basic outlines can also be prepared beforehand. One possibility is to make templates in plywood or hardboard; a second involves the use of a filmstrip projector or epivisor, the necessary image being thrown on the blackboard and outlined in chalk. If wooden boards are in use these outlines can be etched in with the point of the chalk compasses and become permanencies. When not in use these scratched outlines are all but invisible, yet can easily be rediscovered when required.

The overhead projector

This instrument has already been referred to as a possible rival to the blackboard. Its essential principles are described in chapter 7; here its potentialities for teaching will be considered.

It possesses several advantages over the blackboard.

(1) While the master is writing or drawing on the acetate sheet he is facing the class. Equally he can point out details projected on the screen without turning his back on his pupils.

(2) Maps can be built up in stages by placing a series of overlay transparencies over an outline base map. The same applies to diagrams, and the reverse process can also be used very effectively.

(3) An exact replica of a map or diagram supplied to the pupils can be projected on to the screen. This is possible when a spirit duplicator is used, one copy being made on an acetate sheet put through the machine instead of a sheet of paper.

(4) There is no chalk dust.

A general advantage is that the instrument can be used in full daylight. Switching it on does not involve any break in the continuity of the lesson.

Its chief disadvantage is its initial cost, which is at present sufficiently high to preclude its introduction into many schools; and also the all too frequent expense of replacing the quartz–iodine lamps. Other criticisms which have been made refer to its lack of portability and to the relatively small amount of writing which can be accommodated in a 10 in. square to give a sufficiently large image on the screen.

Globes

It is now universally accepted that a physical and possibly a slate globe should form part of the equipment of every room where Geography is taught. Since the earth is approximately spherical a two-dimensional representation of any large part of its surface must necessarily show distortions, and unless precautions are taken this is likely to give rise to misconceptions in the pupils' minds. Here then is the first use for a globe. The reader need only be reminded of the areal comparison of Greenland and Australia, first on a Mercator graticule and then on the globe, for proof of the importance of this point.

The slate globe is useful for marking with chalk such things as ocean currents and world wind systems, explorers' routes and distributions of many kinds.

Perhaps the most dramatic use of a globe is in demonstrating the true character of Great Circle routes. To take one example, pupils who are accustomed to atlas maps have difficulty in believing that the shortest air route from Chicago to Bombay lies across

Greenland, northern Norway, the Aral Sea and Afghanistan. But the truth of this and other examples of the same principle can soon be shown, given a globe and a piece of string.

The globe will prove invaluable for demonstrating the causes of the seasons, of day and night and of the difference of sun time in different parts of the world. For the last of these the best source of light is the sun, the globe being placed with the British Isles uppermost. If the sun proves unco-operative the film-strip projector will provide the necessary light. Further effects will be seen as the globe is turned on its axis or is 'walked' round the source of light, its axis at a constant tilt. For greater detail about this subject refer to the specimen lesson on p. 104.

Maps of different kinds

Not all Geography masters regard wall-maps as essential, but there is fairly wide agreement that they can make a valuable contribution to the success of many lessons. It is important, however, that they should not obscure the blackboard or the projection screen. One of their virtues is the rapidity with which, by their aid, pupils' attention can be focused on the area, feature or town which is the subject of the lesson. To be effective wall-maps must be boldly and clearly printed, and because of this only major physical features and the largest towns can be shown. For detail it is necessary to refer to the atlas. A marked defect of some wall-maps which are on the market is that they are too small for effective class use. Map sets—each consisting of a series of maps of a given region—are particular offenders in this regard.

Wall-maps may be mounted in different ways. For details see Chapter 7, p. 188.

The atlas

This must be regarded as an essential item of a pupil's equipment, perhaps the foremost one. It is part of a geographer's stock in trade, and one has difficulty in thinking of any lesson which could proceed very far without detailed reference to it. In general, geography lessons should not start until the pupils have opened their copies at the right page.

Although atlas work is of fundamental importance, the ability to use the maps properly only comes with practice. To the first-year boy and the slow learner words like 'Physical' and 'Political' have very little meaning, while many boys and girls are perplexed by scales. Again, 'Mollweide' and 'Mercator' are familiar terms at university level, but this is hardly the position in the lower forms of schools.

The list of difficulties could be extended, and there is a very strong case for devoting some lessons to 'How to read an atlas'. When the means of locating position by latitude and longitude is introduced masters have a ready means of enlivening lessons. Link the exercises with topical events: 'Here are a number of references. In each case name the town or country concerned, and the reasons for its appearance in the news.'

Some problems concerning atlases call for comment. In the first place the atlas in use must be suitable for the pupils concerned. Elementary though this point may be, it is frequently ignored, perhaps because of lack of thought or as a result of a general shortage of school equipment. In this connection it should be noted that several publishers have turned their attention to the grading of atlases. Secondly, atlases, like textbooks, rapidly become out of date. Figure 3 illustrates the truth of this remark by reference to African countries since the Second World War.

From this standpoint it is fortunate that atlases have a comparatively short life. Their cost of replacement, however, often depletes departmental allowances, and masters may find that they cannot supply every pupil with an atlas. Floating sets, distributed and collected in the lesson, often provide the means of overcoming this problem, but this practice is far from ideal. Immediately it raises homework problems, and ought never to be contemplated in the middle or senior school. At such levels every pupil should have his own copy of the atlas, otherwise the quality of work will suffer, and the objective of enabling pupils to know the meaning and the limitations of all the different maps in a modern atlas cannot be achieved.

Topographical maps

The value of large-scale topographical maps in local geography and field-work is discussed in chapters 3 and 8. Here other aspects of their use are considered. Those of greatest value are Ordnance Survey maps on the 6 in., $2\frac{1}{2}$ in., 1 in. and $\frac{1}{4}$ in. scales. Bartholomew's $\frac{1}{2}$ in. maps and the few Ordnance Survey maps on the same scale are also very useful.

The essentials of map reading (grid references, conventional signs, scales, measurement of distances, orientation and the represen-

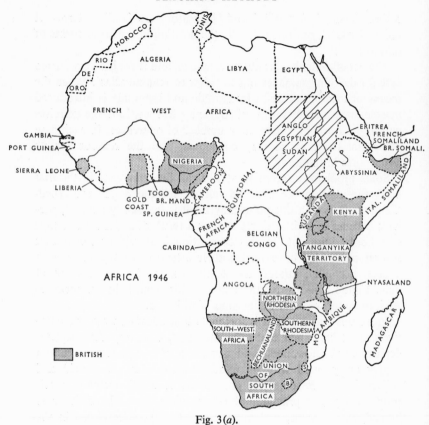

Fig. 3 (a).

tation of relief) are usually introduced in the first form, and are frequently closely linked with the study of the local area. The ability to give accurate grid references and to use symbols correctly is quickly developed in this way, and these aspects acquire real meaning. The pace of progress in map reading naturally varies with the ability of the pupils concerned, but the case is very strong for starting this work with most first-year pupils and for devoting some time to map work in each succeeding year.

The adoption of this procedure has inevitable repercussions on the syllabus as it necessitates the provision of time for map reading. It is important that it should fit appropriately into the course. To leave the seringueiros sweltering in the Amazon forests while a second form studies a contour map of the Lake District would seem to many to be an abuse of syllabus freedom. Where there is no obvious link

Fig. 3(*b*).

why not set aside a definite part of the term for map analysis, concentrating on the landscapes not far from home? Pupils find such work of more interest and relevance than coping with a miscellaneous collection of old examination extracts, occasionally introduced.

Physical Geography offers plenty of scope for illustration by large-scale maps. A great variety of features can be found on those of the Ordnance Survey. Topographical sheets can be used either by way of regional example or for introductory purposes. Pupils might, for example, be asked to describe and account for the detail of a ria. Similarly, one means of beginning the study of limestone country is to inspect the 2½ in. map of Edale and Castleton. The contrast between the abundant surface drainage in the northern part of the area and its absence in the south is spectacular. It positively demands explanation!

67

Map analysis can also be integrated with regional study. An increasing number of textbooks include foreign map extracts, but the emphasis remains on British studies, generally undertaken in the fourth or fifth year. A correspondent observes that most of the major features of the Western Highlands of Scotland can be deduced from the study of appropriate 1 in. Ordnance Survey maps. Clearly seen are the sweep of the mountains down to the sea, the lochs, the minute proportion of good farmland, the choice of sheltered spots for settlement, and the use of seawater rather than land for communication. Again, a study of the Fens cannot fail to be enhanced by the examination of its 1 in. Ordnance Survey maps. The network of drains, the unusual pattern of settlement, the road system, and the concentration of orchards round Wisbech are very prominent features.

The possibility of displaying blocks of adjacent topographical maps is also worthy of note. A transparent protective cover is a necessary safeguard against the eager curiosity of pupils, but wall-maps of this kind will prove very useful, especially if they are of the home region.

Contour lines

Some boys do not easily grasp the basic ideas behind contours, and the Committee therefore thought it wise to include a detailed section on methods of introducing the subject. At an early stage the master must impress on the pupils that a contour line keeps to a fixed height, a principle which can be effectively demonstrated in the field. One pupil attempts to walk across a slope, without climbing or dropping in height, watched and corrected by his friends. The boys then associate the contour with the ground itself rather than with a map or a model. The next stage is to contour the whole slope, using white painted stones or the boys' feet as markers for each contour. If a variety of slopes occurs in the vicinity of the school, it is possible to demonstrate the relationship between steepness and the closeness of the contours.

Where the school is not so favourably placed, some masters make use of a model standing in a large observation tank. Water is run into it to a succession of levels shown by a scale on the inside of the tank. Each contour is then traced on the model by means of pins or stylus marks. Finally the model is laid on the floor so that the boys can, by looking down on it, sketch the contour pattern on a plan.

If this method is dismissed as cumbersome there are several others from which to choose. One of them involves the use of a horizontal pointer rigidly clamped to the upright of a retort stand. By moving the stand round the model a contour line can be traced on its side. Note that the size of the model is somewhat limited by two factors: the base of the stand must be quite clear of the model and a

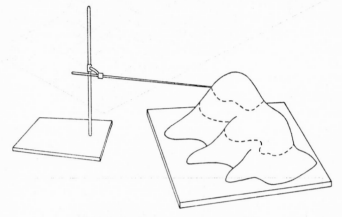

Fig. 4. Tracing a contour on a model.

long arm will be unstable. The boys will naturally learn more from the exercise if they are invited to help in tracing one of the contours and, as in the immersion method, are finally required to sketch the pattern from above. The necessity of extending the arm to take account of valleys, and of withdrawing it where there are spurs will soon make the boys realise the properties of contours (see Fig. 4).

A sectional model, specially made for the purpose, can also be used, and one such example is the subject of Plate 1. Construction begins by drawing a contour sketch map on a sheet of cartridge paper about 18 in. × 24 in. Wood or chipboard sections are then cut out for each contour. (Nine pieces were used in the illustrated model.) Each section is fitted with a peg on its under side and a hole above so that the series can be locked together. At this stage the model will look like a flight of steps, but the outline can soon be smoothed by the removal of the protruding edges. Then the model is coloured and the rivers are shown.

The Committee can also recommend a modified version of the sectional method, one that involves glass or Perspex. Five or six

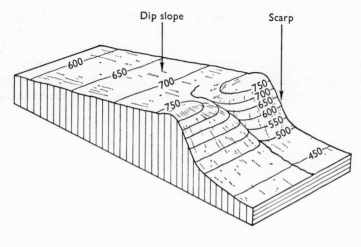

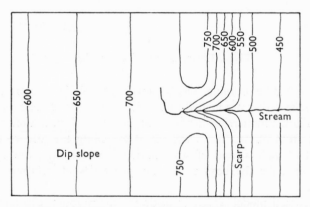

Fig. 5. Teaching contours by block diagram: cuestas.

sheets of a convenient size, for example 18 in. × 18 in., are purchased, preferably with their sharp edges already removed. The first task is to select a map area of the same size and to reproduce its rivers on a sheet of white paper. This will act as the base of the model. A sheet of glass is now placed on the map, and the lowest contour is traced off, using Indian ink and a fine, round-headed nib. This operation is repeated with the other sheets, but on each occasion the next contour in the succession is plotted. It is essential to exercise very great care in this work; check that the area covered by each sheet is EXACTLY

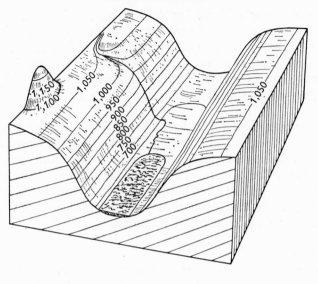

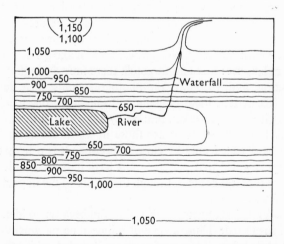

Fig. 6. Teaching contours by block diagram: glacial valleys.

the same as the others. Only by this means will one contour be correctly positioned in relation to its neighbours. India rubbers can be used to separate the sheets of glass when they are finally assembled above the base map. By viewing the result vertically or obliquely pupils see a transparent, three dimensional model.

71

Finally, a method involving block diagrams linked with contour sketch maps is suggested for consideration. It involves no equipment other than paper, but the master must have some idea of perspective and a modicum of artistic ability if he is to prepare the diagrams himself. Figures 5 and 6, on pp. 70–1, illustrate the method, which one member of the Committee has successfully employed for some years.

Many masters pass from basic contour work to the construction of cross sections, using 1 in. or $2\frac{1}{2}$ in. Ordnance Survey sheets for the purpose. Opinion is divided on the better scale, but much can be said in favour of the $2\frac{1}{2}$ in. one for teaching the principles. In any cross-section work it is as well to emphasise that the vertical scale is considerably larger than the horizontal, making it important to mark the exaggeration on the completed profile.

Photographs

Direct field observation is the geographer's ideal, but for many reasons it is not often realised. For the majority of the time we have to rely upon photographs of one kind or another, and it is sobering to reflect how restricted teaching method would be without them. Here our concern is with photographic prints or pictures rather than with transparencies in slide or filmstrip form. Our correspondents are very decided on the qualities which go to make a suitable photograph for class use: first and foremost there must be high quality of reproduction, and, secondly, the photograph must have real point in its subject-matter. Pictures claiming to highlight one locality, but which might have been taken practically anywhere in the world, are hardly likely to appeal. Nor are those in which the subject of the view can be detected only by close inspection. It is a truism of the photographic world that pictures must have impact. This is equally so in a geographical context, though the nature of the impact may be quite different.

Ground-level views. Such pictures often fail because no idea of scale has been suggested. Thus, a view of a limestone pavement conveys much greater realism if human figures are included, whilst the size of a levéed river becomes apparent if there are nearby houses. Pictures must also be up to date. Boys may well miss the geographical point if people's clothes belong to a previous generation, or if cars look like vintage models. It therefore pays the master to prune the school collection from time to time.

Air views. These are of two kinds, the vertical and the oblique.

Extraction of material from vertical air photographs is considered to be beyond the capacity of most school pupils, and stereoscopic work to be of very limited value. An exception occurs when a vertical print covers the same ground as a map, for pupils will then be very interested in checking the latter's accuracy and its cartographic notation. Obliques would seem to be of much wider application, and they are becoming deservedly popular. This is a trend which the Committee welcome, hoping that many more oblique photographs of foreign countries will become available for class use. The attraction of the oblique is in the fact that it is three dimensional, a 'solid' view. Every object is readily recognisable, and attention can be focused immediately on the GEOGRAPHICAL problem involved. In certain respects such shots are superior to direct ground observation where the view is often circumscribed by neighbouring slopes and trees. By contrast, the oblique provides a panoramic view so that the individual feature can be seen in its wider setting.

The class use of photographs. This depends very much on the size of the pictures, as well as the number of copies available. Large, poster-type pictures are sometimes pinned on the walls of the classroom only to become part of the decorative scheme. This is a real possibility, and some means has to be devised of bringing them to the pupils' attention. If the master has a series of individual but related pictures it may be possible to organise an effective wall display. Desks are pushed into the centre of the room, leaving sufficient space under each wall for small groups of pupils to circulate. The latter are given questions to focus attention on important aspects of each picture and they are duly instructed to start. Some means has to be found of phasing pupil movement so that the groups do not converge on the same picture but this is hardly an insuperable difficulty. Experience suggests that this teaching method has real potential. Moreover, its scope is not limited to pictorial matter, for samples, distribution maps and Ordnance Survey sheets can easily be brought into the display. Pupils welcome the freedom from the tyranny of their desks, and the groups often participate in a spirit of friendly rivalry. This method will make the best use of limited teaching resources, as well as ensuring that the investigation is pupil-centred.

Group work with photographs is hardly the norm, and the possibilities of pictorial analysis in ordinary lessons must be considered. The collection of material on a class basis is facilitated by the existence of several textbooks on these lines, old examination questions, and commercial prints. The latter are costly but merit

73

purchase for special purposes. The liability of such prints to be torn or ink-stained in class use can now be minimised, for transparent, protective envelopes are marketed in various sizes by Duraweld Ltd., Sherwood St., Scarborough. The prints are merely slipped into the open end, and their life is thereby extended.

To illustrate the possibilities of pictorial analysis questions about the photograph of the Prairies (Plate 2a) have been included:

(1) The photograph was taken near Portage la Prairie in Canada. Find this town on your atlas map, and name the province concerned.

(2) How can you deduce that this area was settled in fairly recent times? Think of the way in which it differs from a typical English landscape, and try to explain your points.

(3) Some of the fields are in deeper shades of grey than others, while several appear to be white. Why is this? Explain the reasons for using the land in this way.

(4) Comment on the pattern of trees. What does this tell you?

Projection

Most British schools are adequately, if not well, endowed with episcopes, filmstrip and cine projectors. By virtue of this fact, a further means of using pictorial matter is available, but it is one which should complement rather than merely supplement the methods already considered. The successful use of projection depends on a number of important points. First, the room must be effectively blacked out, and the 'dim-out' facilities recently installed in some schools hardly measure up to this requirement unless the projector bulb is very powerful; colour saturation and crispness in black-and-white slides rapidly fall away with the intrusion of light. Secondly, effective class control is imperative before embarking on projection. Inexperienced masters should be warned that high-spirited pupils are unlikely to be tamed by showing them pictures on a screen. A third point to watch is the quality and arrangement of the material. The master should work through illustrative matter himself before projecting it in class. It is an elementary safeguard, but one which can make all the difference between a successful venture and a boring failure. Finally, a word about the length of projection time is not amiss. Experience confirms that it is rarely satisfactory to devote the entire lesson to it. Its use should be integrated with that of other aids or methods relevant to the subject.

The episcope. Although many masters feel that this is an obsolete piece of equipment, others maintain that it still has its place. It can be used, for instance, to show pictures which are not available in slide or filmstrip form, and also book illustrations and small specimens. The detail of large-scale maps can be projected and subjected to analysis, provided that the episcope is very efficient, and the blackout faultless. The latter is vital. Since the light which reaches the projection lens is reflected from the picture, then, unless the light source is very powerful and the optical system of a high order, the image is dull and its details obscure.

The filmstrip and slide projector. Since this projector depends on transmitted light the resultant picture should be crisp and clear. Filmstrips have the advantage of compactness and the orderly presentation of ideas, as well as the virtue of assembling photographs which might not otherwise come on the market. Provided that discrimination is used, many of the marketed strips are well worth purchasing. However, it pays to make use of preview facilities and Education Authority libraries before taking a decision, since strips vary in quality and suitability. One disadvantage of the filmstrip is that it is very difficult to use the pictures in an order other than that determined by the author, unless the master is prepared to cut the strips and house individual frames in transparency holders. Another disadvantage becomes evident when a filmstrip has been in use for some time. Since the surface is unprotected marks and scratches appear on the emulsion, necessitating the replacement of the whole strip.

Many Geography masters nowadays have their own cameras, usually of the 35 mm. type. Apart from taking shots while on holiday or with school parties, they can be used for photographing wall-maps and blackboard diagrams. Masters requiring more detail of this should refer to the article in *Geography*, XLVI, part 3 (July 1961), entitled 'Blackboard and camera' by P. J. M. Bailey. With a modicum of skill and the right equipment amateurs can also make monochrome and colour slides from specimens, book illustrations and picture postcards, although care must be taken not to infringe copyright.

Cine film projectors. The portrayal of movement is the most important function of the cine film as compared with the slide or strip. Herein lies its use in Geography. It is, for instance, difficult to appreciate the work of lumbermen in the equatorial forests or the destructive power of storm waves without seeing the actions involved. Another useful feature stems from the technique of 'panning' whereby a more vivid impression of the size of a landscape or man-made feature can be created than is possible in still photography.

Classroom films must be of such length that they can be effectively used in normal lessons. This precludes the use of films running for more than twenty minutes (two reels) as a time has to be allowed for an introduction and a follow-up. Corresponding members of the Committee are almost unanimous in advocating films of this length.

When time allows many masters show the film through twice in a lesson period, sometimes switching off the sound for the second showing and substituting a commentary of their own. The practice of stopping the film at selected points is not now common, at least during the first showing, as it breaks the essential continuity, of the sound no less than of the picture.

It is important that a film should be accurate and orderly and should possess a high standard of photography. The inclusion of relevant maps and diagrams is also desirable; some of the latter may be animated, designed to simplify, accelerate or slow down natural or mechanical processes. The master should make sure that commercial films really suit his purpose. Titles are occasionally deceptive, but it is only natural for some commercial firms to be more interested in selling their products than in providing good educational fare. A further criterion to be insisted on is that the film should deal with the normal, not with the extraordinary or the purely spectacular. The latter may be interesting but can easily give pupils false ideas, and may therefore be worse than a waste of time.

Since there is a sound track on the vast majority of films, some points about this aspect are relevant. The foremost quality expected of a commentary is that it should be delivered in good, clear English. Some producers try to heighten the sense of reality by making use of local dialect. On occasion, this is practically unintelligible; its unbridled use even causes mirth, and then the audience misses the point. On the other hand, with real thought dialect has its place in films. Another point to consider is the content of the spoken word, for a balance must be struck between technicalities and light-heartedness. Obtrusive background music is universally condemned, and whilst a case exists for the inclusion of genuine local sounds, these should be omitted if there is any risk of interfering with the commentary.

Practice regarding the preview of films varies enormously, although most masters regard this as the ideal. When the detailed subject-matter of the film is already known, the preparatory stage is much more effective, and so, too, is the follow-up. When previewing is out of the question, printed commentaries and catalogues may help.

A script version of the commentary is enclosed with some films, and it would be very useful if this practice were more widespread. The Educational Foundation for Visual Aids publishes comprehensive catalogues of instructional films and filmstrips: Part III is devoted to General Physical and Economic Geography, and Part IV to Regional Geography. The Sound Services catalogue can also be recommended. Details of the addresses, and of publications of a similar nature will be found in appendix C, p. 339.

Geography broadcasts

One cannot fully understand the significance of schools broadcasts, in either sound or vision, unless one relates them to the overall pattern of broadcasting and the listening and watching habits of children and their parents. Though we are primarily concerned here with the application of broadcasting to the teaching of Geography, we must also consider the impact of home listening and viewing on the mental development of children. There is wide agreement that children should be encouraged to view and listen critically, whether in school or at home. It is also true that many evening programmes bring out valuable geographical facts or concepts even though the intention of the producers may be primarily to entertain.

The educational benefit of sound and television broadcasts to schools is fiercely disputed, and not least their value in the teaching of Geography. It must be admitted that even sound broadcasting, which was begun for schools in 1924, is far from being used in every school today, and television is at present used by still fewer (6,000 schools approximately in 1963 in Britain, where there are more than 12 million private receivers and more than 34,000 schools).

Many problems in the use of broadcasts in schools are common to both sound and vision, some of them of a practical and others of a psychological nature. Amongst the former the most obvious is that of time-tabling. Broadcasts at fixed times and of a limited period all too commonly do not fit in either with the school's time-table or with its Geography syllabus. A further difficulty is that very often a special room has to be used for reception, particularly of television. In planning new schools and new Geography departments it is important to see that the Geography room is equipped with means for the reception of both sound and vision. The time-table problem is so widespread that many teachers, when faced with the considerable organisational difficulties involved, tend to shun broadcasts for this reason alone. On the other hand, in schools where it has been found possible to plan a term's or a year's work around one or more broadcast series, teachers report an enrichment of the Geography teaching and an accession of reality into the classroom. To ease the problem the broadcasting authorities usually repeat any given lesson at some other time during the week, whilst so far as sound programmes are concerned the difficulty can be overcome by using a tape recorder (see p. 80).

Far more serious and difficult to refute is the argument that passive watching or listening leaves little impression on the minds of the pupils; this is certainly true when the broadcast is received without adequate preparation or follow-up. The master must not regard the radio or television set as something that makes his work easier or less demanding of skill. They are valuable teaching aids, to be used as the master determines; they are no substitute for the personal contact between him and his pupils.

Of equal weight is the complaint, often made, that programmes vary greatly in value, are not necessarily adjusted to the abilities of pupils, and may contain material which many Geography masters would regard as irrelevant and therefore time-wasting. To enable teachers to decide whether or not to use a broadcast series, and to assist them in making the best use of those which they may consider of value, the broadcasting organisations prepare, a term in advance, booklets of Teachers' Notes, which give a broad outline of each programme throughout the term, together with pictures, maps and short bibliographies. In addition, details of the year's broadcast plans are available in the spring preceding the new school year so that schools desiring to do so can plan ahead. These publications may be obtained either as single copies or in bulk, the notes for teachers being issued free. Pupils' pamphlets are also published, at a small cost, for use with most of the series, and it is strongly advised that they should be supplied to the pupils before the broadcasts are used. Requests for information and published material may be made to:

B.B.C.

B.B.C. Publications, 35 Marylebone High Street, London, W. 1.

The Secretary, School Broadcasting Council for the United Kingdom, 3 Portland Place, London, W. 1.

The Secretary, School Broadcasting Council for Scotland, 5 Queen Street, Edinburgh, 2.

The Secretary, School Broadcasting Council for Wales, 39 Park Place, Cardiff.

Independent Television

The Schools Information Officer, Schools Broadcasting Section, Associated-Rediffusion Ltd., Television House, Kingsway, London, W.C. 2.

The Secretary, Education Department, Associated-Television Ltd., A.T.V. House, 17 Great Cumberland Place, London, W. 1.

The Secretary, Schools Department, Granada T.V. Network Ltd., Granada House, Water Street, Manchester, 3.

In two other ways the broadcasting organisations seek to render more effective the aid they provide. In the first place many television broadcasts for schools are repeated during the holidays to enable teachers to assess their value for school use. Secondly, the B.B.C. has, since 1963, experimented in radio-vision, in which a specially prepared filmstrip is shown in conjunction with a sound-radio broadcast. The latter can be tape-recorded in the school so that it is available for use several times if necessary. In the first year of the venture two filmstrips on the Jurassic limestone belt of Britain were produced, one concentrating on iron ore, the other on Cotswold farming. Notes and filmstrips for these and later programmes are obtainable in the same way as other B.B.C. publications. The technique may well prove to be an important development in method.

Certain other attributes are common to both sound-radio and television broadcasts to schools. Though they are usually pre-recorded the information they convey is generally more up to date, and because of that more accurate, than that provided through other media. There is the sense that what is seen or described is actually happening at the moment, and confidence is inspired by the obvious knowledge and authority of the narrator.

Classroom procedure. Although the impact of a television programme is different in quality from that of a sound-radio programme, both media require the same kind of classroom procedure.

Before the broadcast is received a certain amount of preparation is desirable in order to place the particular lesson within the context of the course that is being followed, and to put the pupils in the right frame of mind to give close attention to what they are to see or hear. They must be given a sense of purpose, and this can be achieved by, for example, posing questions which are to be answered after the broadcast, or starting the build-up of a regional map for completion likewise after the broadcast. Care must be taken, of course, not to anticipate the actual material of the programme itself.

7-2

It is most important that there should be no form of interruption during the programme. Careful editing will have pruned away all extraneous or repetitive matter, so that any diversion of attention is likely to cause pupils to lose the thread of the lesson. Note-making, blackboard work, reference to atlases, questions—all these can but distract. Moreover, it must be remembered that the impact of the programme lies not only in its factual content but also in its emotional appeal. However, because a sound broadcast, unlike a television one, provides no visual images, it may be desirable in the case of the former to display a wall-map for pupils to look at when necessary. For the same reason, the narrator may refer pupils to maps or pictures in the published notes.

Follow-up is essential in order to ensure that pupils have fully understood the broadcast and have grasped the facts and principles presented to them. Misconceptions can be corrected and difficult points explained by means of questions and discussion. The pupils should then be able to answer the questions set, or complete the map begun before the broadcast. Alternatively, they could be asked to produce a written account of the programme, illustrated by maps and/or diagrams; this could form part of a record of the whole series, the assembling of which might well be carried out by the school Geographical Society.

Repetition of broadcast lessons. The chief disadvantage inherent in both sound and television broadcasts is their 'once and for all' character. Although both B.B.C. and I.T.V. usually give a second broadcast of each lesson there is normally no opportunity for the same pupils to see or listen to both. Tape recording of sound broadcasts has already been mentioned. It should be realised that in the ordinary way, because of copyright laws, it is illegal to tape-record a B.B.C. programme. A concession has been obtained, however, which permits the recording of school broadcasts provided the recordings are used only for instructional purposes in class, and that they are destroyed at the end of the school year.

The B.B.C. has had gramophone records made of a limited number of its outstanding school sound broadcasts and these are on free loan to teachers; a catalogue can be obtained from the School Broadcasting Council. There are also a few tape recordings, available to Colleges of Education.

The problem of securing further showings of a television broadcast presents much greater difficulties. A few programmes of both B.B.C. and I.T.V. have been made available on 16 mm. film, but their number is at present very small. Apparatus, analogous to the tape recorder, called 'videotape' is being produced, however, for recording television broadcasts. Its use in schools will no doubt increase.

Sound and television broadcasts compared. Each medium makes its own special demands on the pupils and on the Geography master. In sound broadcasts success depends to a very great extent on the voice of the broadcaster. The subject must be one which lends itself to lucid description and explanation, and the narrator must be able to conjure up vivid pictures in the minds of the pupils. Few could fail to visualise, for example, the Bushmen as described by Laurens van der Post against the Kalahari background. The stimulation of the pupils' imagination may be heightened by the inclusion of natural sound or local music, of dramatised episodes or stories. The reception of sound broadcasts does not necessitate any special arrangement of the class, whilst when radio-vision is used the arrangements are much the same as for any other lesson involving the filmstrip projector.

Television possesses all the advantages of sound radio except that less use of the pupils' imagination is required. This is more than compensated for, however, by the enormous range of visual material which can be introduced into the classroom. This includes film material (telecine) often specially shot, aerial photographs, animated diagrams and still pictures of all kinds. In addition, people can be interviewed at their work, and outside broadcasts can bring industrial and agricultural activities to the pupil. The chief problem involved with television viewing in the classroom concerns the position of the set and the seating arrangement of the class. Although more pessimistic figures have been suggested, most teachers in this country find that a 24 in. screen is adequate for a normal class of 30. It is important that pupils should not sit closer than 5 or 6 ft. from the screen, whilst maximum distance for viewing for children with normal vision is about fifteen times the diameter of the picture. Blackout is unnecessary, but care should be taken to avoid reflections on the screen from the windows.

Television and films. It is often suggested that television programmes in Geography do no more than a good film can do, and that the film is more flexible in application. To a certain extent this is true, especially if the film is always readily available; but the number of good films is small and teachers must book them some weeks ahead. A film is bound to become out of date before its useful life is finished, whereas television material is in most cases fresh and

81

topical. The functions of the two media can obviously overlap, but the occasions on which there is a straight choice between them are very rare.

The programmes

Sound Radio. Three types of programme are likely to be of interest to the Geography master:

(*a*) Geography for Secondary schools for pupils aged 13–15.

(*b*) A Primary school series such as 'Exploration Earth' for pupils aged 10–11.

(*c*) Various talks dealing with topics of current interest or scientific or historical matters (e.g. 'How things began', 'Past and present', 'People, places and things'). Talks having relevance to the Geography syllabus can be selected.

The Geography series (*a*) lasts for the whole school year, and forms a definite course on a particular part of the world. In 1965–6 the subject was the British Isles, based on a series of topics, e.g.

Autumn Term: Landscape—'North Country horizons', hydro-electricity, forestry, Fenlands, North Sea oil, fisheries, food processing, sheep farming, dairy products, beef cattle, Scilly Islands, poultry farming.

'North Country horizons' and one programme in the Spring Term, on the growth of London—'Mithras to Megalopolis'—were radio-vision broadcasts.

The series for 1966–7 dealt with certain regions of Asia: U.S.S.R. in the Autumn Term; India and Pakistan in the Spring Term; Far East and South-east Asia in the Summer Term. Again, two radio-vision programmes were included, one entitled 'Soviet horizons', the other 'A village in India'. The subjects for the Spring Term were: a village in India, Calcutta, Damodar project, Durgapur steelworks, small-scale industry, cotton, jute, surveying Pakistan's resources, transport in the sub-continent.

The Primary school series (*b*), though intended for younger children, can be of value to junior and backward pupils in a Secondary school.

Television. The present policy of the B.B.C. is to produce a Geography series lasting for one term, in each year. For 1965–6 the subject was 'Looking at Australia', intended for pupils aged 12–14. It was designed to supplement a regional study, the earlier programmes dealing primarily with rural life, the later ones with industry and towns. The subject for 1966–7 was 'Changing Britain', designed for the 13–15 age range: and the broadcasts dealt with changes in industry and agriculture, population movements, transport, new towns, airport location, power, water supply, and the use of open spaces.

As with sound broadcasts, teachers have found that individual programmes from Current Affairs and other series have considerable interest and relevance in geographical work.

Of the independent companies only Associated Rediffusion Ltd. has produced Geography programmes, though there have been none since 1962. One major series, spanning three terms, covered a regional approach to the British Isles.

Samples and specimens

One way of adding realism to a lesson is to use specimens. These can be used as an introduction; 'What is this?' may well be an excellent beginning to a lesson. Samples can also be shown at appropriate points during the lesson. The idea of a cotton field or an asbestos mine can be conveyed through pictures, but the impression is deepened and the idea made more vivid if the pupil can examine an actual specimen of a cotton boll with its seeds and mass of lint, or one of chrysotile asbestos with its long silky crystals which can be easily pulled off one by one.

Specimens and samples can be obtained from many sources, but whenever possible the pupils should themselves gather them during field excursions; there are endless possibilities.

The actual use made of specimens during lessons will depend on their size, value and fragility, and on the number of any one kind available. It is largely a matter of common sense on the part of the master whether they are passed round the class for inspection by individual pupils; examined by different groups in turn; distributed simultaneously to pairs or groups of pupils; or projected on to the screen by means of an episcope.

PUPILS' WRITTEN WORK

Using notebooks. Opinions differ widely on the best way of using pupils' notebooks. It is possible to fill the books with dictated notes and closely copied blackboard maps. The argument used in defence of this method is the shortness of teaching time: by no other means will the syllabus be as effectively covered, or can the master be sure that his pupils have satisfactory notes. The Committee are prepared to admit that rare occasions may arise when dictation is useful, but in general they are unanimous in condemning it, believing that while it is in progress the pupils are completely passive and soon become bored.

Comment has already been passed on the value of copying blackboard notes, and with this can be linked the distribution of sheets of typewritten notes to be copied out. Both are sterile as means of provoking thought among pupils. Some masters maintain, however, that, used sparingly, these methods have their place, for they can be used to demonstrate how material should be organised. There is also the point of view that 'handouts' leave more time for active teaching. This has a limited validity if the information in a handout is intended to provide material for interesting exercises. It would be a complete waste of time, however, for pupils merely to copy the information into their notebooks.

Many masters subscribe to the belief that pupils learn most of all through making their own notes during a lesson. And yet it cannot be denied that this method may lead to problems. Boys find real difficulty in deciding which points ought to be recorded. While they hesitate the master has passed to the next point, and they are soon thrown into utter confusion. Some of the ways of anticipating this kind of dilemma have already been discussed (see 'The blackboard' p. 59) but there are others of real importance. A master would be unworthy of his profession if he did not adapt the pace of the lesson to the ability of the pupils. He will repeat important points, and he may well insist that pupils make their notes in an all-purpose 'rough' book. These notes can be recast and expanded either during the remainder of the lesson, or for homework.

Critics of this discussion might well argue that 'memory loading' is implicit in the insistence on note taking, however well this is done. The Committee therefore hasten to observe that notebooks should contain far more than mere notes. Pupils' own observations and deductions from a wide range of material, including distribution maps, statistics and graphs, should also find a place in them. One of our primary aims must be to make the pupils think geographically.

Maps in notebooks. There is a large measure of accord regarding the value of sketch maps in geographical teaching. Differences of opinion arise, however, in the execution of such maps. Should they be traced, map-roll duplicated or drawn freehand? The Committee favour as much practice as possible in freehand drawing, provided that the outlines are not complicated. In the latter case they suggest that some assistance ought to be offered. Badly drawn, inaccurate outlines obviously affect the subsequent insertion of data, so that such maps are rendered valueless.

Some masters insist on map drawing 'rules'. In one school a copy of the points to be observed is glued into each atlas when it is first issued. Here is the list:

(1) Start by using a lead pencil. Mark the outlines lightly, and only proceed when you have a good shape.

(2) Use coloured pencils for shading.

Green is for lowlands.

Yellow and Brown are used for uplands.

Blue marks rivers and lakes.

Red is reserved for frontiers, the position of towns and arrows denoting 'movement',

Colouring must be lightly and neatly applied.

(3) Print names and comments in ink; keeping to horizontal lettering wherever possible.

(4) Check that every map has a printed title, some indication of scale and a key.

The annotated sketch map is of particular interest, partly because it focuses pupils' attention on a wide range of geographical techniques. In the compilation they are obliged to think in spatial terms and of interrelationships, apart from exercising care cartographically. There is a danger, however, that, if the notes are too full, the map may be submerged under a confused mass of overlapping print.

An alternative arrangement is to devote a double page of the notebook to the analytical description of a region or topic. The map is drawn in the centre, and flanked by statistical graphs, notes, and sections, in 'boxes'.

The issue of notebooks. Practice among masters is very varied on this point. Some of them issue one book per pupil in years one to three; and this is used for every aspect of the work. If it is necessary to have distinct sections of material, the book can be divided up as desired. Other masters like their pupils to have two books, the second one for statistical records and definitions, occasional reference to which is comparatively easy. An alternative method is sometimes adopted of keeping material fresh in their pupils' minds. Old notebooks are preserved, so that a complete record of study is available. This raises problems of storage, but the books can be re-issued to their owners for revision purposes.

The correction of notebooks. This is a vexed issue, for large classes and existing staffing ratios mean that marking can become an extremely heavy burden. The Committee do not feel that every piece of work need be corrected, although they are equally aware of the danger of the opposite extreme. Frequent inspection of notebooks is undoubtedly a necessity if pupils' standards are to be maintained. It is also a deterrent for those of our pupils who, in its absence, would fail to complete exercises, either by default or through absence. A popular method of correcting notebooks is to give an overall mark for a section of work, as well as others for specific exercises. In the busy routine of school life the marking of a particular set of books can easily be overlooked. To meet this possibility some masters instruct pupils to number the pages in their notebooks and to provide a table of contents. A column in the table is left blank for the insertion of marks, and the master can therefore see at a glance if the book needs attention.

Homework

Our correspondents in every kind of Secondary school are directed to set homework, although a minority of them see little value in such work, especially in the case of less able pupils. But, if homework has to be set, masters should strive to make it a specific task and one of real geographical value. Some homeworks will be preparatory in nature (see the specimen lesson on the Seasons) or a means of consolidation (see the lesson on Montreal), whilst others are illustrative.

If a preparatory homework only involves reading the next chapter in the textbook, it is of little use. Where a short list of associated questions has been added, however, the position is very much improved, especially in the case of those which demand independent thought and reference to atlases. While the textbook and atlas are the primary sources of information, other possibilities should not be neglected. Personal observation, documentary television programmes, reference books in the school library, and books at home are other sources. It has to be admitted of course that some of these suggestions may be impracticable. In a number of homes, including those of some of the abler pupils, there are few books, and either no television set or no possibility of 'looking in' at the recommended programme. Useful tasks, unaffected by such drawbacks, may well include such things as the construction of bar graphs and divided circles from statistics.

The problem of preparatory homeworks is most acute in the less able forms. Tasks have to be fairly easy, and preferably practical in type or based on direct observation. Here, then, are some possibilities:

(1) Write down a list of all the jobs that you have noticed being done by coloured immigrants. Which countries do you think they come from? Why?

(2) Obtain three labels from food containers (e.g. bottles, jars and cardboard boxes). Stick them in your notebook, and name the foods. State where each of them has come from.

(3) Make a list of eight of the most popular types of car, and find out where each of them is made.

Homeworks which are consolidatory or illustrative in type provide fewer difficulties for the master. In the first place pupils can be asked to draw maps. These are frequently designed to illustrate regional studies and the base map is taken from the textbook or, better still, the atlas. The danger of using the former is that the task then merely involves copying someone else's original work. By instructing pupils to add some points and to omit others the master can ensure that the finished product will more truly serve the purpose of the exercise by invoking some thought from the pupils. If map drawing of this or any other nature is given to less able pupils it is as well to ensure that the notebook reproduction is on approximately the same scale as the original map.

Annotated summary maps, already discussed in general method, are a variant of this kind of homework, but are more suited to brighter pupils.

Written work can also be set, ranging from accounts based on the subject-matter of a film shown in class to imaginative description. After dealing with Moscow or the racial groups in South Africa, pupils can reasonably be asked to put themselves in a news reporter's position, preparing a dispatch for the editor.

Where attention has to be concentrated on impending external examinations pupils are sometimes given an essay question for homework. They prepare the answer in some detail, but are not allowed to refer to notes of any kind when it is written out in the following lesson. In this way pupils learn how to use examination time to the best advantage.

So far no references have been made to 'learning' homeworks. Differences of opinion on their suitability may arise, but it is difficult to see how basic factual knowledge can be absorbed in other ways. Admittedly some facts are retained through practice in handling material and discussing it in class, but this is hardly enough for purposes of serious study. If such homeworks are interspersed with other kinds there need be no fear of a return to the days of 'Cape and

87

Bay' Geography. As a practical point the learning ought to be tested in the next lesson or some pupils will ignore the injunction!

Revision

The arguments used in the last paragraph are also applicable in the case of revision. Every master knows that pupils soon forget much of what they have learned. Revision provides the remedy and, moreover, offers an opportunity of emphasising important points, and of presenting them to pupils in an alternative form. Purposeful revision is by no means synonymous with the mere repetition of all that has gone before.

Several means of consolidating progress are in use. Some masters prefer to pause for this purpose after each group of lessons, while others wait until the end of the course. Perhaps it is best to use a combination of both methods.

Periodic revision often centres round a revision homework and some form of class test, of which two types are commonly used. The first attempts to cover breadth of knowledge by means of single-word answers. The other looks for depth of knowledge, and the ability to think geographically. Paragraph-length answers are expected and the questions are so phrased that pupils have to concentrate on deduction and explanation.

Revision at the end of a course can easily become a boring process and every effort should therefore be made to look at material from a fresh point of view. One means of achieving this is to plan imaginary journeys and to ask pupils to describe the geographical features *en route*. For example, if Canada has been treated regionally attention could be concentrated on a trans-continental railway journey. Similar in conception are exercises based on transects, when attention is given to interrelationships, both physical and human.

Another means involves the use of statistical maps depicting, for example, economic data or the spread of population. The interests of geographical technique are admirably served if the questions demand explanatory analysis. In this way, for instance, it is possible to look anew at Scotland. The majority of masters base their course work on a threefold regional division of that country so that a study of its overall population pattern has much to offer.

Pictures can also be useful in systematic revision. Where they are in slide form, a considerable number of topics can be covered, especially by restricting the number of questions per subject. To a more limited extent the same technique can also be employed with filmstrips. An alternative method is to mount a set of pictures on pieces of cardboard, linking each one with a fundamental question and giving it a reference number. The pupils write down the sequence of numbers, allowing one or two lines for each answer. Sufficient time is allowed to answer the question on the first card received and then all the cards are passed on in a predetermined order. This method brings all the pupils into active participation, but confusion may result unless there is strict control. The work may be marked as a test in the ordinary way. On the other hand it is probably quite as valuable if organised as a basis for discussion, not tied up with marks. The subject-matter of the cards need not necessarily be pictorial. Equally valuable are maps, which may be portions of old atlas maps and diagrams.

OBSERVATIONAL GEOGRAPHY
The weather

For obvious reasons the study of the weather must be included in course work and it is clear that masters rate the maintenance of a meteorological station very highly. So rapidly does our weather change, sometimes with dramatic suddenness, that it can scarcely lack interest. Yet its study involves careful observation, the compilation of detailed records, and subsequent analysis, all useful objectives in themselves. Finally, real awareness and understanding of British weather, supported by statistics, establishes a useful basis of comparison with other climates and meteorological phenomena. Thus figures of temperature and rainfall for places like Winnipeg or Cape Town have greater meaning because of its study.

The understanding of weather increases when data can be displayed in the Geography room. One board, illustrated in Fig. 7, might be used for the latest figures from the school weather station (Plate 4a) and another for monthly averages. Masters having these figures on display are agreeably surprised to note how frequently reference is made to them.

It is often best to choose observers from fourth and fifth form pupils. At this age they should be able to read the instruments accurately and will be studying the British Isles. Observers should work in pairs, forming a rota. Nine o'clock in the morning (G.M.T.) is the official recording time, but this will hardly provide sufficient information for some work, and more frequent observation may be considered necessary for short lengths of time. Gaps in the records, particularly at the week-ends but also for longer periods during school holidays, are very frustrating so that provision should be made to cover them, if possible. Pupils who carry out the work during the holidays must, however, be completely reliable. Incomplete but accurate records are better than misleading ones.

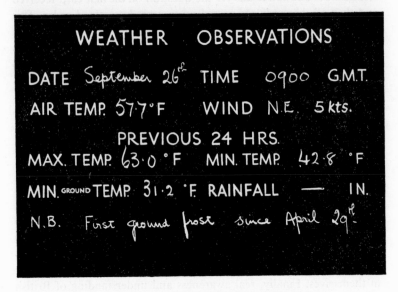

Fig. 7. A display board for details of the daily weather.

The school's observations should be matched against those shown in The Daily Weather Report, issued by the Meteorological Office. The figures given in the report provide some kind of check on the school record, especially if there is an official station in the neighbourhood. Again, by reference to a larger canvas it should be possible to ascertain the longer-term causes of any change.

Real encouragement is given to weather study where the school is linked with sister institutions, or a central organisation. The work itself becomes more purposeful and extra emphasis is placed on careful observation. Two inter-school organisations may be mentioned. One of them caters for schools in the London area, and the pooled information has been used to make a detailed study of London's weather and climate. To participate in the scheme stringent conditions are laid down regarding the siting of the station and the instruments. For example, air and ground temperatures must be measured to the nearest tenth of a degree. Dr T. J. Chandler's research based on these figures is now complete and its results are embodied in his book *The Climate of London* (Hutchinson).

A similar type of scheme was explained in *Weather* (May 1960), xv, no. 5. Schools wishing to join need not install special instruments, and location can be anywhere in the British Isles. The organisation requests the completion and dispatch of a monthly sheet of information, as follows:

1. Precipitation (in inches)
    (*a*) Monthly total.
    (*b*) Number of rain days (0·01 in. or more).
    (*c*) Day with heaviest rainfall.
    (*d*) Amount of rain on that day.
    (*e*) Number of days on which snow fell.
    (*f*) Number of days with snow cover at 09.00 G.M.T. (half ground or more covered).

2. Electrical phenomena
    (*a*) Number of days with thunder and lightning.
    (*b*) Number of days with thunder only.

3. Temperature.
    (*a*) Maximum temperature: (i) date, (ii) temperature.
    (*b*) Minimum temperature: (i) date, (ii) temperature.
    (*c*) Average maximum for month.
    (*d*) Average minimum for month.
    (*e*) Mean monthly temperature.
    (*f*) Number of days with ground frost.
    (*g*) Number of days with air frost.

4. Visibility (at 09.00 G.M.T.)
    (*a*) Number of days of dense fog (visibility below 44 yards).
    (*b*) Number of days with fog including dense fog (visibility below 1,100 yards).
    (*c*) Number of days with good visibility (over 6·25 miles).

5. Cloud (at 09.00 G.M.T.)
    (*a*) Number of days with half or less of sky covered.
    (*b*) Number of days with over half sky covered.
    (*c*) Days with predominance of cumulus cloud.
    (*d*) Days with predominance of stratus cloud.

6. Wind speed at 09.00 G.M.T. (except 6*e*)
    (*a*) Days with wind 0 – 3 kts.
    (*b*) Days with wind 4 – 11 kts.
    (*c*) Days with wind 12 – 21 kts.
    (*d*) Days with wind 22 kts. and over.
    (*e*) Highest wind speed: (i) date, (ii) speed.

7. Sunshine
    Number of hours of sunshine.

8. Wind direction (09.00 G.M.T.). Number of observations
   W., N.W., N., N.E., E., S.E., S., S.W.

9. Special remarks.

Masters may also like to know that schools can become official observers of the Meteorological Office. The figures required are either rainfall alone, or the full range of meteorological phenomena. Very stringent conditions of participation are naturally enforced, and much thought should be given to the matter before submitting an application. Details of the requirements are set out in two leaflets: No. 5, *Taking Weather Observations*, and No. 6, *Rules for Rainfall Observers*, both of which can be obtained free from the Meteorological Office.

Observations of the sun

The important things to ascertain are (*a*) the direction and altitude of the sun at regular intervals during a single day; (*b*) the altitude of the sun at a given time (e.g. noon) in different months of the year. The simplest method is to measure the shadow of a vertical pole as regards both length and direction (the latter as an angle from true north). Alternatively an instrument in the form of a quadrant with a movable arm (see Plate 4*b*) can be used for measuring the sun's elevation directly. The results of these observations demonstrate the relationship between the sun's noon altitude and temperature, e.g. in January as compared with July.

SAMPLE STUDIES

It is essential to consider this aspect of method because Sample Studies have gained wide acceptance in recent years. In making a Sample Study the master selects a single geographical unit (such as a farm, a village, a factory, or a physical feature) and subjects it to detailed investigation. The suitability of a unit partly depends on the amount of information that is available and can be sifted for class use. It must be there in abundance. If the material is carefully chosen, pupils will have a clearer, more interesting and realistic picture of conditions. Moreover, it may be possible to use the sample in generalising about the region as a whole.

Perhaps the most popular of all Sample Study units is the farm. It is important to choose a farm which is typical of its area, and part of whose details are available in map form. The map, preferably on a large scale, should show at least the layout of buildings, the access roads, the position and extent of the fields, and the minor physical features of the locality. Essential information concerns the weather, soils and markets, as well as details of crops and crop yields, numbers and types of livestock, the labour force and the degree of mechanisation. Besides this wealth of factual detail, pupils should also see pictures of the farm, its owner, and the seasonal activities.

The detailed study of a factory involves the collection of a similar amount of material although there are particular dangers to watch in this case, for geographers should not be gathering detailed information about processes and manufacturing techniques. Some of these facts are welcome, but the main concern will be with raw materials, the significance of the site, products, labour and markets.

The techniques of sampling can also be applied to Physical Geography. The detailed study of ONE glacier or ONE stretch of coastline not only grips the attention of the pupils, but teaches them more accurate Physical Geography than do the generalised accounts given in textbooks.

Sample Studies as a teaching method have several commendable features. In the first place they involve the study of actual people and places as the starting point. Good pedagogic precept is therefore followed, for the master moves 'from the particular to the general'. Again, the method can be used without special equipment in ordinary classrooms. Illustrative material can be projected if an episcope is available but this is not essential, and only a blackboard and some display space are really necessary.

From other points of view the method has its dangers and limitations. Prominent among them is the over-zealous use of sampling. Pupils can be given so many of them that they merely go from sample to sample instead of from topic to topic or region to region. The facts of one sample will be confused with those of another, and little of lasting value will be achieved. The keyword here is moderation, and only two or three Sample Studies a term should be attempted, each as different from the others as possible, both in content and approach.

Purists would also argue that no sample is typical, but the problem of rapidly dating material seems more important at this level of instruction. For example, many South American, African and Asiatic countries are undergoing profound and rapid changes, so that a number of the Sample Studies available to us, dealing with aspects of life in these countries, are already quite out of date.

8   93   TOG

Unfortunately, most Geography masters simply cannot afford sufficient time to remedy this situation.

Some masters have experienced difficulty in collecting sample material. Here, therefore, are a number of possible sources. The Geographical Association has published an excellent booklet entitled *Sample Studies*. A number of school textbooks also contain sample studies:

Nelson's *Geography Texts*, edited by W. G. East, volumes 2–8.
Geography for Schools, Books I–V (Heinemann).
How People Live. A series of books edited by A. C. Tubbs (Ward, Lock).
Case Studies in World Geography, ed. R. M. Highsmith (Prentice Hall).
Focal points in Geography, edited by R. Beddis (U.L.P.).
Sample Geography of Great Britain, Burrell and Hancock (Methuen).
Study Geography, book series by Rushby, Bell & Dybeck (Longmans).
Focus on Geographical Activity, Thomas & Patton (McGraw-Hill).

The danger of using outdated information on farms can be minimised by using the Farm Adoption Scheme of the Association for Agriculture (53 Victoria Street, London S.W. 1). The Association supplies details about farms in Britain as well as of those in different parts of the Commonwealth. Bulletins giving news about each farm are sent out at regular intervals, and visits to some of the British farms can also be arranged.

INDIVIDUAL WORK AND GROUP WORK

One of the themes in this chapter has been the importance of pupils actively contributing to class lessons. Whenever time and circumstances allow many masters abandon class instruction as such and pupils work as individuals or in small groups. Responsibility for progress is more fully thrown on the pupils' own shoulders, and experience shows that in the main they respond to the challenge. In one sense, of course, the master is more closely involved than ever, for detailed preparation on his part is essential if such schemes are to succeed. Job cards may have to be made, room displays mounted, and source material collected.

For some topics it is reasonable for the master to expect pupils to find their own material though he would probably be unwise to rely on every child in this respect. He should therefore have the necessary sources available and be prepared to steer the less able pupils in the required direction.

One correspondent introduces his classes to individual work when South America is to be studied. He has made out a full set of exercises and directions to guide the class through its studies. The pupils' attention is directed to the maps, pictures and letterpress of their textbook, to their atlases and to wall displays. During this session of individual work a film is shown and exercises set on it. Due allowance is made for the display of pupil initiative but the emergence of the fundamental points is assured through well-chosen questions. Each is carefully phrased so that its answer forms part of a developing theme.

Another attempt to move away from formal class teaching may be outlined here. Masters who have used this method find its preparation time-consuming and its operation an exacting task. Nevertheless, the boys find such an approach unusually stimulating and the method is at least well worth a trial. Few teachers, however, would be likely to use it more than once or twice a term.

For this method the class is divided into five groups, each with its own leader. The master arranges five different items of group work in different parts of the Geography room laid out so that each task can be completed in eight or so minutes. Here a 1 in. map, there a poster, in one corner a film slide projector with three or four slides, in another corner a photograph and on a board a graph...By going to each station and answering the questions displayed each group gathers information for itself. There is purposeful activity, movement and discussion, the boys are thinking for themselves and the master assumes the dual rôle of organiser and adviser.

Individual work may span several subjects. The artificial division of knowledge is often deplored by educationists, and here is a step towards overcoming it. One member of the Committee, in conjunction with his history and art colleagues, asked second formers to produce a folder on 'Australia: past and present'. The resulting compilation was set out on file paper and enclosed in hard-backed, decorated covers. The project, which lasted for a term, was exhilarating to the pupils, and the results highly commendable.

In this case able pupils were involved, but the idea can readily be adapted to slow learners. An alternative with the latter kind of pupil is to invite them to prepare poster summaries. The master gets the work under way by distributing sheets of drawing paper on which there are templated maps. The pupils insert their own detail, and arrange notes, sketches, and brand-labels around the maps. One advantage of this kind of work is the variety of expression which is afforded. A characteristic of such pupils is their inability to concentrate and in poster work they can quickly change from one form of expression to another, thus reducing the danger of boredom.

Another form of work which may be carried out on either an

individual or a group basis is the project, an example of which has already been given. In project work pupils are more truly left on their own than in most other forms of teaching. They are responsible for the sectional layout of their piece of work, the way in which its subject-matter is handled, and the illustrations. When it has been completed the material is frequently put in a folder.

Few masters doubt the value of project work when it is properly executed, but certain pitfalls have to be watched. One of these is the natural tendency for pupils to reproduce entire paragraphs of print. Such mechanical work does not involve their own thought, and must be accounted of little merit. Similarly, some projects are full of cut-out illustrations that have little or no connection with the subject-matter.

Even when the *written* material is self-expressed and original it can still be unsatisfactory from a geographical point of view. Perhaps an example drawn from a C.S.E. project 'Sugar beet and cane' illustrates the point. Despite earlier warnings by the staff some pupils still spent a great deal of time and effort in describing different kinds of refined sugar!

In some Secondary schools streaming based on ability has been abolished, and the Geography master, along with his colleagues, is presented with a very real problem. So great is the range of ability and so large the groups that normal class instruction is out of the question. Individual, or perhaps group, methods must therefore be employed for all teaching, despite all the difficulties entailed. A full discussion of ways and means of dealing with this situation will be found in the Geography chapter of *Education of the Average Child*, by A. W. Rowe (Methuen).

Model making

Model making is mentioned here as a type of individual work. The range of possibilities is considerable, the most popular being a relief model of the Home Area, but other subjects range from 'Terraced hillsides in China' to 'A Snow scene in Arctic Canada'. Model-making materials are as diverse as subject-matter. Relief models are perhaps best made with cardboard cut-outs. Each layer of card-board is cut to the shape of a contour line, its thickness representing the vertical interval. The layers are glued together, making a step-like landscape before encasing the surface in papiermâché, and painting it. Alternatively plaster of Paris can be used.

There is insufficient space in a book of this nature to take the questions of materials and techniques much further. Masters wishing to embark on this kind of work are recommended to consult *Miniature Building Construction*, and *Miniature Landscape Modelling*, both of which were written by J. H. Ahern and are published by P. Marshall, 19–20 Noel Street, W. 1. Batsford have also published an interesting book entitled *Model Making in Schools* by J. Eves. Then there is *Practical and Experimental Geography* by Balchin and Richards (Methuen) as well as a booklet called *Model Making in School* by G. K. Sewell (National Committee for Audio-Visual Aids in Education).

The Committee is of the opinion that model making cannot normally be done wholly within the time-table, since neither the time allocation nor facilities make this a feasible proposition. However, masters should not ignore model making as a teaching method on this account, for it involves the detailed study of real scenes, as well as *active* pupil participation. To avoid taking too much school time model making might well be split between class and home. Detailed work can be done in the pupils' own time, while advice is given in special lessons set aside for the purpose. Alternatively, model making might well take the form of a post-examination, end of term activity, or be a major interest of the school's Geographical Society.

PROGRAMMED LEARNING

This is a comparatively new teaching method, and one which masters would do well to investigate. Basically, the subject-matter of a programme is broken down into a number of logical steps. At each step the pupil is required to make his response, and immediately afterwards he is informed whether or not the answer is correct.

Programmes are normally of one of two types: the linear programme or the branching programme. In the linear programme the pupil works progressively through the subject-matter, constructing his response at each step and comparing it with the given answer. The answer required usually consists of one or two words. Thus in the statement 'Low latitudes have ...... climates' the word 'tropical' must be filled in. For the linear programme to work successfully the probability of an incorrect response has to be very slight, not more than about 5%.

In the branching programme the pupil is presented with a list of possible answers, seldom more than four, and he has to select the one that he believes is correct. If he selects the right answer, he is led to the next step in the progression. Should the pupil select any of the wrong answers the path leads into a side alley. Here the error is explained, and he can then return to the main sequence. Suppose, for instance, that the programmed question reads: 'What is the six-figure reference of the church at Sutton?' and the correct answer is 645387. If the pupil selects these figures he will be directed to the next question. If, however, he choses 645397 he will be told that the Northing is incorrect, and that he will have to try again. If he chooses 646387 he will be informed that the number of tenths Eastwards has been incorrectly assessed and that another, more careful look at the map is necessary. Most of the Geography programme material so far examined by the Committee has been of the former, or linear type.

Programmed material is currently prepared either in textbook form or for use in a teaching machine. In the case of the linear text the pupil himself has to conceal the right answer until he has made his own response. If he wants to cheat there is nothing to stop him, and in any case 'cheating' has been shown to cause little harm. In any case a final test where no answers are provided would find him out! In the branching text, or 'scrambled textbook', the pupil is referred to a particular page which depends on the answer selected. It is usually more trouble for the pupil to glance at three or four pages than to work out the problem for himself.

Material for use in teaching machines has to be prepared on film or rolls of paper. It is feasible to build one's own linear-type machine, provided that the design is simple. One of the main features must be lid-top spaces: one for displaying the information and the question, another for the pupil's own response, and a third for the correct answer. The latter appears in its space only after the pupil moves his own recorded attempt irretrievably under a 'protective' window.

Machines designed for branching programmes are much more expensive. In this case the pupil records the answer which he has selected by pressing a button, and the machine automatically presents the frame linked with that answer.

It should not be thought that the programmed material is confined to the printed word. Diagrams and photographs can be presented on the paper, or the programme may direct the pupil to examine nearby models and specimens. Machines have also been constructed that can be connected to projectors, thus making it possible to use slides or filmstrips in this work.

It must be emphatically stated that a teaching machine *does not* teach. It is a means, however, of assisting pupils to learn. The programme has to be written up in the first place and this demands considerable knowledge of the subject-matter, as well as of the best means of presenting it for others to digest.

Enthusiasts claim much in the name of programmed learning. They argue that every pupil has to think, and think carefully. If they have not grasped a point correctly this is immediately discovered. In normal class teaching, however, the error may remain undetected for very much longer, perhaps only coming out in an examination answer. Again, when programmed learning is in use the master can turn to other tasks, helping the slower pupils or marking exercises. Experienced masters must also have been faced with the duty of helping individual boys who have been ill, or are new to the form or school. Provided that a suitable programme is available the difficulties can therefore be minimised.

There are, of course, a number of limitations and disadvantages to weigh in the balance. Among them are problems of cost and preparation. In the event of the class use of machines, up to thirty-six or more will be required, an expensive capital outlay. As already stated, teaching machines can be home-built, but this will involve much time and effort on someone's part. Experience suggests that problems of an allied nature arise when programmed texts are favoured. Commercially produced booklets cover a *limited* range of subject-matter, which is a point to bear in mind when there are other calls on the departmental allowance. Sometimes such texts suffer from another defect, topics being pitched at other levels than that required by the master. Self-compilation of material is very interesting, but inevitably time consuming. Moreover, it would be surprising if the master's own programme did not have to be revised in the light of its use.

In view of these considerations the Committee do not regard programmed learning as the panacea for all teaching problems, though they feel that it has real value as a useful addition in the master's armoury. Clearly experiment in the method is to be encouraged.

SPECIMEN LESSONS

The following specimen lessons are offered as examples of various teaching techniques. It is hoped that they may suggest ways of approaching some of the many problems which arise in the organisation of a lesson or group of lessons.

The first group is essentially a town sample study. Montreal is chosen because it is such an excellent example of a route centre and river port.

A. A SERIES OF LESSONS ABOUT MONTREAL

Content. The Geography of Montreal, Canada's largest city.

Knowledge assumed. The general layout of the physical features and human geography of the St Lawrence Basin and surrounding regions.

Age and Ability of the Class. Thirteen- and fourteen-year olds 'A' and 'B' streams in a Grammar school.

Equipment. An episcope or filmstrip projector; a large wall-map of Canada; pupils' own atlases, and blackboards. Two outlines, one the subject of Fig. 8, the other showing the site of Montreal, have already been prepared.

Fig. 8. Sketch map to show why Montreal is an important town. The outline. This can be prepared before the lesson begins.

Part 1. Introduction

A thousand miles from Canada's eastern sea board stands Montreal, the biggest city in Canada. (Over 2,000,000 inhabitants). The master projects pictures, such as those shown in Plates 2 *b*, 3 *a*, *b* and the pupils are asked to study their atlases to establish importance as rail and manufacturing centre.

Part 2. The choice of site on an island

'To discover why this site was chosen, we must go back as far as 1535. This, by the way, is no exception, for past conditions have often influenced later town growth. Geographers often glance back.

'Why, then, did the French explorers choose a site near the Lachine rapids, so called because they thought that the St Lawrence might lead to China?'

(The Lachine rapids prevented further navigation upstream; the island was good defence against hostile Indians; the volcanic hill on the island gave a good look-out). 'The hill was called Mont Réal (Mount Royal), and the settlement at its foot became known as Montreal.'

Part 3. Montreal, a route centre

The pupils are now asked to name important physical features in the surrounding area: The Ottawa, Richelieu River, Adirondack Mountains, St Lawrence Seaway etc. (Fig. 9).

As each one is correctly named, the word is printed on the blackboard map.

Following this their attention is focused on the routes which converge at Montreal: 'From looking at the blackboard map what advantage can you see in Montreal's position? Think of influences which would certainly cause the original settlement to grow in importance.' 'What products move along these routes?' (Cereals from the Prairies, using the Ottawa valley route; timber and dairy products. Foreign cotton, rubber, sugar and oil come up the St Lawrence.)

Arrows and names of products are marked on the blackboard, as the facts emerge (Fig. 10).

It could be noted here that Montreal is the site chosen for EXPO 67.

Part 4. Montreal, industrial centre and port

'Last lesson we discovered several reasons for the growth of Montreal. What were they?' 'Now let us think of the kind of industries which might develop because of such activities. Suggest some possibilities.'

(Flour milling, paper making, tyres, sugar refining, and oil refining.)

'What are other contributory factors? Think what a factory manager would consider as important.'

(Power supplies from Laurentian Shield; easy access to deep sea transport facilities.)

During the course of the questioning establish that Montreal was once the effective head of navigation. The pupils will have heard this term before, so that the idea can be used to help them in answering the present question.

101

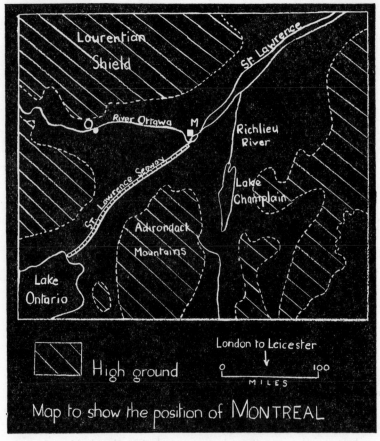

Fig. 9. The place-names are added.

'From what *disadvantages* does Montreal suffer as a port?'
(Ice, usually for four or five months from late November.)

Part 5. Individual book work

The principal items:

(1) The map (see Fig. 11). The main facts have been erased, and replaced by question marks. The pupils use their textbooks and atlases if they have forgotten any of the names.

(2) Brief answers to the following questions. Some of the questions are designed to give the necessary detail for Montreal, but others attempt to consolidate principles of more general application.

(a) 'Why is Montreal so named?'
(b) 'Why did settlement start there?'

102

Fig. 10. Arrows indicating the flow of the trade of Montreal are inserted.

(c) 'Montreal was once the head of navigation. Define this term.'
'Why is it important for this to be far up-river?'

(d) 'Describe the trade of Montreal. How has it been affected by the St Lawrence Seaway?'

(e) 'Name some of Montreal's industries. What features do many of them have in common?'

(These are typical port industries.)

Part 6. Follow up

Possibly done at home. In the case of a regional syllabus, ask the pupils to undertake another town study on similar lines, e.g. Toronto or Vancouver. The results of the investigation could then be compared and contrasted with the Montreal material. If a systematic syllabus is followed Paris or London might be useful comparative studies.

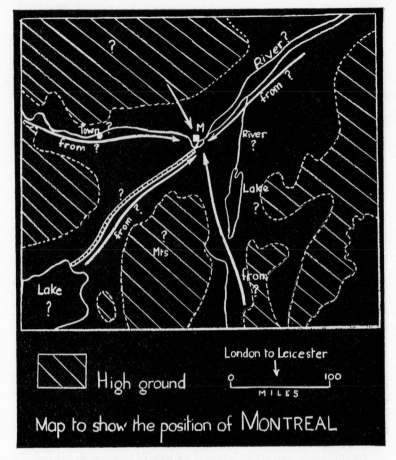

Fig. 11. The map is prepared for the pupils to put into their notebooks. Memory and atlas work will be needed to complete the map.

B. A SERIES OF LESSONS ABOUT THE REVERSAL OF THE SEASONS IN THE SOUTHERN HEMISPHERE

Content. To answer the questions: 'Why do places in the Southern Hemisphere have their winter while we enjoy summer (and vice versa)?' 'What are the effects on human life of the Reversal of the Seasons?'

Knowledge assumed. Fundamental facts about latitude and the annual movement of the earth.

Age and ability of the class. Twelve- or thirteen-year-old pupils, 'A' to 'C' streams in a Grammar school.

Equipment. A free-standing globe, blackboards, and graph paper (one sheet per pupil).

Part 1. Introduction

Preparatory homework: to graph the seasonal temperatures for Algiers and Capetown, using the same axes.

Algiers

J.	F.	M.	A.	M.	J.	J.	A.	S.	O.	N.	D.	
53	55	58	61	66	71	77	76	75	69	62	56	°F
$11\frac{1}{2}$	13	$14\frac{1}{2}$	16	19	$21\frac{1}{2}$	25	$24\frac{1}{2}$	24	$20\frac{1}{2}$	$16\frac{1}{2}$	$13\frac{1}{2}$	°C

Capetown

J.	F.	M.	A.	M.	J.	J.	A.	S.	O.	N.	D.	
69	70	68	63	59	56	55	56	57	61	64	67	°F
$20\frac{1}{2}$	21	20	17	15	$13\frac{1}{2}$	13	$13\frac{1}{2}$	14	16	18	$19\frac{1}{2}$	°C

The pupils are asked to state five points about the graphs.

The graphs and answers are subsequently marked. It is surprising to find that even intelligent pupils will state that 'Capetown has a cold summer and a hot winter'. Such mistakes make a useful starting-point for the lesson.

The graphs are glued in the pupils' notebooks, and they note the five *correct* points.

Part 2. Explanation of the facts

Use the filmstrip projector to represent the sun. The master walks round it, holding the model globe in its true plane. He shows that this angle has been the effect of tilting the Northern Hemisphere towards the projector beam in June, and the Southern Hemisphere away from it. Also demonstrated is the opposite position in December, as well as the intermediate positions of March and September when, relative to the sun, the earth has no tilt.

These points are now consolidated by means of blackboard work, the effort being concentrated on the situation in June (see Fig. 12). The pupils are closely questioned, and given every opportunity to supply information.

On completion, the diagram is transferred into the pupils' notebooks, and they are instructed to draw another diagram illustrating conditions on 22 December.

Part 3. The effects of the Reversal

By question and answer techniques the pupils enumerate the effects:

(i) Christmas is outdoor picnic time in Australia.

(ii) The M.C.C. plays in Australia in our winter.

(iii) Wealthy people spend our winter months in South Africa and thus enjoy continuous summer.

(iv) South African and Australian harvests occur at the same time as our spring. Thus they can put their fruit on the British market 'out of season'.

Finally, the pupils draw up their own account of these effects.

105

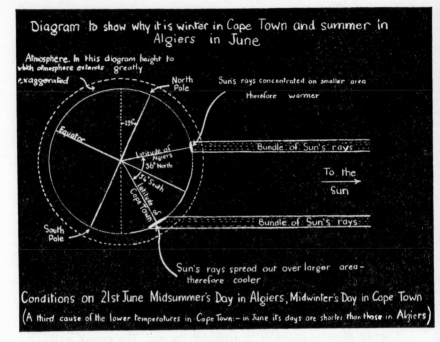

Fig. 12. Blackboard work: specimen lesson on the reversal of the seasons.

C. A SERIES OF LESSONS ON GHANA AND CACAO FARMING

Content. Ghana and cacao farming.

Knowledge assumed. Salient facts about the geography of West Africa including some information regarding African problems and living standards. Also assumed is the awareness that international trading is the way in which nations can earn foreign currency to buy goods they themselves are unable to produce.

Age and ability of class. Fourteen-year-olds, 'C' stream in a small Secondary Modern school.

Equipment. Slides, or filmstrips on West Africa, and some means of projecting them. (The projector can be set up in a corner of the room, and groups or individuals can view West African scenes.) Episcope (to assist in map-making). Atlases and textbooks (considerable variety, and, in the case of the most suitable ones, several copies of the same book). Magazine articles, leaflets, charts, specimens (the last three obtainable from the chocolate manufacturing companies, the Ghana High Commissioner, and the Commonwealth Institute). Modelling materials—paper, glue, etc., for chart and map making.

Method. Bars of chocolate, tins of cocoa, and advertisements for these products, are exhibited and discussed. Soon, the question of ingredients arises, and the dominant position of Ghana as the world's main supplier of cocoa is made clear. 'What do we already know about West Africa and Ghana?' (By questioning and discussion, class recapitulates its knowledge.)

'What do you expect to be the main difference between a Ghana cacao farm and a farm in Britain?' (After time for thought, and noting ideas, pupils discuss the points.)

'We are now going to study cacao farming in Ghana. Make up your mind whether you will either:

(1) prepare an illustrated book, entitled 'Ghana: Cacao and Chocolate'; or

(2) draw scenes of Ghana farming and the farmers at work; or

(3) prepare maps and charts; or

(4) construct a model.

'As soon as you have made up your mind, take a card from the box dealing with that topic and start. If you want some help, and I'm busy with someone else, look at the display on cacao farming until it is your turn.'

The card assignments:

Box 1. An illustrated book

(a) Write an illustrated essay on *one* of the following:

'Home life in Ghana'
'Education in Ghana'
'Food and clothes in Ghana'

(b) Find out about the following, and note your discoveries: customs, food recipes, insects and animals in Ghana.

(c) Find out about the history of Ghana: its discovery, slavery, British rule, and independence. Write down the main facts you discover.

(d) What is the meaning of co-operation? The farmer hands over the selling of his crops to a co-operative marketing board. How does this help him? Write down the answers to the questions.

(e) Write an account of life on a cacao farm.

(f) Explain how chocolate is made.

(g) Write a short playlet which some of you can act, and which will tell us about the life of a cacao farmer's family.

(h) Write a conversation between two cacao farmers, telling of their problems and successes.

Box 2. Drawing scenes of Ghana farming and farmers at work

(j) Draw a picture showing the farmer harvesting his crop.

(k) Paint a picture showing womenfolk removing the beans from the pods.

(l) Paint a series of pictures to show how the crop is dried.

(m) Make a sketch showing the lorry being loaded with sacks of beans.

(n) Make a drawing to show a ship being loaded with sacks of beans.

(o) Make a drawing to show some of the other crops grown on a cacao farm.

107

Box 3. Maps and charts

(*p*) Find out which other countries grow cacao and show these on the outline maps of the world provided. Name each one. Try to name its capital and chief port.

(*q*) Make a list of cocoa and chocolate firms in Britain. Where are their factories? Make a map to show the position of the factory towns and illustrate your map with as many of the firms' advertisements as you can discover.

(*r*) Make a copy of the chart 'A year's work of a cacao farmer'.

(*s*) Construct a graph to show the increase in Ghana's cacao production over the last sixty years.

(*t*) Draw a map of the whole journey that the sacks of cacao beans will make from the farm to the town in Britain where it will be manufactured.

(*u*) On the map of West Africa provided mark some of its different countries. Mount this map on cardboard and cut it up to make a jigsaw puzzle. Practise putting it together again.

Box 4. Models

Construct a model of a cacao farm.

When all is complete a generous selection of the material will be mounted and displayed for the whole class to study. This is followed by a test. *Note.* Some of the work started in this lesson series would certainly have to be completed either as homework or as an activity outside the time-table.

D. A SERIES OF LESSONS ON THE VEGETATION OF AFRICA

Content. Vegetation belts of Africa, emphasising those north of the Equator.

Age and ability of class. Thirteen- to fourteen-years old, slowest stream in a Croydon Secondary Modern school.

Equipment. Atlases, wall map of Africa, blackboard with outline map of Africa, cine projector, film 'Destination Cape Town' (colour; sound). Notebooks, with outline map of Africa.

Part 1. The Film

(1) Before the film is shown ask some questions:
'How far apart are London and Croydon?'
'How far apart are Brighton and Croydon?'
'How long do these journeys take by car?'
'Find Algiers and Cape Town on a map of Africa in your atlases.'
'Use the scale to find the distance between these two towns. Mark with a dot, and name, both these towns on your notebook map of Africa.'

(2) Indicate the route that the car will follow in the film. Do this on the wall-map, and then draw it on the blackboard map of Africa.

(3) Now copy this route on to your notebook map.

(4) Show the film 'Destination Cape Town'. It runs for 25 minutes.

(5) After the film is shown, consolidate the ideas by questioning:

'What kind of vegetation zones did the car travel through?' (As *the areas* are mentioned, annotate the blackboard map with such words as 'Mediterranean Area', 'Atlas Mountains', 'Sahara Desert', 'Tropical Grasslands' and 'Rain Forest'.)

'Where were grapes seen growing?' (In the Mediterranean area.)

'Who lives in this area?' (Both Europeans, and people of Arab stock.)

'What mountains were crossed?' (Atlas; Hoggar.)

'What desert was crossed?' (Sahara.)

'Were there any people in the desert?' (Yes, but only a few.)

'Why were there so few?' (Lack of water.)

'Did the film show any sources of water in the desert?' (Wells.)

'When the vegetation began to increase, what did it look like?' (Tall grass, with scattered isolated trees.)

'More people were now to be seen. How did they obtain a living?' (Farming.)

'How could we tell when the car left the grassland?' (The road was cut through forest.)

'Can you describe this forest?' (Dense, dark green, damp.)

'What difficulties did the car encounter in this region?' (Flooded roads, log roads, many rivers to cross, overhanging trees making use of headlights necessary.)

'Was the forest region inhabited?' (Yes.)

'What sort of clothes did the men here wear?' (Semi-European.)

'What is the chief cause of the differences between desert, grassland and rain forest?' (Amount of rainfall.)

Part 2. The follow-up lesson

(1) Write the following words on the blackboard, but keep them out of sight until after the discussion.

Mediterranean coast. Grapes, oranges, olives. Sunny weather.

The Sahara Desert. Sandy, stony and largely barren.

The Tropical Grasslands. Tall grasses and isolated trees. Some villages.

The Rain Forest. Crowded with trees. Heavy rainfall throughout the year.

(2) Start the lesson itself by recapitulating the main points demonstrated in the film. This is by means of question and answer.

(3) Reveal the blackboard information, and ask the pupils to write two sentences about each of the vegetation zones through which the car travelled.

(4) Instruct the pupils to annotate their notebook map, showing the main vegetation belts. The *boundaries* of the belts are indicated on the blackboard version but that is all.

5

SIXTH-FORM GEOGRAPHY

The position of Geography

Just as the teaching of Geography in schools has made rapid strides in the twentieth century, following upon its recognition as a university discipline, so its rôle has steadily increased in sixth-form work. Although, it must be admitted, in some schools advanced Geography is still neglected, looked upon with some impatience if not with suspicion by the headmaster unacquainted with modern developments in the subject, and perhaps with some faint-heartedness on the part of the Geography master, generally, it is true to say, the subject is now established as a major element of the sixth-form curriculum. As we noted in Chapter 2, the progression from accurate observation via recording and classification to interpretation, so characteristic of the best scientific investigations, is now widely applied to Geography, a subject which, with its close regard for human relationships, fits well into an Arts subject course. Thus Geography at once finds itself not only a major subject for sixth-form study, but one which has footholds in both the humanistic and the scientific fields.

But in addition to this function as a main subject there is a need for the balancing of the specialist courses by means of general background work. By gathering together the threads of knowledge obtained from the experiments of natural science, from the investigations of history, archaeology and language study, and indeed, from all branches of human research, Geography attempts to form and understand the pattern and picture of man's life on the earth. Thus Geography, as a unifying science, can occupy a pivotal position between the Arts and the Science courses.

Here then are two functions of Geography in the sixth form—as a main study in either the Arts or Science courses, and as a background subject for all sixth-form scholars.

Possible courses

Entry into the sixth form in the more affluent society of today is open to a far greater proportion of the 16-year-old age group than

110

in the past when family necessity obliged boys to leave school at the end of their fifth year and become wage-earners. Moreover, not only is the entry more numerous, but it covers a far wider range of academic ability or even academic intent. Over recent years, therefore, the task of the sixth-form master has become steadily more complex, courses having to be designed for several categories of scholar, such as:

(1) The normal 'Advanced' level student whose course extends over two years with Geography as one of two, three, or four main subjects, on either the Arts or the Science side.

(2) The more advanced student working for 'Advanced' level but with the intention of also sitting the 'Special' paper. Such pupils form an élite within the first group; they need closer supervision by the teacher and must read more widely and deeply.

(3) The boy who has sat an early 'Ordinary' level, followed by 'Advanced' level in two years, but who is too immature at the latter stage to take the 'Special' paper. Such a student will need a third year during which he can cover the more advanced work for the latter paper, re-sitting the 'Advanced' level paper along with the 'Special' paper, at the end of that year.

(4) The post-'Advanced' level pupil working for University Open Scholarships or University places. Such pupils are few in number in any one year, and may be regarded as exceptional. They will demand special treatment, and should be able to devote extra periods to the subject.

(5) The one-year Geography pupil who does not aspire to the 'Advanced' level certificate and who is working for some specific professional examination, e.g. Sandhurst or Cranwell. Many of these examinations have their own particular syllabuses in Geography, and thus each student will need individual attention.

(6) The General Course students, either taking Geography as part of a general background course subsidiary to their main subjects, as already suggested, or staying on at school without any desire or necessity to specialise, but merely wishing to continue their studies. Often they are also re-sitting 'Ordinary' level subjects.

To reconcile all these diverse aims is no easy matter for those who are responsible for the organisation of sixth-form work in general, and for the Geography course in particular. Time-tabling alone presents an enormous problem and the task of the Geography master is also often complicated by the enforced combination of upper and lower sixth forms for one or more periods per week, a practice to be deprecated.

9-2

Such problems are not, of course, peculiar to the Geography master. In every subject, the demands for more varied courses are increasing, and it may well be that some form of integrated course is now becoming necessary if modern demands are to be met.

Geography could well be taken as a background subject subsidiary to a number of other main subjects, and in this case there would be a certain amount of bias towards those aspects of Geography which throw light upon the companion subjects taken in the course. A Modern Languages course requires a knowledge of the physical and human background to the countries whose languages are being studied. Here, both subjects will benefit, for the original work of de Martonne, Jean Brunhes, and Alexander von Humboldt are excellent examples of both Geography and style. A similarly geographical emphasis can be given in History, Mathematics and Classics courses.

At present, however, such integrated courses are rare, and generally regarded as experimental, and the basic sixth-form course is governed by an examination syllabus; but the alert Geography master will be aware of the numerous applications of his subject within the advanced work of the school. For convenience, therefore, we may group the courses under two heads—the 'Specialist Course', and the 'General Course.'

THE SPECIALIST COURSE

The syllabus

Today, the syllabuses for the 'Advanced' level of the General Certificate on the whole provide a satisfactory basis for sixth-form work. There are, nevertheless, a number of important points which must be considered by the sixth-form master when preparing his course.

Though the syllabuses prescribed by the University Examination Boards are similar in content, widespread discrepancies in interpretation are reflected in the examination papers set. All examining boards include, and thus all specialist sixth-form courses must provide for:

Physical Geography—Geomorphology, Meteorology and Climatology; also Bio-geography (though this last aspect has been somewhat neglected in the past).
Human Geography—both Social and Economic Geography, while some include Historical Geography.

Map work and Practical Geography.
Regional Geography—generally of two major areas.

Limits. These broad headings cover an enormous range of material and often the Geography teacher is left in some doubt as to the form his course should take. The section on Human Geography is expressed so vaguely, or the pattern of question papers offers so very limited a choice of detailed questions, that the master is obliged to cover a wide variety of work in order that his pupils should be adequately prepared for the examination. It therefore seems natural that he should seek for some guidance from past examination papers. This is a wise practice provided it does not lead to question 'spotting' (see Chapter 6, p. 162).

What modifications to the syllabus or examination papers are possible in order to limit the amount of material a student needs to cover in detail? Some suggestions are:

(1) Within each broad division of the Geography syllabus a list should be given of those matters on which detailed questions may be set.

(2) The examination papers should contain such a wide choice of questions that any student who has followed a well-planned course can find material with which he is conversant.

(3) Detailed studies of marginal subjects, which could lead the student outside Geography altogether, should be omitted.

Overlap. If, as in a minority of cases, the sixth-form course is regarded as a progressive stage from 'Ordinary' level to a university career, then the course must be adjusted accordingly. In recent years, many teachers have expressed anxiety at an apparent overlap between sixth-form Geography and the courses at the universities. Former pupils have complained that much of their first-year work in the university was mere repetition, whilst, at the same time, university teachers were concerned at the academic deficiencies and attitudes of first-year Geography students. This particular problem was the subject of study by a special committee set up by the Geographical Association in 1960, whose report was published as a Supplementary Paper in November 1962. Evidence and reasons for overlap were considered, as well as textbooks used in sixth forms and examinations in both the universities and the schools. In their conclusion to the report, the Committee stated:

There is a genuine problem of overlap, particularly in Physical Geography.
The existence of overlap is recognised by both school and university teachers.

There should be clearer recognition by both schools and universities of each other's difficulties and points of view, and a greater appreciation that the tasks of the schools and universities are complementary. . .

Intense competition for limited university places is an important factor placing strain on Sixth Form teachers and pupils, tempting them to undertake too advanced work too soon. . .

It is right to expect that students entering universities should have had a good general, rather than a narrow specialist, education. Universities should make it known to the schools that they expect candidates for entry to be able to express themselves clearly in their own language and to have a reasonable background of attainment in such subjects as Mathematics, a modern foreign language, Science, History, Economics, in addition to Geography. Action should be taken from both school and university sides to ensure that university entrance requirements, Advanced and Scholarship (Special) papers, and examination questions are framed with this end in view.

Continuing care should be exercised to ensure that questions of appropriate form, content and standard are set at Advanced and Scholarship Levels of the General Certificate of Education.

The problem of overlap is not limited to the upper end of the scale, between Sixth Form and University. Several correspondents, and some of the Committee, have expressed concern at the repetitive nature of the course from 'Ordinary' to 'Advanced' Level. Syllabuses for the former examination require knowledge of most of the branches of Geography enumerated for the 'Advanced' Level examination, through the regional work may be varied. This leads to a form of 'evolutionary re-capitulation' whereby the original work is repeated in the Sixth Form, and each topic is taken a stage further.

The basic facts of Physical, Human and Regional Geography do not vary from stage to stage in the scholar's course. It is the method of handling these facts in order to establish ideas and principles which provides the varied and more stimulating diet of the sixth-form geographer.

It has been suggested that one means of avoiding an undesirable overlap between the work for 'Ordinary' and that for 'Advanced' level would be by gearing the syllabus for the fourth and fifth years to an anticipation of sixth-form work. An example of how this can be done may be seen in appendix A, Syllabus 2, which caters for just this possibility. Such a scheme is practicable, though many teachers might experience difficulty in regard to its detailed application, since the existing 'Ordinary' level syllabuses already cover the main range of geographical topics. In addition, the practice could well result in a situation in which a large proportion of the pupils have virtually chosen their sixth-form courses, if any, by the age of 13 or 14—

a tendency towards specialisation at far too early an age. The door to a possible 'Advanced' level course in Geography should not be closed before the pupil enters the sixth form, which is what might well happen if the work for the 'Ordinary' level were too closely linked to the 'Advanced' level course. Such a practice was deprecated in the Crowther Report.

Resultant courses

In the light of the foregoing arguments, the syllabus must generally cover a period of two years and aim at being both stimulating and challenging. The Geography master is governed by the number of periods available and the extent to which he may have to tolerate the upper and lower sixth forms having combined periods. The latter problem is not an insuperable one, however, as will be seen. The number of periods varies from school to school, the minimum quoted to the Committee being six per week whilst the maximum was ten. A reasonable allotment of time would seem to be five hours per week for each form, with additional time available for Scholarship work and for those working for the 'Special' paper. Two distinct approaches are possible, with variations between, and both seem to find favour:

Course 1

Year 1: General Principles of Geography (the Basic Course):
  1. Physical: Term 1: Geomorphology
               Term 2: Meteorology, Climatology and Bio-geography.
  2. Human: Term 3: Social and Economic Geography.

Year 2: Regional Geography—regions to run consecutively or concurrently.

N.B. The techniques of map work are practised throughout both years.

This form of course has two main disadvantages. First, where upper and lower sixth forms are combined, every other year one group is studying the more advanced concepts of regionalism before obtaining a sound basis in the general principles of systematic Geography. Secondly, the diet lacks variety in that all the work in each term is devoted to one branch of Geography, surely a dull process for the geographer whose chief interests within the subject may lie in a different direction. It must also be noted that if this pattern is adopted the sharing of sixth-form teaching between two or more members of the staff is very difficult during any one term.

115

Course 2

Year 1

1. Physical Geography—Climatology and Bio-geography.
2. Human Geography—Social Geography—primitive societies and agricultural communities.
   Economic Geography—crops.
3. Region 1.

Year 2

1. Physical Geography—Geomorphology.
2. Human Geography—Economic Geography—minerals, power, manufacturing industries and communications.
   Urban Geography and settlement.
   Historical Geography.
3. Region 2.

N.B. Once again, map work is used through the course, and in both Course 1 and Course 2 time must be found for Practical Geography.

In the latter course, in both years, the branches of Geography run concurrently, thus allowing of variety within the week's work and the participation of several members of the staff, dependent on their particular preferences. In addition, should it be unavoidable that upper and lower sixth forms are combined entirely, or for selected periods of the week, the two years are interchangeable. A further advantage is that, by this means, Geography appears in its wholeness, no one branch appearing to be isolated from the rest, and the overall interaction of man and his environment is emphasised, man becoming neither dominant nor subordinate in the pattern. On the other hand, many teachers feel that the big disadvantage of this type of course is that the students have too many aspects to consider at the same time, insufficient time being devoted to any one branch. It may also be a disadvantage for field-work if Geomorphology is left to Year 2.

There is, however, one further consideration to be taken into account here. If a section of the Geography sixth form is likely to leave after one year, then the Geography master will feel obliged to ensure that such boys leave with something gained from their one-year course—something of real value to them in later life. This means that the course that they follow must be a unit in itself, and this will be easier if the first-year course follows such a plan. The study of the general principles of world Geography will cover very much the same ground for specialist students as it does for those leaving early and there may well be difficulties in separating these students in

116

a small school, except for one or two periods per week. An amalgamated course is therefore often desirable closely following Course 1 above:

Year 1
  General Principles of Geography:
  (a) Physical Geography:
    (i) Geomorphology.
    (ii) Meteorology and Climatology.
    (iii) Bio-geography.
  (b) Human Geography:
    (i) Social Geography.
    (ii) Economic Geography.
  Here the two courses would diverge:

Specialist: Non-Specialists:
  (iii) Political Geography   Geography of World
  (iv) Historical Geography   Problems

To this should be added map work and Practical Geography of all kinds to both courses.

Year 2—Specialists—Regional Geography.

Branches of study

There are specific problems associated with the teaching of each of the branches of Geography, and these must be considered in some detail.

Map work. Map work, it is increasingly recognised, is not merely a branch of Geography—an exercise in itself. It is a geographer's technique—an aid to his work—and, as such, must be integrated with every aspect of the subject. Throughout his course, therefore, the sixth-form scholar should be encouraged to recognise the importance of mapping and the interpretation of maps to his understanding of the systematic and regional branches of his subject. To possess the technique of drawing a map to show any particular distribution effectively is an invaluable asset, and in local studies and practical Geography many schools insist on the students carrying out practical surveying and the drawing of maps from first principles. At least one examination board includes a practical paper on this aspect of the work.

The converse is also true; the ability to translate and understand maps must be acquired, though not *in vacuo*. It should be a natural technique in dealing with any aspect of Geography. To quote some simple examples, local studies, which are now an important part of sixth-form work, cannot be carried out without constant reference to the local Ordnance Survey sheets. Sheet analysis, involving cross-sections, transects and field work, slope analysis and the relating of Geological, Land Use and topographical sheets to one another, are invaluable techniques and, some masters find, the ideal type of work immediately after 'Ordinary' level for the jaded intellectual appetite, providing a welcome practical break from the hard factual learning of the fifth form. Here the boy is brought back to basic Geography. In Physical Geography, glacial morphology becomes far more real and logical if interpreted from the 1 in. Tourist sheets of the Lake District and Snowdonia. The Daily Weather Map and the synoptic chart will form an inevitable part of the course in Meteorology, as will the use of isotherms, isohyets and isobars be familiar in Climatology. Land Use maps, dot maps and isopleths find their natural place in Economic Geography. The ability to use these maps, to draw them, and instinctively to resort to them for evidence, is part of the Geography course, and does not form a course in itself. Some schools do, however, devote a specific part of their course to map work. This may be advisable in a revision period immediately before the public examinations, and may be needed where the university board calls for a knowledge of map projections, but otherwise such a course should not be necessary.

Practical Geography. Within every syllabus, it is recognised today that time must be found for practical work. This may take two forms —the practical techniques of mapping and the handling of statistics in the form of statistical diagrams, and direct observational work in the field. Both of these are now considered as essential parts of the sixth-form course, and, as such, play a part in the 'Advanced' level examination, where more than one university board sets questions on this work in a separate paper.

The importance of field-work of all kinds has been stressed in chapter 2, and details of courses may be found in chapter 8. Field-work, where the student is presented with a setting from which he must sift the facts by observation, where he must collect and correlate his data, and then devise his own methods of presentation and his own interpretations, reveals the use of true scientific technique and helps to establish the sense of intellectual discipline in the mind of the sixth-form pupil. Often, the genuine curiosity of the boy will be stirred, lending greater enthusiasm to his later studies. Such work in the field, with its training in techniques and attitudes, is vital to sixth-form work, and a place must be found for it within the planned course. Some teachers like to use a field course as an introduction to sixth-form work, but most prefer to have completed at least two terms of the basic sixth-form course in Physical Geography, especially Geomorphology, before embarking on an extended field course. The ideal would seem to be to combine, if time can be found, local study as introductory work, where the pupil is brought back to basic, first-hand principles, and a field course in a more distant environment at the end of the first year, where these principles can be applied. Some University boards demand written accounts of these as part of their 'Advanced' level requirements.

Physical Geography. In their broad content, the syllabuses of the university examining boards are in agreement in their requirements in this main branch of Geography, and only in detail are there any important variations. A course in Physical Geography is recognised as being essential in the grounding of the geographer, though the actual content of such a course, as we have seen, can vary considerably in detail. Although the universities include, under this broad head, Geomorphology, Climatology, Meteorology, Oceanography, and the geography of soils and plants, and require all five to be studied in the sixth form, these five usually receive very unequal attention and treatment. In order to pass the examination for most boards, it is possible, unfortunately, to concentrate upon just one of these branches, usually either Geomorphology or Climatology, and merely touch upon the others. Indeed, Oceanography and the geography of soils and plants are usually treated quite superficially if not neglected altogether, and many teachers tend to avoid Meteorology as far as possible. In many schools, this practice even reaches the extent of totally ignoring all but the one branch selected, despite the fact that this limits the candidate's choice of question in the examination, and produces a very incomplete geographer. Of the two branches, Geomorphology is usually the favoured subject, and at both Universities and Colleges of Education it has been found that many incoming students have a very imperfect idea of climate or perhaps none at all. Possibly this is due to the difficulty of teaching the subject, with its need for a knowledge of Meteorology and therefore of Physics and Mathematics; possibly to the intangible nature of its subject-matter. Be this as it may there is a great need for a better balance in the teaching of the main branches of Physical Geography.

It is in this section of the syllabus also that the practice of question 'spotting' appears to be most prevalent. Individual topics are

119

selected from the Geomorphology or Climatology syllabuses as occurring frequently in the examination papers, and are taught in great detail, to the detriment of many other aspects and the overall picture as well. By the time they reach 'Advanced' level, most sixth-form pupils taught on this basis have a very thorough knowledge of glacial morphology, igneous activity, limestone scenery, ocean currents and 'Mediterranean' climates, but all too often know only imperfectly where these fit into the broad field of Physical Geography, or how they form part of an overall pattern of the physical environment. Both Geomorphology and Climatology are best understood if their study follows a logical sequence of cause and effect. One brick must be placed upon another in the structure. There is a wholeness to Physical Geography, though the exact pattern of approach may be varied; and this unity should be evident to the specialist geographer in the sixth form. It is a basic part of the course, not a series of isolated Sample Studies, chosen at random.

The school of thought currently dominant, however, regards regional synthesis and analysis as the core of the subject, and it is often suggested that Physical Geography should arise from regional studies in some form of integrated course. Most geographers would in fact agree with the belief in the fundamental importance of Regional Geography, but it must be insisted that, until a firm basis in the systematic branches has been established, the student lacks the necessary principles and techniques to enable him to recognise and evaluate the characteristics of any region.

Two further considerations relevant to the teaching of Physical Geography may be mentioned here, though they have been stated more fully elsewhere. First, there are the dangers of over-attention to detail, and obsession with the workings of physical processes leading beyond the strict realms of Geography, often involving overlap with university courses. In avoiding this, the Geography master must establish his own limits within each topic. It is in Physical Geography that the greatest danger of this occurs. Secondly, map work should form an integral part of this section of the course, constant references being made to examples illustrated on particular sheets—the Swiss 1:50,000 Jungfrau sheet for glaciers, the Ordnance Survey 1 in. Snowdon sheet for glacial erosion features, the Ordnance Survey 1 in. Torquay and Plymouth sheets for ria coasts, and the French 1:50,000 Le Puy sheet or the Geological and Ordnance Survey 1 in. sheets of Arran, for igneous intrusions. A wider use of maps from overseas is to be recommended here, for the sixth-form scholar should be familiar with the different mapping techniques of other countries.

Before leaving references to the Physical Geography course, it is as well to remember that field-work on any scale requires a certain basic knowledge of physical processes, and thus it is necessary to ensure that a minimum amount of map work and Physical Geography has been covered before embarking on an important field course.

Many correspondents have raised the question of the extent to which Geology should be taught as part of the sixth-form geographer's training. Time is short obviously, yet Geomorphology, and even much Regional Geography, become so much more intelligible with a basic knowledge of the various branches of Geology. It is also true that every geographer is, to some degree, an amateur geologist, and most teachers continue to take an interest in it long after their own student days are over. How far then should the sixth-form scholar be expected to understand the various aspects of this other science? Place must surely be found for some such work in the Physical Geography course. Rocks are made of minerals, and minerals of elements, and the formation of these can well fit into its appropriate place in the sixth-form geographer's course, without detailed considerations of Petrology, Mineralogy or Crystallography. Earth processes become more intelligible with some knowledge of the geological time scale, without undue emphasis on Stratigraphy, and some mention of fossils must be made without delving into the biological detail of Palaeontology. Each will find its place in the Geography course, without any section of the work being set aside as being Geology, and thus irrelevant to the geographer's studies. The task of the geographer is to explain the existing landscape, both physical and cultural. The use of Geology is valid if it leads to, or assists in, this.

Human Geography. In this branch of Geography, the published syllabuses of the examining boards for the 'Advanced' level are at their least satisfactory. An enormous range of the social, historical and economic aspects of the subject is envisaged and it is left to the sixth-form master to make his own choices. He may therefore feel compelled to embark upon a wide range of work which will often be covered very superficially, and loaded with bare factual learning of distributions and factors of production. This part of the course often becomes a mere memory process, usually aided by great volumes of hand-out material to compensate for any inadequacy or dating of textbooks and for the lack of time for the course. Judicious selection is clearly necessary—some crops, probably the main staples, such as rice, wheat, maize and millet, sugar, tea, coffee, cacao, and a few industrial crops such as rubber, cotton and oil seeds; animal products such as wool and meat; some minerals—iron, copper, aluminium; power resources in the form of coal, oil and hydro-electricity; manufacturing, transport and settlement—a kaleidoscope of topics needing integration. This may be helped by some reference to past examination papers. In the present state of the syllabuses, it is difficult to see what else the master can do, though it is surely incumbent upon him to formulate the course into a coherent, logical whole, and thus once again avoid the dangers of fragmentation of the subject.

As we have already seen, in the more advanced human societies, man is no longer entirely at the mercy of his physical environment and, though the extent to which he can control nature is limited, his activities conform more and more to conditions imposed by his fellow men—his social environment. Thus the student can arrive at a full appreciation of the life and work of mankind only if he has a grounding in the physical environment, and superimposes upon this the economic conditions which modify the influence of that environment. The operation of economic laws must be given full weight in the study of Human Geography, as a counter-balance to the physical laws, if complete 'determinism' is to be avoided (see chapter 3, p. 46).

The course in Human Geography must therefore aim to place man in his physical setting, starting with the least sophisticated societies, where environmental 'determinism' is most apparent, and leading from there through the more advanced societies and economies to considerations of commercial agriculture, the raw materials of the industrial society, the manufacturing regions (but not processes), and communications, to an understanding of world trade and economic interdependence.

Once again, in connection with this study, the use and construction of maps and the use of statistics are important. Dot maps, isopleths, statistical diagrams and graphs, and maps of all kinds and types of distribution, are vital to this part of the course, and must be fully integrated into it. It is an interesting exercise to conclude such work with an attempt to divide the world into various types of economic region, and this may well serve as an introduction to regionalism, as well as aiding the development of a concept of geographical conditions on a world scale.

Regional Geography. Throughout the development of Geography as an academic discipline, two broad methods have been recognised —'General' Geography and 'Special' Geography—today known as Systematic and Regional Geography. To this day, there are varying opinions as to the relative importance of these two branches, but modern geographers are in agreement that Regional Geography is a vital and indispensable part of the subject, and, many believe, the culminating branch, the final product of the separate systematic studies. In 1935 Sir Halford Mackinder stated: 'Geography presents regions to be philosophically viewed in all their aspects interlocked.'

Whether one believes in the overriding importance of Regional Geography or not, there is little doubt that either in the recognition and interpretation of regions (the analytical approach), or in the systematic delimitation of regions (the synthetic approach), a sound basis in the systematic branches of the subject is necessary.

Thus Regional Geography is the natural complementary approach to the other branches within the sixth-form syllabus, as in other levels within the school, and might be said to summarise them.

For reasons given in Chapters 2 and 3 and for simplicity of delimitation, regional work is usually based upon a continental and national division of the world. Continents and countries are the main units of study, and it is this pattern which has been adopted by the university examining boards in their regional syllabuses. Generally, two broad regions are required for the 'Advanced' level examination, though the grouping of these varies from board to board.

In addition, emphasis has changed with the changing world situation. Western, or North-Western, Europe is often prescribed, rather than the whole of Europe, as the continent has become more complex of study, and Russia, the Monsoon Lands of Asia, or the Far East are recognised as regions for study, rather than a simple continental division such as Asia. At the same time as such parts of the world are becoming more important and more complex, thus suggesting concentration on more limited areas, the speed of modern transport and the tendency for major blocs to become economically and politically delimited seems to suggest a grouping of regional studies around one major area. The changing emphasis is reflected in the flexible pattern of regional work set by the university boards.

Whatever the detailed regional requirements are, there is a minimum spread of knowledge needed to appreciate Geography as a coherent academic discipline, and this applies both to the systematic branches and to Regional Geography. The sixth-form geographer should therefore be expected to have a grasp not only of broad patterns over the world as a whole, but of detailed patterns within one or two major units within that world framework, applying to those regions the principles and techniques of the systematic branches for their evaluation.

Although certain regions are deserving of special recognition as a result of their world significance, the teacher is left with a considerable choice as to the regions studied by his own sixth form. Usually, the set syllabus is planned so that one developed and one less developed continent must be studied at least, and this is to be commended in that the former continents present a complexity of human and economic patterns, and the latter present dominantly physical patterns. These require different approaches. In the former, the cultural landscape results from the social environment; in the latter, the physical environment still to a great extent sets the scene for the Human Geography. Such contrasting regional studies will stimulate and interest the sixth-form scholar and, in addition, will give him a greater range of material upon which further comparisons can be based.

Selection of the regional studies should also be made in the light of the relative importance of the areas prescribed in the present-day world. A citizen of the British Isles should not leave school without a sound knowledge of the geography of his own country and of Western Europe. With the rise in the twentieth century of other great powers destined by virtue of their economic potential to play a vital part in the future of the world, a knowledge of Russia, the United States of America, or China, is of considerable importance. Then, for their historical significance, the cradles of the great civilisations merit study—Ancient Egypt, Greece, Palestine, China, Central America and India. It is true to say, however, that, with the development of new territories throughout the world, most regions or continents have, or have had, major parts to play in the governance of our globe, and thus every region set down by the university boards for study will have much to commend it on these grounds. Quite clearly they cannot all be studied, for such congestion would result in superficiality and the loss of that all-important aspect of study in depth. Selection is inevitable, and, though this is perhaps unfortunate, omission is also.

There are a number of further factors likely to influence the choice of region for any particular sixth-form course. With a limited number of regions prescribed for the 'Ordinary' level examination of any particular board, the sixth-form teacher can either repeat these regional studies, attempting to ensure examination success by repetition and familiarity, or he can vary the work and broaden the understanding of the student by presenting new regional studies. Sometimes such repetition cannot be avoided, for the same regions are required for both the 'Ordinary' and 'Advanced' level examinations. This is often true in the case of Western Europe and the British Isles. It is the opinion of the Committee, however, that, wherever possible, the advantages gained as a result of the interest taken in the study of new regions in the sixth form improve the examination chances of the pupils. They thereby broaden their world knowledge and approach regional work with fresh minds clear of any preconceptions.

Another important consideration is that of textbooks. Regional Geography textbooks suitable for 'Advanced' level studies are increasing in number, though they are often inadequate in themselves and are costly. With University boards changing their prescribed regions at regular intervals, the master may be faced with a large financial outlay from his precious grant allocation, which may well be 'frozen' in the form of textbooks which are temporarily useless in some years, and may even become out of date before being of use again. This is particularly true where the sixth form has large numbers in any one year. Thus, the master will tend to return, time and time again, to the regions for which he is best equipped with books. This tendency may be furthered by the natural predilections and interests of the Geography staff. There is a danger here of staleness, the use of out-of-date material, and the selection of a region for expediency's sake. An interesting and stimulating way of partially overcoming this and many other problems of regional selection is that of allowing each individual member of the sixth form to select his own regions from those prescribed for the examination. The work can then be conducted in small tutorial groups, as is described later in this chapter, a wide range of textbooks can be carried by the department with few lying useless in any one year, and fewer boys are competing for the use of any one book. In addition, in discussions and class-work in other branches of Geography, examples can be drawn upon from all parts of the world.

Within the broad regions studied, two approaches are possible and necessary. The overall region itself must be considered along systematic lines—the structure, relief, climate, the natural vegetation, the agriculture, the distribution of population, and so on—and also its smaller units considered as regions in their own right. Many teachers would deprecate the stereotyped systematic approach listed above, though there is little doubt that a sound knowledge of distributions within the continent is essential. An approach through emphasis on the dominant distributions can be far more stimulating than one which is formal and stereotyped.

Geography is the study of place and it is a frequent defect of the sixth-form course that, while pupils can interpret the Geography of a country, they are unable to locate places correctly. We have come far from the 'Capes and Bays Geography' of our predecessors, but some basic learning of position is essential before one can proceed to the higher flights of geographical thought. This is particularly true in Regional Geography, and it is sometimes an awareness of this danger which leads the Geography master to adopt the same regions for 'Advanced' level as for 'Ordinary' level, for then he can hope that the factual learning of place has been already acquired.

The division of a country into regions presents many problems. For ease of delimitation, textbooks and syllabuses generally adopt the national state as the unit of study, with one or two notable exceptions, though the national frontiers pay little regard, in many cases, to the true geographical regions. Thus Europe is studied country by country, even though, for example, the coalfield of Nord and Pas de Calais in northern France is similar in its industrial pattern to the other side of the border in Belgium, in the Sambre valley. Is it not better to study this sub-Hercynian industrial belt as one unit? The Rhine Rift Valley is shared by France and Germany, and the Alps by France, Italy, Germany, Austria and Switzerland. The frontier between Spain and Portugal by no means coincides with any natural or significant geographical divide, and Denmark, physically, is a northern extension of the North German Plain. In every case, a national pattern of study will involve needless repetition. Some continents and countries lend themselves to regional division better than others, and these might well be taken as 'sample studies' of the regional technique. In 1960 Professor E. W. Gilbert said:

Now geography is, in my view, the art of recognising, describing and interpreting the personalities of regions. Regions, like individuals, have very different characters; moreover, the characters of regions...are constantly changing and developing.[1]

[1] 'The idea of the region', by E. W. Gilbert, The Herbertson Memorial Lecture, Geography, XLV (1960), pp. 157–75.

The delimitation of such regions is a difficult task, often outside the capabilities of the sixth-form scholar, but he should be able to acquire the 'feel' of a country, to recognise regional characteristics in well-defined areas, describe them and map them, and attempt to find reasons for them. Here he can apply basic geographical principles which can be exhibited in the tackling of examination questions on Regional Geography.

But, in the past, questions have been set which required far too detailed knowledge of particular, and often ill-defined, regions, questions impossible for even the able pupil to answer unless he had made a special study of them. This makes regional studies of continents an exhaustive and exhausting exercise. The division of a country into regions is not easy, but some regions within any country are quite definite and the sixth-form pupil could be expected to have knowledge of them. Similarly, he could be expected to demonstrate his appreciation of regional characteristics when he is presented with a sufficiently large choice of questions and regions.

Whatever the regions studied, and whatever the approach, the purpose of Regional Geography is the better understanding of a complex whole, the world, by the study of its constituent parts. Thus, though many of the major world problems have particular application within selected regions—colour and race in North America and in the Republic of South Africa, population and food in South-east Asia, development of mineral resources in Latin America, and the effects of ideologies on economic patterns as shown in Eastern Europe, and Soviet Russia and China—they must be regarded as 'sample studies' of the whole. Studies of these in their regional settings are not only essential to a true, up-to-date understanding of the particular countries and continents, but equip the sixth-form geographer to appreciate the problem in similar areas and throughout the world. Thus, as with all branches of Geography, there must be constant attention to accuracy and current developments, for by sound, enlightened regional studies the geographer is able to appreciate the wholeness of his subject and its value as an academic discipline.

'Special' paper and scholarship work

Expansion in the number of university places and in the size of sixth forms have led to a natural increase in the number of Geography students aspiring to university places. Oxford and Cambridge Universities have also increased the number of Open Awards in

Geography, and so the 'Special' paper (formerly the 'Scholarship' level paper) of the General Certificate has come to assume considerable importance in the work of the sixth-form master, and an increasing minority of pupils has also become significant in requiring preparation for the University Open Award examinations.

It is difficult to separate these two examinations from the point of view of either syllabus or method. The 'Special' paper, of the General Certificate, sat at the same time as the 'Advanced' level, and therefore after two years in the sixth form generally, consists of a closer examination of the subject-matter prescribed for the latter examination. The Open Scholarship papers can cover the whole range of geographical thought, both in the systematic branches and in the regional, though a wide choice is catered for.

It is at this level, often using two or three lesson periods per week, that more advanced concepts can be discussed and evaluated. The pupil who works at this level should have more detailed knowledge, and more power to apply the general principles he has studied. This necessitates a considerably more detailed study of a region, or regions, a wider acquaintance with geographical literature, a closer appreciation of principles and mechanisms behind physical and human phenomena, and some understanding of the development of geographical thought.

Regional Geography. At both the 'Special' and Open Scholarship levels, a wide choice of region is offered. The student is likely to find that his regional studies for 'Advanced' level give him adequate coverage, though the knowledge required will be of greater depth. With time so limited in the few periods available for this work, it is seldom practicable for the scholar to be introduced to new regional studies, except in perhaps a superficial way as a means of broadening his world knowledge and increasing his range of examples in support of the systematic studies. Thus, as far as true regional work is concerned, a certain amount of time must be set aside for a more careful appraisal of the essential characteristics of the regions already studied, and a more thorough analysis of the present-day problems within those areas. Regions, where man is concerned, are dynamic units. They are constantly changing, as regards both their limits and their character, and the scholarship student should be able to appreciate this changing pattern. This is possible only where there is reference to a wealth of geographical literature, in the form of textbooks, magazine articles and the daily press. Such detailed regional work is also the opportunity for the consideration of more advanced concepts of Geography, such as the problems of regional delimitation, the different types of region—the 'natural' region and the 'geographic' region, for example—and the ideas of 'possibilism', 'probablism' and 'determinism'.

Systematic Geography. In the systematic branches, there are aspects which we have seen might, or should, be omitted from the normal 'Advanced' level course, but which would form valuable studies at this level, especially for the Open Scholarship candidate. In addition, many of the subjects treated in a relatively simple form at 'Advanced' level need to be considered in greater detail. Such topics as Political Geography, and the geographical bases of states, frontiers and nations, might well be included. Race is a topic which rarely enters the 'Advanced' level work, but this, together with certain aspects of Geology (especially Stratigraphy), of Meteorology (e.g. air mass analysis) and of Bio-geography (e.g. plant and animal adaptation), might all be studied. Many physical features and processes could well be examined in more detail—the development of soils, the causes of depressions and their movement, world problem climates, and theories of continental drift, to name but a few. Here is the opportunity to pursue the interests of the pupils and the master at will, delving deeply along lines suggested by the enthusiasms of the group. Once again, however, a wealth of geographical literature is necessary for the success of such work.

World problems. A further section of the time available must be devoted to a consideration of the geographical aspects of present-day world problems, and this will lead to a wider appreciation of areas of the world outside the scholar's regional coverage. World food and population problems probably start in South-east Asia, China and Japan, but, before the subject is exhausted, Africa, Italy and Britain will have been mentioned, and the studies will have led on to soils and soil erosion, tropical climates and aridity, standards of living and economic tariffs. Indeed, here is a whole integrated section for the course. Political controversies will lead to ideas of self-sufficiency, distribution of mineral resources on a world scale, conflicts of ideologies, and national economic planning. 'Colour' problems involve the 'Deep South' of the United States, apartheid in the Republic of South Africa and the difficulties of the 'Cape Coloureds' and 'Poor Whites', and the 'All White' policy of Australia, as well as leading to the whole aspect of white settlement in the tropics. The importance of the Polar regions will serve to introduce air routes, glaciology, and modern ideas of Meteorology; and study of minorities will raise a wide variety of political and historical problems, especially with regard to Europe. The list is long, but here again the master must make a judicious selection from the great variety of subjects available. The good scholarship candidate will be expected to be able to discuss vital problems of the day. To be in a position to do so he must ensure that his grounding in geographical principles is sound; and he must keep abreast of the times by close study of the daily press and of magazines.

Methodology. Scholars at this level are aiming at a university career, and generally hoping to read Geography as their main subject. It is reasonable to expect, therefore, that they will begin to think more deeply about their subject as an academic discipline, and the master might well introduce some considerations of the development of the subject historically, and of its methodology. Work such as this can be most challenging to the able sixth-form scholar, and a philosophic counterpart to the more practical assessments of modern world problems. A short course on the historical development of geographic thought, referring to Classical conceptions, the Renaissance, Humboldt, Ritter and Ratzel, and the French school of Vidal de la Blache and Jean Brunhes, the ideas of Mackinder and Herbertson and more recently of Hartshorne, will bring him to a re-assessment of the subject, and give him some idea of the various approaches to the work. Topics such as regions of all kinds, 'determinism', and the relationship of Geography to other disciplines, especially History, will also be included in this section of the work, bringing about a very real appreciation of the true place of Geography. Such work as this is both stimulating and far-reaching, but it is not suggested that a great deal of time should be spent upon it. The place for this is in the university. However, some discussion along the lines suggested would be valuable, both to produce the mature candidate ready for his university place, and to equip him for the Open Scholarship examination. Questions such as 'To what extent should Geography be regarded as a science?' or 'Consider the value of *either* Geology *or* History as a background for Geography' call for some very real thought about the nature and method of the subject by the potential university scholar.

Scholarship methods. Formal teaching or lecturing to the scholarship sixth form is unnecessary, and probably the least successful way of approaching the work. Numbers will usually be small, and the intellectual level of the boys will be such that they are fully cognisant of facts and principles, and are able to apply them to the formulation of ideas and arguments. The master, having aimed at fostering the spirit of discovery throughout the sixth-form course, must now turn the products of this into a clear ability to handle the material in the form of opinion and argument. Tutorial groups for discussion and oral dispute; papers read by pupils or the master, the latter sometimes deliberately appearing obtuse or sceptical until overwhelmed by weight of enlightened opinion; essays and criticisms; the study of newspaper reports and leaders; all these provide means whereby the mental stature of the scholar will grow. And all the time, there is the encouragement to push forward his own boundaries of knowledge by reading and observation.

Sixth-form methods

We have already seen that, at this level, the acquisition of facts, though still of vital importance, is secondary to the handling of them. The ability to do this is the true test of the good sixth-form pupil, and thus the methods adopted in sixth-form work must foster this particular aim.

Formal lessons. It is inevitable that some facts and ideas must be transmitted by direct teaching or lecturing. In the first few months of the sixth-form course, the master is often anxious to see that his pupils have a firm grounding in the basic geographical principles and methods. The preparation and presentation of lessons for this purpose will be an important task. It is essential that the pupils are precise in their knowledge, and the master's lessons will give clear-cut statements and enunciate basic principles, illustrated from slides, filmstrips and maps. Conflicting ideas will generally be avoided at first, while the pupils are finding their feet, but, although such formal lessons are necessary, they should be varied in type. Visiting masters, discussions, and the use of films and broadcast talks may all be used to provide a change of approach, and, though throughout the course lessons of the more formal type will always be necessary, and indeed welcomed by the pupils, there is implicit in them a grave danger of 'spoon-feeding'. Many young students have been known to arrive at University or College of Education suffering from the ill-effects of such a process. Through lack of time or initiative, the teacher has lectured without discussion, forcing the pace along narrow lines to the detriment of the pupils' general education. More enlightened masters prefer to move quickly into the background as imparters of information.

Tutorials and seminars. One of the most valuable aspects of sixth-form Geography arises from the greater freedom brought about by the reduced numbers, and thus the closer personal relationship between pupil and master, wherein ideas and opinions can be discussed. With a large sixth form, this advantage is lost unless a system of seminars or tutorials is adopted. By breaking the form down into smaller units for particular aspects of the work, individual problems can be tackled, and the master is likely to gain a much clearer impression of the progress of each student. Arranging tutorial groups is not easy within a limited time-table allocation, but the enterprising Geography master will use some of the periods of the week for smaller groups when the rest of the form are engaged on other individual research projects along lines previously suggested. This method of teaching is especially valuable in regional work, where one is often concerned with subjective assessments which vary from scholar to scholar. By this method also, as has been suggested, the pupils can select their regional studies so that there is little competition for textbooks or library books and each person has something to contribute to general discussions. Certain it is that, at some time in the sixth-form course, the Geography master will need to deal with small groups of two or three boys, simply because of their varying speeds and abilities, and these periods offer the best opportunities for dealing with matters of controversy and for encouraging pupils to formulate ideas and to express them in public.

Textbooks. From the formal instruction to which he has largely been accustomed throughout his school course up to the fifth form, the sixth-form scholar must now learn to cover a great deal of the work in his own private studies. The aim in an advanced course should be to create an atmosphere of friendly co-operation between the master and the individual student in the joint investigation of the many points of interest that will arise. There should be no problem of class or work discipline. The scholar should be interested and stimulated to want to delve further, and should therefore cover a great deal of ground on his own initiative. His chief source of information will be the textbook, a convenient standard which is common to the whole class and which has been selected for its particular relevance to the course. But textbooks are not infallible and the pupil should be encouraged to recognise their limitation and be prepared to test the accuracy of the information he obtains from them.

Selection of the class textbook is not an easy matter at this level, and it is rare indeed that the Geography master finds the book which exactly suits his needs. Two criteria should always be adopted—all statements in the work should be fully authenticated by reference to specific examples; and sources of examples and statistics should be quoted to enable the pupil, if in any doubt, to check their reliability by reading the original source material. Textbooks which give suggestions for further reading on every major aspect are also of great value at this level, when the student is just learning of the wealth of geographical literature at his command. The textbook with information which is obviously out of date is both misleading and useless.

The pupil who has confined himself to a thorough study of one textbook is certain to be very limited in outlook. There are many standard texts for particular geographical topics, but inevitably on any controversial matter they express only their authors' opinions. They may present most persuasive arguments in support of their own particular views and even select evidence to suit these arguments, discounting or failing to quote evidence to the contrary. Toynbee, Griffith Taylor, Huntington and Brunhes will be read by good sixth-form scholars, but reliance on any one of them, or on any one textbook, is to be avoided, and the pupils should be encouraged to look further afield in whatever aspect they are studying.

Further, no textbook covers all the aspects of any one branch of Geography fully. Inevitably there are sections where the textbook has but superficial coverage and another work suits the course better. Thus, many Geography masters have found that a course of planned reading, following the pattern of the assignment method described in chapter 4, serves as a means of avoiding over-attention to one specific textbook and brings before the pupil different points and varied ideas.

Notes. Great importance should be attached not only to the matter of the student's individual work, but also to his method of study and the arrangement of his records. A valuable part of his training is lost unless he is required first to plan his work, and then to present the results in an orderly and systematic form. This is to be achieved in two ways.

In the first place, the majority of Geography textbooks cannot be read, except by the rare scholar, without some form of note-making. Much that has been read will immediately be lost. On the other hand, it is pointless to repeat in note form that which is presented so much better in the textbook. The student should therefore be encouraged to develop a technique of making clear, succinct notes, which will later be of value, incorporating all the material gleaned from various sources, and quoting references to the particular texts used. Such notes can best be organised on a loose-leaf basis. In this work also, the student should be encouraged to prepare neat, simple and relevant sketch maps (see chapter 4).

Essays. The second method is the set essay, an essential feature of which is the accurate use of geographical terminology as applied to any aspect of the subject. It has been said that 'Reading maketh a full man; conference a ready man; and writing an exact man'. Some of the work will require facts, and this is valid where examination preparation is necessary and memory must be tested. The question commencing 'Give an account of...' is common and the pupil must have practice in the orderly presentation of material. But this is no real test of the good sixth-form scholar. He should also be able to use his facts to present logical argument and opinion, and therefore the question should be 'Assess the significance of...', or 'To what extent is...', or simply 'Discuss...', where subjective assessment is called for and the student is encouraged to show well-supported opinions. Such questions can test not only factual knowledge, but also the capacity for orderly, methodical thinking and the ability to weigh up evidence in support of arguments. Such a question as 'Show the extent to which landscape can be said to be controlled by climate' involves knowledge of both climate and the various agents of erosion and an ability to weigh the effects of the former against the agencies of earth movements and rock type. A pupil cannot regurgitate the textbook merely, when answering such a question as 'How would you convince an enlightened sceptic that much of Britain has at some time been subject to glaciation?' This requires more than mere factual knowledge.

The correct approach to any scientific problem is to collect facts, to make observations, and from these to arrive at broad generalisations which, by the test of time and example, can become established as principles. This process is most exciting to the good Geography scholar and a most valuable exercise in his training. He must have a desire to unearth the principles behind particular instances, and to refuse to accept generalised statements without some scrutiny of the facts on which they are based. This aim can be furthered in the process of essay composition. He can start with a bold generalisation, and then seek to support it with evidence, perhaps in the process finding missing links in his argument; or he can take a simple distribution and deduce from the facts some geographical principle, or some interpretative conclusion.

Whatever form the essay may take, clearness of expression will stem from an orderly mind and a disciplined approach to the subject. Although geographical content must be the pre-eminent consideration, emphasis should also be given to fluent and accurate expression of ideas and matter in clear and concise English. There has been a regrettable tendency of recent years for specialist subjects to overlook the literary limitations of their scholars.

Supervision. At first, the individual work will be carried out with the assistance, and under the constant direction, of the master, but, as the course proceeds, assistance should be needed and given less, until, during the concluding months, the student may be left very much to his own devices, the master confining himself to directing his pupil to the appropriate sources, and offering criticisms of his finished work. This last point cannot be over-stressed. Pupils gain a great deal from the criticism of their written work, and will only give of their best if such work is marked and returned promptly. In order to keep a close eye on his pupils' progress, therefore, the Geography master must be punctilious in this matter. Students soon become discouraged and apathetic if their written work is never returned.

Equipment. All forms of individual work—reading, notes, essays and practical work—are dependent upon the resources of the Geography department and the school library. In particular, books and maps are essential, whether in the school or from an easily accessible public library. The training involved in tracing information to the relevant sources, and in extracting just what is required for the student's purpose, is of the greatest value, not merely as preparation for university work in Geography, but as a contribution to the mental equipment of all sixth-form pupils. But it will be obvious that, to obtain such results, the information must be readily available, and at all times the library facilities must be of the highest order. These considerations, together with the need for practical work indicated below, justify the allocation of a special room for sixth-form Geography studies, where books and equipment are always available for private work.

Practical work. Although individual activities such as those already described may be regarded as essential to advanced course work, most of them are concerned with second-hand data obtained from books and maps. The importance of the practical approach, obtaining material from first-hand observations, cannot be over-emphasised (see Chapter 1). Whatever the place of Geography in the sixth-form course, whether it be the main subject of specialisation, or taken as a more general cultural or background subject, the importance of individual first-hand studies, map work, field-work, and, above all, Local Geography, has been increasingly recognised in recent years, and may now be accepted without question. Such practical work, besides giving a realistic basis to sixth-form Geography, provides valuable opportunities for acquiring those habits of accuracy in observation and expression which, as has been suggested above, is one of the chief aims of the course. Local surveys, at this level, are now required by one of the university examining boards, and such work must therefore be included in the syllabus. Each student should be required to produce his own record of work accomplished, and this will usually take the form of a map, or series of maps, accompanied by a text. The type of study and its content are to a great extent determined by the local environment. Further reference to work of this kind will be found in Chapter 8.

Research. Geographers are particularly fortunate that, in their own subject, opportunities for original investigations are unlimited. Much of this research is suitable for students still at school, either as an individual or as a group project. Thus the young scholar can be introduced to the thrill of new discovery, and of drawing his own conclusions from his own researches. There is, for example, a great deal which can be accomplished in local studies which can add usefully to local knowledge. A careful analysis of traffic density and the types of load and vehicle can be of value in road planning; many sixth forms have contributed to the most recent Land Use survey; recordings of meteorological data, especially of rainfall, are always of great value to the Meteorological Office; but more original work in the form of such things as micro-climate measurements, the careful measurement of hill slopes and river profiles, of beach recession and wave action, and of run-off and evapo-transpiration, even though applied to particular local problems, can add usefully to a much wider field of knowledge. Some schools have carried out measurements of local weather in special locations in the Cairngorms, comparing conditions in corries and on the plateau. Another school has undertaken hydrographic surveys of many of the Scottish inland lochs. Most useful work can be performed where human or physical phenomena are changing rapidly—the meander erosion of a river, the changing pattern of the landscape where new towns are established, the effects of the flooding of valleys for water supply, and the effects of new farm practices upon fauna and flora. Where man is concerned, the landscape is never static, and work in recording present-day distributions will prove valuable in the future.

Some projects can be carried out by individuals, but in many schools the work is undertaken as a co-operative effort where a team organises a major survey, perhaps using helpers from junior forms. Such enterprises can be effective in many ways—in work in the local area or further afield, for an exhibition or for a published monograph. Reference to this kind of activity is made in Chapter 8, but, at this age in particular, most pupils will have 'enthusiasms' in one direction or another, some for architecture or for other of the fine arts, some for Geology or Archaeology, others for practical mechanical work. All these, and other 'bents', can be harnessed to the survey team and the direction of these different interests towards a common and worthy aim is of the greatest value to the pupils as a preparation for community living.

One school has carried out a great deal of work at the Somerset Record Office, where Geography scholars and History scholars have produced original notes from the Tithe Map of 1839, and work of this type can well be carried out in other Record Offices in some of which there are well-appointed students' rooms. Many documents will form the basis for fascinating studies for both geographers and historians, though generally schoolboys will find language and palaeographic difficulties if the work involves material written before the eighteenth century.

Much of this work, however, cannot be fitted into the school time-table, and must therefore be an extracurricular activity. However, in the post-'Advanced'-level examination period, which in some schools and under some boards can be quite lengthy, many boys would welcome such an exercise, and derive a great deal of benefit from it. It is during this period that the co-operation of other departments might well be obtained.

During school vacations, research projects can be undertaken further afield. One school has carried out valuable studies in Iceland, and another, as shown in chapter 8, spent much of a summer vacation in Corsica. Research work of any kind is a valuable exercise and can stimulate even the most indolent pupils to work in the common cause.

THE GENERAL COURSE

Many schools elect to have a General Studies course for all members of the sixth form. As a subject which has its roots in both the Sciences and the Humanities, Geography has a great deal to contribute and it is often left to the Geography master, therefore, to organise and supervise such a course. When this is the case, he must realise that his Geography scholars are merely part of the great body of sixth-form pupils for whom the course is planned. It must cater for all interests and tastes; a course of study wherein each member is able to contribute his own specialist knowledge, and gain from the ideas and experiences of his fellows. One must not confuse this course with that planned for the non-examination Geography student, which has already been discussed.

With such a range of knowledge and specialisms within his group, the master who organises General Studies needs to take a great deal of care in the planning of the work. Any superficiality or apparent lack of coherence or preparation will lead to an attitude by students and staff alike of cynical boredom, and the whole course might well become a total waste of time and effort. There must be some sense of purpose and logical planning to the work, the whole following a coherent, exciting pattern.

Either for each term, or for the whole year, there should be a theme which would serve to integrate the contributions made by the various specialisms represented in the group. Within that theme, opportunities should arise for every member of the group to play a part, and many of the school staff could also be called in for individual lectures. Problems of Africa or South-East Asia pose an enormous range of questions which can be only partially answered in terms of Geography. A study of Nationalism on a world scale calls for contributions from many branches of knowledge, ranging from History and the development of the nation state, to Applied Science represented by, for example, the modern technology of oil pumping and refining and its significance to the Arab states, the distillation of seawater and the development of the state of Israel, and the uses of new sources of power. A particular civilisation or period, often a subject of great complexity, can be used as a terminal or yearly theme, giving coherence to the many aspects which must be analysed and evaluated. Contributions on the geographical background, the historical pattern, biographical details of men of letters and science, technological advances, and political and economic organisation, all have their part in such a course, and, with careful planning and preparation, the Geography master can devise an integrated study of great value to the whole of the sixth form, and a gain to their general culture.

The planning and detail of a course which will cover all the aspects of world affairs suggested above depends very much on the time which can be allocated to it. If the study is to be taken seriously the work must be coherent and comprehensive, and an adequate allowance of time must be claimed. If, however, no more than two periods per week can be allocated, it is probably better to probe one or two major problems to some depth, even at the expense of their apparent isolation from each other.

6

EXAMINATIONS

Examinations figure prominently in the life of every school, for many a stimulus to work, though for others a regrettable necessity. Candidates and their parents await the results with anxiety, knowing full well these will be carefully scrutinised by employer or selection board.

A suitably devised examination in Geography should test the candidate's knowledge of geographical facts, his grasp of fundamental principles, his skill in practical work, his powers of observation, his knowledge of geographical methods, and his understanding of the geographical point of view.

INTERNAL EXAMINATIONS

Examinations set and marked within the school fulfil at least three purposes:

(i) To evaluate the performance of pupils at suitable intervals and keep a record of their academic progress. This record helps in placing them in the stream, or even school, which is most appropriate to their aptitude and attainment.

(ii) To stimulate pupils to revise the work they have previously done and to ensure as far as possible that they have built adequate foundations for further study before they advance to the next stage of the work.

(iii) To give pupils practice in examination procedures and techniques. This helps to prepare them for external examinations of one kind or another, which they will almost inevitably face at some stages of their school life and during their subsequent career.

Types of question

The questions set in examinations must obviously differ according to the ages and abilities of the pupils in the form being examined. The following are among the important types of question:

(i) *The practical question.*

(*a*) Interpretation of geographical material such as maps, including Ordnance Survey maps; pictures; data represented graphically by devices such as divided circles, pie graphs, bar graphs, columns, histograms, or pictographs, and statistics such as those dealing with climate, population densities, Land Use and other aspects of Economic Geography.

(*b*) Construction of diagrams or the drawing of sketch maps in order to represent information provided and to demonstrate ability to make use of various cartographical devices such as dot maps or flow line maps.

(ii) *The short-answer question.* This may require completion of an outline map; insertion of names or features on a map; writing of short sentences; or even a choice between a number of alternative words or names.

(iii) *The essay,* which may be of greater length the older, or more able, the pupils.

Clearly the last two of these types can be combined with (i*a*). Moreover, it is common practice to set questions which have several parts, each of which represents a different type of question, and there is much to commend this course.

Marking

An efficient technique for the marking of examinations is of great importance. It is very desirable that masters should have confidence in the assessments made of their pupils. Experience and experiment combine to produce the ability to assess pupils fairly. The allocation of marks to short answers is relatively simple, but to assess answers either wholly or partly in essay form requires much greater judgement on the part of the teacher. Furthermore, in marking the essays, there arises in the minds of many teachers a conflict between judging the pupil's geographical knowledge and taking into account his ability to spell correctly and express himself clearly. It should be remembered that it is primarily Geography which is being examined, but poor English, or bad Art in a sketch map, will nevertheless carry some penalties into Geography.

Reliability in marking can be increased by taking care in framing the questions. They should be so constructed that only one form of answer is acceptable and no doubt is left in the mind of the candidate as to what he is required to do. The questions should be fair and carefully arranged. Where there is a choice of questions they should be well balanced in subject-matter, difficulty and length of time required for answering. Questions should give adequate and fairly distributed cover to the syllabus.

The form of the examinations will also vary according to the frequency of their occurrence, the significance of the results in the school as a whole, and the ages and abilities of the pupils who are being tested.

For younger or less able pupils more questions requiring short answers should be provided, but even here the question which requires some logical presentation of facts will find a place. Some teachers consider that insertion of information on outline maps is a useful test of the amount of geographical knowledge that has been acquired. There is a growing opinion, however, that outline maps are better used to provide facts from which candidates may work. It has also been suggested that candidates should be allowed to take atlases into the examination room and this is being done for some C.S.E. examinations.

For older examinees the proportion of essay-type answers might reasonably be greater, corresponding to a longer time allocation for the examination. However, the use of maps and practical exercises should not be forgotten.

In a large school, where there is more than one master in the department, it might be beneficial, in the upper forms at least, to share the marking in such a way that one master marks all of one year or marks the same sections of all papers. Some masters advocate completion of all the scripts from a whole form before going on to another, whilst others prefer to mark one question only at a time in order to ensure an even standard. Whichever method is adopted, it is wise to prepare a detailed mark scheme, because all answers will not be accurately valued by impression, and a good scheme will enable the master to maintain an even standard of marking.

Sketch maps

A geographical essay makes suitable use of maps, cross-sections and other diagrams. At an early stage of his study the pupil should recognise these as essential and integral parts of the answer. They represent the geographer's shorthand and can, at times, replace much verbose description. In the type of question which begins 'Explain the distribution of. . . ' a map would often be the best means of locating the subject-matter and would be more effective than many lengthy paragraphs. Such maps and diagrams must form part of the answer and neither be placed hopefully at the beginning nor be appended hurriedly at the end. They should not be crowded with more detail than is necessary and should be of sufficiently large size to be clear.

Sketch maps generally state or illustrate one special point and so the range of detail upon any one map should be limited. In senior forms and in external examinations, rather more complex illustrative material is likely to be demanded, and it is prudent to expect the lower and middle forms to acquire gradually the habit of drawing clear maps.

Outline maps

Where an outline map is provided on which information is to be inserted, a certain amount of detail should be included. For example, 'Name five of the towns whose position is indicated by a dot' is better than 'Mark and name Oxford, Birmingham, Brighton, Edinburgh and Cardiff' on a blank outline map of Great Britain. The latter would be a fairer test if some physical features and suitable rivers were also marked, or if the towns chosen were closely related to well-defined coastal features.

The use made of outline maps should be limited in any one examination so as not to unbalance the paper.

Ordnance Survey maps

Most masters would include questions, graded according to the age of the forms, on maps from at least the two main scales (1:63,360 and 1:25,000) of Ordnance Survey maps. Such questions are often made compulsory. The map extracts produced for examination boards and available fairly cheaply from the Ordnance Survey are very useful.

Content and balance of question paper

Where there is a choice of questions on the paper, each should require the same amount of attention and carry an equal number of marks. If it is desired to introduce questions of greater or lower value these should either be made compulsory or put into separate sections of the paper within which all questions do have equal value.

All questions should be asked as briefly and precisely as possible. There should be no overlapping of subject-matter between one question and another: it is no test of the pupil's knowledge if he is asked to present identical answers to two separate questions.

One should be careful too, particularly in the middle and upper forms, not to set the type of question which invites the reproduction of notes: this is better done in a class test, if at all. The examination, while it must test factual knowledge learned, is an occasion when the use made of that knowledge is rightly the subject of enquiry. In the lower forms of Grammar schools and in some Modern schools, questions requiring application of knowledge will not constitute such a large part of an examination paper. Questions of this type could very well be put into a separate section of the paper, thereby helping to indicate to the pupil the way in which he should present his answers.

Examples of examination papers set in schools

Paper I. This follows the syllabus No. 1 set out on p. 287 and was used for a first form in its Summer Term examination.

Length of paper—1½ hours.

Answer all the questions.

1. (Map work)

   (*a*) Express the scale 1 in. to a mile as a representative fraction.

   (*b*) Draw the symbols used by the Ordnance Survey on 1 in. maps to show the following: (i) a major road, (ii) a bus station, (iii) a Youth Hostel, (iv) a prominent hill-top—1,255 ft.

   (*c*) Draw a simple contour map with 50 ft. intervals to represent this three-dimensional diagram:

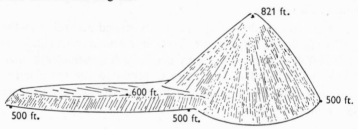

2. (The local district)

   (*a*) What equipment is used to record the weather in our locality? How is the equipment placed to obtain readings? (5 lines.)

   (*b*) Name *three* different kinds of sedimentary rocks which outcrop within two or three miles of school.

   (*c*) Describe the layout of Longthorpe Lane Farm, the way in which the land is used and the destination of its crops. (10 lines.)

3. (Selected parts of the world)

   On the outline map provided, mark and name: the Equator and the two Tropics, Longitude 90° E. and the Greenwich meridian. The black lines on the map indicate the boundaries of the great climate and vegetation regions which we have studied. Shade and name a Hot Desert in South America, two areas with Mediterranean climate in Australia, and one wheat-producing area of world importance.

   Finally, mark in the two rectangles the direction of the prevailing winds.

4. (Selected parts of the world)

Describe *either* Life in Kufra, a Saharan oasis, *or* work on a Malayan rubber plantation.

In your answer, mention the physical background and the climate, as well as the activities of the people. (10–12 lines.)

5. (North America)

Explain the meaning of the following terms, giving as much detail as possible:

(*a*) The Canadian Shield.

(*b*) The Cordillera.

(*c*) A Continental type of climate.

(*d*) The 49th Parallel.

(*e*) The St Lawrence Seaway.

(*f*) The Deep South.

(*g*) A Boll.

(*h*) The Middle West.

(*i*) Marketing corn 'on the Hoof'.

(*j*) The Hudson–Mohawk Gap.

(Two or three sentences for each section.)

Paper II. This was also set to a First Form but to one in a Comprehensive school following syllabus No. 3, on p. 300.

The length of the paper was two teaching periods (80 min.).

Answer Questions 1 and 2.

From the remaining questions (3, 4, 5, 6, 7), answer three questions.

Write as much as you can and draw pictures and diagrams wherever possible.

1. On the outline map of the British Isles:

(*a*) Shade and name *four* areas of highland,

(*b*) Draw in and name *two* rivers,

(*c*) Shade and name *two* coalfields,

(*d*) Mark and name any *four* fishing ports.

2. On map 2:

(*a*) In which direction is the river flowing?

(*b*) How many miles long is the river?

(*c*) How many feet does the river drop from its source to the sea?

3. Write all you know about:

(*a*) Trawling,   and (*b*) Drifting

Draw and label a trawl net.

4. Imagine you own *two* farms.

Farm 1 is in East Anglia (in the East of Britain).

Farm 2 is in the Welsh Mountains or the Highlands of Scotland (in the West of Britain).

(*a*) What will be the main differences in the relief between Farm 1 and Farm 2?

(*b*) What will be the main differences in the climate between Farm 1 and Farm 2?

(*c*) What farm animals would keep on Farm 1? What farm animals would you keep on Farm 2?

(*d*) What crops would you grow on Farm 1? What crops would you grow on Farm 2?

(*e*) Which farm would you prefer and why?

5. Choose *either* the Yorks, Notts, Derby coalfield, *or* the South Wales coalfield, *or* the Lancashire coalfield:

(*a*) Draw a large sketch map of the coalfield.

(*b*) Put on the sketch map any *four* industrial towns.

(*c*) Write a few lines on the industries of the coalfield.

(*d*) Draw a clearly labelled diagram of a coal-mine.

6. Write all you know about CROFTING in the Highlands of Scotland. Illustrate your answer with drawings.

7. Choose *one* of the commodities COTTON and WOOL.

(*a*) Give one reason for development and concentration of its manufacture in *either* the West Riding of Yorkshire *or* Lancashire.

(*b*) Name any *three* towns where the commodity chosen is manufactured.

(*c*) What is made from the commodity?

Paper III. This is based on a systematic syllabus (No. 2 on p. 291) and was used in a Grammar school, second form.

Length of paper 1½ hours.

Answer Question 1 and three others.

1. This is compulsory. Answers to be written on the Answer Sheet provided.

(*a*) Draw in the river and the tributaries which pass through settlements at *A* and *B*.

(*b*) On the map, label the following features in the appropriate spaces: Spur, Conical Hill, Ridge, Valley, Uniform Slope, Dry Valley, Sea, Confluence.

(*c*) Shade lightly all the land between 50 and 100 ft.

(*d*) Shade more heavily all the land between 100 and 200 ft.

(*e*) If the scale were 2½ in. to 1 mile, what would be the R.F.?

(*f*) If the R.F. were 1:190,080, what would be the scale expressed in words?

(*g*) What is the compass bearing from *A* to *B*?

(*h*) What is the direction from *B* to *A*?

(*i*) In the frame provided, draw a cross-section along the line *X–Y*.

2. (i) What is the difference between weathering and erosion?

(ii) Giving examples, describe different kinds of weathering of rocks.

(iii) What is meant by the following terms:

(*a*) corrosion, (*b*) deposition, (*c*) transportation.

3. (*a*) Explain the formation of, and (*b*) describe in full, the distinctive characteristics of a river valley in *either* its: (i) Valley (Middle or Mature)

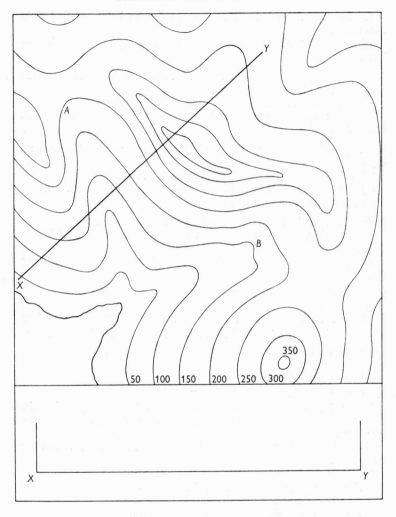

stage, *or* (ii) Torrent (Young or Mountain) stage, under the sub-headings of:

> Cross-section
> Profile
> Tributary Pattern
> Interfluvial areas (Inter-stream areas)
> Human activities

4. (*a*) Describe briefly, with aid of labelled diagrams, how and why fold mountains are eroded so that anticlinal hills become anticlinal valleys and synclinal valleys become synclinal hills.

147

(*b*) Describe five of the advantages to human beings of Old Fold Mountains.

(*c*) Describe the disadvantages to human beings of Old Fold Mountains.

5. (*a*) Describe the world distribution and chief characteristics of the glaciated shield lands of the world.

(*b*) Of what value are these to man?

(*c*) What disadvantages do they possess so far as human activities are concerned?

6. Drawing labelled diagrams to illustrate your answer, describe and explain:

(*a*) What is meant by lateral, medial and terminal moraines.

(*b*) The characteristic features of the cross-section of a glacial valley.

(*c*) How man makes use of glaciated valleys.

7. (*a*) Describe the formation of Young Fold Mountains.

(*b*) Describe, with brief notes, *five* physical characteristics of Young Fold Mountains.

(*c*) Describe the advantages of these Mountains to the people who live there.

8. World map—see separate sheet.

Paper IV. This was set for a third form in a Secondary Modern school and was designed for the lower stream in that year (see syllabus No. 5 on p. 314).

Length of paper $1\frac{1}{2}$ hours.

1. On the map of the world:

(*a*) The following countries are shaded—name them correctly. Canada, Malaya, Soviet Union, New Zealand, Argentina, Cuba, Egypt, Kenya, Norway, Japan.

(*b*) Shade in yellow an area of hot desert and in green an area of hot wet jungle.

(*c*) Write the following letters in suitable places:

F—where French is spoken (outside France).

E—where English is spoken (outside Britain).

B—where most people's skins are dark brown.

L—where most people's skins are light brown.

Y—where most people's skins are yellowish.

C—a Communist country (other than Russia).

D—a Commonwealth country (other than Britain).

N—a NATO country (other than Britain).

2. On the map of the British Isles:

(*a*) Name *three* of the towns marked by dots. These towns are Dublin, Manchester, Edinburgh, Southampton, Belfast, Newcastle.

(*b*) Write Kent, Yorkshire and Cornwall in the correct places—these counties are marked *A*, *B* and *C*.

148

(*c*) Name the North Sea and the English Channel.

(*d*) The following are islands or groups of islands: Hebrides, Isle of Wight, Anglesey, Isle of Man. Name two of these.

(*e*) The line of crosses represents a line of hills between Croydon and Redhill. Write their name next to the line of crosses.

Answer the questions on your answer paper. Number each question correctly.

3. Pair the following capitals and countries correctly:

Tokyo—Jamaica   Kingston—Canada
Delhi—Japan   Ottawa—India

4. In which part of the U.S.A. (S.E., S.W., N.W., N.E.) do most American coloured people live?

5. Name a crop which is exported to Britain from that part of the United States.

6. What is the meaning of the word 'Apartheid'?

7. Name a country which had to leave the Commonwealth because of apartheid.

8. Which of the world's countries has the largest population?

9. In England, we look south to see the sun at midday—in which direction would you look if you lived in Australia?

10. What is the Ruhr?

11. Why is the Nile so important to Egypt?

12. Why is the Suez Canal so important to Britain?

13. What is a fiord?

14. Tractors are used to pull ploughs in England. What are often used in India?

15. What is the main food crop of South-east Asia?

16. How can the weather cause a famine in India?

17. Write down the names of the following countries in the order of position from north to south: Sweden, Greece, Switzerland, Germany.

18. Similarly write down the following three North American cities: Los Angeles, Vancouver, San Francisco.

19. Pair the following areas and countries correctly:

Alps—Chile   Prairies—Russia
Ukraine—England   Andes—Switzerland
Fens—Canada

Answer only *one* of the following:

20. Write three paragraphs about the foreigners you have met (e.g. how they differed from us, how they are like us, their homes, what you thought of them).

21. Write one paragraph on each of: deserts, jungles, tropical grasslands.

22. Write a paragraph each on farming and coalmining in Britain.

EXTERNAL EXAMINATIONS

The most important of the external examinations taken by pupils in Secondary schools are those for the General Certificate of Education and for the newer Certificate of Secondary Education. A number of other examinations are also of some importance.

General Certificate of Education (G.C.E.) papers

In England and Wales all the eight Boards examining for the G.C.E. set papers in Geography at both 'Ordinary' and 'Advanced' levels. There are also 'Special' papers set on the Advanced syllabus but differing in the character of the questions set.

The syllabuses of these Boards show a broad measure of agreement, but there are some points of difference on matters such as number and length of papers, attitude towards a practical examination, and the methods chosen for assessing field-work.

The Committee is of the opinion that 'Ordinary' level papers, taken by pupils aged about 16, should not be as long as 3 hours. A single paper, even of this length, does not allow a sufficient number of questions to be answered to cover the syllabus satisfactorily. The majority of the Boards do in fact set two papers, the length of which varies from $1\frac{1}{2}$ to $2\frac{1}{2}$ hours. It is felt to be better if the examination consists of two papers each lasting 2 hours.

Although only one Board describes one of its papers as 'Practical' others include similar questions. Such questions involve exercises such as section drawing, calculation of gradients, interpretation of weather or population statistics, or construction of diagrams from data provided.

Field-work. Some of the work most difficult to test is field-work. Some boards make no reference to this in their 'Ordinary' level Geography syllabus. One encourages candidates to make observations in the field, whilst another sets an optional section on field-work. The clearest demand for field-work comes in syllabuses which state that candidates should, where possible, make a study of their home area or some area of which they can have first-hand knowledge. An example of a question relating to field-work was one set by the London Board for 'Ordinary' level in summer 1960.

For a small area (e.g. around your school or one which you studied on a geographical field excursion) describe:
 (a) The geographical features you studied.
 (b) The Ordnance Survey maps you used.
 (c) The ways in which you made your field studies.
(N.B. This question *must* be answered from your own outdoor field work and the maps and notes made by yourself.)

Another example was set by the Oxford Board in autumn 1961.

Write an account of your home (or school) district to show how the relief is related to the types of rocks, and how this has affected transport routes.

This latter question could undoubtedly be answered without any experience in the field, but only a very exceptional candidate would be able to compete with those who had done work as outlined in chapter 8.

At 'Advanced' level the majority of Boards do refer in their syllabuses to the need for field study and one of the others expects pupils to be familiar with the map of their own locality for the purpose of illustrating the principles of Physical and Human Geography. One Board asks for records of candidates' own field-work to be submitted.

This Committee feels that there should be at least one question relating to field-work or local Geography at both 'Ordinary' and 'Advanced' level in the G.C.E. Ideally there would be some form of oral assessment of the work performed, but this would depend upon availability of examiners.

The syllabus: 'Ordinary' level. All the G.C.E. Examining Boards set a compulsory question requiring candidates to interpret topographical maps. Usually the scales of the maps which must be studied are stated and in the opinion of the Committee the syllabuses should always give this information. Normally a study will be made of maps on the scales of 1:63,360 and 1:25,000, the most commonly used and readily available of the Ordnance Survey maps. Some time allowance should be given to the candidates for studying the map before commencing to answer the paper. Although the Committee agrees with the practice of setting a compulsory map-reading question it is felt that syllabuses should always make it clear that this is the

Board's intention. It is also felt that candidates should be given some information as to the relative rating of this question in comparison with the others.

Some Boards state that they will require the interpretation of geographical pictures. In this connection the importance of good reproduction must be stressed; the Boards should declare in the syllabus their intention to use photographs.

The study of the British Isles is rightly common ground, while land forms, weather and climate, natural vegetation and the inter-relations between these factors and human development find a place in all the syllabuses. Even in these matters, however, some of the syllabuses are much less precise than others and will leave the less experienced teacher in some doubt as to what aspects of the subject it is really intended to examine. A study of previous papers may go some way towards solving this problem.

For regions outside the British Isles there is much variation in the methods of determining the areas of which knowledge is to be required. Two Boards do not ask for any other region to be studied. The remaining Boards seem to base their policy on one of three main principles: (*a*) to leave the selection in the hands of the master, setting a fairly large number of questions and offering a wide choice; (*b*) to specify a particular region, such as North America, for detailed study, a different region being prescribed every year or two years; (*c*) to nominate two or three regions and to allow the master to choose. It is, of course, clear that some method must be adopted to restrict the areas of the earth's surface which are to be studied in detail. In so far as it leaves the choice in the hands of the master and encourages him to make a broad study of several continental or sub-continental areas for the purposes of comparison, the first method is undoubtedly the best, though it may be open to abuse. One Board says 'The questions will not demand comparisons of areas drawn from different continents...'. The second method takes out of the master's hands the decision as to what shall be the culmination of the five-year course of study and obviously it presupposes the availability in the school of all the necessary textbooks. The third method has much to commend it, especially as the regions offered for choice frequently include Western Europe, the U.S.A. and Canada, South America, Asia and the U.S.S.R.

It is a common practice for most Boards to use an outline map of the world, or a substantial part of the world, on which they require certain information to be inserted. The geographical significance of some of the information required is at times rather obscure. In some cases this map is linked with written work. Frequently when a second part is added requiring an essay-type answer, the map provided is of a regional area. It is often unavoidable that the results of the second part depend upon a reasonably correct interpretation of the first part, and it is thought that in such cases the question might well be optional. Provided that such map questions are not a substitute for the candidate's own sketch maps, they do provide a good test of factual knowledge.

The drawing of sketch maps should be encouraged and they should be recognised as integral parts of answers. Candidates should not be required to attempt to draw difficult shapes, nor outlines of large areas. A demand to 'draw a sketch map of Scotland' or 'Ireland' is unreasonable: a blank outline map of such an area should be provided and the candidates should be asked to fill in a certain amount of detail. In such a way the question would test the candidate's geographical knowledge and his power to apply it and not merely his ability to reproduce a shape. The statement by one of the Boards at the head of their question paper is worth noting: 'Credit will be given for appropriate sketch maps but you should not make them too elaborate.'

The syllabus: ' *Advanced* ' *level.* Several Boards now set three papers and the compulsory map-reading question has, in these cases, been transferred from the Physical Geography paper to one of a more practical nature. This raises the status of work on interpretation of the Ordnance Survey maps—a study which is so important to the understanding of both Physical and Human Geography. The Committee believes that here, as at 'Ordinary' level, the maps on the scales 1:63,360 and 1:25,000 are the most suitable for general topographic study.

There is close resemblance between the different Boards in that they all require study of Physical Geography, but the amount of detail provided in their syllabuses shows much variation. In most cases not only the surface features of the earth, oceanography, climate, natural vegetation and soils are prescribed, but a study is to be made of how these are associated with general Human Geography. It is quite usual, however, for some purely physical questions to be set. The study of weather reports is mentioned in some syllabuses and varied questions are set on meteorological topics.

The emphasis placed on map projections varies. Three Boards make no mention of them in their syllabuses: the others refer to an understanding of the properties and uses of projections, but only one specifies the projections which are to be studied. It seems reasonable to expect simple projections to be recognised and their properties understood. The problems which face compilers of atlases should be appreciated, but detailed knowledge of properties of the many projections now used cannot be expected.

In the section of a syllabus variously described as 'Human', 'Social' or 'General' Geography the absence of precise statement can lead to overloading of the sixth-form curriculum (see chapter 5). World distributions of crops and minerals are frequently asked for: it is left to the master to select the items for study. In order that his pupils should be adequately prepared, he must choose a wide variety of both crops and minerals, and not only is a knowledge of the cultivation or methods of extraction required but also some acquaintance with their position in international trade. It is felt by many teachers that a list should be given in the syllabus from which examples could be chosen. If this were done students could practise applying the principles of Economic Geography rather than merely learning and reproducing a mass of facts.

In the report (1960) by the Geography Panel set up by the Board of the Faculty of Science of the University of Birmingham to enquire into the suitability of 'Advanced' level syllabuses in Science as a preparation for direct entry into First Degree courses, it was suggested (Appendix G) that the following should be included under the heading 'Human Geography', 'The principal factors affecting the distribution and production of the major foodstuffs and products of economic importance of plant and animal origin, illustrated from the following: wheat, oats, maize, rice, potatoes, sugar beet and sugar cane, cocoa, tea, oil-producing plants, cotton, rubber, vines, pigs, cattle, sheep, fish' and 'the principal factors affecting the occurrence, extraction and processing of the following major minerals of economic importance: coal, petroleum, nuclear fuels, aluminium, copper, iron, lead, tin and zinc'.

It is, however, in Regional Geography that most variation is evident in the syllabuses; there are almost as many ways of specifying the regions required as there are Boards. A study of the British Isles is not compulsory with all Boards. This omission is not, perhaps, as serious as it may appear at first sight. The British Isles will have been dealt with regionally in a certain amount of detail at 'Ordinary' level towards the end of the first five years of the pupil's Secondary school career. Britain will form the basis of much of the work to be covered in the Physical Geography section. Also, almost all of the map-reading work will be chosen from within its boundaries. In the section which is described as 'Human', or 'General' Geography once again, much of the material and many of the examples must come from the British Isles. However, in the five syllabuses in which study of the British Isles is not compulsory, they can be chosen with western Europe as a selected region.

The main considerations when selecting regions for study should be parity of importance and variety. It would be better to study contrasting regions, e.g. Australasia and western Europe, or North America and southern Europe, rather than western Europe and North America. The availability of textbooks suitable for sixth-form pupils has been a limiting factor in the choice of regions but this is becoming less important as textbooks on all continental areas, written for this level, are now published.

In general, the 'Advanced' level syllabuses provide a satisfactory basis for sixth-form work. Whether sufficient time is allowed for a proper completion of this work is largely a matter of school organisation; one Board suggests 'that not less than five hours a week are necessary'. This would seem a reasonable allocation of time.

Special Papers. In 1963 the Scholarship level was replaced by the 'Special' papers which are designed to test the potential university entrant. These papers are set on the 'Advanced' level syllabuses but the questions are more difficult and searching. Wider reading and a more mature outlook are necessary to answer these questions satisfactorily. It is interesting to note that some university departments regarded 'Advanced' level results as a more useful means of assessment than achievements at 'Scholarship' level; whether this will remain so with the Special papers time alone can tell.

Certificate of Secondary Education

The Certificate of Secondary Education was established in 1963 and fourteen regional Boards, covering the whole of England and Wales, were established.

Every school entering candidates is free to choose one of three alternative methods by which these candidates are to be examined:

(*a*) an external examination based on a syllabus prepared by the Board—known as Mode 1;

(*b*) an external examination on a syllabus submitted by the school or by a group of schools and approved by the Board—Mode 2;

(c) an examination set and marked internally in the school (or group of schools) but moderated under arrangements made by the Boards—Mode 3.

Each Board established Subject Panels, composed wholly of practising teachers, whose first task was to draw up syllabuses on which Mode 1 examinations are based. *The Examinations Bulletin No. 1— The Certificate of Secondary Education*—issued by the Secondary School Examinations Council, states specifically, 'The responsibility of the schools will be to decide which of the available facilities will best meet the needs of their pupils', and that it is the responsibility of teachers 'to ensure that what is examined is what they want to teach'.

The syllabuses. In the main, the general considerations behind the syllabuses are those which are recognised by all who construct syllabuses for a five-year course in Geography. There is, in the C.S.E. syllabuses, much that is to be found in those for G.C.E. 'Ordinary' level and other external examinations, though the new methods of examining provide the greatest contrast with the established external examinations.

All Boards require a study of the Ordnance Survey map, using the 1:63,360 and the 1:25,000 scales. One, however, further requires knowledge of the 1:10,560 map. Two Boards provide a key to the conventional signs for use during the examination but others expect candidates to know them. Instead of written questions, one Board sets an Oral Map-Reading Test and this too includes the provision of a key to the symbols. Some Boards include in their map-reading section an appropriate photograph so that simple relationships may be deduced. Whether the drawing of sections will be required in connection with this map question is not stated in some syllabuses, whereas others include a definite statement that they will not be required.

The study of the Home Region has been emphasised by all Boards, and it is examined in various ways. Sometimes it is part of the study of the geographical area covered by the Board and is examined by a written paper. In some syllabuses, it forms part or the whole of the course work submitted by each pupil for examination.

All the Boards have followed the well-established pattern of requiring a fairly detailed study of the British Isles, though in one case it is an optional alternative set against (a) field or project work, and (b) the Ordnance Survey map and regional study (through Ordnance Survey maps) of three selected regions of the British

Isles. The approach to the study of Britain shows a considerable variety of method, ranging from the systematic to the regional. One Board states its requirements as:

The British Isles. A knowledge will be expected of: physical features, climate (including common weather situations), major population centres, chief industries including fishing and agriculture, communications and trade. There will be a wide choice of questions so that candidates need not necessarily cover all regions or aspects in detail.

But another Board states

Whilst a certain amount of general treatment will be necessary, the main emphasis will be on selected regions or topics.

A third requires

(i) Agricultural studies in their regional settings to include East Anglia, South East England, South West England, (ii) Industrial studies in their regional settings to include North East England, the Midlands, South Wales, (iii) studies of life in Highland areas to include the Highlands of Scotland, the Lake District, Central and North Wales, (iv) one general study selected from: the fishing industry, textile manufacturing, distribution of population, power resources.

The remaining sections in the syllabuses cover the whole of the content of Geography but the Boards have recognised the difficulty that schools have in preparing candidates for an examination in all of them. The choices as to the section or sections which shall be presented by the candidates for examination have been left to the master and these are considerable as the following examples show.

(i) South-east Board—Paper II
Part A. World Map   5%
      Physical Geography   short answers   15%
      Human Geography

Part B. Two of the following sections: 30% each
   (1) Literary Geography—one of four books (e.g. *A Town Like Alice* —Neville Shute).
   (2) Physical Geography.
   (3) Human Geography of contrasting regions (one of six pairs of regions).
   (4) Major Natural Regions—one of each of the following types: Cold, Cool Temperate, Warm Temperate, Hot.
   (5) Commodities (nineteen are listed).
   (6) Meteorology.
   (7) Field-work or project or library studies or local geology.

and later may be included

(8) World Problems (*a*) Problems created by nature.
     (*b*) International Groupings related to world problems.
(ii) East Midlands Board—Paper II—three of the following sections
 (*a*) World Map.
 (*b*) Meteorology, Weather and Climate.
 (*c*) Land Forms.
 (*d*) Main Climatic Types and products associated with them.
 (*e*) World Problems—four nominated, e.g. soil erosion.
 (*f*) World Topics—three given, e.g. irrigation.
 (*g*) Regional studies of either the U.S.A. or the U.S.S.R.

Field-work has been stressed in all the syllabuses, though often it is linked with course work or project work. Most Boards leave the choice of topic in either of these sections to the decision of the teacher but some make suggestions of lines that may be followed and of methods that might be suitable for presenting the study. One Board has asked that candidates be prepared for an oral examination in Field Study or Local Geography—this section, however, is an optional one.

Suggested by the Southern Board (Syllabus A), in this connection, is:

A folder, loose leaf file, or notebook should be submitted, containing individual work on some aspects of local geography and/or field work, not necessarily of the home area or school area.

Maps, diagrams, models and specimens relating to the region studied, and individual records of observations made and data collected relating to such topics as relief, drainage, structure, weather, vegetation and human activities of the region would be suitable material for assessment.

A programme of field work might well include some of the following:

(i) A full-scale transect chart, showing relationships between surface rock, drainage, land use, settlement, communications.
(ii) A traverse between two points with a schedule of questions to be answered, based on observations.
(iii) A comparative study of two or more settlements.
(iv) A journey through an industrial area.
(v) An industrial visit, such as a factory site, with emphasis on geographical material.
(vi) A detailed examination of a selected rural or urban area.
(vii) An annotated sketch of the landscape from a stated view point.
(viii) Simple surveys, e.g. compass traverse.
(ix) Identification of physical features.
(x) Weather records.

For project work some Boards offer suggestions for the guidance of masters presenting candidates. The North Region Board states that:

The following suggestions are given to candidates offering a project:

(i) Growth of an industry in one of the six Northern Counties.
(ii) Study of the human geography of Africa within the tropics.
(iii) Food supply in India and Pakistan.
(iv) Select two of the following: Snowy River Scheme, Kariba Dam, St Lawrence Seaway, Tennessee Valley Authority, Saharan Oil and Natural Gas.
(v) The development of a river basin in the Northern Region.

Most Boards make the submission of records of field-work or local study a compulsory part of the examination.

The examination papers. Many new features have been introduced in the examination papers for this Certificate that are not usual in 'Ordinary' level examinations. Considerable emphasis has been laid on questions of a practical type. One of the general objects of a C.S.E. course is that pupils should be able to handle source material of all kinds. The short answer type of question is also used frequently and many questions require the insertion of factual knowledge on an outline map. The third type of question (see p. 141)—the essay type—is, in general, little used.

Because of the wide syllabuses, the generous choice of sections and sub-sections within the question papers and the intention of the Boards to explore as many methods of examining as they can, the question papers are often very long, with many outline maps, tables or extracts of statistics, and photographs. The provision by many Boards of extra time to study these papers in the examination room before the start of the examination is a welcome and necessary feature.

Other external examinations

Examinations of several other bodies such as the College of Preceptors, the Royal Society of Arts, and the Union of Educational Institutions are still taken in some schools. Some of these examinations may be attempted at the end of a four-year course, but a five-year Secondary school course is now completed by most pupils who take external examinations. Syllabuses for these examinations usually follow a pattern similar to that of the G.C.E. Emphasis is laid upon a study of the British Isles in detail and only a general knowledge of the world is required, with some familiarity with Ordnance Survey maps on the scales of 1:63,360 and 1:25,000.

Preparation for external examinations

The problem of preparing pupils for external examinations needs careful thought. It can be seen from the school syllabuses set out in Appendix A that most of the concentrated study for the 'Ordinary' level of the G.C.E. and for the C.S.E. examinations comes during the fourth and fifth years of the Secondary school course. After the end of the fifth year the majority of our pupils leave school and both the examinations themselves and the revision required before them provide a sound culmination to a school career.

Where examining bodies allow the candidates a wide choice of questions, the master can devote more attention to those parts of his own syllabus that he considers important or to which he can bring his own specialist knowledge and interests. In the sixth form the 'Advanced' level syllabuses are broad enough to allow a wide scope; frequently, in fact, so some critics complain, too wide to permit more than a superficial study of many topics.

Revision for examinations always presents many problems. For 'Ordinary' level forms, some masters find that they cannot reserve any time for revision, whilst others can provide only homework time. Frequently masters manage to complete the teaching programme early in the summer term and devote several weeks to revision and consolidation before the examination.

Since all the examination Boards have either a separate paper, or part of a paper, devoted to General Geography (Physical and Human), and as much of the work on these aspects of the subject may have been studied in the junior forms as matter incidental to regional study, revision of these topics may be treated systematically towards the end of the course. For example, glaciation may have been considered in work on Norway, North Germany or Switzerland. It can now be treated as a separate topic, with the examples taken not only from the regions formerly studied, but also from the rest of the world. A general study of world climate, vegetation and economic products will serve partly as a means of revising general knowledge of regions which have already been studied.

One of the most important features of any programme of revision should be practice in answering examination questions. This should be given as often as possible in class, for not only is this a more reliable test of the pupils' own revision but it also gives practice in answering questions within their time limit. He will be helped to avoid many of the common errors. Loose expressions such as 'the right climate', 'lush pastures', 'convenience for raw materials', 'fertile soil', 'good communications' and so on, can be pointed out and the need for relevance and careful explanation emphasised.

Many sketch maps accompanying examination answers are inadequately drawn and this is often attributable to lack of practice. Sketch maps should have a heading, an indication of scale and direction, and a key. They should be neither too large nor too small: half a page of examination paper is usually an appropriate size to allow detail to be entered neatly without crowding. All sketch maps should include certain locating features, which should be named. It is of course essential that the sketch maps meet the needs of the question. Their relevance may be judged by the extent to which they either add to the written part of the answer or replace much writing.

During revision time it should be stressed that sketch maps need to be bold, clear and not over-elaborate. It may be noted that printing names is preferable to writing them as legibility is so often a casualty of speed. It is noteworthy how frequently the examiners still complain about the bad presentation and inadequacy of sketch maps.

Choice of questions

The choice of question is obviously a decision that ultimately the pupil himself has to make, but he should be advised that it is better to choose questions which he feels able to answer correctly and fully than to select one for which he can offer only vague knowledge. Credit is given for all material that is correct and there is usually no positive deduction for errors.

Careful reading of the questions is essential, but the selection from the candidate's store of knowledge of the relevant material required to answer the question is a matter of practice. Many pupils tend to substitute a question—one which fits in with their own knowledge—which may have little bearing on the actual topic which they should be discussing.

There are some types of questions which suggest by their wording that they do not require a lot of factual knowledge. These are very often chosen by pupils whose revision has not been too thorough, and very seldom is it a tactic that succeeds. In all answers a certain amount of factual information is required before useful conclusions can be drawn. It is of little use to describe the uneven distribution of population in Scotland or Norway without giving examples of centres of dense populations and indicating some reasons for their locations. To describe an area shown on an Ordnance Survey map as having been glaciated without giving some evidence for the assertion by locating glacial features does not show much understanding of the map evidence. When describing climate either statistics should be quoted or some means of comparison used: without these it is very easy to be vague, using terms like 'hot' or 'cold' which may have varied interpretations.

Answers to questions inviting comparisons and contrasts need careful planning. So many boys treat these as two separate parts of the questions, but may add as an afterthought at the end of the answer a note to the effect that 'so it can be seen' or, more encouragingly, 'you can see how the two areas can be compared or contrasted'. Comparisons and contrasts should be made throughout the whole answer as each point is considered. This type of answer should be written in essay form: pupils should be warned against the habit of setting out their information in columns—this may be a suitable method for note taking but not for examinations.

In all examination questions there are operative words which indicate quite clearly what particular emphasis is desired and what particular area is to be discussed. The opening word or phrase of the question, such as 'Explain', 'Give an account of...' 'Describe', 'Compare and contrast', has its own particular meaning. Some questions are subdivided and in such cases the answer should be similarly arranged, using the same notation or subheadings. Other questions imply subdivision and can be treated similarly. It must be emphasised, too, that logical presentation of an answer demands a reasonable standard of written English.

The period of revision before an examination need not therefore be merely a time to recollect information taught and learnt during previous years. It can also be a time to ensure that examination techniques are mastered.

During this stage of preparation most masters make considerable use of questions from previous examination papers. Much can be gained from study of these: very often more than from the briefly worded syllabus. The members of this Committee, with many years of experience in preparing candidates for external examinations, feel, however, that they must deprecate the use of past papers for the purpose of deducing the topics most likely to occur in the actual paper for which pupils are being prepared. This practice can only be justified on a most cynical view of the purposes of education, and if the deductions are wrong the outcome will be disastrous from all points of view.

Some Boards publish comments annually on the performance of candidates at their summer examinations: these can be most helpful to all masters. It is the policy of this Association to press for such publication by all Boards. Some Boards also divulge their scheme for the allocation of marks to the various questions. This knowledge is extremely useful, particularly during the revision period, as it means that the emphasis can be distributed appropriately and the candidates can be forewarned as to the best allocation of their time when answering the paper.

7

EQUIPMENT

The wide range of Geography and the variety of methods which teachers of the subject may employ have already been discussed. It follows that the best teaching of the subject will involve the use of a wide range of material.

Some aids to the practical teaching of Geography were known even in the nineteenth century and the equipment of several of the old Grammar schools included examples of apparatus which are essential features of modern Geography rooms. There has been steady development during the present century and the essentials of good Geography rooms are now widely recognised and incorporated in new schools.

Although, as described in chapters 2 and 8, there is no doubt that field-work is vital, it is impossible for teacher or pupils to go out and see very much of the world which is the geographer's province. Thus it is desirable, to as great an extent as possible, to bring the world into the classroom. Means of attempting this involve the use of many maps, pictures, photographs, samples, filmstrips, films, slides and books. Only in special rooms and with adequate stores can this material be available and ready for effective use as required. Any attempt to carry material from room to room fritters away much of the time and energy of both staff and pupils. It also means that materials require to be renewed at too frequent intervals and unnecessary expense is incurred. But, apart from the saving of time or labour, there are many stronger reasons which account for the fact that the need for Geography rooms is now so clearly recognised. Showing filmstrips as an integral part of lessons is only possible if projector, screen and blackout are permanently available. Map rails and large areas of blackboard may frequently be needed; they will not be provided in every room in a school. Good tables are vital when large map sheets are being used. Tracing tables or sand trays can only be available in a special room. Displays of maps, charts and

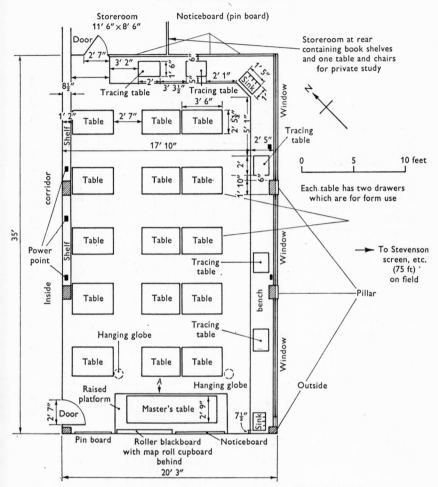

Fig. 13. Geography room plan. A Grammar–Technical school for over
700 including over 120 in the sixth form.

samples need large wall spaces and display cases. A good teacher can
only be expected to make use of very many of these things to the
best advantage if equipment is readily available.

An equally cogent reason for the provision of Geography rooms
which are both well equipped and of adequate size lies in the fact
that the rooms will nowadays often be functioning as workshops or
laboratories rather than simple class-teaching rooms. The general atmosphere of the room can stimulate imagination and give inspiration

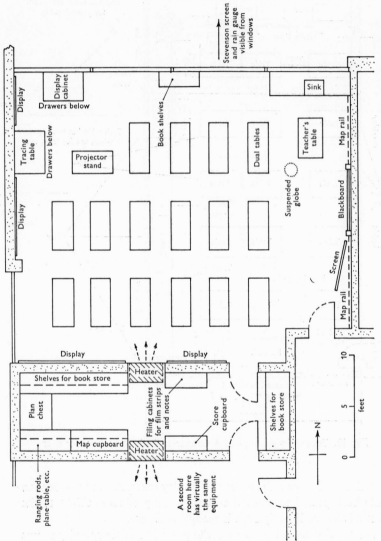

Fig. 14. Geography room plan. A girls' High school with nearly 700 pupils including 88 in the sixth form.

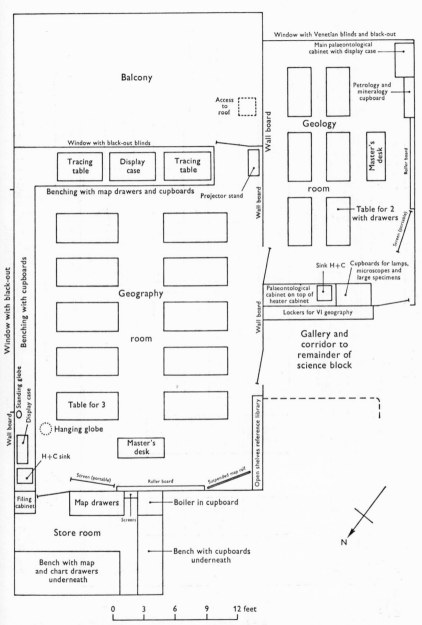

Fig. 15. Geography room plan. A Grammar school for over 800 boys including 180 in the sixth form. Of the boys in the sixth form 31 take Geography and 23 take Geology.

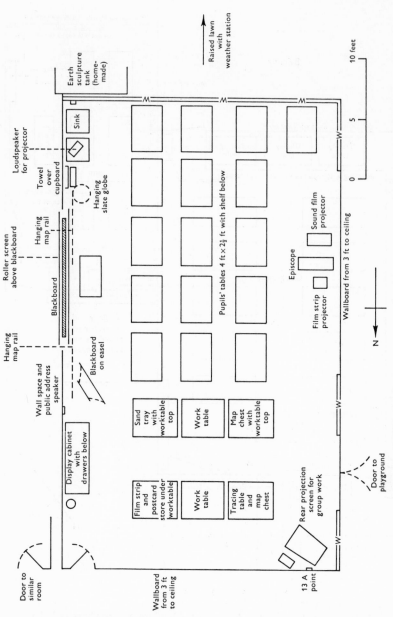

Fig. 16. Geography room plan. Girls' Comprehensive school for over 2,000 pupils including 175 in the sixth form (about 75 in the academic sixth).

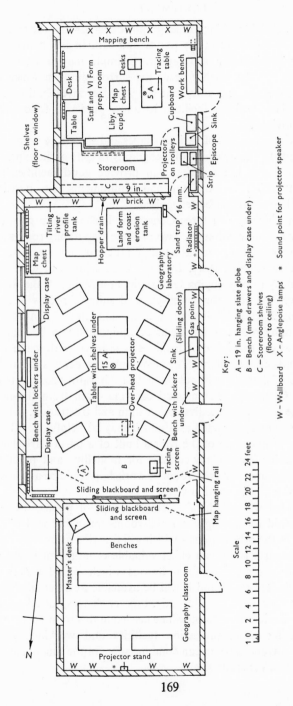

Fig. 17. Geography room plan. A Grammar school for over 800 boys. There are 210 in: he sixth form including the full two-year 'A' level course in Geography.

Mapping bench

Desk

Staff and VI Form prep. room

Desks

Map chest

Tracing table

Liby. cupd.

5 A

Cupboard

Work bench

Table

Shelves (floor to window)

Storeroom

Projectors on trolleys

Strip

Episcope

Sink

9 in.

Tilting river profile tank

Hopper drain

Land form and coast erosion tank

16 mm.

Sand trap

Radiator

Geography laboratory

Map chest

Display case

Bench with lockers under

Display case

Tables with shelves under

15 A

Over-head projector

Sink

Bench with lockers under

(Sliding doors)

Gas point

W brick W

Key:

A — 19 in. hanging slate globe
B — Bench (map drawers and display case under)
C — Storeroom shelves
        (floor to ceiling)
W — Wallboard   X — Anglepoise lamps   * — Sound point for projector speaker

Tracing screen

B

A

Sliding blackboard and screen

Sliding blackboard and screen

Map hanging rail

0 2 4 6 8 10 12 14 16 18 20 22 24 feet

Scale

Master's desk

Benches

Geography classroom

Projector stand

N

169

to the pupils. Good teaching of Geography demands that the teacher not only has an interest in his pupils and skill in his profession, but that he is himself a geographer. Example may often be as useful as precept; the teacher needs the surroundings in which he can work with maps and carry out geographical investigation and experiment. The need for facilities to allow pupils to follow this example is obvious.

In older schools, rooms of various shapes and sizes have been very usefully adapted to the teaching of Geography in spite of the expense. In a new building, the architect can provide good facilities for Geography teaching from the start and requirements as to position and size of the rooms can be recognised.

Schools in which two or three Geography lessons are in progress concurrently are quite common. Two or three Geography rooms are needed and should be planned as a unit, on the same level if possible, together with a suitable store. In some large schools at least five classes are likely to be studying Geography at any time of the week. In such cases, the need for a well-planned suite of rooms is even more obvious. Each individual room in the suite must be in itself a good Geography room. A few items of equipment may be shared, but on the whole the value of facilities is reduced if they are not constantly and easily available. The Geography teacher has to handle a large mass of material without the aid of laboratory assistants or technicians. Continual fetching and carrying, even from the next room, can be a cause of needless exhaustion and frustration. Where several rooms are constructed as a unit it may be helpful, for those who wish it, to have one of the rooms built of a particularly large size, thus making it especially suitable for modelling and practical work. Many features of a craft room or workshop could be available, including a work bench with a vice.

For advanced work with fairly small groups of pupils, there is much to be said for having one small room—probably well under half the size of the other rooms—which will function as an advanced laboratory. Such a room can effect valuable economy of space by accommodating some sixth-form lessons which would otherwise occupy a full-sized room and it will be available at other times for staff use and sixth-form private study. Library shelves, for advanced textbooks and reference books, will be needed in this room; also map storage, tracing table, projection facilities and working space. Possibly this advanced room can combine some of the functions of a store if it is of a generous size.

Size

Geography teaching groups are usually similar in size to those for the majority of subjects. Recognition of the value of practical work with reduced numbers, as in Craft and Science subjects, is unfortunately rare. Therefore the Geography room must be large enough to serve three purposes at the same time. Adequate formal teaching space is needed with provision for tables rather than desks. Space for some work at tracing tables or modelling tables must be available at the same time. There should be adequate storage for maps and other equipment in frequent use. Thus only rooms of something between 960 square feet and 1,200 square feet can be regarded as satisfactory. This means that, if the school has a series of standard rooms in a classroom block, the Geography rooms must be elsewhere. In a new building they may be incorporated in the section of the building where there are other craft rooms, workshops or laboratories. In an old building, a room which has been used for another practical subject may be made into a good Geography room.

Adequate teaching space requires a gap of about 10 ft. between the front tables and the blackboard.

If the room has also to function as a form base then pupils' lockers should be provided in the corridor outside.

Store

A storeroom is needed and it must be well fitted out and easy to reach. Often there can be access from the main Geography room but, as all but the smallest schools will require more than one room, a door leading from another room, or a corridor, will be an asset. The real value of a store depends not only upon its size but upon the use made of the space. Large cupboards for general supplies, storage of equipment and models should be provided. The rest of the wall space should be fitted with a variety of shelving. Small shelves, some quite high up, can accommodate such things as sets of textbooks, magazines and duplicated maps. Shelves at lower level can provide a working surface where, for example, a duplicator can be available. Below this level large shelves can be designed to store large sheets of drawing paper.

Aspect and access

There is an advantage, for purposes of observing the apparent movement and altitude of the sun, in a room with south-facing

171

windows, but means of providing shade against bright sunlight will be needed. A recessed balcony, with access from the room, is excellent. If a good view of the local area is available, a top-floor position may be chosen and a model or orientation table provided at the window.

Considerations of aspect must be weighed against those of access. A direct way to the school grounds or to a good flat-roof space will be an advantage for meteorological work. Thus a ground-floor position may be chosen, with the additional advantage that it will be easy to take classes out for field-work without disturbing other classes.

Lighting

Good lighting, both natural and artificial, is needed to provide clear even light in all parts of the room for map-reading. As in most classrooms, the largest windows will probably provide light to the pupils' left hand when they sit at tables. Because of the need for large areas of display space, the windows, if any, on other sides of the room might be of the clerestory type. Special lighting should be provided to illuminate the blackboards and wall maps. Light switches should be conveniently placed. A master switch controlling all lights can be useful and some teachers advocate a dimmer or a light at the back of the room shaded from the screen so that notes can be taken in subdued light whilst a projector is in use.

Electric plug sockets should be available around the room. A radio is to be expected, but in new buildings may well be provided by a loudspeaker system throughout the school. A connection for a television aerial should be considered as experience in the use of this medium is accumulated.

Blackout

Whether blinds or curtains are chosen it should be possible to provide complete darkness if needed. Even a small amount of light can greatly reduce the value of colour slides or films and can mean that use of an episcope is far from satisfactory.

The most satisfactory blinds are spring-loaded and they can be fitted with the edges running in slots so that excellent blackout results. It is, however, essential to ensure that operation of such blinds is really efficient. Curtains are simpler to operate and maintain. They may be either black or of some dark colour. Two thicknesses of material will probably be needed and it will be an advantage if each curtain is held firmly against the sides of the windows. A good lightproofing where curtains meet is best achieved if the curtain rails overlap for about 9 in.

Ventilation

Close-fitting blinds prevent entry of air, and, if curtains are used, windows must be closed in order to prevent the wind blowing the curtains apart. Therefore some means of ventilation other than through the blackout material must be provided. The need for this may be especially obvious when a room is crowded for a special lecture or meeting of a school geographical society. Some new schools have air conditioning which provides for this need. In other cases special ventilators or extractor fans may be installed.

Sink

Somewhere in the room there should be a good sink with hot and cold water. A roller towel and soap dish should be fitted to provide for the obvious need for washing of hands and cleaning up after certain types of modelling. It will be sensible to have a waste pipe which is accessible and has an easily detachable section: clay or plaster can be a cause of blockage. The sink may be fitted in a teacher's demonstration bench but is probably better in a corner of the room. Alongside it there should be a working surface with a good hard top. Slate might be chosen but a table covered by metal sheeting, as is used in many pottery rooms, would be excellent.

Gas

If 'Advanced' level Geology is likely to be taught in any of the rooms then a gas connection should be provided, but not otherwise.

FURNITURE AND FITTINGS

Blackboard

That the best of all teaching aids is a blackboard is nowhere more true than in a Geography room. A very considerable surface area should include some sliding or roller sections. A roller blackboard can easily be adjusted so that most of the work can be done at a convenient height. Maps can be moved round and retained for future use; sections of the surface can be painted with outline maps of the world or British Isles or can have a squared ruling suitable for graphs or diagrams. However the roller board is not very popular ('Geography room survey 1957', J. A. Morris and R. Cole, *Geography*, XLII, p. 241).

Three or four fixed boards will be useful at the teaching end of the room. Sliding boards of the same size can be fitted in front. These should slide horizontally and be reversible and detachable. Outline maps in frequent demand can be available on the sliding sections or on square boards kept for use as needed. Part of the blackboard should have a squared surface, preferably of 2 in. squares, with lines incised rather than printed on the board, since they are then scarcely visible to the class and the finished drawing is so much the clearer.

The nature of the surface is vital. Green and other colours have been used but the Committee is unanimous in preferring traditional black. Texture should be really smooth for production of bold, precise mapwork. Many wooden boards are not satisfactory. A glass surface is excellent and good qualities are now being claimed for a metal board surfaced with matt vitreous enamel. Some asbestos composition boards have a good surface.

A narrow chalk shelf should be fitted below the blackboards. If the board is not fixed vertically, but is given a slight slope outwards at the top, chalk dust will fall more easily from it, and a clean surface is more readily maintained.

Display board

Wall space which is not occupied by blackboards, windows or other fittings should be covered with a fairly soft wall board which will take drawing pins well. This display board can occupy entire sections of wall from ceiling to floor or at least down to the level of the tables or cupboards along the wall. Perhaps it is an advantage to have low furniture below the board so that pupils are kept at a distance from material on display. Some movable sections of pegboard, with a supply of pegs, hooks and clips, will enable an attractive finish to be given to special displays. The fitting of a series of folding or hinged boards, a device frequently used in wallpaper showrooms, will provide additional surface area and a means of featuring a special series of pictures or maps.

Picture frames

Some loose-backed picture frames are useful for display of pictures and maps. Some of these, including good examples of interesting maps drawn by pupils, can well be hung in various parts of the school.

Map bars

Two or three map bars are commonly fitted at the front of the room above the blackboard but some teachers prefer fittings across a corner or at the side where hanging wall maps do not obscure pupils' view of blackboards. Cords running over pulleys enable the bar to be raised and lowered. These cords come down at the sides clear of the blackboards. Pins may be used to fix maps to the bar but hooks sliding in a groove along the length of the bar are very much better. They do not damage the maps and are readily adapted for maps of various sizes. Most folding wall maps have eyelets fitted. Plastic rails and clips provide another good method of supporting maps and wall charts of any size (see appendix C).

Tables

The greater part of the floor space should be occupied by pupils' tables and chairs. The Committee favour dual tables which give a reasonable working surface but yet achieve some economy of floor space. The arrangement of tables will depend upon the shape of the room, other furniture and individual choice. For most purposes a formal and regular alignment of tables, as shown in the plans of rooms, will be convenient. For some project work or special activities and for exhibitions, tables will perhaps be grouped or may line the walls of the room. Dual tables should have a flat top at least 2 ft. 6 in. × 4 ft. The dimension of at least 2 ft. 6 in. from front to back is most important. The surface should be hard and there may be advantages in choice of a hard plastic such as is often used for school dining room tables. Each pupil may have atlas, map and exercise book in use at the same time and full-sized sheets of the Ordnance Survey 1 in. series will be in use from time to time. If the size of room is adequate, tables above this minimum size will be an advantage. A shelf below the back of the table is for pupils working in the room to put satchels and books which they bring from other classes. As noted earlier, if the room must be used as a form base, lockers for book storage should be outside in a corridor.

Inkwells fitted in the tables are not advised; a supply of ink for fountain pens should be available at the side of the room. At least one firm manufactures a special 'filling station' with this in mind. If inkwells are needed on the tables, they should be strong, heavy and unspillable, and a tray on which they may be collected and kept out of the way will be an asset. A pencil sharpener may be fitted on a side table.

Individual desk lights or illuminating tracing frames in each desk have been fitted but are not likely to be in frequent demand, except, perhaps, by sixth-form pupils.

Staff table or demonstration bench

A staff table with some drawer space is obviously required. Some teachers may prefer a demonstration bench. This can include some map drawers, cupboards and a tracing frame. A shallow display cupboard can be built into the front.

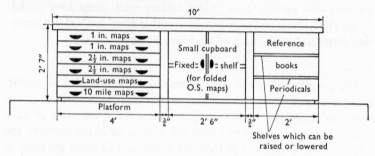

Fig. 18. Detail of a staff table incorporating storage space.

Tracing table

Among the large items of furniture in the working areas of the rooms away from the pupils' tables, tracing tables will be prominent. At least one large one should be provided in each room. A plate glass top should be illuminated evenly from below. Provision of strong wooden covers will allow it to be converted into a working table when desired. If the glass is clear and an opening is provided at the side, the fitting can also be regarded as a display case. On the other hand, it should be realised that frosted glass gives more even illumination. The space under the tracing frame should be used for cupboards or for extra map drawers.

Sand tray

A sand tray should be lined with suitable sheet metal, preferably zinc, and should be about 9 in. to 1 ft. deep. As in the case of the tracing frame, some wooden covers will make it available for other purposes when desired. A clean silver sand or thoroughly washed sand should be used.

Modelling tables

One or two modelling tables should be provided; those with smooth hard tops are best. A metal or plastic finish may be suitable. The object is to have a surface which cannot easily be cut or damaged and which can easily be cleaned. There are advantages in having uniform dimensions for these tables together with other major items such as tracing table, map chest and sand tray. The furniture can then be grouped usefully in an island block or along a wall. If fitted benches with hardwood top along a whole wall, as in other science laboratories, are chosen, cupboards and shelving should be built under the benches. One Local Authority has a very satisfactory range of items constructed so that a base either with legs or five large map drawers can be supplied with any of the following alternative top units: two more map drawers; tracing table; sand tray; or filmstrip and postcard drawers (*School Furniture*, published for the Inner London Education Authority by the Staples Press Ltd.).

STORAGE

Maps

All the rooms in any active Geography Department will have considerable space for storage of maps. The essential characteristics of a practical map chest spring from its dimensions. The area of the drawers must be adequate to accommodate, flat and unfolded, the largest sheets likely to be used, those of the so-called 'National Atlas' scale of 1 in. to 10 miles which are 33 in. × 42½ in. Thus a drawer 34 in. × 45 in. (Antiquarian size) is convenient. For storage of Ordnance Survey plans, maps of the 1:25,000 series, 1 in. geological sheets and other relatively small sheets, a slat, which can be inserted in grooves and so divide the drawer into two parts, will be useful.

Depth of drawers should certainly not be more than about 3 in. and 2 in. is much better. The drawers must have convenient handles and run easily. There should be slots at each side of the fronts of the drawers to take clear labels. On top of a map chest there can be a very useful working surface.

Each of the Geography rooms needs a map chest. Some additional map storage will be advantageous at a central point, in the largest of the rooms, in the storeroom, if this is large, or in an advanced laboratory.

A cupboard with large free-sliding drop-fronted shelves may provide an alternative means of map storage. Such a fitting must be at low level if maps are to be easily handled and identified.

Drawings

It is quite likely that pupils, especially in senior forms, will work on fairly large sheets for the making of maps or drawings. A set of shallow drawers for sheets up to 30 in. × 22 in. (Imperial size) will accommodate work in progress and allow for storage of some worthwhile pieces of finished work. Drawers of the same type are likely to be supplied for Art and Technical Drawing purposes.

Pictures

Most Geography teachers accumulate collections of photographs, pictures and pamphlets. These need sorting out and classifying. They then require a flexible system of storage which makes it possible to take out material on any given area or topic both quickly and easily. Ready availability is the measure of the value of such material. Storage in specially made files is excellent. Most commercial filing systems are suitable, but may require expensive filing cabinets. These, however, may be well worth while as they will last indefinitely and really provide what is needed. The 'Railex' system is convenient and has the advantage that it can be installed in cupboards. Although not so convenient or durable, pocket files or stout envelopes may be used for the same purpose. Box files have the disadvantage that the material upon any given subject will rarely happen to fill exactly one file and much space may be wasted. Convenient shelving for the files will be needed.

Slides

Satisfactory storage and classification of 2 in. slides needs special provision of suitable boxes or drawers. The portability of a slide box is combined with the compactness and convenience of drawers by using a series of small drawers which stack on top of one another.

Some boxes are fitted with grooves to hold each slide. This increases the space needed and is not essential. If divisions run from back to front of the box, grooves in these can be used for adjustable separators which enable slides to be grouped in various ways.

If an automatic projector is to be used, it may be possible to plan storage in magazines.

Map extracts and duplicated material

Sets of Ordnance Survey map extracts can be kept in files or stout envelopes. Supplies of duplicated maps and other material require similar facilities. If filing cabinets are inadequate for the quantity of material which some teachers may wish to have available then really strong cardboard boxes can be employed. They should be of uniform size and might be specially ordered from a box-making firm. Boxes large enough to take about a hundred foolscap sheets folded in half need to be 7 in. × 9 in. × $1\frac{1}{2}$ in. An adequate run of suitable shelving is again obviously required.

Mapographs

Map rollers, such as the 'Mapograph', are in frequent use in most schools. The boxes in which they are supplied can be stacked so that the rollers can be identified and taken out very easily. This is yet another use for good cupboards or shelving.

Filmstrips

Filmstrips are probably already available in the majority of schools and their number is likely to increase. They are best kept in shallow drawers which are provided with partitions. The filmstrip containers are usually clearly labelled but it may be found useful to mark the title of the strip in the bottom of the partition where it should be kept. Thus strips are returned to their correct place in the filmstrip library and also it is simple to see which strips have been taken out for use. If several members of staff are using the strips it is convenient to provide a number of cotton reels bearing their names. When a strip is borrowed an appropriate reel is simply put into its place so that the strip is readily located should there be another demand for it.

The notes which accompany the strips should be kept nearby, classified and arranged in the same order as the strips.

Sets of steel drawers can be obtained with some shallow drawers for strips and some deeper drawers below in which the notes can be kept in order standing on edge. Such drawer units are usually lockable, which may be an asset for a filmstrip library.

Equipment for practical work

Some cupboards or drawers are likely to house the great variety of small items needed for practical work. Adequate allowance should be made for this, remembering that a combination of large and small drawers and shelves is more useful than a complete series of a standard size. Items such as scissors, paintbrushes, mapping pens, and cutting knives can be kept in wooden blocks provided with suitably sized holes.

Model-making may involve the use of plaster of Paris and perhaps clay. Mixing basins and modelling boards are needed. Storage of the materials is convenient in bins which should fit under a table.

Incorporation of every one of these fittings and furnishings into any one Geography room is perhaps neither possible nor desirable. However, the Committee feels that all the items merit very careful consideration and that the vast majority, will, in some form, be available in all good new rooms. If financial difficulty limits provision of adequate facilities it is suggested that the first essential should be a good-sized room with a really useful store. Unless these are available no amount of equipment can remedy the disadvantages of inadequate space.

In old buildings, a very great deal can be done to equip a room. In fact it is not uncommon to find that sizes of rooms and stores are larger in old buildings than in new. Emphasis will probably be upon the purchase of good furnishings and fittings rather than upon any structural alterations. This will very clearly be so if new premises are to be provided in the future. There is every justification for obtaining some first-class furnishings if it is known that these can later be transferred to a new room.

PROJECTION FACILITIES

Film projectors

Very nearly all schools now at least have access to a film projector. It is rapidly becoming usual to have at least one on the school premises and often it is housed in the Geography department, where it is likely to be most frequently used.

The 16 mm. film size is at present used for nearly all films available from Local Authorities and from commercial sources for school use. A sound projector should certainly be chosen.

A good machine, although expensive, is well worth while. Weight and portability should be considered. Good even illumination and clear sound are to be expected. The erection and operation of the machine should be simple. A socket for a microphone is provided on most machines and some have apparatus for recording a magnetic sound track, which can be temporarily superimposed upon an existing optical sound track, so that any commentary can be provided.

In rooms where films are frequently shown, the provision of a fitted lead and place where a loudspeaker can hang semi-permanently in a corner of the room will contribute to the ready availability which is so often the measure of the real value of equipment. A projector stand, with lockable cover, can contribute to the same end. Good use can be made of the lower part of the stand by fitting shelves or cupboards. If it cannot remain in place all the time then the stand should take the form of a wheeled trolley.

Amateurs use 8 mm. film a good deal, mainly on grounds of relative cheapness of the film itself, and an 8 mm. projector can be useful for showing films taken privately. It will be very appropriate if the school possesses its own cine camera. The low cost, combined with improving standards of technical performance, may well lead to greater use of 8 mm. films and projectors in school.

Short 8 mm. films, running for 3–5 minutes or even less, are now being made for educational use and they may prove helpful in Geography teaching. They are supplied in convenient cassettes and may be in the form of a loop film for use in a special projector. This is built into a unit which incorporates a small rear-projection screen for showing in daylight. Operation is simple and the film can easily be repeated as often as desired.

Filmstrip and slide projectors

Virtually all schools possess a slide projector. In the majority of cases there is at least one in the Geography department; large departments will have the exclusive use of two or three machines.

Slides of 2 in. × 2 in. made from 35 mm. film, and filmstrip using the same film base, are used for very nearly all the new material of this type likely to be used in schools. The projector, adaptable for showing either filmstrip or slides, should be portable and robust. A carrying case is a great convenience and in the long run an economy if the machine is likely to be used in various rooms. Good illumination is essential. The power of the lamp may be chosen in relation to available blackout but frequently a lamp of at least 750 watts is advisable, remembering that projection of coloured material, already probably more used than black and white, requires a good light. With a lamp of this size the projector should have a cooling fan.

One or two simple precautions should be taken in using such

projectors, to avoid risk of damage to the machine and to obtain the best results with the class:

(1) A loop of the cable passed around the leg of the desk or table on which the machine stands will prevent it from being pulled to the floor should someone accidentally trip over the cable.

(2) The projector should never be moved while switched on as the vibration may well cause the bulb to 'short'.

(3) Should a fault occur the projector should never be opened whilst hot, as the rush of cold air can damage the bulb or the lenses.

(4) Projection from the back of the class will give a large image. It will also make for ease of discipline.

In recent years increasingly efficient daylight projectors have come on to the market. The day may not be far distant when it will be possible to project reasonably good pictures, both monochrome and colour, in full daylight. The projector could then be used when and where desired and the problem of doing written or map work with projected material would solve itself. Anyone considering the use of a daylight projector is advised to make thorough tests of the equipment under varying conditions of external lighting before making a final decision.

Episcope

For projection of pictures or drawings an episcope is required. Many masters will build up their own picture collections. Where pictures are in constant use it is advisable to have these cut out, mounted on cardboard and filed in a card index. Pictures suitable for use with an episcope should not as a rule exceed 6 in. × 6 in. if the whole surface is to be illuminated for projection.

An episcope requires a highly efficient reflector system, a large-aperture lens, good definition and efficient ventilation. The fulfilling of these requirements, together with the fact that a transformer may be incorporated, may well result in considerable total weight. This does not encourage use of the episcope if it has to be moved about at all. A second factor against it is that, even with the best models, a really good result is obtained only if there is absolute blackout. Despite these disadvantages the episcope is still invaluable to many teachers. If a new one is to be introduced to a school, steps should be taken to ensure that its drawbacks in terms of weight and blackout requirements are as far as possible minimised.

Some types of episcope allow pictures, maps or other material to be placed on top of the machine rather than upon a platform below it. There are at least two advantages. First, material is less likely to be damaged. Secondly, there is no limit to the size of sheet which may be used.

Overhead projector

This instrument is best handled in a permanent position or upon a trolley. It could very conveniently be kept in a desk with a recessed well such as is used by typists. The number of overhead projectors in schools is not yet large but the machines have obviously great potential value in the hands of skilled and enthusiastic teachers. Blackout is not necessary for satisfactory results. Anything written or drawn, in black ink or in colour, upon sheets of cellulose acetate supported on a glass plate, will be projected on to the screen. Work can be done on the acetate in colour, using transparent inks, paints, chinagraph crayons or felt-tipped marker pens. Solid areas of colour are produced by the use of adhesive pieces of plastic foil cut to shape and attached to the acetate.

Machines may be fitted with scroll attachments. A 50 ft. acetate roll can then be turned through the machine and either be used as a blackboard or carry a sequence of material prepared in advance.

Transparency mounts, 10 in. × 10 in., are available for work which is to be filed for future use. Drafting tape is used to hinge overlays to the acetate.

Illustrations can be produced from printed matter by the use of a copying machine. A commercial service will produce material in this way, but each transparency will at present cost several shillings. A transparency can also easily be made on a spirit duplicator by substituting a sheet of cellulose acetate for the normal paper.

This versatile projector could virtually take the place of a blackboard. It could solve the problem of chalk dust for the teacher of any subject! It also has the advantage that the teacher faces his class whilst writing, drawing or explaining material.

The particular attractions of the instrument for a Geography master include:

(1) The fact that material can be prepared in advance and may therefore be of a more detailed and precise nature than is normally possible on a blackboard. A wide range of material may be stored for future use.

(2) The fact that transparencies showing a number of different features can, separately or together, be laid over the same base map. The solid geology, drift geology, soils, vegetation or population

distribution of an area could each in turn be examined in relation to a base map. The base map could be entirely in black, colours being used upon the other maps. Subsequently any two or more of the overlays could be studied in combination. Thus interrelationships are considered and a region is studied by a process of synthesis. The instrument can thus contribute to some characteristic methods of the geographer.

Screen

As in the case of the projectors, the screen should always be as nearly ready for use as possible. A fixed screen or a section of the wall suitably surfaced meets this requirement but does take up space which might be put to other uses. There is also the likelihood that the surface will easily become dirty and so cleaning and maintenance costs may be high.

In the unfortunate cases where projectors must be used in a variety of rooms, a portable screen is essential. Screen widths of 4–6 ft., when open, are fairly adequate for small classrooms and the closed screen is reasonably portable. Larger screens are better when in use but less easy to carry.

For a Geography room, a roller screen will probably be first choice. It can be mounted over the centre blackboards, leaving others still available at the side, or may be across a corner of the room if it is felt that diagonal projection is more suited to the shape of the room and the arrangement of the pupils' tables. Spring-loaded screens are pulled down and return automatically to their case when released. Very effective and reliable results are achieved by using simple pulleys and cords to let the screen down. There is little to go wrong and if there is trouble it is very easy to remedy.

Silver and beaded screens reflect more light to those seated directly in front of them but their efficiency falls off rapidly for those seated at the sides. They are to be avoided if the room is wide but allows only a short distance between projector and screen. In long, narrow rooms this disadvantage is less serious. The silver screen is not good for projection of coloured material.

A plain white screen has many advantages in spite of its rather lower efficiency as a reflector. It is relatively simple and cheap. The surface is not easily damaged. Resurfacing is not difficult: white paint is all that is needed on a fixed screen. The screen is not strongly directional, so that pupils at the sides will have a good view provided they are not at at very narrow angle to the surface.

A large screen is a very great advantage. One of the objects in using films and slides is to try to bring the world into the classroom in cases where it is impossible to take the class out to see for themselves. Pictures should convey as much realism and detail as possible. They are more likely to succeed in these respects if they are large and bright. With good material, a modern projector in a classroom with efficient blackout can fill a screen at least 8 or 10 ft. wide. From a good 2 in. slide, much interesting, attractive and realistic detail can be derived in this way.

If at all possible the screen should be square to accommodate vertical frames, but it should not be reduced in width to achieve this.

It is very convenient to have a torch projecting an arrow to the screen in order to point precisely to features which are to be noted and studied. This is a facility which a few schools afford.

Rear projection involves an arrangement of mirror and translucent screen, in a box. Effective equipment is not difficult to construct but it may not be portable. Commercial units are available with a collapsible 'box' incorporating screen, mirror and projection aperture. Such equipment can be used in any classroom without blackout and gives fair results. The unit can be dismantled and carried to other rooms fairly easily.

Rear projection will perhaps be chosen if a large number of rooms do need to be used, but in terms of brilliance, clarity and reality it cannot compete with good front projection and good blackout.

Films

Most of the films used are likely to be 16 mm. sound films. Colour films are steadily replacing black-and-white. It is, therefore, unlikely that schools will have many, if any, of their own films: the cost is quite out of proportion to frequency of use. Some Local Education Authorities may have a good library and make it really easy for schools to borrow films. Teachers will also be well advised to consider other sources of film such as those listed in appendix C, and others mentioned in the press from time to time.

The cassettes containing short 8 mm. films are convenient. Such films deal with one single topic only, and might be run through two or more times during a single lesson.

Filmstrips

An excellent range of filmstrips is available for Geography. The cost is not great and strips may be used more often in part than as a whole. A Geography department should possess a good basic library of filmstrips. This should be built up steadily and carefully, taking advantage of the facilities provided by most producing firms for the previewing of strips before purchase. The Local Education Authority may well have a filmstrip library which can loan additional special strips but this is no substitute for a set of strips ready to hand in the room where the teaching is done.

A few teachers make their own filmstrips and provision of dark-room facilities will be a great encouragement to such interest and enthusiasm. It may, for instance, be possible to provide particularly good blackout in a room which is intended as an advanced Geography laboratory, or in a store room.

A filmstrip made by the teacher himself will possess great advantages as he will choose just the features required and will have a much more detailed knowledge of the views shown than is normally the case with a commercially purchased strip. On the other hand, he must not be tempted to include frames which are of interest to himself but are not really likely to either instruct or interest the pupils! One case in which a strip made in the school has particular value is when a field excursion or local survey can be used as the basis for the material.

Slides

Slides made from 35 mm. film can be used much more flexibly than a filmstrip. Some teachers would even advocate cutting film-strips up and mounting each frame separately as a slide. In this case it is best to purchase a filmstrip which has double-size frames (24 mm. × 36 mm.). There is, however, a good deal of time needed to keep a slide collection in order and to select and take out the particular slides needed for various purposes. It is increasingly common to find teachers taking their own 35 mm. pictures, often in colour and building up personal slide collections. Pictures taken by the teacher can be made much more meaningful to pupils than can a purchased filmstrip. This process is likely to continue among keen teachers in spite of the considerable expense, towards which neither school nor taxation authorities make contribution.

Slides of the 2 in. size, usually in colour, can be purchased from an increasing number of commercial firms. Some of the geological survey pictures are available as 2 in. slides from the Geological Museum, South Kensington. Some firms supply slides specifically chosen for geographical reasons. They may be bought either singly or in sets dealing with particular topics or regions.

It is not difficult to make useful slides by photographing in colour carefully drawn blackboard diagrams. The diagrams should be bold and colours used with systematic purpose.

Pictures and magazines

In appendix C, a number of periodicals and other sources of good pictures are listed. In the course of time a large range of such material can be collected. As the collection increases so it becomes vital to select the best and most useful items, classify them, and store them so that they are really easy to pick out when needed. Conversely there is much to be said for ruthless discarding of unwanted material.

Mounting of small pictures is advantageous if they are in frequent use. They can be used in sets which can be passed round a class and they are easy to store and index.

OTHER GEOGRAPHY ROOM EQUIPMENT

Aerial photographs

These are of two types—obliques and verticals. The former have the advantage of familiarity, and are therefore valuable in illustrating a scene which can then be discussed with the pupils. They have the disadvantage, however, of having patches of 'dead ground', and also of not being analogous to maps. The uses of both of these are becoming increasingly realised, for they are both accurate and non-selective—they are true slices of reality, and thus are invaluable in any regional work. In sixth-form studies, the use of stereo pairs can also be attempted, providing exciting reality to what otherwise might appear merely as another form of map. (Sources of aerial photographs are given in appendix C.)

Globes

A really good globe is a very high priority for any Geography room. A diameter of at least 12 in. is to be expected and a 19 in. globe is very much better. Some globes for school use are of 24 in.

diameter. The Committee would stress the value of a 'slate' surface on which outlines of continents are permanently printed in white. Lines of latitude and longitude are best incised into the surface but not printed white. Political and relief globes also have their uses and it may well be that more than one globe should be provided. Special globes can give prominence to items such as sea and air routes of the world.

The globe is far better made of metal or unbreakable plastic than of plaster, which is so easily damaged. If the globe is mounted on a small stand it is useful if it can easily be detached. The hanging globe, balanced by counterweights or mounted on a spring-loaded roller, is found very convenient in many schools. It has, however, some critics, and the choice of mounting is ultimately an individual matter.

It is now possible to make globes of light plastic material. They can be inflated for use and stored away easily if not required. If a room is, for instance, provided with slate-surface and relief globes it might be useful to have an inflatable political globe.

Illuminated globes are impressive and attractive but their cost puts them beyond the range of normal equipment.

Provision of small globes, about 6 in. diameter, for each pupil, or at least on each dual table, is strongly recommended by some teachers, but is not at present very common. There is much to be said for allowing pupils to handle globes frequently themselves, rather than having the globe associated only with the teacher.

A valuable adjunct to a rolling globe, in this age of air transport when teaching of Great Circle routes should assume importance, would be a transparent hemisphere of rigid plastic, on which soft wax pencils can easily be used, to fit loosely over the globe in any position.

Wall-maps

Some form of wall-map is likely to be in frequent use. A roller map has the advantage of an attractive appearance when in good condition. It needs considerable storage space, either hanging vertically from hooks or in a special rack or cupboard, and may deteriorate rapidly if not carefully handled. For most purposes, the Committee strongly favour folding wall-maps. These are usually dissected and mounted upon cloth. They have eyelets to go on to the hooks of a map bar. They can be clearly labelled and stored vertically in sets upon a partitioned shelf or in a drawer.

A wall-map showing relief of the continents and most major areas studied will be a first requirement. The choice between layer-coloured maps and those with some system of shading to stress relief is partly an individual matter, but the Committee feels that shading is often an advantage, particularly for pupils of limited ability.

A set of maps of uniform scale of a given area enables aspects of climate, vegetation, economic development and population distribution to be compared with the basic relief map. It is not useful to have such a series of maps mounted together on a single bar: they should be available separately or to be put up side by side in such combinations as may be required.

The general appearance of the map should be bold, and a fairly large size is an advantage, but it need not be expected that all the printing should be legible from the back of the classroom. A use for roller maps arises if it is possible to have a smaller battery of the most important maps mounted upon spring rollers in a convenient place near the front of the room.

Topographical maps

The maps produced by the Ordnance Survey of Great Britain should form the basis of the school map collection in the Geography room. They can be obtained direct from the Director General of the Ordnance Survey, Chessington, Surrey, who will also supply particulars of the terms on which maps may be obtained at reduced rates for educational purposes. Examples of all available scales of maps should be obtained together with class-teaching sets of local maps on several scales. The Ordnance Survey plans on the scale of about 50 in. to 1 mile, actually 1:1,250, show detail of urban areas which is fascinating to children, especially when they see their own houses represented. These maps are particularly useful if early stages of mapwork teaching are approached through plans of rooms and houses. If the school is in an area covered by these plans, a series of sheets should be available for the surrounding area. These can make an excellent wall display when map work is being introduced. A class set of the school itself may be well worth while.

A few sheets of the 25 in. (1:2,500) plan are interesting for comparison. The 6 in. to the mile map is still the largest scale available for some rural areas and good local coverage on this scale should be obtained in such cases. In urban schools at least one copy of the local sheets is needed for purposes of comparison and illustration. The 6 in. maps will also be needed for of field-work. Their value in land-use survey has been demonstrated very clearly both in the Land

Utilisation Survey of England and Wales carried out in the 1930s and in the new survey started during 1960. Exercises in such survey may well form a part of field-work both in the local area and on longer journeys.

The most important maps, in the school, numerically, will be those on the scales of about $2\frac{1}{2}$ in. to 1 mile (1:25,000) and 1 in. to 1 mile. Class sets of the local map on each scale should be a priority. A reference collection of 1 in. maps should be built up, aiming ultimately to cover the whole of Great Britain. In the early stages, maps of the local region and examples of particular types of topography should be chosen. (For example the maps of areas described by booklets in the Geographical Association's *British Landscape through Maps* series with, in some cases, accompanying sets of exercises.) Maps of the local region may be used to 'wallpaper' a corridor.

For use in G.C.E. and other examinations the Ordnance Survey produce special extracts from $2\frac{1}{2}$ in. and 1 in. maps. Extracts which have been used in the school for examinations can be retained as teaching sets and additional copies can be obtained. The Ordnance Survey will, on request, supply a list of the extracts which are currently available for purchase. This list frequently changes but in the course of time maps showing varied aspects of British Geography can be obtained. The extracts are cheaper than the full sheets and are convenient to handle in class.

Some schools have a library of 1 in. maps available, on payment of a fairly substantial deposit, for loan to pupils.

When a particular 1 in. sheet is being reprinted the Ordnance Survey have an arrangement with the Geographical Association, to whom enquiries should be directed, to make available water and contour pulls of the map. Advantage should be taken of this facility.

Some $\frac{1}{2}$ in. and $\frac{1}{4}$ in. (now 1:250,000) maps will be in the collection. So will a good many of the 10 miles to 1 in. (actually 1:625,000) series, covering Britain in two sheets and showing features such as geology, types of farming, coal and iron, density of population etc. Examples of some of the special maps on smaller scales (for example Roman Britain) should also be included.

Other maps examples of which should be stocked include Land Use maps. Some sheets of the first Land Use Survey may still be available on the 1 in. scale. The organisers of the new survey have chosen the $2\frac{1}{2}$ in. scale for publication. The $\frac{1}{2}$ in. to 1 mile maps produced by Messrs Bartholomew are clear and attractively layer-coloured. Some Local Authorities, through their Engineering or Planning Department, have up-to-date local plans available. One or two sheets of the maps produced by the Soil Survey of Great Britain will be of interest. A number of representative geological maps, available through the Ordnance Survey, should include those of the local area on the 1 in. scale if available. Some areas are covered by 6 in. geological maps which, although reprinted from an old survey, are of value. Descriptive monographs are available with some of these maps.

A few foreign maps, comparable to our Ordnance Survey series, should be selected, bearing in mind the regions studied in detail by 'Advanced' level pupils (see chapter 6) and the value of the maps to illustrate aspects of Physical Geography.

The majority of the maps will be ordered 'paperflat'. They are best used flat and the room should be equipped, as described, for storage and use of such sheets. Binding the edges of the maps prolongs their life, makes them easier to handle and improves appearance. Special binding tape should be used. Map edge binding machines are available (see appendix C for Map Binding Machines). For field excursions and for a reference collection the folded style is preferable. The mounted and folded version is more durable than paper folded style but the cost is obviously greater than the latter and may not be justified.

Models

Various working models are available to illustrate processes germane to the study of Geography; for instance, an orrery showing movements of the moon and the earth in relation to the sun. Such things are expensive and certainly not basic items of equipment.

Models made by groups of pupils, either in class or as a Geography Society activity, will be simpler but of greater value.

Plastic relief models of various parts of Britain and of some maps used in map work books can be purchased. Similar models can be made by pupils. They can be coloured to show information such as height, communications or geology.

As already noted, the making of models requires adequate space and working surfaces. Materials required will include things such as clay, plaster of Paris, balsawood, cardboard of various types, moulder's sand, 'plasticine' and paints. Some models have been made in concrete: others in polystyrene. Wire, nails and screws may be needed from time to time and a simple tool kit should be assembled. A small engineer's vice attached to a work table will be useful. A few fretsaws will be in demand, particularly for cutting out relief models. A treadle-operated fretsaw very much aids such work.

Supplies of base boards for models should include some of asbestos or some similar material which will not be affected by moisture from clay or papiermâché. Various buckets, bowls, scissors, cutting knives, steel rulers, paint brushes and jars will have their uses. Sponges, cloths and a brush and pan greatly aid the clearing up processes.

A small glass trough, of the aquarium type, may be useful in the teaching of contours by partially submerging a simple relief model made by some pupils.

Meteorological apparatus

Setting up of a school weather station is usually undertaken by a Geography master. A good range of really accurate instruments should be the ultimate aim but, if this cannot be achieved all at once, a great deal of stimulating and informative work can be done with simple apparatus.

A maximum and minimum thermometer should be obtained if possible. A rain gauge requires only a 5 in. diameter plastic funnel, a bottle and a purchased measuring cylinder. A weather vane is easily made. Wind speed, visibility, cloud type and general weather conditions can be noted without instruments. A barometer may be in the Science department.

Even though equipment is to be simple and perhaps made by pupils it is worth while consulting the stringent requirements laid down by the Meteorological Office (*Meteorological Observers' Handbook*, H.M.S.O.). This will ensure that work is on the right lines and enable more accurate work to be done when instruments can be obtained.

A Stevenson screen should be obtained as soon as possible. Purchase is expensive but construction of the double-louvred sides is not easy for pupils. One supplier has available a 'Make-it-yourself' kit which is an excellent compromise. The screen should be sited according to Meteorological Office instructions.

A wet- and dry-bulb thermometer to measure humidity can be added without great expense, as also can the separate instruments needed for official observation of maximum and minimum temperatures. Thermometers should have been tested by the National

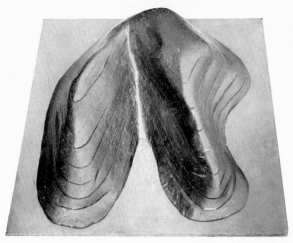

1. Wooden model for teaching contours:

(*a*) the assembled model;

(*b*) the model opened to show the '300 ft.' contour;

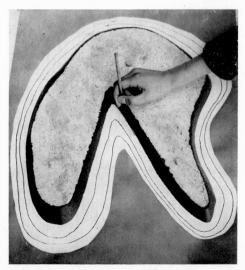

(*c*) drawing in the '300 ft. contour on a map.

2. (a) Wheat harvesting near Portage La Prairie: example of a photograph that can be subjected to geographical analysis.

(b) The St Lawrence Seaway near Montreal.

3. (a) View of Montreal showing the docks and St Lawrence River.

(b) The docks and business quarter.

4. (a) 'The Weather Station'.

(b) Instrument for measuring the angular height of the sun.

5. (a) A Geography room in a new school. This corner of the Geography room at Queen Mary's Grammar School, Walsall, shows some of the display facilities and the end of the series of cupboards, with work bench above, which line one side of the room (see Fig. 15). A sink with hot and cold water is fitted. The door leads to a good storeroom. At the back of the room there is an excellent tracing table and a door leads out to a special south-facing observation balcony. Adjoining this main Geography room is a slightly smaller room specially fitted and equipped for Geology. The rooms are part of the science block of the school.

(b) Geography laboratory. This is a general view of the larger of two rooms at Northgate Grammar School, Ipswich (see Fig. 17). The door leads to a store room. Many excellent items have been provided to make a good room in an old building. At the back of the laboratory there are river profile and coast erosion tanks (a photograph showing these more clearly appeared in *Geography and Education*, H.M.S.O. 1960).

6. (*a*) Furniture. These special items of furniture are part of the range designed and made for the I.L.E.A. The right-hand unit has two shallow drawers, one of which is specially fitted for storage of filmstrips or for postcards or other pictures. To the left is an eight-drawer map chest with shallow drawers large enough for any Ordnance Survey map to lie flat. The top of this unit, containing two drawers, may be interchanged with the top of the filmstrip storage unit. Two other top units, to fit either base, provide for tracing (see Plate 6*c*) and for a sand tray. All units are 4 ft. × 3 ft. × 3 ft., and have a working surface on top. Between the two units is a modelling table to the same dimensions.

(*b*) Geography room table. This is the flat-topped dual table designed for the I.L.E.A. for use in Geography and History rooms. To the left is a display case with cupboard units below. It has a flat glass top and is illuminated by strip lighting.

(*c*) Map chest. This is one item in the I.L.E.A. range of furniture (see Plate 6*a*). Recesses on the front of the drawers combine the functions of handles and label slots. The top is an unbroken piece of ground glass illuminated from below by strip lighting. Wooden covers, one of which is in place, can be placed over the glass to provide a working surface.

7. (a) Geography room in a rather older building. Each table in this Geography room in Albright Girls' School, Oldbury, is provided with a small globe. The screen is painted on part of the blackboard area. The sliding reversible blackboards carry some prepared outlines.

(b) Reference library. This new room is well provided with adjustable shelving on which reference books, periodicals and other source materials will be kept. Diagonal mounting of a map bar has been chosen in this case.

8. (*a*) Front of a Geography laboratory. The fixed screen has two vertically sliding black-boards in front of it. The hanging globe is slate surfaced. There are map bars, at a slight angle, at both sides of the room. The staff demonstration bench contains drawers and storage cupboards. The advantage of clerestory windows along one side of the room is apparent in terms of increased wall space. The open door leads to a second room also used for geography.

(*b*) Simple surveying instruments. Part of an exhibition at an Annual Conference of the Geographical Association.

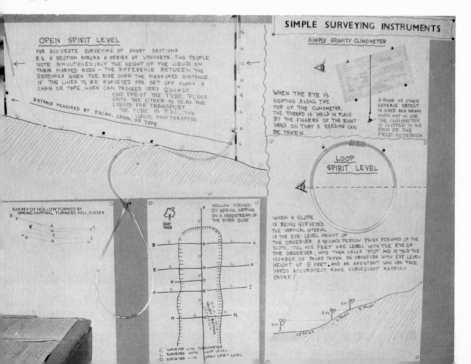

Physical Laboratory. Sunshine recorders vary in price according to type. A wind speed indicator (anemometer) may be purchased or possibly constructed. The whirling cup type is probably most suitable. A barograph, thermograph and hygrograph will also be useful in time.

Whatever instruments are used it will be important to have suitable blank sheets or a book for recording regular observations at least once a day. Several firms produce these or they may be duplicated (see appendix C—Teaching Material in Connection with Weather Study).

The interest of the school records is greatly increased if the school receives the *Daily Weather Map*. This is posted daily from the Meteorological Office, who will supply details of subscription charges including special rates for schools.

Surveying equipment

In Secondary schools it is often found that surveying arouses great interest and at the same time gives a practical demonstration of elementary geometry and trigonometry. This has been recognised by several of the C.S.E. Boards in their syllabuses. Here is real Practical Geography, and children even in their first year will find a simple chain survey or compass traverse well within their power. Second-year pupils will tackle plane-table survey and simple contouring, and the third and fourth years will produce very good results using the prismatic compass and model theodolite.

The compass must be purchased, and a chain or tape forms part of the equipment of every school, but the other survey apparatus is generally too expensive, even if the simplest models are required.[1] Most of the instruments can be fairly easily constructed in the school workshops, or in the Geography room, if it is well equipped. When making these instruments, the teacher should remember to use brass, or some other non-magnetic material, for any parts that may affect a compass which is being used near them.

Ranging poles. These are the first requirements for marking ends of base lines, etc. The standard pole is made of a straight-grained wood, such as ash, 1 in. in diameter and 6 ft. long. One end is pointed and shod with sheet iron. The pole is painted in contrasting colours, generally red, white, black, repeating, each band of colour being 1 ft. wide.

[1] Good second-hand instruments may be obtained from: Charles Frank Ltd., 67–75 Saltmarket, Glasgow, C. 2.

A more easily seen marker is the 'Belisha Beacon'. The constructional details of this are shown in Fig. 19. Two discs of metal or plywood, *A* and *B*, are halved together at right-angles. Two slots at right-angles are then cut in the top of the ranging pole, the discs forced in and held in place by screws. These discs are then painted yellow, which is very easily seen over long distances by the naked eye, if the paint is kept clean. The appearance from the side of these discs is that of a sphere, but any errors due to their size will be negligible.

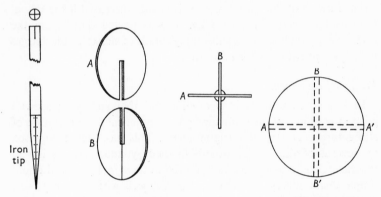

Fig. 19. Ranging poles.   Fig. 20. Offset pole.

The levelling stave. This is usually a telescopic instrument, but for most elementary surveys it is sufficient to have a 12 ft. length of two-by-one painted white, with the feet and inches marked off in red. Such a length of wood is, however, inconvenient for transport and storage, and certainly two jointed 6 ft. lengths would be handier when travelling.

Measuring right-angles. For taking offsets, a convenient means of obtaining a right-angle is required. The simplest method is to drill two $\frac{1}{8}$ in. holes at right-angles through the top of one of the ranging poles (see Fig. 20). If small children are to use this method, then a special short model can be made with the holes about $4\frac{1}{2}$ ft. from the ground. Accurate offset right-angles can be quickly measured by compass, with ranging poles. Insert two poles along the main traverse line, take the bearing from one to the other, and an angle of 90° from that line is easily measured by the compass, a ranging pole then being inserted along the offset line.

194

Optical square. This is a very accurate method of obtaining a right-angle. It is particularly useful in setting out a circular running track, or the semicircular ends for a track. Two small mirrors, about $1\frac{1}{2}$ in. square, *L* and *M*, are fixed by means of metal clips to a base-board (Fig. 21). The angle between the mirrors is 45°. The top half of the mirror *M* has been scraped clear of the backing so that it is clear glass. The object, *A*, say a ranging pole at one end of a base

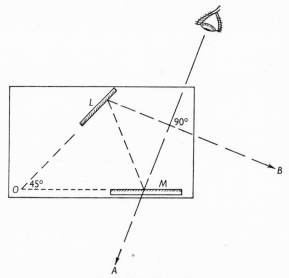

Fig. 21. Optical square.

line *AB*, is viewed through the top clear portion of *M*. The surveyor moves until he sees the reflected image of *B* coincident with *A*. Then the angle subtended at their point of intersection by the rays from the ends of the base line is 90° and this point is on the circumference of the circle of which *AB* is a diameter.

Clinometer. This is a very simple instrument (Fig. 22) and can be made by every child in one ordinary classroom period. It consists of a rectangular piece of wood—plywood or hardboard—about 10 in. long and 5 in. wide. A line *AB* is drawn parallel to one long edge and about $\frac{1}{2}$ in. from it. A small round-headed brass screw is partly screwed in at *A* and a small ring, such as is used at the end of a curtain wire, is put in at *B*. These two form a ring-and-bead sight. A protractor is fixed so that its reference line coincides with the line through *AB* and its centre is at *C*. It is actually better if the protractor is drawn on good quality paper. Then the zero can be put at the bottom of the curve and 90° along the line *AB*. When this is done, readings are taken off directly without any mental arithmetic being involved. At *C* is a small screw to which is fastened a piece of twine or thread. To this is attached a weight *D*, such as a ½ in. nut. This acts as a plumb bob when sights are being taken.

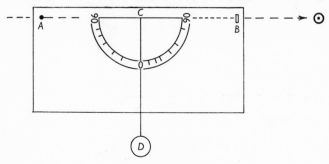

Fig. 22. Clinometer.

On the reverse side of the rectangle it may be found useful to affix a sheet of paper on which is given a brief description of how to use the instrument for finding the height of a distant object, by taking angles of elevation from the ends of a measured horizontal base line which is pointing towards the object.

The sextant. This instrument should be in every Geography room. Not only is it valuable for survey work, but it is most useful when dealing with Latitude in ordinary class teaching. Daily 'shootings' of the sun at noon can be made by the first-year children and a record kept. Thus the movement of the sun can be graphed and the explanation of the seasons is made easier.

The essentials of the sextant (Fig. 23) are:

(1) A sector-shaped base of plywood or metal, as shown. If metal is used, only a framework is required, since it will be sufficiently strong and rigid without extra weight at the centre.

(2) An arm, *AD*, pivoted at *A*, so that it can move freely over the arc *BC*. In this arm is cut a small rectangular opening through which the scale can be read. Through two small holes, *L* and *M*, is stretched a fine wire which is then soldered to the back of the arm. This acts as a hair-line for increasing the accuracy of the readings.

(3) A small mirror fixed firmly to the arm at *A*. The front face of the mirror must coincide with the centre line of the arm, and the hairline *LM*.

196

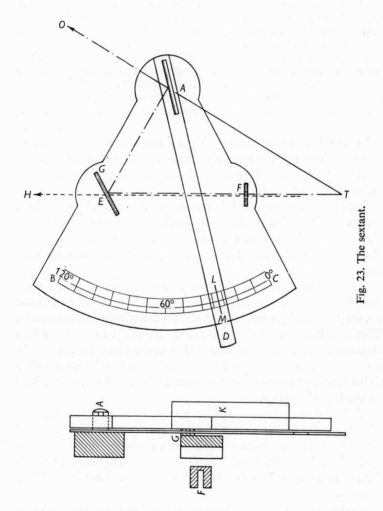

Fig. 23. The sextant.

(4) A second mirror at *E* is parallel to the line *AC*. The upper (or outer) half of the mirror is scraped clear so that the horizon *H* can be viewed directly. The reflection of the object *O* is seen alongside this in the mirror half of *E*. The mirror is mounted at the outer end, at *G*, in such a way that a gap is left to accommodate the arm *AD* when readings are taken near that end of the scale (see elevation in the Fig.).

(5) A back-sight *F*. This may be a simple slit in a piece of blackened brass, or a small ring-sight.

(6) The scale *BC*. This is marked off from zero, at *C*, to 120° at *B*. The angle *BAC* is 60°, but it will be found that when the angle of elevation *OTH* is 30° the angle *CAD* is only 15°. Thus, when the scale is marked off, each five degrees on the protractor becomes ten degrees on the scale.

(7) A handle *K* (in the elevation) fixed across the back of the sextant.

In the side elevation, the back-sight *F* is shown moved forward so that the mirror *E* can be more plainly seen. A piece of blue cellophane stuck to this back-sight is a good protection against glare when shooting the sun.

With this instrument and the clinometer, it is a good plan to have the children working in pairs, one to hold the instrument and do the sighting, the other to take the readings. A reversal of role both gives them practice in taking readings and provides a check on each reading.

Plane table, alidade and Indian clinometer. Collectively, these instruments can provide both horizontal and vertical triangulations; i.e. they are a substitute for a theodolite, though much less accurate. They are, however, much more readily improvised than is a model theodolite (see paragraph below). Successful plane tabling can be done using a drawing board supported on a wood tripod with a fixing screw, to clamp or unclamp the table, and a carpenter's level to check horizontality.

An alidade may be formed from a 12 in. wood ruler into the ends of which have been driven two large sewing needles, the forward one with point uppermost, the rear one with the eye uppermost, as a back-sight. The ruler should be slit centrally lengthwise to within 1 in. of its ends to allow rays to be drawn on the paper immediately beneath.

An Indian clinometer is a more ambitious instrument to copy, but can be simplified. The essential minimum is three wood strips. The horizontal one has a central slit for positioning over rays drawn by alidade; the rear vertical one has a single $\frac{1}{8}$ in. hole at 4 in. height; the forward vertical has a central slit $\frac{1}{4}$ in. wide, and its scales of degrees and tangents should be copied from a commercial model.

A needle held in one hand can be used instead of the horizontal sighter, against the forward vertical.

The theodolite. A plan and side elevation of this instrument are shown in Fig. 24. We require to be able to read angles in both the vertical and horizontal planes. Vertical angles are easily taken with the base of the instrument levelled. Horizontal angles must be referred either to Magnetic North, or to one end of the base line as zero.

The model consists of:

(1) The base *F*. This is the top of the tripod stand, and about 4 ft. high. The tops of the legs are not shown in the diagram.

(2) *E*, a disc of plywood, about ⅜ in. in thickness, and 8 in. in diameter. On the outer rim of this disc is fixed the horizontal scale, reading in both directions from 0° to 360°. When setting up the instrument, some way must be found of aligning the zero line either with the Magnetic North or the base line. Once this has been done, however, the disc *E* must be clamped to the base so that any movement of the disc *D* will not disturb it. This is accomplished by sinking the head of a ¼ in. bolt into the disc *E*. A thin brass plate is screwed to *E* so holding the bolt and *E* together. To allow the bolt to move relative to the base, a curved slot is cut for it in *F*, so as to allow *E* about 20° freedom of movement. A wing nut on the bolt, *M*, clamps *F* and *E* together when the centre line of *E* has been correctly aligned.

(3) *D*, a disc of plywood similar to *E* in thickness but about 6 in. in diameter. To *D* is glued and screwed the spacer *C* so that the centre line of *C* coincides with the diameter of *D*.

(4) *C*, a piece of plywood 4 in. by ½ in. by ¾ in. in thickness. This holds the two pieces, *B*, ½ in. apart, while being sufficiently thick to give them rigidity.

(5) *B*, two identical pieces of plywood, 4 in. by ⅜ in. by 6–8 in. in height. This height allows a fairly wide angle of movement to the clinometer which they support.

(6) *B*, *C* and *D* are firmly glued and screwed together. They provide the support for the clinometer, *A*, and enable it to be turned smoothly and without jerkiness about the centre bolt. The wing nut, *G*, provides the adjustment for tightness.

(7) The protractor *L* is fixed to one face of *B* so that its centre is at *H*, and its diameter is parallel to *OP* when the instrument has been levelled and *OP* is horizontal

(8) The clinometer, *A*, is a rectangle of plywood with a ring-and-bead sight as shown. It is fixed rigidly to a ¼ in. bolt, *H*, by means of the setscrews, *S*. Washers of cork between *A* and *B* provide sufficient friction to make the movement of *A* smooth at the same time that it is being sufficiently firmly held to remain in any given position without difficulty.

(9) The pointer *J* is a needle, brazed, or a force fit, in a small hole drilled in *H*.

(10) The pointer for the scale on E is made from a needle driven eye-end first into the disc D along the centre line of D, i.e. the centre line of the instrument.

The two protractors for this instrument are difficult to make and they may best be provided in the form of circular celluloid protractors fixed to the wood by means of countersunk screws.

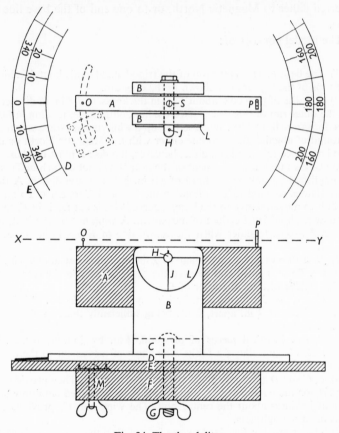

Fig. 24. The theodolite.

It may be pointed out that, if the scale reading of the base line be observed and the angular difference measured, there is no need for movement of E relative to F. On the other hand, the adjustment of E described above not only gives useful practice in manipulation but saves calculation and greater opportunity for error.

The instrument may be levelled with small spirit levels, but, if one is to be fixed to the base, the best type to use is the circular one, with a small central circle engraved in the glass top, in which the bubble is centred.

Experimental erosion tank

This is by no means a priority item but the Geographical Association Survey in 1957 noted 'one aristocrat of Geography Rooms boasted "a tilting river profile tank" and "a land form and coast erosion tank with weirs and wave paddle"'. These are properly made plate glass tanks with water supply and drainage fittings. Several cases are known of simple tanks being made out-of-doors. Wood, roofing felt and polythene can be used but brick and cement would be more durable and satisfactory in use.

Soil survey

An important item of equipment is an auger 1 in. or $1\frac{1}{2}$ in. in diameter and about 2 ft. long which can be purchased at most tool stores. A longer handle is preferable and if this cannot be purchased it may be possible to have an extension made in the school metalwork room, so that soil samples can be taken down to depths of 6 ft. in suitable material. The soil samples can be most useful if brought back to the school.

An indicator for testing the pH value of soils is sold by British Drug Houses or the School Science department may be able to produce the items required. Elaborate soil-testing kits can also be purchased.

Pens and drawing equipment

It is not unreasonable to expect pupils to possess their own pen, pencils, ruler, rubber and coloured crayons, but more specialised equipment must be provided by the school.

An exceedingly useful device is the UNO pen. A selection of pens and lettering stencils can be very well used both in labelling stock and equipment and by pupils drawing special maps. A rather larger number of pens in a medium size, say No. 3, will enable pupils to use them for map outlines. With such a pen even a very untidy pupil can produce a neat, clear outline map on a tracing frame with very little practice. The pupil both surprises and greatly encourages himself. A supply of special ink will be mainly black but red and blue are also useful.

Various types of felt pens, using special ink, are most useful for indexing, labelling wall displays and making quick posters. Some sets are available quite cheaply with three colours of ink and a felt brush to dip into each. It is worth having at least one felt-tipped fountain pen, of which several makes are on the market.

Mapping pens and indian ink will be supplied in all Geography rooms for use from time to time. A selection of lettering pens may also be available.

For special purposes and in Geography Society work a simple pantograph for making alterations of scale can be an asset. This need not be a very expensive item.

Duplicators

For administrative purposes, preparation of excursion notes and supply of maps and diagrams with which pupils are to work during lessons and for homework, some sort of duplicator is used by virtually all Geography teachers (see appendix C, Sources of Maps).

Simple but very convenient results are obtained with embossed rubber rockers or spring-loaded rollers. Outlines of the continents, maps of many parts of the world and maps of various local districts of Britain are available. Rollers are usually made to produce maps fitting conveniently on to a page of an 8 in. × 6½ in. exercise book. They are reliable, durable and easy to use.

In practice the choice of duplicating machines is between various ranges of stencil duplicators and spirit duplicators. The jellygraph is now little used and offset-litho machines are a present beyond the scope of most schools.

The majority of schools are now equipped with a stencil duplicating machine. A good electric model is well worth while. Very often this is housed in the school office, which is quite satisfactory provided that it is really freely available to serve the teachers' needs. High-quality results can be obtained if teachers ensure that they have the right stencils, styluses and backing plates. Stencils suitable for typed material may not be the best for map drawing; the advice of the manufacturer should be sought. A device to hold the stencils is valuable to teachers who make considerable use of duplicated diagrams. With care, stencils can be stored between folded sheets of paper over many years and thousands of copies can be obtained from each. An index number on each diagram and upon the appropriate paper folder makes it easy to select stencils needed for additional supplies of maps. They are conveniently kept in a good steel filing cabinet.

It should be noted that some firms sell stencils with prepared outlines and also provide a service for making stencils by photographic means.

Spirit duplicators use master sheets of highly glazed paper and special carbons. The diagram is drawn on the master paper, using a hard pencil or ballpoint pen and a glass or other hard surface as a backing. If required, carbons of several colours can be used for one diagram. The master sheets are quickly prepared and easy to use. It is an advantage to be able to work easily in a number of colours but even with top-quality materials the process only allows about two hundred copies to be made before the carbon on the master sheet is exhausted. If a spirit duplicator is frequently used it should be housed in a Geography room.

Photocopying equipment has now come within the budget of some schools. It is of greatest value where the original document contains complex or finely drawn material which could not be copied on a stencil or spirit duplicator or where only a few copies are needed. Anything up to foolscap size can be accommodated on the size of machine which a school is likely to purchase. The cost of each copy is only a few pence. Photographs can be copied as well as almost any map or diagram. A large negative of the photograph enables very fine copies to be made but quite acceptable results can be produced working from a good print.

Some machines can produce copies upon safety film. This is invaluable if an overhead projector is in use. Very finely drawn maps or diagrams may be thrown on the screen at the same time as the identical material is in the hands of the pupils.

Copying processes making use of infra-red light are only satisfactory if the original is printed in certain types of ink. Electrostatic processes give very high-quality copies by entirely dry methods but costs of machines are prohibitive. If this type of process is developed it could be very useful to the Geography teacher.

Radio, television and tape recorders

Radio is now available in most schools and very useful Geography programmes are available. Sometimes individual radio sets are provided for a classroom but many new schools have a central radio receiver wired to loudspeakers permanently fixed in each room. Whichever is the case the essential requirement is that the programme be available without trouble or fuss.

Television sets are slowly but steadily increasing in numbers in schools. A set is likely to be kept in a particular place for use by various departments.

Most schools now have a tape recorder available somewhere. Provided this is the case, no special provision is needed for Geography.

Foucault pendulum

Considerable interest can be stimulated by this apparatus to demonstrate the earth's rotation. Given a fairly deep stair well effective results can be obtained with a fine strong wire and a 14 lb. weight.

GEOGRAPHY MUSEUMS

School museum

In addition to visits to public museums (chapter 9) an entrance lobby or large corridor in a school may provide an excellent site for a school museum. If conditions are ideal and considerable space is available it may be possible to have co-ordinated exhibits beginning with Astronomy at one end and extending through Geology, Pre-history and History to Modern Life, displaying industrial processes and materials and exhibiting conditions of life in the regions of the world. The greatest possible thought should be given to classification and arrangement of the exhibits. Glass-fronted cupboards and glass-topped display cases should be used according to the shape of the space available. Exhibits should generally be between 3 ft. and 6 ft. from the ground. Space below the display shelves should be fitted with lockable cupboards and shallow drawers for storage of additional material. There should be opportunity for pupils not only to look at exhibits but to put together displays for various purposes so that the museum is a changing and living element in the life of the school and one to which geographers make a good contribution.

Geography room museum

Some display in the Geography rooms should be possible but it will be less permanent than that in the school museum, depending on the work in progress. Equally important in the Geography room or store will be the collection of specimens available for display and for class use as required. Boxes and packets of uniform shape and size with clear, convenient means of labelling greatly aid storage of the collection. Small plastic boxes, in a series of shallow drawers, enable storage and display to be combined effectively. Plastic bags may also be used to good purpose and are inexpensive. Narrow strips of paper made with a thin wire running along the middle provide means of holding the bag shut and of labelling the specimen.

The building up of a good collection of material will take time.

The Commonwealth Institute have a large range of specimens on sale and geological specimens can be obtained commercially. Some firms will supply raw materials and examples of products either free or for a small charge. School field excursions and visits will add to the collection and individual pupils may make very welcome contributions from time to time. An adopted ship may bring examples of materials from various countries.

In or near some Geography rooms there are permanent or semi-permanent exhibits which are of interest. They give general background atmosphere to the study of the subject as well as making specific contributions from time to time. Compass directions can be clearly marked upon ceiling or floor. A mosaic of 1 in. or larger-scale local maps has already been mentioned as fitting well on some corridor walls. In other spaces, large maps of, say, Herbertson's Natural Regions or names of great explorers and geographers can be painted to good effect.

PUPILS' EQUIPMENT

Atlases

There is no doubt that ideally every child should have a good atlas. Perhaps this is even more important than a good textbook. That the ideal is not always reached is largely a matter of finance.

The atlas has to serve at least two purposes. One view is that it is of the same nature as a dictionary. As a corresponding member of the Committee puts it, he looks for 'a work of reference rather than a teaching atlas'. But another correspondent says 'I prefer a teaching atlas to a reference atlas for normal class use'. Each teacher must make his own choice or decide on a suitable compromise. There is considerable weight of opinion in favour of the view that the maps should be clear, well drawn and not too elaborate. Even in a reference atlas, the pages should not be overloaded with names to the extent of being confused. In a teaching atlas, the amount of material might be very much reduced. Correspondents also suggest the possibility of having, perhaps for year 2 use, an atlas of the southern continents only. In practice, the majority of school atlases do effect a compromise between reference and teaching requirements.

The most important maps are the relief maps and these should include quite large-scale maps of Britain and of some very densely populated parts of other countries. Colouring should be clear, simple, conventional and tasteful. A uniform system of colouring throughout the atlas is desirable as far as possible. Hill shading is useful and effective for some areas.

Political maps will appear and for teaching purposes a range of other maps will be very welcome showing things such as population, distribution, vegetation, climate and economic features. Local supplements are useful.

Care should have been taken in selection of projections and a note of the one used should be given under each map. A variety of projections can be of interest.

Choice of different atlases for different school years or different ranges of ability is quite common, partly on the ground that a really clear simple atlas is best at first, and partly on grounds of expense. For pupils in years 4 and 5 a more detailed atlas is often provided. Sixth-form pupils should have a good reference atlas if possible. For some sixth-form Regional Geography, it is well worth ordering atlases produced for use in the country being studied. Firms in Britain produce atlases for Africa, Canada and Australia and other examples may be obtainable. Every atlas should have a clear and appropriate index.

An alternative plan is to supply one atlas to each pupil to last for the whole of his Secondary school career. It has been suggested that the Education Authority should present each child with an atlas on his entry into a Secondary school. Some schools issue pupils with atlases to be kept at home whilst others are available as class sets in the Geography room.

There is general agreement that the overall page size of the atlas should be kept as small as the provision of good maps will allow. A large atlas is easily damaged in a satchel. For the same reason an atlas requires a particularly robust binding.

Textbooks

The ever-changing range of books available and the infinite variety of teachers' requirements make it quite impossible to give more than very general comment upon this exceedingly important matter.

Size, binding and cost of books must all be considered in relation to their probable life.

Obviously the book should as far as possible be graded to the age and ability of the pupils. Correspondents stress, above all, the need for clarity. The text should be concise and well written, but not long or wordy. Similarly diagrams, of which there should be a good number, should be clear and purposeful but not overburdened with detail. Photographs should be selected primarily for their teaching value and only secondarily for artistic quality. They should as far as possible be an integral part of the text. Good-quality printing makes its value especially obvious in the appearance of photographs. Some statistical information and some stimulating questions and exercises will generally be welcome. A really adequate index adds greatly to the value of the book.

Questions and exercises are sometimes interspersed among the text. This may help teachers who make regular use of questions from the book. The more normal practice of having questions and exercises at the ends of chapters makes for greater flexibility.

Geography textbooks are particularly prone to becoming outdated. Nevertheless, it is quite likely that many of them may have to serve for up to ten years. Thought should be given to a numbering and issuing system. Labels on which pupils insert their names may also carry a space for a book number. It is useful to write the number of the book on the edges of the pages or in bold black figures, with a felt tip pen, upon the cover. The latter method is good for atlases which are too thin to take a number upon the edge. If these numbers are put on when the books are new then doubts and confusion may be avoided later on.

Few teachers find quite the ideal text book. Some say they could only do so by writing their own! Even then, satisfaction might be short-lived, for the teacher's own ideas and methods should be constantly subject to worth-while changes and developments. One teacher likes many Sample Studies, another chooses systematic accounts; one likes brief, orderly presentation of facts, another looks for interest value and a good style of descriptive writing. The value of a textbook to a particular teacher is never proved until that teacher has actually used the book with a class (see also chapter 4).

Stationery

In the first three years pupils are likely to use exercise books at least 8 in. × 6½ in. and possibly 9 in. × 7 in. in size. Some teachers like alternate lined and plain pages so that maps need not be drawn over lines. Others abhor the disorder which such books produce as pupils strive to keep written material in step with maps, drawings and diagrams.

From the fourth year pupils following academic courses may have at least two different exercise books for different branches of work.

15-2

A separate homework book may be used. Some teachers choose loose-leaf files for at least part of the work at this stage. Provided pupils are capable of keeping the files in good order, the loose leaves make organisation of work more flexible and much reduce the weight of material to be carried about for marking. Stiff-backed notebooks may be introduced at this stage.

In the sixth form, the variety of materials used will almost certainly include loose-leaf files.

Other stationery needed will include tracing paper in sheets the size of an exercise book and a larger size. Graph paper in the same sizes may include both $\frac{1}{10}$ in. and 1 in. rulings for various graphs or diagrams. Good quality white drawing paper, in Imperial (30 in. × 22 in.) sheets, will provide for large maps or diagrams. In addition 22 in. × 15 in. and 11 in. × 15 in. sizes are useful. Cheaper coloured drawing paper and sugar paper are usually supplied in Imperial size. White card and strawboard sheets will be useful in various thicknesses. A thick strawboard of at least twelve sheets, serves very well for building up relief models if cut by fret-saw. Coloured gummed paper is useful.

GEOGRAPHY LIBRARIES

Books are the life blood of education. The wide scope of the subject brings the Geography teacher into contact with an extensive range of material. This will be especially true in sixth-form work and where project and topic methods of teaching are employed.

School library

Some Geography books will have a place in every school library. Whether the majority of those needed are kept in a central library or where the subject is taught may be a matter of school policy or the choice may be open to the teacher. In a centrally housed library, the Dewey classification is likely to be used and this is not very appropriate to Geography. Also, it may be felt that it is difficult to introduce pupils to books unless the two meet frequently under the subject teachers' guidance. There is, however, much to be said for allowing pupils to see and use the whole range of books appropriate to all branches of knowledge in one place. Knowledge should not be unduly divided into subjects and the geographer should be one of the first to recognise this. The actual selection of books will depend upon experience and up-to-date contact with publishers' catalogues, reviews and visits to exhibitions and other libraries. Reference books, textbooks, guide books, travel and adventure books and fiction all have their place.

Departmental library

Choice or circumstance may result in the bulk of a school's geographical books being kept in or near a Geography room. Suitable shelving, preferably adjustable, is needed. Wooden shelves supported by steel spurs hooked into slotted wall bars are convenient. Glass-fronted cupboards are costly but may be needed for some books. The system of classification adopted could be that of the Association of American Geographers or that used in the library of the Geographical Association.

Geography room libraries

Where the books are divided among a number of Geography rooms, each room should have a small collection of books or magazines chosen either for reference or on grounds of interest value. Magazines and topic books may be included. Certainly there should be a good reference atlas, a gazetteer, an economic atlas and a good year book. These basic reference books will include volumes such as *Whitaker's Almanack*, the *Statesman's Yearbook*, the *Oxford Economic Atlas of the World* and a variety of good advanced reference atlases.

Schools, often through the library, take several magazines which serve first for general interest and information and then may be kept in a Geography room either as background material or for the sake of the pictures they contain.

Box files are the most convenient way of storing pamphlets. Reference atlases in the school or departmental library should include several of the best general atlases which can be afforded. Some of these will be general world atlases. Others will be chosen in order to give good coverage to particular regions. Throughout the school it is important to have good maps of the British Isles available. The *Atlas of England and Wales* (Bartholomew), which gives maps of all areas on the scale of $\frac{1}{2}$ in. to 1 mile, will be of much interest in a library. The *Atlas of Britain and Northern Ireland* (Oxford), though expensive, will prove invaluable, whilst the *Complete Atlas of the British Isles* (Reader's Digest) also has much to recommend it. It may be well worth while purchasing copies of school or reference atlases produced in some of the European countries for their own use. For certain other parts of the world, too, sixth-form students will find useful the atlases produced for the area being studied.

TEACHING GEOGRAPHY IN ORDINARY CLASSROOMS

It is still unfortunately necessary for many Geography lessons to take place in ordinary classrooms. Some schools have no Geography room; many do not have enough Geography rooms to accommodate all Geography lessons; some schools are organised in such a way that masters move to classes rather than vice versa.

This chapter is not irrelevant to such cases. Those who face such circumstances should select the items which they feel to be most essential and which can either be made available in the rooms which are to be used regularly for Geography or can be taken by the itinerant master from room to room. Every effort should be made to provide at least some equipment, especially in cases where a class will have no lessons at all in a Geography room.

In ordinary classrooms where Geography is to be taught for a large part of the week, it is suggested that at least the following should be available:

(1) Pin boards on the walls, large enough to take the biggest sheets of the Ordnance Survey map series.

(2) One complete class set of a local 1 in. map.

(3) A complete set of wall maps together with a map bar or hooks in order to display them. As a very minimum there should be one map of each continent.

(4) Several large atlases and some reference books.

(5) A globe.

(6) Basic Mapograph rolls together with a handle and ink pad. Outlines of the world, the British Isles and each continent would be a first objective.

Other items will be housed in the main Geography room or in a store. They should be immediately available on demand for use in any room where Geography is taught. The advantage of access to a store directly from a corridor as well as through a Geography room is apparent here. It may be helpful for monitors to be organised to dispatch equipment to the place where it is required and, what is perhaps more important, to ensure its return after use.

Ordnance maps, wall-maps, atlases, reference books, globes and mapographs are all portable. So too are projectors, folding screens and many other items. Given a willing spirit, the limiting factors are time and energy. The master must plan lessons carefully and arrange to take to the rooms the items which he feels to be most essential for each period.

8

FIELD-WORK

It is now widely accepted that good Geography teaching must include some field-work at every stage throughout school and college courses. Behind such an insistence there are four clear educational reasons.

In the first place pupils have 'to look, to think, to analyse and to record' when they are in the field. Thus engaged they are following a learning process which has been valued scientifically for a very long time. The landscape itself is the geographer's laboratory, and it is this learning process out of doors which gives reality to the subject and saves it from being arid and theoretical. Secondly, such first-hand experience simultaneously brings into play all the learning faculties, whether of sight, hearing, smell or touch. In such a way vivid impressions are created, and these can be put to profitable use by the teacher on subsequent occasions whether he is dealing with conditions at home or abroad. So this first-hand knowledge can be said to provide a standard of reference—a yardstick for comparative purposes. Then again, field experience ensures that the technical language of the subject has a precise meaning. The master must insist that an accurate geographical vocabulary is employed both when points are being made in the field and during the follow-up. Finally, it is only too well known how 'blinkered' pupils can be, whether in town or in the country. They spend a day out but return home with only a very general and superficial impression of what they have seen! In field-work they must therefore be encouraged to acquire an 'eye for country'. This will sharpen observation and help to cultivate powers of seeing geographically.

The ultimate aim in geographical field-work is to describe the patterns and relationships in the landscape. The pupil should be able to analyse and describe those elements which produce marked contrasts, e.g. between neighbouring limestone and gritstone country. He has 'observed little bits of geology, soil, weather, plant life, animal life, homes, farms, crops, roads, etc.; he has pieced together the jig-saw', and these fall into patterns which distinguish one part of the

211

country from another. On the road to this goal many lesser objectives are attained: the acquisition of techniques; the relationship of map to land, and the observation of processes. What a host of possibilities there are: watching a fast stream sweeping round a meander, or turf sods slipping down the slope behind a sapping spring; knowing and understanding the way a farm works with its crops, its livestock and seasonal calendar!

Some Geography masters feel that they cannot conscientiously afford adequate time for field-work. After all, they argue, it demands much careful study and even research on their part, as well as room in a syllabus already strained to the limit. To such points we would reply most vigorously. In the first place increasing recognition of the value of field-work is being given by examining boards. Either there are questions on written papers, or the submission of a thesis or long essay is invited. The Committee fully recommend the preparation of an account of practical field-work, and its submission to a visiting examiner who can in addition conduct an oral examination and inspect specimens, field sketches and field notebooks. They are also pleased to note that such requirements are no longer confined to some of the 'Advanced' level syllabuses, for field-work certainly occupies a prominent place in the C.S.E. examination. Quite apart from this increasing recognition, field-work can be commended for its beneficial influence on the rest of a pupil's work. His interest in Geography will grow, and he should write better answers to other questions on examination papers because of his field experience. It often has a very marked influence on attitudes.

The preparation required for taking classes into the field is inevitably time-consuming. The master whose pupils work well in the classroom knows that this success has been achieved through wise and careful planning of the course, and of the individual periods themselves. In the same way, field-work necessitates careful preparation: the leader must have a thorough knowledge and understanding of the countryside into which the pupils will go. He must be clear in his own mind what features are worthy of attention, and he must know from experience how long each portion of the study will take. Indeed it can be asserted that the teacher should have walked the country himself, stop-watch in hand. And yet it is also a precept that the lesson plan should not become a strait-jacket. Therefore the programme has to be very adaptable, allowing for the vagaries of the British climate and other unforeseen difficulties.

TERMINOLOGY

Some confusion has arisen regarding the precise meaning of words like local geography, local studies, environmental studies, local survey, field classes, school journeys and school camps. The committee therefore define *Local Studies* to be the use, particularly in the first forms, of those elements of the Geography of the locality near school or home which the pupils know well. It does not necessarily involve taking or sending the class out of doors, although it may very well do so. *Local Survey* is understood to cover the collection and analysis of data obtained in an outdoor survey of the locality, sometimes carried out in collaboration with other subject departments. Because this work is often performed by members of the Geographical Society, non-examination forms or other groups and does not feature in every course, it will be considered after *Field-work* or *Field Classes*. The latter terms describe outdoor work in which observation, recording and analysis are particularly concerned with the landscape in a number of its aspects. This puts them on a very different plane from *School Journeys* or *Excursions* which convey thoughts of happy holidays and days of relaxation. There should be fun and pleasure in field-work, but it is not worth so much time and effort unless the central purpose of the operation is educational.

PROVISION OF THE TIME FOR FIELD-WORK

Field-work can be organised in sessions varying in length from a double period to many days. The circumstances of schools vary so much that it is difficult to generalise, but for the majority of those situated in towns it is usually impracticable to get out for less than a half day. Some headmasters have agreed to arrange the timetable so that there is a double period of Geography at the end of the afternoon, thus allowing field classes to be carried on after school. The practical problem of providing sufficient time during the day at the expense of other subjects is very real. What, then, ought to be the aim? First it is generally agreed that field-work should be done in every year of a Secondary course, the frequency varying from year to year, depending on the topics in the syllabus which are conveniently illustrated in the field. Every pupil should have a minimum of one full day's field-work per year, although many teachers like to take junior forms out for one day a term. It should be a regular time-tabled feature, otherwise good field-work habits are not estab-

213

lished. Such habits develop more easily with juniors than with middle school pupils.

Unfortunately, many schools do not achieve these standards and have to be satisfied with the occasional field day, taken whenever opportunity allows. Then it is necessary to make special arrangements since pupils and Geography staff have to be freed of normal routine. Staffing difficulties are greater when Local Education Authorities require a staff/pupil ratio of 1 to 20 in the field, and supervision by both a master and a mistress where mixed classes are involved. Help is therefore especially welcome in the form of old pupils, geographer prefects or other sixth formers. If the teacher is to avoid unpopularity with his colleagues he must seek those times in the year which are least inconvenient for all concerned, possibly during the period after summer examinations and the G.C.E. Another solution is to choose those days when the Geography master would be teaching his sixth form for the most part. Pupils at this level can safely be left to work on their own at least occasionally.

At sixth-form level, when more field-work than ever is necessary, the problem of finding time for it becomes even more acute. A number of topics might conceivably be covered at week-ends, but if, as is probable, some of the party are in school teams, such occasions cannot be used if field-work is deemed to be obligatory. Apart from making use of occasional days, the master is thrown back on the idea of a field week in holiday time. Although there are staff who feel that this is an unjustifiable burden, it seems almost impossible to suggest an alternative.

DAY OR HALF-DAY EXERCISES

The nature of the programme will naturally vary according to the age, aptitude and field experience of the pupils concerned.

The boys should be occupied in practical work for much of the time, and those in the higher forms may be left increasingly to work on their own, whether individually or in small groups. Even these, however, will need fairly close supervision to ensure that exercises set are carried out. The very worst type of field course is that conducted from the softly padded comfort of a luxury coach, the teacher with microphone constantly in hand and pupils ready with pencil and notebook. A compromise must be sought in which the master helps the pupils to solve problems by their own efforts. In the following paragraphs attention is therefore given to some of the many exercises which have been worked with real success.

Field mapping. Since map work is so fundamental in geographical studies its use in the field should begin in the first year. A useful exercise involves a sketch map depicting contours and several key features. This is given to the pupils. While the teacher draws attention to different elements in the view, the pupils insert outline shapes

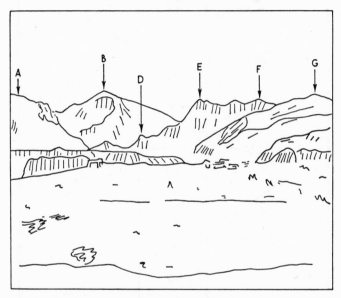

Fig. 25. View from M.R. 477525 looking up the Nantlle Valley.

(1) Name and give heights of *A, B, D, E, F, G*.
(2) Mark T.S. and *C* on the sketch to indicate 'truncated spur' and 'cwm'.
(3) Indicate (*a*) the canalised course of the River Llyfni, (*b*) slate tips.
(4) In what direction are you looking?

or append appropriate names. A variant of the exercise is to supply each pupil with the Ordnance Survey map that covers the full extent of the area seen from a given viewpoint, and an outline field sketch of this view. The maps have to be read in order to find place-names and grid references to be written against the features shown (Fig. 25).

Senior pupils can also learn much from exercises in elementary surveying, the object being to produce sketch maps of particular features. The quickest exercise is the compass traverse, in which bearings are observed with a hand-held compass and distances are worked out by measuring chains and tapes, or string, knotted at

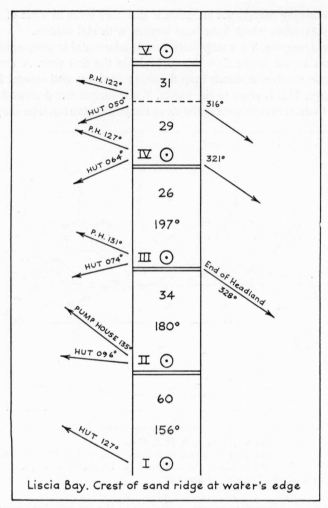

Liscia Bay. Crest of sand ridge at water's edge

Fig. 26. Page from Field Log Book of compass traverse along crest of sandspit drawn on sketch map of Liscia Bay, Corsica.

1 ft. intervals. Observations are recorded in field notebooks (Fig. 26) for use in the follow-up (Fig. 27).

Similarly, middle and upper school boys might well be employed on making scale diagrams, based on actual field measurement; for example, of the profile and cross-section of a valley. Angles of slope can be measured with an Abney level, either a scientifically accurate instrument or one made from a protractor, its bob-line suspended from a central point. Alternatively there are possibilities in simple levelling. If survey poles are unobtainable pupils can be asked to stand in their stead. One home-made level used in such work consists of a continuous circle of polythene tubing half-filled with coloured liquid. A simple sighting cross attached to a bulldog clip which moves up and down the pole completes the equipment, crude but effective!

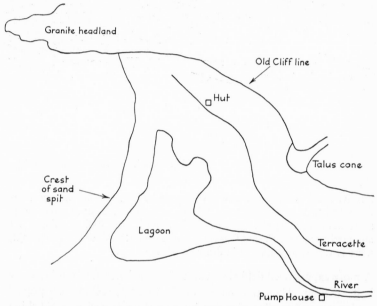

Fig. 27. A sketch map based on compass traverse observations (made by sixth-form boys at Liscia Bay in Corsica).

Field sketching. This is of considerable value in middle and upper school work. The main type is the detailed sketch (Fig. 28), which takes some time to draw. This may be of a complete landscape or a single landform, but the principle is the same: the very process of attempting to sketch it makes the pupils observe the detail more closely. Indeed, such details might otherwise have gone completely unobserved! During his early days the pupil must be taught the elements of field sketching. The late G. E. Hutchings had in *Landscape Drawing* some pertinent observations to make on this score:

Geography students and other observers of country often complain that they have no aptitude for drawing and that they are therefore denied this valuable means of recording observations. They need have no such

217

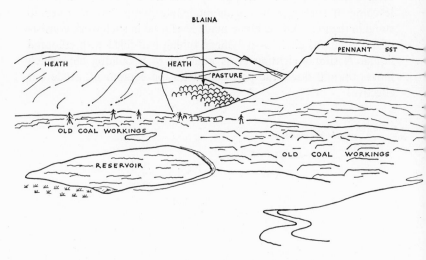

Fig. 28. Field sketch: looking southwards acr

misgivings. Drawing is something which can be learnt by anyone who cares to study its principles and undertake much practice. Learning to draw is, more than anything else, a matter of learning how to look at things... 'I am nearly convinced', said Ruskin, 'that when once we see keenly enough, there is very little difficulty in drawing what we see.'

A more experienced field class can be left to sketch for 20 minutes or half an hour. Then the master ought to help, seeking the pupils' explanation of details which they have inserted, as well as establishing the general relationships in the view. The other type of sketch, which can be quickly dismissed, has a very different purpose. It is rapidly drawn and annotated, serving as a 'shorthand' method of recording points made in discussion and oral work.

Farm studies. These are appropriate at all ages, but particularly in the first forms. Such field experience provides a yardstick that will serve as a basis of comparison with Sample Studies of farms all over the world. The ready co-operation of a farmer is essential, one who will allow a considerable number of youngsters to look over his property and is prepared to answer a barrage of questions. It is much better for pupils to obtain the information from the farmer than second hand via the teacher. And yet the latter may be called upon to initiate the discussion! Pupils can become curiously shy on first meeting other people, and the master must also ensure that a full range of ques-

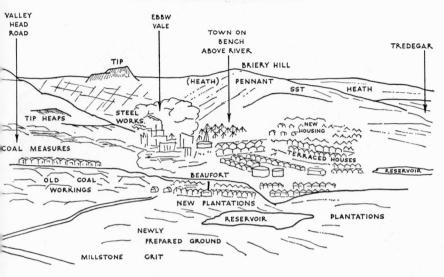

head of the valley towards Ebbw Vale.

tions is put. If his intervention has its danger, junior pupils can be given a duplicated sketch map of the farm round the edge of which are panels headed with questions. Senior pupils may be instructed to have a list of more obvious farm questions in their field notebooks. Here is one such example:

Farm name
Number of acres.
Position of farm: height above sea level, aspect, shelter, accessibility
Soil type and depth
How are the fields drained?
Field boundaries: walls, hedges, fences
Acreage under each crop
Livestock breeds and numbers
Machinery
What does the farmer produce for sale?
What must he buy in to keep the farm running?
What markets does he use?
Number of workers
Wintering of stock
Water and power supplies
Farm management and economy

This list may be extended for the more detailed studies required at sixth-form level. Fig. 29 is appended to show the kind of mapping appropriate in farm study.

219

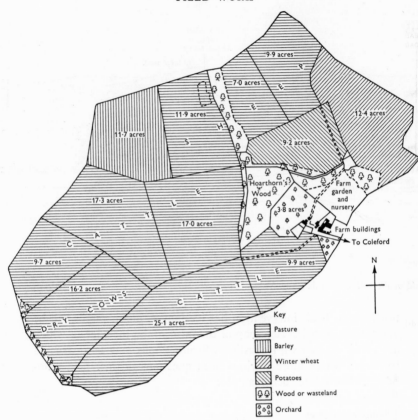

Fig. 29. Hoarthorns Farm, near Coleford, Gloucestershire.

Settlement studies. A useful project for pupils at any age is the study of a local settlement. Every pupil should have an outline sketch map of the locality on a fairly large scale, i.e. at least 6 in. to 1 mile, and, sometimes, up to 25 in. to 1 mile (Fig. 30). On this he is asked to insert the outline shape of buildings, or to record more detailed facts: age, function, and type of building material used. This often calls for the use of a colour 'key' which the pupil may be left to design for himself. For larger settlements it may be desirable to divide the form into groups, each under a leader responsible for one particular aspect of the study. Apart from the aspects already mentioned, other groups can be observing the site of the settlement, its accessibility and services. If its shape or form is closely related to such physical features as steep banks, floodable areas or

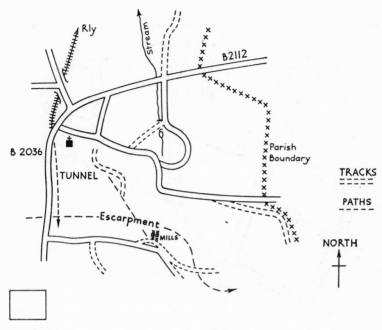

PRINT VERY SMALL

SHARP PENCIL POINT

MARK EACH BUILDING
FIRST BY A SMALL SQUARE
THIS SIZE —▫

Age of Buildings		Use of Buildings		Made of	
1	1945 TILL NOW	R	House (Residence)	F	Flint
2	1918 – 1939	H	Pub, Hotel	S	Stone
3	1901 – 1914	S	Shop	W	Wood
4	1850 – 1900	W	Workshop	B	Brick
5	1800 – 1850	P	Public Building	O	Other
X	VERY OLD				

BESIDE EACH SQUARE MARK THE LETTER

Fig. 30. A sketch map of Clayton village.

terraces these can be measured and mapped at middle or senior school level. Figs. 31 and 32 illustrate the kind of urban analysis which is within the grasp of sixth-formers.

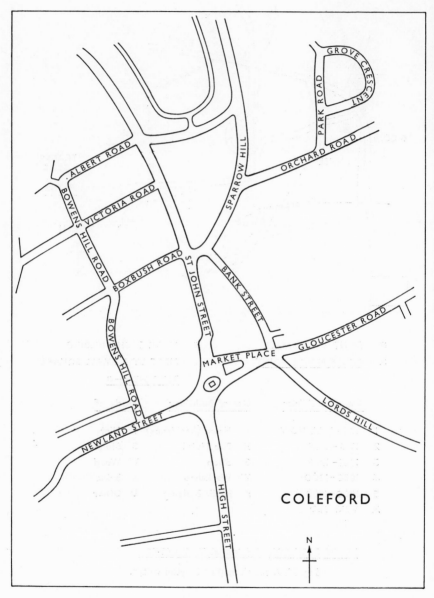

Fig. 31. Coleford.

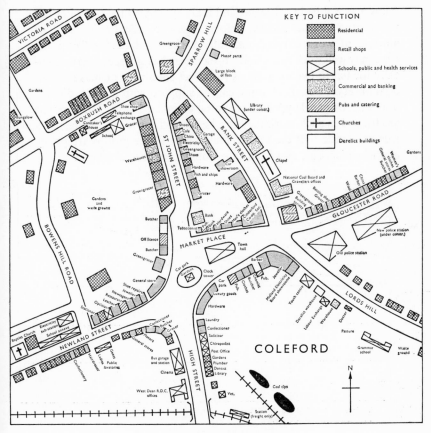

Fig. 32. Coleford. Detail of centre.

Transects. The success of these exercises depends in large measure on the ability of participants to recognise certain spatial phenomena, and this is in itself will be a valuable element of the pupils' general education. They must be knowledgeable on such matters as the rocks, soils, plants and crops of the district concerned—a problem which the master must have resolved before the exercise is under way. In addition, he will have to give some consideration to the line of the transect, seeking to select one which will encompass a variety of landforms or built-up environments. 'Accessibility' along the line is something else to watch: landowners are unlikely to welcome the prospect of boys climbing over walls or striding across their arable land. Even footpaths marked on Ordnance Survey

223   16-2

maps may not be in existence, and it always pays if the organiser has walked the transect himself before others are asked to do so. The amount of work entailed naturally varies; with junior forms the class may well work as a whole, its members being dispatched periodically for ten to twenty minutes to collect specimens or make individual observations. Each pupil can be supplied with a sheet, divided into various panels which have to be completed (Fig. 33). If pupils are trained in such work they can be sent off for longer periods, but it is axiomatic that the master must know where groups are going, and a rendezvous, at a fixed time, must have been arranged.

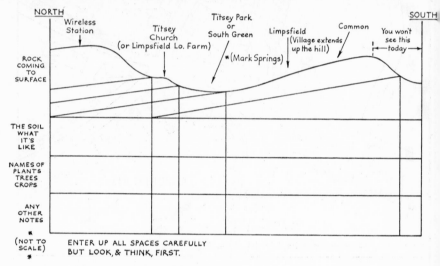

Fig. 33. Titsey Hill to Limpsfield Common—changes in scenery.

Transect work may either be concerned with a single type of phenomenon or involve most of the elements in the physical and cultural landscape. A soil transect could in itself form the basis of an afternoon's field-work with juniors. This should be preceded by preliminary teaching on the nature of soil itself, and demonstrations of sample taking, either with augur or by trowel-made exposure. In the same way, a vegetation transect can be mounted, a useful means of testing plant identification. One type of questionnaire for completion in the study of plant communities is illustrated in Fig. 34.

More detailed, general transects are particularly suitable for senior pupils and the results provide the most satisfactory form of

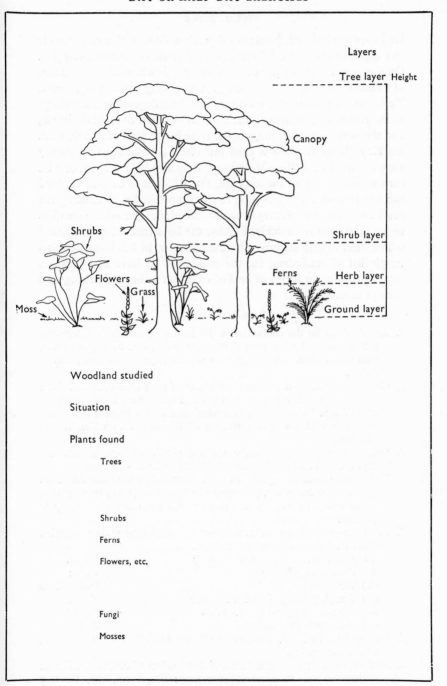

Fig. 34. Woodland study.

landscape analysis obtainable in a short time. Observation can be made to a depth of about one kilometre on either side of the transect line. On average, a team of three sixth-form pupils will work about 2 km. of transect (i.e. 4 sq km. of country) in a working day of 6 or 7 hours. Variations are inevitable, however, and these depend on such things as the nature of the ground, the amount of detail thought desirable, and the organisation of the project. Here is one plan of attack. Each working group is given a card on which is sellotaped its survey area, cut from an outline $2\frac{1}{2}$ in. map. They also have a $2\frac{1}{2}$ in. or 6 in. card-mounted map of the same locality, which is to be used for land use observations. The adoption of the simplified key devised by the first Land Utilisation Survey is recommended, since it enables essentials to be plotted fairly quickly. Finally, the boys themselves are issued with a sheet of instructions, reproduced below. In this instance it is a simple list of reminders, for the pupils should have had previous experience of most forms of field observation before embarking on a general transect.

TRANSECT SURVEY

1. Relief—describe the characteristic landforms; particularly interesting features should be described in more detail, e.g. incised meander, river cliff, corrie. Add a diagram and a sketch, map position, measure slopes.
2. Geology—describe the nature and range of rock type observed; from suitable exposures measure and mark in on map the angle and direction of dip. Obtain fresh, non-weathered rock samples; label each specimen with the grid reference of the site from which it was obtained.
3. Soils—where possible describe the soil profile—colour, texture and depth. Obtain labelled samples from the different horizons.
4. Vegetation—note the species in each community; note the dominant species in (i) tree cover, (ii) coppice or bush cover, (iii) ground plants. Observe related features at the transition from one community to another.
5. Land use—mark in on the map the land use under the main categories. Estimate percentage under each type.
   - (i) Arable (including rotation grass) — Brown
   - (ii) Permanent pasture — Green
   - (iii) Woodland — Dark Green
   - (iv) Rough grazing—heath and moor — Yellow
   - (v) Houses with gardens, orchards — Purple
   - (vi) Densely built over — Red
6. Farms—location, size, type, crop rotations, markets, labour, livestock, mechanisation etc.
7. Settlement—describe the nature and distribution of settlement. Larger settlements can be studied more fully: size, form, site, building

materials, age of buildings, function of buildings, utilities available—gas, electricity, water, telephone. Enquire about service centres used —choose sample items for questions, e.g. where they obtain meat, vegetables, clothes, electrical goods, entertainment—cinema, theatre, secondary education, library. Describe the form and frequency of transport services to these centres.

In the follow-up of the exercise each group is made responsible for the collation of material relating to one particular aspect of the survey. Each group assembles the facts which have been discovered together with sketch maps and samples and is then required to devise (with teacher guidance) the most effective means of displaying the material. A striking demonstration of changing relationships and patterns will also emerge if results are treated in the same way, and mounted, as in Fig. 35. This illustration, originally in colour and of wall size, was completed by senior pupils in the evening after they had been in the field.

Industrial visits. There is some divergence of opinion on the value of factory or industrial visits, and whether or not they should be regarded as geographical field-work. Some correspondents claim that they should not be undertaken by geographers; but the majority view is that they are of considerable value and interest.

There are, of course, a number of difficulties in the way of a successful visit. Many teachers complain that guides employ a standard patter which is rarely geographical. Often they cannot be heard because of the noise of machinery and managements are naturally more concerned with recruitment and advertising than objective study. It sometimes happens, too, that the visit is very long, leading to boredom and tiredness. Moreover, some works are more impressive and worth while than others. If the boys are to stand looking at walls displaying only moving dials, flickering lights, switches and levers, as in a power station, little purpose has been served. Some, though by no means all, factory processes are too complicated to be understood on a short visit.

Careful selection of factories is therefore essential. Every pupil should, if possible, go down a coal mine and visit a large works, e.g. an iron and steel plant. If these visits can take place when the pupils are studying the more industrialised northern continents, so much the better. It has also been found that correspondence with firms can obviate some of the difficulties. The master should tactfully but firmly draw attention to the points in which his party will be interested. Some managements supply very useful preliminary notes

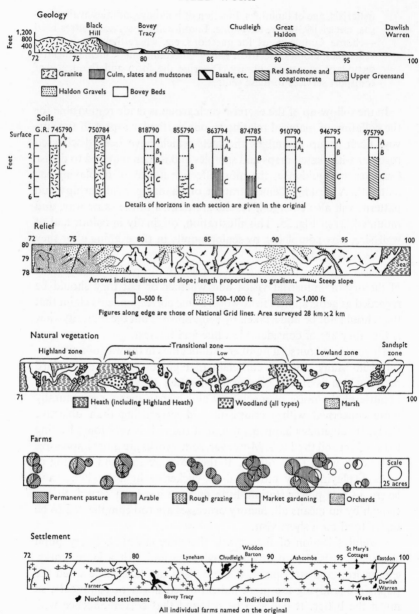

Fig. 35. Transect survey. The diagrammatic assembly of material observed on a transect survey is a useful exercise producing a document that can be the basis of much fruitful analysis of relationships.

detailing the size of their plant, its labour force, fuel, type of mechanisation, means of transport, sources of raw materials and markets. It can be a salutary experience to learn that the vital factor of location is often not so deterministic as some textbooks would have one believe.

When a long journey to the field study area is involved, as is often the case for schools in the metropolis, its geographical possibilities should not be neglected. In fact it is helpful to the tone of the whole day if the outward journey is occupied with some work. A useful practice is to have items to mark on maps and short questions to answer.

Five or six types of field exercises have now been detailed. The number of single-day programmes which could be envisaged is almost limitless; the two examples which follow illustrate the nature of the hand-outs and the general organisation:

FIELD DAY PROGRAMMES

A Secondary Modern school. Field-work locality: the Northern Weald

Purpose of this journey

   (i) To study the shape of land around Merstham, and between Merstham and Nutfield.
  (ii) To map a strip of land showing how it is used.
 (iii) To study and map the two villages of Merstham and Nutfield.

Timing

  9.30   Leave school
10.05   Train dep. East Croydon
10.31   Train arr. Merstham
Discussion and Plans
10.45–11.45 Study at Merstham Village
11.45   Walk via Limeworks to Tollsworth Manor—sketching
12.15   Start land-use map strip
12.50   LUNCH BREAK—Warwick Wold
  1.45   Continue land-use map strip
  2.40   Nutfield Church
  2.50   Discussion
  3.00–4.00 Study of Nutfield Village—sketching
  4.00–4.30 TEA BREAK
Conference
Walk to Merstham—2 miles
  6.02   Train dep. Merstham
  6.18   Arrive East Croydon

Groups

Leaders underlined. Keep with your group.
Each group will be responsible for (i) completing land-use strip map, (ii) a section of village surveys.

Butler	Osborne	Dando	Spalding	Rees	Tilley
Anscombe	Allan	Barrow	Grace	Stevens	Howe
Walker	Lower	Pharoah	Smith	Read	Taylor
Williams	Ware	Webzell	Doncaster	Howie	Harris

Note on the day

This is arranged as a serious day's work. Your full co-operation is required all day. Look after everything, especially maps and notes. Help to make the day a pleasant one for everyone. It is a long day, therefore challenging, and we expect every boy to brace up cheerfully to the 7 miles of work involved.

Follow-up

(i) Approximately 6 lessons in school will be devoted to the follow-up of this in your Fieldwork Folders.

(ii) A programme of tasks will be set immediately. These will constitute Section 4 of this year's Field Survey Exhibition.

A Grammar school. Form 3. Field-work locality: north of Gosport

THIS CIRCULAR IS TO BE TAKEN HOME AND SHOWN TO YOUR PARENTS

The coach will leave school at 9.00 a.m. after registration and will return at approx. 6.00 p.m., stopping at various points in Gosport. The object of this trip is to make a transect on foot across various types of rocks: mainly sandstones, clays and chalk, noting changes in the landforms, soils, vegetation and land use. A detailed study of a village will also be made. The whole day is a working day and pupils are asked to remember this and to co-operate fully. A great deal of preparation has been put into this trip.

Each pupil must bring:

A packed lunch
Rough notebook
Pencil, rubber and pocket-knife
Maps and instruction/questionnaire sheet
Four large paper or plastic bags for plant and flower specimens
A few pieces of string
Four small containers for rock and soil samples
A small haversack or satchel to carry these things.

Clothing

School uniform
Stout shoes (walking 5–6 miles)
Raincoat or cape

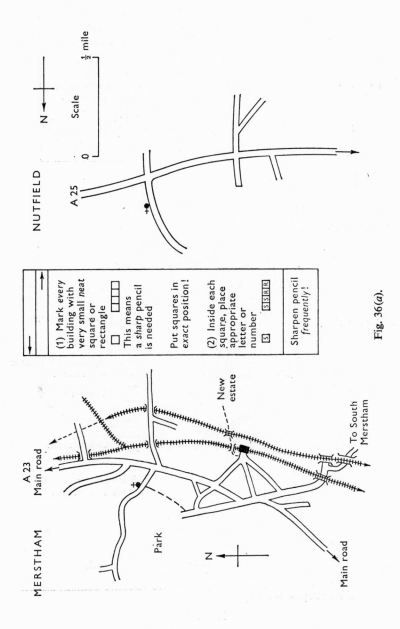

Fig. 36(a).

NUTFIELD

A 25

N

Scale

0   ½ mile

MERSTHAM

A 23
Main road

New estate

To South Merstham

Park

N

Main road

(1) Mark every building with very small *neat* square or rectangle

This means a sharp pencil is needed

Put squares in *exact* position!

(2) Inside each square, place appropriate letter or number

S   S S R R

Sharpen pencil *frequently!*

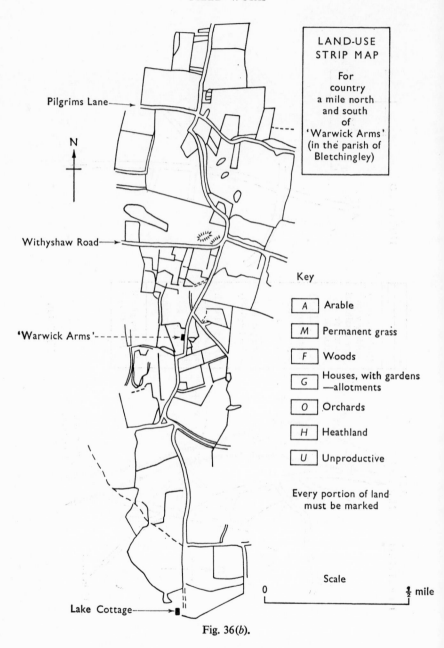

Pilgrims Lane→

N

Withyshaw Road→

'Warwick Arms'------→

Lake Cottage→

LAND-USE
STRIP MAP

For
country
a mile north
and south
of
'Warwick Arms'
(in the parish of
Bletchingley)

Key

A	Arable
M	Permanent grass
F	Woods
G	Houses, with gardens
	—allotments
O	Orchards
H	Heathland
U	Unproductive

Every portion of land
must be marked

Scale

0   ½ mile

Fig. 36(b).

Please check these items off on the evening before so that you are ready in the morning.

Questionnaire

These questions are to be answered in your rough notebooks in addition to the other notes you make. Set aside special pages for the answers so that they are together.

Outward journey on the coach

(1) Note the time that the coach leaves the school.

(2) As the journey proceeds make a note of the route by stages.

(3) At what state is the tide in Fareham Creek? Note the time and when you get back look up the times of high and low water today.

(4) What kind of building has taken place on Portsdown Hill? Why has it had to take place and spoil such a beautiful area?

(5) Describe the nature of the building development along the main road from Purbrook to Horndean. Do you think it is good or bad? Give your reasons.

(6) From Horndean onwards for about five miles the underlying rock is chalk. What appear to be the chief characteristics of chalk country? Use headings of (*a*) shape of the ground, (*b*) land use including crops grown, (*c*) vegetation.

(7) From Petersfield onwards the underlying rock is sandstone. What changes do you see in land use and vegetation compared with the Chalk country?

ORGANISATIONAL ASPECTS OF DAY EXERCISES

Route planning

Besides considering which features are to be studied thought has to be given to the walking distances involved. Work must not suffer through fatigue. Some correspondents have definite views on this but it is difficult to generalise for distances will vary according to age of pupils, type of work, and terrain. One opinion is that 'more than five miles is hiking and not intensive field work'. Notions of the maximum distance for 11- to 12-year-olds range from 1½ to 5 miles, for ages 13–14 from 4 to 8 miles, and for more senior pupils from 5 to 15 miles. Some features are difficult of access and necessitate a long tramp; should this take most of the day the value of the exercise is open to doubt. Even on a short route, where much exploration and effort is involved, conservation of pupil energy must be watched.

Another factor to bring into the reckoning is the need for refreshment during the day. Are suitable cafés open *en route*, or must the pupils be warned to bring their own food? If the latter is the case, giant bottles of 'pop' should be actively discouraged; great care should be taken to see that no litter is left behind.

Insurance and legal matters

Before embarking on the field day it is important to have made arrangements for insurance. Practice here is very varied: it may be that the Local Authority has a comprehensive policy which covers all school parties against accident and third party claims. If such is the case notification of excursions must be given to the Local Education Authority before the actual day. Sometimes only pupils are covered, in which case the master must take out a comprehensive policy to protect himself against personal accident and third party claims made by parents.

From time to time, claims have been made against members of the A.M.A. on account of alleged liability for accidents to pupils. The policy of the Association has been repeatedly stated, viz. that the A.M.A. gives full legal and professional protection to any member whose current subscription is paid when such a claim is made, unless the Association considers that there are special circumstances which, in its opinion, would make it improper to use the funds of the Association in his defence. It is necessary, in view of recent cases successfully contested by the A.M.A., to re-emphasise this protection, and to assure members that they are fully protected by the Association against such liability whether arising during the time when school is in session or during such out-of-school activities as call for the voluntary supervision of a master.

There is need to repeat the obvious advice that, while he is in charge of pupils, a member is *in loco parentis*, and that he must consequently give them such measure of supervision and guidance as is consonant with their age and intelligence. This advice is axiomatic, and, if followed reasonably, will effectively rule out the great majority of claims arising out of accidents to pupils.

But cases do, nevertheless, arise in which claims are made in good faith and which an individual member could only resist at considerable expense and at risk of injury to his professional standing. Members are therefore assured that in all proper cases the Association affords full protection to the member by undertaking his defence and reimbursing him for any damages not exceeding £25,000 which may be awarded against him. This protection goes far beyond that which can be given by an insurance company: the Association is quick to discern any threat in such cases to a member's professional standing and will refuse to come to any settlement based on commercial considerations. Moreover, there is at the call of the Association a body of skilled legal and professional advice which cannot be obtained by the mere protection of an insurance policy.

Claims are often made against the governing body, headmaster and assistant master jointly. In such cases, the Association is careful to protect the master against any settlement agreed to by the other parties which might react adversely upon his financial and professional position. Provided members take due care in school or on out-of-school activities, they are fully protected by their Association, and the experience of recent years emphasises both the value of that protection, which has never yet failed, and the freedom from anxiety and from financial stress that it confers.

Immediately any accident occurs, members must notify Headquarters and thereafter follow implicitly the instructions given.

In order to reduce the number of unnecessary claims and to protect themselves against the inconvenience of appearing in Court, members are advised whenever possible to get parents to sign indemnification forms in connection with excursions, school camps and tours within Great Britain and Northern Ireland. This is not a condition of Association cover but it is a method by which members can help the Association by reducing the extent of its liability for the cover given. Cruises, tours and camps in countries outside Great Britain and Northern Ireland fall into a different category in view of the difficulty of contesting cases abroad and the differing legal positions in other countries. It is all the more important that for such tours, etc., parents should sign indemnification forms; in addition, a special insurance policy should be arranged. (see p. 386). Below is a suitable form of wording for an indemnification form.

In consideration of Mr .... undertaking to take my son ....
.... on (i) .... I promise to indemnify the said Mr
.... against any claims damages or costs which he may become liable to pay in consequence of any injury or damage to or illness of my said son occurring during the aforementioned (ii) ....
or while under the charge of the said Mr .... for the purpose thereof.

I further promise that for the consideration aforesaid I will not hold the said Mr .... responsible for any loss from whatever cause arising and will indemnify him in respect of any expenditure reasonably incurred by him in consequence of any accident to or illness of my said son or otherwise for his benefit.

Date ....   Signed ....
                                                      (6d. stamp)

235

(i) Insert here particulars of the activity it is required to cover, with dates.

(ii) Insert the relevant activity, e.g. tour, excursion.

The first paragraph is necessary because a parent cannot assign (or waive) the rights of a minor. The second paragraph clears the master of any financial obligation he might otherwise incur to the parent.

Finance

This is another vexed issue, and it remains so because of the very varied regulations of Local Authorities and Governing Bodies. In some schools the parents will have to find the full cost of transport, but in others only a nominal sum or even a complete subsidy will be the rule. The Geography master's attitude must be unequivocal: field-work is essential and the authority should cover the cost. Geographical field observation is on a par with experiments in the chemistry laboratory, and pupils have to be put in a position to undertake the work. The principle is already accepted by many authorities. Where, unfortunately, this is not yet the case, there is no alternative to asking parents to contribute. In schools where much field-work has been undertaken and pupils have had several outings each year progressively getting further afield, parents have been very co-operative and have regularly paid anything from 1*s*. 6*d*. to 6*s*. per trip, although a few hold rigidly to the principle that 'everything must be provided'. There is of course always provision for those who genuinely cannot afford to pay.

Whilst considering this issue, it may be as well to give thought to the financial aspect of longer field courses, for these may involve board and lodging, educational fees, and transport costs. When pupils attend Field Study Centre Courses run by resident staff, most authorities give financial assistance, ranging from complete coverage of all expenses to the cost of transport and tuition only. However, should the same accommodation be used for courses devised and run by school masters, no assistance is given by some authorities! The logic of this position is incomprehensible: not only are those masters the fully trained, highly qualified employees of the authority, but they inevitably know their charges better. Pupils are familiar with their teachers' methods, and are at ease to argue and discuss. Furthermore, a teacher's course is geared to the immediate needs of his pupils. This is said with all deference to the Field Centre Staffs, who know their country so very well. They are, in fact, generally appreciative when school staff run their own course. In the circumstances, then, it is felt that at the least Local Education

Authorities and Governing Bodies should bear the cost of transport, insurance, maps and materials, as well as all the master's own expenses.

Clothing

Many staff are of the opinion that school uniform should be compulsory, so far as junior forms are concerned. The only modifications apply to the need for stout, waterproof boots or shoes, and some form of rainwear. The arguments in favour of such regulations are that school uniform will not be spoiled on the outings envisaged, and that it will set the right tone for work. With senior pupils one ought to relax the rules: journeys will be longer, and more energetic programmes are involved. Pak-a-macs or capes, pullovers, scarfs and even gloves are called for, especially in cold weather or in mountainous areas. Materials should be carried in haversacks or small rucksacks, but certainly not in suitcases. Both hands must be free.

Pupil preparation

Some time must be devoted to 'briefing' the pupils, both on the administrative arrangements and on the objectives of the forthcoming expedition. There need be no confusion if all the information is repeated on duplicated hand-outs. While the itinerary is under discussion, some advice on pupil equipment should be offered. This includes a lead pencil and two coloured ones, a sharpener or knife, a mapboard (made of plywood or hardboard not more than 12 in. × 14 in., together with bulldog clips and elastic bands), a protractor, pocket notebook, sample containers, and several polythene bags. Particular individuals, such as group leaders, might also be asked to bring trowels, measuring string and geological hammers.

Back at school: the follow-up

If the field impressions are to be of lasting value, follow-up work will be regarded as indispensable. It is axiomatic that more time will have to be devoted to the topic when juniors are concerned because they will be learning the necessary techniques. With seniors, a deadline for the completion of the work can be announced, so encouraging them to organise their own time. Generally speaking, the follow-up will include the completion of fair copies of maps, transects, diagrams or sections. The written part of the record may be in the form of essay, notes, or answers to a questionnaire.

A display of field-work material can be most rewarding, particularly so since, in order to make it effective, the pupils learn to explore the best methods of graphical record. The use of statistical diagrams and various mapping techniques is often a necessary part of the school syllabus; how better can it be taught (see Fig. 35)?

Besides preparing material for exhibitions, some have found the preparation of a written account for publication to be very profitable. Pupils are keen to see the results of their work in print and become more careful about the accuracy of their conclusions and the preciseness and quality of their expression. In some schools, field-work is found in a supplement to the school magazine. Yet another application of the conclusions is in the preparation of lecturettes to be given to fellow pupils, to the Geographical Society or to parents.

FIELD COURSES

These are basically longer periods when the activities already considered are continued for successive days. Nevertheless, the planning, preparation and execution of such courses clearly involves many other considerations and attention is now turned to them.

Location of area for study

A number of diverse factors influence choice of area, but a primary one is the desirability of taking the pupils to an environment markedly different from the home region, or from those visited during single-day outings. If the Geography syllabus provides for pupils to attend several field weeks during their school career masters should build up a varied selection of suitable localities. Any one of these should provide a study theme which will form the basis of the course. A focal point of interest will serve as a framework for other activities. This is an important point in planning, for whilst pleasure will be gained through the mastery of techniques a richer academic satisfaction will come from application of those techniques in the analysis of a facet of Geography. Well-chosen centres will permit the identification of small regions, as well as the promotion of systematic studies within the landscape. A third factor is sometimes even more crucial, the availability of accommodation. If the master has good fortune on his side and there is some choice, preference should be given to a route centre from which most of the region is easily accessible.

Accommodation

Many kinds of accommodation are available, ranging from Youth Hostels to hotels. Apart from facilities offered by the Field Studies Council and the Scottish Field Studies Association, places can be obtained in C.H.A., Holiday Fellowship, Y.M.C.A. and Y.W.C.A. premises (see appendix D). Some schools also use college hostels during vacations, and here there might be a partial solution to the ever-increasing pressure on accommodation at limited times in the year, particularly Easter. Many teachers also use the Y.H.A., but others find their hostels unsuitable because of the amount of time absorbed in domestic chores and the lack of rooms for studying. However, attention must be drawn to the increasing provision of special facilities (see *Youth Hostels for Field Studies*, Y.H.A. 1963) by the movement (see appendix D). Finally, there are a number of guest houses up and down the country which cater for field parties and are only too willing to help.

The majority of correspondents do not favour basing field-work on camps, for two reasons. They want better facilities for mapping and other work than they believe can be obtained in camp and, after a hard day in the field, they want their pupils to be catered for. However, some masters have operated from camps to their own satisfaction, in some instances through having a large organisation and the provision of adequate facilities. Others have run small camps and been satisfied with a more limited amount of field-work. Then map drawing has to be left almost entirely until the pupils are back at school.

There are those who advocate roughing it on a field course in a spirit of adventure. However, it would appear that the ideas behind the adventure course and field study do not easily blend when only one week in the year is devoted to them. Facing up to the elements and grappling with difficult physical conditions with spirit and re-source should certainly be encouraged, but the quality of field observations and correlations will inevitably be less satisfactory under adverse conditions.

Transport

The form of transport used will depend very much on the size of party, but, whatever the numbers, much is to be said in favour of using a coach, utility bus or Land-Rover. Door-to-door transport, apart from its natural convenience, enables one to take more equipment than might otherwise be used. As this transport is available during the whole course, it can be used to get one rapidly to the area of the day's study. This can be done either for the whole party or for groups of pupils along a line of transect. When the driver is not the party leader, the vehicle can also be used to extend the scope of the day's work or to limit walking to the most desirable sections of the route.

Teacher preparation

In addition to points already mentioned in connection with day excursions, some others need to be borne in mind. The arrangement of the programme must be as flexible as possible so that, for example, time will not be wasted in climbing to a vantage point on a day when it is enveloped in low cloud. To provide against persistently adverse conditions, the plan must include a foul-weather programme. In such circumstances walking-distances can be reduced by well-planned use of the vehicle or by using short cuts previously investigated by the master.

A master is well advised to seek local contacts, both to improve his own knowledge of the region and to secure assistance in conducting the actual programme. Among potential sources of help are university dons, local teachers, the clergy, county archivists, and government officials. A farm visit is well worth while, and in this connection a first contact should be the County Agricultural Advisory Officer. Note, too, the facilities of the Association of Agriculture at 53 Victoria Street, S.W. 1. Others who might prove helpful are Officers of the Forestry Commission, as well as local quarry managers, industrialists and business people.

Balance within the programme

Instruction, investigation, and relaxation must all be kept in nice balance. In the first part of the week the party might well operate as a single unit, under the direct supervision of the master. He will introduce the major features and also some detailed studies typical of the region. This is also a good time for farm and other visits. On subsequent days the emphasis should change, work now being largely in the form of personal assignments. As a rule, boys should be in teams of three. A larger number has obvious drawbacks while a smaller number is prejudicial to safety. When sickness or injury occurs one boy should always stay with the incapacitated member while the third goes for help.

240

Some time in the evenings should also be given to study. Much of the follow-up has to be done very soon after the actual exercise, otherwise jottings will mean nothing. Furthermore, fifth- or sixth-formers may well have difficulty in fitting this work into the crowded routine of term time. The opinion has been put forward that since the field course is being run in holiday time it is too much of an imposition to use evenings in this way. Certainly there should be time for relaxation, and something can be said in favour of a half-day break in the middle of the week, but much of the value of the course will be lost without evening study. To forgo any follow-up is clearly folly.

To complete the course the teacher might well organise a summary tour of the local countryside or an urban study of its chief town. It has been said that the latter often epitomises the Geography of the whole region. Alternatively, the party could journey *outside* the region, thus appreciating its distinctive qualities better through the study of a contrasting area. For instance, the climax of a week in the Lake District might come through devoting some time to the Cumberland coalfield. Throughout the last day, while one is exploring industrial landscapes, unravelling the development of Maryport or Workington and visiting Calder Hall, there is a backcloth of mountains. More dramatic perhaps is the beginning and end of the day, when the party passes from one physical and cultural environment into the other. Yet another possibility is to organise an air trip across the area of study. The best time of day for this is early evening when the atmosphere is often clearest, features are prominent because of the low angle of the sun, and bumpiness is reduced.

TYPICAL FIELD COURSES

(1) *Norbury Manor Secondary Boys' School*

Lower fifth forms. Secondary Modern school. Previous experience fourteen field journeys.

Base. Preston Montford Field Centre. 26 May–2 June.

Time-table (handed to members of the party)

Monday 26 May meet at Norbury Station 12.35 p.m. sharp.
Via Victoria, Inner Circle
Paddington dep. 2.10 p.m.
Via Banbury, Birmingham, Wolverhampton.
Arr. Shrewsbury 5.47 p.m.
Bus to Montford Br. arr. approx. 6.30 p.m.
Evening. Discussion sitting on R. Severn bank, plans for week.

Tuesday to Sunday inclusive: The days in the field will not necessarily follow the order given, but will be fitted in to suit the other arrangements of the Centre.

(i) Simple transect work—Ruyton area and panorama.

(ii) Snailbeach via Hope, Round Hill and Stiperstones; south-west Shropshire hills as an upland area; geology of Lower Palaeozoic; dependence of landforms on structure. Walking distance 8½ miles.

(iii) Day in Shrewsbury—Town study; history, site, functions.

(iv) Day in the Breiddens—Structure and relief of isolated igneous hills, and settlement.

(v) Day in Llanymynech district—especially for Carboniferous Limestone.

(vi) Day mainly by motor transport. A more extensive view of the geology and geography of the region. Patterns of settlement; kettle drift south of Shrewsbury; rift valley and Pre-Cambrian hills at Church Stretton including Caer Caradoc and Long Mynd; scarpland topography of Wenlock Edge; Silurian limestone fossils; early industrial development (iron and coal) about Coalbrookdale and the Wrekin; Ironbridge gorge and post-glacial changes in the Severn drainage; Viroconium—important Roman fort and frontier town. Distance 60 miles plus 5 miles walking.

Monday 2 June:

Bus to Shrewsbury. Train dep. 9.33 a.m. via Wolverhampton, Birmingham, Banbury, Oxford, Reading, Guildford.

Arr. Redhill 2.33 p.m.

Arr. East Croydon 3.04 p.m.

Working arrangements

Most of our work will be done on foot. Transport will be used mainly only to get you to working areas. It is hoped all boys will carry out tasks conscientiously. We want to leave Shropshire with a pretty clear impression in our minds of this unit of country.

Evenings

These will be used for a Conference plus individual work on notebooks and on Exhibition tasks. As much as possible of this we want to get completed while we are away. All previous Lower Fifth Forms have spent the evenings in this way, and the outdoor work all day will keep you perfectly fit.

Bed-time is 10.30 and this means *sleep*.

This week's course is a demanding one. You will not be getting much free time, so don't expect it. I hope all boys will accept these arrangements loyally and get down to solid work throughout the week. If you approach the week's work in the right spirit, you will also find you thoroughly enjoy yourselves.

Train journeys

These are invaluable for 'British Isles' work. Sketch maps will be issued to help you utilise these fully. Don't waste these journeys. The return

242

journey will help you (during its latter stages) to contrast our local countryside immediately.

Notices also included instructions on uniform, equipment, kit, pocket money, behaviour, mealtimes and domestic arrangements, warning about care of maps, a legal disclaimer and information on the Field Studies Council in general and Preston Montford in particular, concluding with the following:

Preston Montford Field Centre lies on the right bank of the River Severn in the fertile agricultural plain of North Shropshire, where dairy farming is the main human activity but where crops and sheep-rearing are also important. Near at hand, to the west and south, ranges of hills rise to nearly 1,700 feet, showing a delightful diversity of landscapes; here the conditions of life are harder, and rocks and weather play a ruling part in the livelihood of the scattered inhabitants. Our course will deal with the contrast between these two kinds of rural scenery, lowland and upland, as a background to everyday life.

You already have a pretty good idea of the 'geological succession' and of the marked influence of geological formations on all the overlying physical and human landscapes. In this area the rocks from Triassic back (or 'down') to Pre-Cambrian also include Igneous; the whole picture is further complicated by widespread Drift of the Ice Ages, etc. So we can expect all sorts of involved problems which will certainly exercise our minds considerably. It remains for us all to see how far we can get to grips with it.

(2) *Latymer Upper School. Sixth Form*

(a) *Base*. Dawlish. 23–30 April.

Saturday. Travel to Dawlish by coach, leaving school at 9 a.m. 7 p.m. dinner followed by introductory talk.

Sunday. Coastal morphology on Dawlish Warren and on cliffs and stacks between there and Teignmouth. Tuition in field techniques.

Monday. Dartmoor. Study of a compact and distinctive regional unit: its landforms, geology and soils, vegetation, farming, mining and settlements. Dawlish to Haytor for morphology, soils and vegetation; to Widecombe for village study; via Postbridge to Two Bridges to visit Beardown Farm, owner Mr R. Gallup; to Lee Moor kaolin quarry. After dinner; write up notes, short briefing for transect study.

Tuesday. 9 a.m. Coach leaves to set groups out along line of transect from coast to moor. Note time and place of rendezvous for picking up in late afternoon. After dinner: each group will be responsible for collecting, analysing, mapping and graphing information on one aspect of study along whole line of transect.

Wednesday. Urban study of Plymouth. Half day free in Plymouth.

243

Thursday. 9 a.m. Coach leaves to take groups out to villages and towns. Groups will be told time and place of rendezvous for picking up in late afternoon.

Evening. Symposium. Groups reporting on settlement studies.

Friday. Lowland Devon. Visit to a dairy farm, Mr T. A. Bagley at Seematon Farm; visit to a horticultural property in Bishopsteignton; Urban study of Exeter; weather permitting an airflight from Exeter Airport following the coast from Exmouth to Plymouth, a left-hand and a right-hand circuit of Plymouth, Tavistock, crossing Dartmoor to come down Tuesday's transect line to Dawlish, two circuits of Exeter.

Saturday. Return home. E.T.A. Latymer approx. 5 p.m.

A similar pattern of programme for sixth-form field weeks has been tried in the following areas:

(b) Forest of Dean. Based on Littledean

Day 1. Travel by coach, leaving school at 9 a.m. Late afternoon field sketching on Littledean Hill. After dinner a talk on geology and geomorphology of region.

Day 2. a.m. Walk through Cinderford analysing settlement geography.
p.m. Geomorphological study on route Littledean—Cinderford—Mitcheldean—Longhope—May Hill—Huntley—Oakle Street—Westbury—Littledean partly by coach, and partly on foot.

Day 3.
8.40 prompt Coach leaves Guest House.
9.00 Northern United Colliery for half the group.
9.15 Princess Royal Colliery for other half, underground visit.
2.00 Meet Mr Jennings, Head Forester, at Speech House for botanical geography and forestry industry.
4.00 Meet Deputy Gaveller of Forest in Coleford to learn how to obtain the grant of a gale.
5.00 Visit a Free Miner on his gale.

Day 4. Transect Survey across north of Forest and over R. Wye.

Day 5. Visits to Mr Simmons's upland farm at Mitcheldean and to Mr Warlock's dairy farm at Westbury-on-Severn.

Day 6. Village studies.

Day 7. Study of a contrasting region. Littledean—Monmouth—Abergavenny—Crickhowell—Ebbw Vale—Pontypool—Usk—Wye Valley—Littledean.

Day 8. a.m. An urban study of Gloucester.
p.m. Return home.

(c) Peak District. Based on either Hope or Castleton

Day 1. Travel to Hope.

Day 2. a.m. Visit to 'The Farm', Bamford, run by Mr F. R. Platts.
p.m. Tuition in field techniques during a walk along Bamford Edge.

Day 3. A day on Limestone. via Tideswell and Millers' Dale to Buxton to visit Mr Lomas's farm at King Sterndale; coach to Peak Dale for study of a limestone settlement; walk to Hope via Perry Dale, Giants Hole, the Winnats; visit to Treak Cliff Cavern, return via Mam Tor.

Day 4. A day on gritstone and Coal Measures.
a.m. Visit to Orgreave Colliery and Brookhouse Colliery.
p.m. Walk across grit, arriving at Aston Hall Farm, Hope, to be shown his farm by Mr J. Dalton at about 4.30.

Day 5. A transect survey.

Day 6. a.m. Urban study of Sheffield.
p.m. Visit to Parkgate Iron and Steel works, Rotherham.

Day 7. Village studies.

Day 8. Return home.

(3) *Cambridgeshire High School, Cambridge*

Fifth form and first- and second-year sixth-form pupils, 30 in party.

Base. Whitby.

Sunday. Study of site and growth of Whitby. Starting with the monastic foundation on the East Cliff and a survey from the cliff top of the immediate coastal scenery. This is necessary to bring out a contrast later with the modern seaside development on the West Cliff, where conditions are physically very different. Move down to the bridge and see the port development, and styles and layout of buildings associated with the port—variety of periods still extant, crowding of building for physical and economic reasons, jumbled street plan, difficulty of adapting to modern traffic conditions. Along west side of harbour—port activities, merchant warehouses and usual paraphernalia of a major port. Invasion by fun fairs, hot dog stalls etc., which are kept off the better-class sea front. Up to main sea front—promenade, big hotels—typical of this type of seaside development. Show how beach and access to it is linked with this development. Influence of a fault between east and west sides of the harbour. Developed area behind the sea front showing infilling by lower-class residential housing, which has spread away to the west. Contrast with very limited development east of river.

Monday to Wednesday. Three days to study various aspects of Eskdale: river features and development as a river valley; glaciation and effects of periglacial lakes; land use and settlement contrasts between the dales and surrounding moorlands. Routes used:
(a) Coach along A169 to 856986—views over Newtondale overflow channel. Coach down minor road into Goathland—study of village siting, etc. Walk from Goathland down the Eller Beck to Beck Hole and up Westbeck to 815004. Northwards along minor road to Egton and back to Whitby. This route enables one to see many of the overflow channels at different altitudes.
(b) Walk up Glaisdale by minor road to 732023, over Glaisdale Rigg and down east side of Fryup Dale to Lealholm. Study of moraines

245

at Glaisdale and Lealholm, the lake basin form of the dales whose exits were ice-blocked; agriculture, vegetation and settlement contrasts between dales and intervening moors. Contrast between form of ice-blocked dales and Murk Esk valley seen on previous day.

(c) Transect studies of Eskdale by individual groups put out and collected by coach. Information collated by groups in the evening.

The three days should give a general impression of: (i) the evolution of drainage in the Esk system during and after the Pleistocene, (ii) the form of the Esk from source to mouth and the reasons for the different forms of the valley in its various sections, (iii) settlement, land use, vegetation and soils in an environment typical of Upland Britain.

Thursday and Friday—coastal studies north and south of Whitby, the Vale of Pickering, Tees-side.

(a) Southwards down A171 to Scarborough, turning off at intervals to study coastal features by short walks, e.g. Robin Hood's Bay. Walk from Scalby Mills into Scarborough. Development of Scarborough as a seaside resort in relation to physical and historical factors offering a contrast to Whitby. This is done in a much more superficial way than Whitby as the town is not so compact and time is limited. Coach from Scarborough to Seamer, across Vale of Pickering to Staxton, along A64 to Sherburn, north to Brompton, east to Ayton (A170), up Forge Valley to Hackness and east to pick up A171. This latter part enables one to tie up the glacial overflow story and also to see a drained lowland, which these particular pupils could contrast with the Fens.

(b) A northward run by coach along A174, again branching off at such points as Runswick and Staithes to see coastal scenery and settlement. During the week the boys see the greater part of the coast from the mouth of the Tees to Scarborough: the part near Whitby in detail, the rest in overall view. Turn inland at Brotton along A173, skirting north edge of the moors, to see something of iron ore mining (now discontinued); into and around Middlesbrough; across the estuary to Billingham chemical works; pointing out the salient features of the industrial landscape. In the afternoon a visit to a steel works on Tees-side. This experience is particularly valuable for the fifth form pupils whose home environment is a non-industrial one.

LOCAL SURVEYS

Time permitting, much more can be achieved by this means than on a shorter, intensive field course. Although few of our correspondents have found time for local survey, they attach great value to the idea. The following details are intended to act purely as suggestions.

(a) Observe the nature of the rocks and their angles of dip. Exposures occur particularly in quarries, and on the sides of railway cuttings: collect samples.

(b) Build a scale model to illustrate the lie of the land, and the relationship of relief and settlement.

(c) Maintain a record of changes in river level and volume. Map the details of its course.

(d) Keep weather records. Calculate mean statistics, and plot results on graphs and diagrams.

(e) Visit open spaces in the locality. Note the details of their plant communities, and collect specimens.

(f) Map the growth of the district, tracing details from old maps. Consult the local librarian and County Archivist. Growth could be depicted either on a series of maps or by means of a composite one, different colours representing stages in development.

(g) Use field observation to complement suggestion (f). Record the *type* of building materials and dates of construction. These results could be mapped.

(h) Map the built-up area, and analyse the *functions* in it:

 (1) Classified house type (a) blocks of flats, (b) terrace houses, with or without gardens, age of building noted, (c) semi-detached houses, (d) cottages with small gardens, (e) detached houses with gardens, (f) large detached houses, set in the midst of extensive grounds, (g) large houses which have been subdivided.

 (2) Commercial buildings: retail shops according to type. Warehouses.

 (3) Places of entertainment: cinemas, theatres, cafes, restaurants, night clubs, amusement arcades, betting shops.

 (4) Other service centres: churches, schools, hospitals, clinics, town hall, library, museum, police station, fire station, etc.

 (5) Factories. See Figs. 31 and 32 (pp. 222–3) for an urban analysis based on this principle.

(i) Map and analyse the pattern of communications. Concentrate on roads, railways, and navigable waterways, constructing flow-maps of various phenomena. Ascertain the kind of goods passing through the local goods yard and British Road Services depots.

(j) Visit factories, and discover the source of their raw materials, the destination of their products, the power in use, and kind of labour force.

(k) Ascertain as much as possible about local newspaper circulation.

(l) Make collections of material relating to the locality: postcards, photographs, newspaper cuttings, etc.

Note. The concepts which can be realised through such study, e.g. 'The Urban Field', emerge from consideration of suggestions (i)–(k).

POSTSCRIPT: FIELD-WORK AND GEOGRAPHY

Among the oft repeated maxims of our subject is that of learning one's Geography through the soles of one's boots. The necessity of such outdoor work has been strongly stressed, and no apology is offered for this insistence. 'Geography' means far more than merely 'to describe the earth' but accurate description of a landscape actually seen is the essential first step.

9

EXHIBITIONS, SOCIETIES AND
FOREIGN TRAVEL

THE GEOGRAPHY EXHIBITION

A useful means of stimulating interest in Geography, not only in class and the school generally but also among parents and the public, is to mount a Geography Exhibition.

To some masters this is the climax of the year, serving as an incentive to pupils to produce good work. It compels pupils and staff to reach their goal and not leave projects half completed. An exhibition of some kind is a valuable feature in all types of school, but particularly so for pupils who are not working towards a public examination. One teacher correspondent goes so far as to say 'without it our school's Geography course would be barren, colourless, feeble'.

Geography Exhibitions seem most frequently to be based on field-work or on local surveys but they are also concerned with aspects of the school course or projects of topical interest (in recent years, the Common Market and African Independence). In the latter type especially, there must be a unifying theme. Exhibitions should be concerned with a single continent, region or topic. The sense of unity in the whole exhibit can also be helped by the use of a uniform system of caption writing.

Many teachers may remember the field survey exhibitions organised by Mr H. C. Wilks and the Norbury Manor Secondary Boys' School (*Geography*, Jan. 1956). The following section is a copy of one of the preparatory leaflets issued by Mr Wilks.

NORBURY MANOR SECONDARY BOYS' SCHOOL
FIELD SURVEY CLUB

SURVEY OF BRASTED, KENT

TO BOYS: Please study this leaflet very carefully.

You are expected to understand fully the tasks which are allotted to you, to seek further advice about these at the fixed times (see Notice Board), to get on with them and see that they are completed by the dates shown. Failure to carry out these instructions means that you are letting the whole Club down badly.

Please ask your Parents to look at this leaflet.

Task programme

No.	Title	Boy responsible	Completed by
1.	6 in. map—25 ft. contours	Hardman	12 Jan.
2.	6 in. map—relief sections	Hardman	1 Feb.
3.	6 in. map—geology (with specimens from geological museum)	Hardman	12 Jan.
4.	6 in. map—land use	Stevens	1 March

(Field-work for no. 4 will have to be done by *all* boys)

*5.	6 in. map—woodlands	Miles	1 Feb.
*6.	6 in. map—buildings: age	Francis (with Lewis, Arnold)	1 Feb.
*7.	6 in. map—buildings: use	Francis (with Lewis, Arnold)	1 Feb
*8.	6 in. map—plant transect lines (2)	Miles, Vokes	1 Feb.
*9.	6 in. map—water map	Lardent	1 Feb.
*10.	6 in. map—weather facts map	Lardent	1 Feb.
*11.	6 in. map—population distribution	Plant	1 Jan.
*12.	25 in. map—village⎱	to be arranged	
*13.	25 in. map—village⎰		
14.	Graph—population growth	Plant	12 Jan.
15.	Graph—rainfall and temperature	Plant	1 Feb.
16.	1/25,000 map—bus and train traffic	Plant	1 March
17.	Traffic census (to be carried out by the whole group)		1 May
18.	1/25,000—local government map	Francis	12 Jan.
19.	Historical maps—prehistoric, Roman	Vokes	1 Feb.
20.	Historical maps—Saxon	Vokes	1 Feb.
21.	Historical maps—Manorial	Vokes	1 March
22.	Historical maps—enclosures	Vokes	1 March
23.	Historical maps—19th and 20th centuries	Vokes	1 May

(For nos. 19–23 the duplicated map will be used)

23 a.	Historical map—the tithe map	Francis, H. C. W.	31 March
24.	6 in. relief model of the area, coloured for land use	Hardman Vokes	31 March 31 May
	This is a big job but should be most impressive when finished.		
25.	Various other models (small)	to be arranged	
26.	Plant transect belts with specimens	Vokes, Miles, Lee	15 June
27.	Pictures—sketches—photos to illustrate any of the foregoing. Also as complete a pictorial survey of Brasted as possible	Plant, Lardent, Miles, etc.	15 June 15 June
28.	Church, old houses, etc. (plans, drawings, etc.)	Miles, Vokes	12 Jan.
29.	Farms—3 'type' farms (complete surveys)	Lee, Hicks	31 May plus later work on current crops
30.	Card index for Croydon	Hicks, Plant	12 Jan.
31.	Parish organisations	Miles, Stevens	15 Jan.
32.	Shopping and market facilities	Miles, Hicks	1 March

No.	Title	Boy responsible	Completed by
33.	Occupational survey and journey to work (to be arranged by liaison with the Parish Council. All boys will have to help on this)		31 May
34.	Schools survey	Hicks	1 March
35.	Public open spaces; N.T. lands	Lewis, Francis	12 Jan.
36.	Factories, workshops, quarries	Lewis, Francis	1 Feb.
37.	Power supplies	Lewis, Francis	1 March
38.	Public houses and inn signs	Vokes	31 May
39.	Place-names	Francis	1 April
40.	Historical date-line (will involve library visits)	Vokes, Plant	15 May
41.	Soil profiles	Lee, Hicks	31 March

* Tracings will be needed for these from the printed map.

All boys will be expected to help each other in different ways.

NOTES

This list of tasks will enable us to present a balanced, fairly complete picture of the parish. We don't want any holes in the picture.

We rely on you to complete tasks by the date shown. (Work that 'piles up' is done badly, or not at all.)

DON'T LEAVE IT—GET ON WITH IT

Many of these jobs will require guidance. Come to get it.

The timing of the tasks is arranged to spread the work evenly through the year.

This survey was never intended to become a burden and need not become so if you keep up-to-date.

Further days out

You are expected to attend all of them. Absence is unfair to other people including our friends in Brasted, and to your organiser.

Keep these dates free

Friday 30 December, Saturday 28 January, Saturday 25 February, Saturday 17 March.

Meet at West Croydon at 11 a.m. Return home will become later as daylight hours extend.

In Easter holidays. 5–7 April, staying at Crockham Hill (see special instructions).

Summer term—to be fixed later.

Log-books

In these you keep a *very brief* record of:
(i) Matters discussed at Wednesday meetings.
(ii) Work done on Saturday journeys.
(iii) Work done by yourself on tasks or at Brasted.

Entering up your log-book should not take more than ten minutes a week, and *they will be checked every Tuesday.*

Maps

The 6 in. maps and 1/25,000 maps are expensive. Maps used outdoors must be kept clean and dry. Pencils should be sharp and pencil-marks kept small and neat.

(Lee and Francis are each responsible for one outdoor set.)

The sets of maps kept at school or loaned for tasks *must not in any case be folded,* and should not be kept rolled longer than possible.

The Duplicated Map. This may be used for rough notes. Don't waste, as the number of copies is limited.

VERY IMPORTANT—PLEASE CONSIDER THIS CAREFULLY

It is clear that the people living in Brasted are not only interested in our work but are affording us, most kindly, encouragement, facilities and hospitality of many kinds.

Your loyalty and hard work, therefore, are owing not only to your school, but also to the Parish of Brasted. Many Brasted people will be looking forward to seeing the results of your work in the Exhibition in July—it must be first class.

The tasks in this programme were chosen by, or given to, individual boys when they were out in the field. Between Easter and Whitsun, on two nights a week for about an hour, voluntary groups of three or four boys from particular forms mounted and annotated illustrations, labelled specimens, sorted items, etc. They called these groups 'Working Parties'. As many different boys as possible were enlisted to help in this way.

Norbury Manor School produced a very fine guide to the exhibition. Financially this was a self-balancing item; a twenty-four page sixpenny guide including eight pages of advertisements. The whole project involved a very large amount of work, which was therefore delegated to boys and to colleagues.

The following officers were appointed:

(i) Exhibition Secretary. His jobs included completing a catalogue which served as a check list for the organiser, helping with advertising correspondence, helping with special invitation correspondence, preparation and supervision of 'Visitors' Book', control of all Stewards.

(ii) Programme Manager. A master. To control the sale of programmes, to push sales, to supervise programme sellers.

(iii) Sign-Writers. This was handled by a master with assistants.

(iv) Handicraft. The Handicraft master helped the boys construct the fittings.

(v) Caretaker (a 3A boy). His job was to wage constant war on mess, go to and from the store room and prevent chaos. He was able to co-opt other boys to help. So far from being a menial task, this officer's work was of the highest importance and required intelligence.

(vi) Typing and Duplicating. Most of the Exhibition circulars were printed by parents.

(vii) Stewards (all fifth-formers—senior Geography pupils). Their job was to help visitors.

During the Exhibition boys took their own parents round, besides acting as stewards for other visitors. A popular feature (partly because adults were able to rest their feet) was the series of short talks given by the stewards. These were illustrated by colour slides and showed pupils actively engaged in field-work.

Other exhibitions

Other exhibitions have been based on work done throughout the year. One on Africa, at a Lancashire Grammar school, took the form of a Wall Atlas. Individual pupils or groups were each responsible for a topic such as relief, climate, vegetation, agriculture, mining or peoples, illustrating it by maps and large pictures or posters. Samples obtained from the Commonwealth Institute and elsewhere were arranged according to their regions. Some of the materials were from a Commonwealth Institute Study Kit. The literature in this kit was not just displayed itself but was used by the pupils as a source of information for their own displays, which included graphs, diagrams, sketches, annotated pictures, models and dioramas. At such an exhibition pupils' notebooks can be displayed, for parents are always interested to inspect these and to compare standards of work. Another feature might be a film show; for example the film *Twilight Forest* would suit the African theme. It could be projected silently in a dark corner of the room.

SCHOOL GEOGRAPHICAL SOCIETIES

Geography, properly taught, arouses an interest in pupils which will not be confined to the classroom. By means of a Geographical Society this can be maintained or even further developed.

Although societies of this nature are not to be found in every Secondary school, many of them possess an organisation of some kind which is concerned with different aspects of the subject, particularly those not studied in formal lessons. Sometimes geographers merely form one section of a wider-ranging society, while in other cases there is a Field Club or Exploration Society. But it is in an autonomous Geographical Society that the best work can be done.

As far as possible the society should be run by pupils themselves, or through a committee composed of pupils and members of staff. The amount of direct teacher supervision will vary from year to year according to pupil membership, but background guidance is always beneficial, if not essential. This does not preclude boys and girls from taking an active part in organisation: committee membership is a valuable experience in itself, and positions such as the secretaryship or chairmanship offer opportunities of real responsibility. Thus the conduct of meetings, the hiring and posting of films, as well as part of the entertainment of visiting speakers, ought to be undertaken by the senior pupils of the society.

In the majority of schools membership of the society is open to all. However, since it is difficult to present programmes which are at one and the same time of real interest to a wide age range, some masters are in favour of having junior and senior branches. In others, membership is restricted to the middle and upper school.

The majority of schools make no charge for membership, but others levy anything from 3*d*. a year to 6*d*. a week, or institute specific charges to defray expenses such as film hire. A case can be argued, however, for the small weekly levy. Some films, of outstanding value, cost up to £4 to hire, and this amount may be beyond the sum which can be raised at a single meeting. Again, it occasionally happens that a field trip is envisaged which will require a subsidy to put the cost within pupils' means. The existence of funds, perhaps more than anything else, makes it possible for ambitious and experimental programmes to take place. Since attendance is not compulsory there can be no certainty that the income from admission charges to meetings will by itself be sufficient to meet the costs.

In general, meetings are held immediately after school, either once a week or fortnightly. Boarding schools sometimes make use of Saturday evenings. Because large numbers of day school boys leave by bus immediately after last lesson, some societies meet during the lunch hour. An arrangement adopted in a minority of establishments overcomes such limitations: ordinary time-tables on several afternoons a term are cancelled, and the time is devoted to various society meetings.

Suggested activities

(i) Debates and discussions, often related to current affairs.

(ii) Talks by visiting speakers who have either travelled or whose work and interests enable them to give a talk with real geographical stimulus. These may be other members of staff, parents, Old Boys, local university staff, local officials or industrialists, members of cultural societies, or overseas students. In addition, speakers can be requested from the sources listed in appendix C.

(iii) Talks, lecturettes or papers read by members of the society. Boys will gain both in confidence and in a greater technical mastery of their subject by giving these illustrated talks.

(iv) Brains Trusts.

(v) Quizzes.

(vi) Joint meetings with other school societies, including competitions run on the lines of a 'Top of the Form' programme.

(vii) Film shows. Good film material is available which cannot find its place in the teaching syllabus. Teachers should be cautioned, however, against over-reliance on this item; in some schools the society has collapsed through lack of support, possibly because of the boredom of a film-dominated programme (see chapter 4, p. 76).

(viii) Model-making, mapping and the annotation of specimens for the Geography Museum, for an Exhibition or for use in Geography teaching. This may involve sessions in the local reference library.

(ix) A Local Survey, described in the latter part of the previous chapter (p. 246) can be in the hands of a group of society members. Its organisation, as well as the analysis, mapping and display of results, can therefore take place during society meetings.

(x) The running of a school meteorological station can, at least for part of the year, be undertaken by the society. In some schools there are two meteorological stations, one for use in junior school teaching and the other, which may be manned by the society, for senior studies. Interesting comparisons can be made if they are mounted in contrasting sites within the school premises; for instance, on a roof-top and in the middle of the playing fields. The school records are of even greater value if further comparisons can be made through participation in one of the national or regional schemes arranged for the exchange of observations (see chapter 4, p. 91).

(xi) The production of 8 mm. films on geographical topics suitable for use in teaching, e.g. erosion along the Trent; Jarrow's industries.

(xii) Taped accounts of the local area may be recorded and subsequently exchanged with foreign schools or those in other regions.

(xiii) Another enterprising activity has been the production of a school geographical magazine. It included articles written by industrialists, travellers and boys, quizzes, competitions and crosswords. It was duplicated, and was paid for by tradesmen's advertisements.

(xiv) Plane tabling and compass traversing is an activity that many teachers find impossible to work into their sixth-form course. If any is to be undertaken, it must therefore come into the society programme.

(xv) Making use of the Ship Adoption Scheme along the lines outlined in the following paragraphs.

(xvi) A Christmas dinner or 'Continental supper' is the highlight of the winter programme in some societies.

(xvii) Invitations to foreign students to take part in informal group discussions and a subsequent meal.

(xviii) The organisation, particularly at junior level, of pen friendships or overseas correspondence. The study of the Commonwealth or foreign countries can be really stimulated in this way. Among the areas with which British children have been corresponding are Czechoslovakia, Ceylon, The West Indies, and West Africa. As far as has been ascertained there is not much interchange of ideas with older Commonwealth countries or the U.S.A., a regrettable situation. Correspondence with children of certain nationalities may present language difficulties, but letter writing to French and German children is a regular practice in many schools, and there is no reason why the geographical side of such correspondence cannot be encouraged. Finally, it should be pointed out, children of other countries, even of Primary school age, are often only too pleased to practise their English.

(xix) Visits of different kinds: to factories, quarries, coal mines, museums etc.

(xx) Cross-country hikes.

(xxi) Where it is feasible, helicopter or aeroplane flights over the vicinity. This is naturally one of the most popular items of all!

SHIP ADOPTION

It has long been customary for teachers of Geography to make use of the Shipping News in the daily press for the purpose of studying shipping routes and allied topics. It is also desirable, however, for direct contacts to be established between schools and ships. In general it is educationally more profitable to follow the voyages of a tramp ship than of a liner on a regular route, for the former traverse the oceans and visit ports that never appear on liner schedules. Moreover, personal contact between pupils and the merchant service provides a human interest in itself.

Considerations of this kind led to the formation of the British Ship Adoption Society early in 1936. Now there are over 800 member schools, each of which is 'paired' with a vessel. Unfortunately, the Society has had a waiting list for many years on account of the difficulty of securing sufficient ships' Masters to participate in the scheme. Interested teachers should write to the Secretary of the Society at H.Q. Ship 'Wellington', Temple Stairs, Victoria Embankment, London, W.C. 2, to ascertain the latest position concerning ship adoption.

Correspondence is the medium through which the adoption mainly works. The school sends letters, and receives replies. The ship's letters provide much material for study and this inevitably gives rise to numerous questions that are incorporated in the following mail. Correspondence naturally tends to be sporadic, but a considerable quantity of information is collected after a relatively short time, and the teacher's problem then becomes how to use it.

Material which accumulates may be classified as follows:

(a) *General and miscellaneous*. Details of the ship, its age, tonnage, engines, fuel, equipment, cargo storage etc.

(b) *Human*. The Master, his career and personal history; officers and crew; life on board; duties and spare-time hobbies; incidents of the voyage, both amusing and exciting, which sketch the background of the seaman's life.

(c) *Geographical*. Routes followed, ports visited, canal transit; pictures of people and life in ports and in other lands; details regarding methods of production of commodities; the ship's log, instruments, weather observations, maps, charts and the like.

It may be added that pictures, postcards, specimens and other objects of interest are often sent by the ships, while schools usually show their interest in the ship by sending, especially at Christmas time, some gift to mark their appreciation. As 'adoption' proceeds many opportunities of interesting and profitable exchange arise.

It is difficult to dogmatise on the way in which teachers ought to use this wealth of material, for the circumstances in schools will differ so markedly. To mention the correspondence casually, for instance or merely to post it on a board is to do the scheme and the ship a gross injustice. The following suggestions are therefore tentative in nature but are made in the hope that they may of some service.

(1) One or more of a group of senior boys (possibly from the Geographical Society) might be appointed to take charge of the correspondence. Duties would include dealing with all incoming correspondence, displaying it, and selecting material for posting to the ship.

(2) Extracts from newly arrived mail could be read to the school at morning assembly.

(3) Duplicated summaries might be prepared, and distributed to classes. They can be dealt with in the Geography lesson, perhaps being illustrated with the aid of the epidiascope and specimens. A home-work might well be allotted for the preparation of subsequent questions and letters.

(4) A filing system should be established, so that documents, letters, photographs, etc., are available when required. One of the most valuable features of adoption is that the personal element can reinforce, in a very special way, points being made in normal lessons.

The quarterly bulletin of the British Ship Adoption Society, *Our Merchant Ships*, is an interesting publication and a valuable adjunct to both ship adoption and geographical work. It contains first-hand accounts, usually written by Masters or other officers in adopted ships, of voyages, ports, peoples and commodities as well as descriptions of the growth of important shipping lines and of their part in keeping the wheels of trade turning. It is hoped to make the bulletin available in quantity for use in classes. The Society has also published, under the title *Seafarers, Ships and Cargoes*, edited by L. Brooks and R. H. Duce (University of London Press), a book of selected first-hand accounts, and this is available as a background reader.

A recent addition to the Society's services is the provision of a library of 35 mm. transparencies and connected tape recordings. One set, for instance, is of a passage through the Suez Canal, and consists of colour transparencies and a tape that runs for 30 minutes. The tape was recorded on board a vessel actually going through the Canal and includes many shipboard noises and a short history of the waterway as told by the Egyptian pilot. The Society is also collecting descriptive articles on various ports of the world written by its sea-faring friends. These descriptions, accompanied by maps, will be available for issue to member schools as teaching aids.

From what has been written it will be clear that the Society needs its income. At present the annual subscription is £5. 5s., paid in the majority of cases by the Local Authority which 'sponsors' the school's membership.

FOREIGN TRAVEL

Many Geography masters, in addition to normal routine, organise foreign tours for their pupils during the school holidays. Those who feel able to do this and who get enjoyment from it are providing pupils with a valuable opportunity to widen their experience and to make the Geography of foreign parts really come alive. These holidays are often organised by geographers in conjunction with modern language colleagues, and both expect the benefit to their subjects to be incidental to the holiday, but none the less quite definite. On the other hand, some teachers are not disposed to run foreign trips without giving them a more positive geographical content; in fact making them foreign field courses.

In the preparation of all types of foreign visits the teachers would be well advised to use the facilities of the School Journey Association of London, 23 Southampton Place, London, W.C. 1. The Association publishes for its members a very useful pamphlet entitled *How to Promote a Continental School Journey*. This gives good advice to those inexperienced in leading parties overseas, dealing with the selection of the season for foreign travel, dates to be avoided, choice of centre and types of accommodation on the continent. It gives advice on costing and makes suggestions on preliminary arrangements such as letters to parents, deposits and payments, collective passports, tickets and reservations, insurance, meetings with parents and the preparation of a guide book.

The Central Bureau for Educational Visits and Exchanges, 55A Duke Street, Grosvenor Square, London, W. 1., also provides a service of information, advice and assistance. It is controlled by a Board of Trustees representative of various sections of the education service and teachers' associations, and is grant-maintained by the Ministry of Education and the Scottish Education Department. The bureau is particularly concerned with exchanges and with facilities for individual young people to attend international meetings and work camps, short courses and study tours in Europe and North Africa. However, amongst other publications it produces one entitled *Travel Notes for Group Leaders*. This contains information concerning collective certificates, concessionary fares, inexpensive shipping accommodation, air travel and insurance. Copies are available free to teachers, who are requested to send a foolscap, stamped addressed envelope.

Examples

One party which has done foreign field-work went from Barrow-in-Furness Grammar school to spend a month in Iceland in 1959. With their van and stores they embarked at Leith for Reykjavík. Their first camp was at the foot of Baula, a rhyolitic mountain, which they climbed. Camp 2 was near a corrie Glacier, the Glerarvalshnukur. Subsequent activities included a town survey of Akureyri, slope mapping of the area south of Lake Myvatn, which abounded in varied volcanic features, and an exhaustive survey of types of building in Reykjavik. A colour film was made of the 1,000 mile journey through Iceland. Five articles on the expedition were published in the *Barrow Evening Mail*. Three surveys were prepared for publication and papers were read to the school geographical society on numerous other Icelandic topics. The expedition, of ten boys and two masters, was made possible by the hard work of the school's Parent Committee, by the kind support of the people of Barrow and by the material generosity of over thirty commercial firms or industries.

In 1962 a party of four masters and nineteen boys from Latymer Upper School went on a geographical and biological expedition to Corsica. The cost of the $3\frac{1}{2}$-week expedition was kept down to £31 per head, with grants from the Royal Geographical Society and the Royal Society, material aid from three large companies and by travelling in the cheapest way possible. The whole enterprise provided adventure and demanded resource, initiative, stamina, and pluck rarely taxed to the same degree on field-work in Britain. The expedition camped for four or five days in each of four contrasting environments on the island. Botanical and geographical surveys were carried out along selected transects near each camp site.

The first camp was on the banks of the Golo River and gave access to part of the Chataigneraie in the schistose hill country of the east of the island. The second site was again on the Golo but near its source in the granite heart of the island. To work a cross-valley transect, the boys climbed in both directions to over 6,000 ft., working up through maquis, juniper shrubs, a zone of chestnut trees, Corsican pines and, finally, across high pastures to the rocky summits. The third camp was ideally sited on a dried lagoon, behind the dunes of a west coast bay. Here careful mapping of numerous landforms involved compass traverses and survey-pole levelling. Within a very short distance of the camp were fine terraces, talus cones, the typical Mediterranean summer sand-bar blocking the mouth of a small river, raised beaches and numerous other coastal features. The slopes inland gave the botanists some dense maquis to study. The fourth camp was in the more cultivated north-west of the island where several distinctive hilltop villages were studied.

Apart from observational work, the boys carried out many enquiries. They were furnished with questionnaires providing the French vocabulary for over fifty geographical queries. The boys surprised themselves in that they were able to conduct such protracted and profitable conversations. Although this was only a schoolboy expedition, the published report shows that they carried out what can genuinely be called original research.

In recent years groups from Charterhouse have gone on similar expeditions to a Saharan oasis in Tunisia, an Azores island, Lapland, Stromboli, the Lofoten Islands and the Carpathians. These expeditions have been self-supporting and, in each case, all-inclusive cost per head has been below £30 for about 3 weeks. Individual boys were responsible for research in geomorphology, biology or aspects of human geography and, where base-maps existed, forces were combined to produce a land use survey.

Fairly typical of the holiday tours are those run by Bancroft's School, if one type can be picked out from a very varied assortment. Most of their tours have taken place during the Easter holidays although some have occurred in the summer time and, in every case, the underlying principle has been that the tours should be of some cultural value apart from being holidays, this justifying the organisation by the school. Hence, the bases have been at such varied centres as Champery in Valais, Switzerland; Carcassonne in South-west France; Blanes in North-east Spain; Venice, and Bellagio on Lake Como, in Italy; Souillac on the River Dordogne; and again in Italy at Florence and Naples.

On these tours, parties number from 30 to 45 and are divided into groups with leaders who are responsible for checking numbers on the way out and for organisation in other ways. Party members are given a duplicated booklet of maps, notes and instructions. Besides a detailed itinerary, time-table, and information about reservations and meals, they are given notes on geographical and historical features to be seen on the journey. General information supplied covers money regulations and rates of exchange, postage, business hours, a short 'phrase book' of language aids on Italian or Spanish trips, and instructions on clothing, luggage and school rules.

Three or four coach excursions will be organised from the holiday base, but much of the rest of the time will be free for individual exploration, although freedom in regard to bathing, wandering in the mountains or other sources of danger will be limited by special regulations. The programme at Souillac serves as an example of the organisation; there the party stayed at a hotel for a fortnight. One excursion took them down the Dordogne to Beynac, visiting châteaux and attractive settlements. The second excursion was to the Lascaux Caves; the next was across the Causses to the grottoes of Lacave and Padirac and the last excursion went well up the Dordogne to the dams and power stations of the gorge section of the river, including a specially arranged visit to the barrage at Chastang. For the rest, the boys were given the following notes:

There will be much to see in and around Souillac, chiefly along the river, for this area is quite unique—the topography with its caves and gorges, the quick changes of vegetation, the intensive farming which might almost be called horticulture, the buildings of stone and the dress and customs of the people. There will be much free time and it is hoped that the members of the party will attempt to absorb as much of the local characteristics as possible...

10

THE GEOGRAPHY MASTER

INTRODUCTION

There is no doubt that the key to effective teaching is the creation in the child of genuine interest, and the desire to know more. Inspired teaching generates wonder, wonder promotes interest, and interest creates a thirst for knowledge. With the world and its peoples as his material, the Geography master fails completely if he is unable to stimulate such a chain process in the child, for only this will lead to real education. In content alone the subject has all that is necessary to appeal to the youthful mind, and to this can be added a wide and interesting range of methods and materials for illustration. But such a wealth of resources, while enhancing for the Geography master the possibility of making the subject meaningful to the child, demands from him the exercise of much skill and judgement. Not only has he to appreciate the possibilities of various teaching media but he must also have a considerable breadth of knowledge, a ready understanding of matters of immediate moment, and a wide interest in many other subjects (e.g. Physics, Chemistry, Biology, Economics and History) which impinge on his own specialism. To these attributes he must add a power of realistic description by the spoken word and an ability to make children think logically. Some of these qualities are necessary in every teacher, but they are, perhaps, of even more importance to the Geography master.

In the early part of the twentieth century, some of the most efficient teachers of Geography possessed no academic qualification in the subject. In many cases, this was because these teachers took their courses before any degrees or qualifications in Geography had been instituted. The number of such schoolmasters has steadily diminished. There is no doubt, however, that the long delay in the recognition of Geography as a principal subject for university degrees had an adverse influence upon the status of Geography teaching. Today, it is considered desirable that teachers of Geography should possess a university degree, or at least an academic diploma in the subject, but it should also be recognised that academic distinction is not enough, and that graduates in other subjects, both in Arts and

262

Sciences, who have made a thorough post-graduate study of Geography, and students from Colleges of Education who have taken Geography as a main subject, may well prove equally effective as teachers of the subject.

THE TRAINING OF THE GEOGRAPHY MASTER

The object of his training is twofold: first to learn the techniques which any good teacher must possess and, secondly, to pursue geographical studies in some depth. He must have a broad view of the subject in all its aspects, a firm understanding of its principles, and an infectious enthusiasm for its study. At the present time recruitment is from two possible sources: (1) those trained for three years in one of the colleges of education, and (2) graduates of a university. The latter group includes Honours graduates who have taken a three-year course for their degree followed by a fourth year of professional training in a university department of education, Pass or General Degree students of a university who have taken a fourth year of professional training, and Honours graduates who have entered teaching without any professional training. The latter practice is, however, discouraged by the teaching profession and by the Department of Education and Science. An exciting new development must also be mentioned, though it blurs the one-time distinction between the university graduate and the college-trained, certificated teacher. This is the institution of Bachelor of Education courses at colleges of education; having successfully completed the normal three-year course the abler students may graduate after an extra twelve months' study.

Many of the necessary teaching skills can be acquired during school practice, although this raises a number of problems, both for the student and for the master. Inevitably, the time available for practice is inadequate, and it is important to use it to the best possible advantage. The ideal procedure would be for the student to have experience in several types of school, both primary and secondary, but this is not always possible.

It is axiomatic that a student should be given the opportunity of observing and working under the direction of a successful teacher. From the latter he will learn many of the special techniques, as well as the handling of equipment such as globes, projectors, maps and pictures. By itself, however, observation is of small value to the beginner. After all, he has a very limited experience and will be unable to appreciate many of the methods and much of the skill which is demonstrated. If student practice is to be really worth while, the beginner must be eased gently and slowly into the classroom. Ideally he should start by being in charge of a class for a few minutes while the master, on some pretext or other, goes out. After the first uncertain steps, and indeed at regular intervals throughout the early weeks, the master ought to hold brief post-mortems: explaining, discussing, and encouraging the student.

Such thorough grounding depends on the goodwill of the member of staff concerned, for his prime responsibility is the teaching of Geography. As a rule, masters are very willing to help students in every possible way, but such work is additional to the busy routine of a normal working day, and time both for marking and for the general administration of their department may well have to be sacrificed.

With all the goodwill possible, the teacher still has to ask himself some searching questions when a student arrives. 'What will least interfere with the general routine?', and 'Which classes can be handed over to him?' These problems are difficult to resolve. The student may, for example, be given charge of several lower and more backward streams, but such a procedure is fair neither to the student nor, in many cases, to the pupils concerned: the less able pupils are most in need of experienced help. No, the student ought to be allowed to teach pupils extending across a wide range of ability and through several age-groups. No school can afford to put beginners in charge of G.C.E. or C.S.E. fifth forms, but they should be given a fair cross-section of the others.

Equally important is the decision over the length of time that the student is to be in charge of a class. The varied practice regarded as so essential cannot be obtained merely by taking isolated lessons. What the student needs is at least a month of full control, and a well-defined section of the syllabus to cover. This will give him an opportunity to develop ideas and to ascertain the amount of his material being absorbed by the class. Most important of all, he will learn to appreciate the importance of working to a time schedule. The effects of failing to do this may be serious, especially when a prepared lesson overruns the allotted time. In this case pupils' lesson notes will be incomplete and unbalanced. Finishing them for homework might then be necessary but would obviously be highly unsatisfactory.

THE QUALIFIED TEACHER

It is not long before the new teacher, faced with regular class teaching, realises that content is often less important than method. And, though the latter will depend very much on the personality and training of the individual concerned, to be successful it must necessarily have certain purposes in mind.

The first aim will always be to create interest. This can best be achieved by looking afresh at each lesson and deciding which of the available media will most effectively illustrate the theme. Will it be the textbook, maps, atlases, models, pictures, specimens, filmstrips, slides, moving film, television, or a radio broadcast? If the list seems long we should be the more grateful for it gives us the chance of real variety in our presentation.

Since so much of our lesson material lies outside the pupils' experience, mental images will have to be created for their benefit. Obviously, these must be as real and as accurate as possible, so that the good teacher is not merely adept in manipulating teaching aids, but can also portray scenes and events by vivid oral description. This can be aided by the judicious use of passages read from books of travel, and it is here that the gift of analogy is so very important. A bare statement that the temperature in Siberia falls to $-59\,°F$ ($-51\,°C$) will mean little to the child. Qualify it, however, by comparing this figure with a typical recording from the school meteorological station, and reading an extract from some descriptive work like Hann's, and reality is given to the whole concept:

It is hardly possible to describe the terrible cold one has to endure; one has to experience it to appreciate it. The quicksilver freezes solid and can can be cut and hammered like lead; iron becomes brittle, and the hatchet breaks like glass; wood, depending upon the degree of moisture in it, becomes harder than iron and withstands the axe so that only completely dry wood can be split. Every step in the dry snow can be heard for long distances; the bursting of the ice cover and the frozen ground sound like the cannonading of distant batteries.

Good teaching method also involves a concern to see things from the child's point of view. Simple concepts, unquestioned in the adult mind, often mean something very different to the young Secondary school pupil. The Geography master must realise the extent of the pupils' understanding and get down to a child's level. He must be aware of misconceptions and should never pursue his course regardless of the understanding of the class. By questioning the pupils, he will soon see the difficulties, and this demands an awareness of every individual child. Jargon, clichés, and gross generalisations are to be avoided—geographers are very guilty of all of these—and even common terms need careful definition and explanation. Simple phrases such as 'a warm climate', 'suitable physical conditions', and 'ease of access', all need explanation and qualification, if used at all. Choice of suitable teaching material will overcome this problem to a limited extent, and this is one reason why intensive and extensive preparation become so necessary.

KEEPING UP TO DATE

As part of his preparation, the good teacher has to find time to keep himself up to date. A lesson which uses topical material, like the birth of new volcanoes off southern Iceland, or an earthquake at Skopje, immediately captures the interest of the class. The use of such information requires alertness, flexibility, and adaptability on the part of the master. Of course, many of the more mundane data of Human Geography are also rapidly changing, though less dramatically! Textbooks and atlases soon get out of date, and if slavishly followed by the master may well be responsible for the repetition of errors through several generations of pupils.

The good teacher knows where to go for additional material, and makes a point of availing himself of it. National newspapers, periodicals, and annual publications, such as the *Statesman's Year-Book, Philips' Geographical Digest*, and the *Statistical Year Book* of the United Nations, are sources which he will constantly use.

Every year a number of organisations offer courses with a similar end in view: to help in keeping staff up to date in both fact and method. The Department of Education and Science sponsors some work of this nature, the details of which will be found in circulars to schools. So, too, do the Field Studies Council and the Geographical Association.

The last-named is particularly active in these spheres. The highlight of its activities is the Annual Conference, held in London during the Christmas holidays. Apart from lectures by distinguished academic geographers or teachers on particular aspects of their subject, there are book exhibitions, and displays of work and equipment. Two of the themes recently exploited from this standpoint were 'Overhead projectors' and 'Field work for C.S.E. classes'. The Spring Conference is organised differently: a city or town is chosen as the meeting place for a series of lectures and discussions on the surrounding region, and as a centre for field outings. Among other activities of the Association two call for special mention. First, individual members in need of professional help can contact headquarters, where the matter will be settled directly, or passed to the specialised sub-committee concerned for its comment. Secondly, there are the local branches of the Association at a more personal level. These are active in many parts of the country, and provide an admirable meeting ground for local geographers, be they specialist members of school staffs or otherwise. No account of the Association would be complete, though, without a reference to its quarterly periodical *Geography*, formerly *The Geographical Teacher*. In it will be found a wide range of articles, including many on teaching problems, as well as a section devoted to 'This changing world'.

CONCLUSION

In Geography the wealth of subject-matter and of teaching aids creates endless possibilities, but materials and methods of any kind are useless unless matched by initiative and drive in the master. He must approach his teaching in a spirit of adventure, always prepared to try new ideas though never hesitating to discard those which prove unsatisfactory. He must recognise that on him falls great responsibility. It is his task to implant a real consciousness of the ever-changing world, something dynamic which can raise his pupils' sights above the confines of their immediate locality and lead them towards the genuine understanding and sympathy so desperately needed in the world.

11

GEOGRAPHY AND CAREERS

The study of Geography develops attitudes of mind and outlook of value in a wide variety of occupations, though it does not always lead directly to a particular type of post in which the subject has a direct vocational use. Geography as an educational instrument encourages clear thinking, broad-mindedness and a wide human outlook. Its value in fitting a person for a responsible position is being increasingly recognised at graduate level. Even below graduate level, the value of Geography in developing certain techniques and habits of work should also be appreciated.

THE UNIVERSITY-TRAINED GEOGRAPHER

(1) *Courses leading to graduation*

The careers opportunities of the Geography graduate are influenced to some extent by the sudsidiary subjects of his degree course. These will depend on his choice of Advanced level subjects. For certain specialist posts, a B.Sc. degree in Geography is preferred to a B.A., usually because a Science subject or Mathematics is required at subsidiary level, but the Arts graduate can widen his careers opportunities by taking post-graduate courses.

In the school sixth form, Geography is often combined with Arts rather than Science subjects and there is perhaps some argument for more Science combinations with Geography where certain careers are envisaged. There is no ideal combination of subjects with Geography for the Advanced level examinations, but a wide variety of possible alternatives exists on both Arts and Science sides. It should be possible for Geography to be combined with either Science or Arts subjects or even with both. A broad background of Ordinary level subjects is very desirable for potential geographers as Geography has such wide ramifications. Details of Matriculation, Faculty and Honours School requirements may be obtained by reference to the relevant sources. It is necessary to find out these details as early as possible and constant checking is necessary as they are changing so quickly.

As an alternative to a straight Geography degree, some may consider the courses in Town and Country Planning such as are offered, for example at Manchester University, or Land Use Studies, as at Durham University. Full details and regulations for these courses and degrees can be obtained from the universities concerned.

(2) *Graduate careers: the major fields*

In the past most Geography graduates have gone into teaching but there is an increasing tendency for geographers to enter other fields. A recent survey of careers taken up by Geography graduates of two Cambridge colleges suggests that only about one-third of the men go into teaching, the majority using their Geography either professionally or as a liberal background in a great variety of other occupations. A higher proportion of graduates of the provincial universities enter teaching, particularly in the case of women. Even so, about one half of the male Geography graduates of all the universities in the United Kingdom now find employment in occupations other than teaching in schools. These fields are clearly now of major importance for the future graduate in Geography. They may be divided into two groups: those for which a knowledge of Geography is demanded or preferred and those in which geographers compete along with graduates in other subjects. Specialised fields in the first category are Surveying, Mapwork, and Town and Country Planning.

(3) *Careers directly involving Geography: a review*

(*a*) *Teaching.* Many university graduates, together with college students who gain the B.Ed., intend to take up teaching as a career. The vast majority of schools of all types offer posts, recognising that Geography is an essential subject in a good education. Among them are Grammar, Secondary Modern, Technical, Comprehensive, Multilateral and Bi-lateral Institutions. The well-qualified geographer may hope to lecture in a College of Education after having had some experience in schools, while a few honours graduates of high academic ability become university lecturers. There are also many teaching posts overseas, especially in developing countries, as well as a limited number of openings in the instructor branches of the Services.

(*b*) *Surveying.* The type of survey work most suitable for geographers is land surveying, and those interested should at an early stage obtain the necessary information from an appropriate institution, such as the Royal Institute of Chartered Surveyors. Most of the survey work for graduates is overseas and is conducted by Government Departments. These include the Directorate of Overseas Surveys and the Survey Departments of the Overseas Territories. The Directorate of Overseas Surveys is a branch of the Home Civil Service and its staff are paid and taxed from the United Kingdom. Details may be obtained from the booklet *Survey Appointments Overseas* published under the authority of Her Majesty's Stationery Office. Other survey posts overseas are offered by survey departments in territories formerly under the Colonial Office.

The British Antarctic Survey has opportunities for graduate geographers, and those with survey experience can be considered for the post of Topographical Surveyor. Vacancies also occur for geographers who are interested in Geomorphology and in the field of Meteorology. Details may be obtained from the Personnel Officer, British Antarctic Survey, 30 Gillingham Street, London, S.W. 1.

The Soil Survey of England and Wales employs several geographers, though their lack of Chemistry and/or Physics is somewhat of a disadvantage. There is no regular annual intake of staff, but vacancies are filled as and when they occur; they rarely amount to more than one or two each year. A First Class Honours Degree is a normal requirement, though Upper Second Class Honours graduates are accepted under exceptional conditions. A degree with Physical Geography and Geology is acceptable. The work lies mainly in the field, and is concerned with the production of soil maps and reports. The headquarters of the Soil Survey of England and Wales is at the Rothamsted Experimental Station, Harpenden, Hertfordshire. On occasion, members of the Survey of England and Wales have been seconded overseas for short periods; the Colonial Pool of Soil Surveyors in the Ministry of Overseas Development undertakes to make surveys in some of the smaller colonial territories.

(*c*) *Cartography*. The production of maps offers some openings for Geography graduates. The Admiralty Hydrographic Department employs geographers as Civil Hydrographic Officers to prepare and correct Admiralty charts. These Officers are responsible for the calculation and plotting of projections and geodetic data and make use of original surveys, observations and hydrographic and navigational reports.

The Directorate of Military Surveys also employs graduates with Geography degrees, preferably including cartography or surveying. Mathematics or Modern Languages are desirable. The appointments are as Map Research Officers in the Map Library at the War Office. There are also very occasional vacancies for Assistant Map Officers in both the Records and Computing Sections at the Directorate of Overseas Surveys. Geography graduates are eligible, but for the Computing Section their degree courses must have included Mathematics. Those employed in the Records Section are specialist librarians and for this section competitition is very severe. Map curators are employed by some University Geography Departments and private map publishers may very occasionally employ a Geography graduate in the Editorial Department.

(*d*) *Town and country planning.* Geography graduates wishing to enter Town and Country Planning will aim at election to Associate Membership of the Town Planning Institute, one of the requirements for which is two years practical experience in a suitable office. Most County Planning Authorities and a number of cities now employ geographers and the necessary practical experience is often obtained in their offices, particularly in the Planning Departments of large cities. These Departments are responsible for drawing up long-term development plans to be submitted for Government approval. Trainees undertake surveys, conduct research, study population movements and social developments and learn about the legal and financial aspects of planning.

Geography graduates interested in planning may also seek employment and obtain their practical training with the Ministry of Housing and Local Government. This Department is concerned with studying the implications of the development plans put forward by the Local Authorities and perhaps does not provide quite such useful training as the more constructive work carried out by the Local Authority Offices. Graduates with at least Second Class Honours in Geography are eligible for employment under the Ministry as Assistant Research Officers. They will be concerned primarily with the analysis and presentation of data on populations, employment and economic resources. At the age of 30 years they will be eligible for appointment as Planning Officers, provided that they have had three years' planning experience and become Corporate Members of the Town Planning Institute.

Other Government posts for qualified town and country planners may be found in the Commonwealth and in H.M. Overseas Civil Service. There are also occasional posts in private consultants' offices, in a few large industrial enterprises, and in teaching in the Planning Schools of Universities and Colleges.

19-2

(e) *Agricultural research.* Another field in which the graduate geographer can apply his specialist knowledge is the Research Group of the Agricultural Land Service under the Ministry of Agriculture, Fisheries and Food. At least Second Class Honours is demanded and experience of field-work or country planning, land classification or agricultural economics, and a knowledge of agricultural and rural conditions are considered as additional qualifications. The duties of Assistant Research Officers and Research Assistants in the Department include organising and carrying out research projects, and obtaining information on the restoration of surface mineral workings. The total number of staff employed in the Research Group is small, and vacancies occur very infrequently.

(f) *Miscellaneous.* There are certain other opportunities for the graduate geographer to apply his knowledge. The Joint Intelligence Bureau sometimes employs geographers for research into the geographical and other features of foreign countries. B.Sc. Geography graduates have, on rare occasions, obtained posts in the Meteorological Branch of the Air Ministry. Employment may occasionally be found under the Field Studies Council as Wardens or Field Assistants and geomorphologists and biogeographers are sometimes required by Government bodies within the Commonwealth. Recent opportunities for geographers in Africa have included Locust Survey and work in research institutes such as the Rhodes–Livingstone Institute as well as in the Ghana Department of Agriculture (Soil Survey and Land Use Division). Other opportunities for work in the field are likely to develop in this continent.

All the above-mentioned opportunities are those in which a specialist knowledge of Geography is important to a greater or lesser degree. It should be emphasised that the requirements given for particular types of posts are those obtaining at the time of writing. When pupils now at school have graduated they may have changed considerably and those interested should write to the appropriate sources for the latest information.

(4) *Careers in which Geography counts as an initial qualification*

In this group Geography is a qualification rather than a requirement and the geographer competes for posts along with graduates in other subjects. The group is a wide one and the opportunities are much more numerous than in the more specialised fields described above, apart from teaching. The indications are that geographers do not use their subject as a specialist qualification for a particular type of post but as a liberal education fitting them for a wide range of possible careers from which they may choose. A recent survey of posts taken up by male Geography graduates immediately after graduation in all the universities of the United Kingdom shows, apart from teaching, some bias towards Government Service, industry and commerce.

(a) *Government service.* Posts in Government Service include those in the various classes of the Home Civil Service, in the Overseas Civil Service, and in the Foreign Office. It has to be admitted that there are comparatively few vacancies in the latter category and evidence of ability to learn foreign languages is required. At home a man's service is in the Foreign Office, and abroad, in diplomatic, commercial, information and consular posts.

There are also opportunities in the Administrative Branch of the Overseas Civil Service. Although there is no niche within this Branch in which a geographer's special knowledge could be put to particular use, many candidates in recent years have been geographers. Details may be obtained from the booklet *Appointments Overseas* published by Her Majesty's Stationery Office.

Geography graduates may also compete for the Special Department Classes of the Home Civil Service. The post of 'Assistant Postal Controller' might well appeal to the Geography graduate as it is concerned with problems bearing to some extent on Geography and involves much travelling over the country. There may also be interesting opportunities at Government Communications Headquarters at Oakley, Priors Road, Cheltenham, Glos. This comes under the Scientific Civil Service and the work is interesting, stimulating and extending, but the direct bearing on Geography is very limited. Only a few posts are available each year and service may be anywhere in the United Kingdom or Overseas. There is also graduate recruitment to the Executive Class of the Home Civil Service and Branch B of the Foreign Service.

(b) *Business.* It has been claimed that, for certain posts in industry, commerce and a few allied fields, the geographer has a competitive asset in the nature and content of his academic education. Admittedly, qualities of personality and character count for much in such fields as industrial and commercial management, but the geographer has two important advantages in his knowledge of the world and in the way he has learnt to approach problems from all angles. Certainly geographers are going into posts of this kind and recent examples of actual cases include the following:

Personnel management in a large sugar-marketing company
Trade representative for an ink manufacturer
Freight Traffic Manager with a large air line
Trade representative for a drug firm
A post in the Commercial Department of a large steel firm
Market Research

There could be some mutual attraction between geographers and posts of this kind. A recent survey of careers taken up by Cambridge men graduates showed that 45 out of a total of 162 entered business, industry and commerce, more choosing these kinds of posts than any other type. Also the proportion of the total Geography graduate output in the country entering these fields is fairly high. For the better trainee posts in industry and commerce, however, competition is keen and considerable stress is laid on qualities of personality and interests.

(c) *Other posts.* In addition to the kind of posts indicated above, geographers have found employment in a vast number of different fields, though admittedly often only in small numbers. Amongst this host of diverse occupations we may include transport, publishing, journalism, social work, accountancy, librarianship, banking, insurance, advertising, missionary work, work in museums, the Services, university administration, the B.B.C., the United Nations. Further training or study for institutes' examinations may be necessary for many such posts, but clearly the field of opportunities for geographers is extremely wide.

In our rapidly changing and developing world there are ever increasing opportunities for geographers. They have already entered many different fields of employment, but it is for geographers themselves to demonstrate even more the relevance of their specialist skills and knowledge in the world at large.

THE NON-GRADUATE GEOGRAPHER

(a) *Teaching.* Under this heading we must mention first and foremost the openings in our schools, qualification being by means of three-year courses at the colleges of education. Basic qualifications for entry are five Ordinary level passes and some evidence of Advanced level study. So popular is the subject, however, that many colleges are now demanding a pass in Geography at the higher level. It is also true that pupils offering subsidiary Mathematics or Science are in a somewhat stronger position to secure entrance, other things being equal, than boys with an uninspired mark in Geography alone. College-trained geographers either apply their specialist knowledge in Secondary Modern and Comprehensive schools on the one hand, or may enter the field of primary education on the other. In the latter case they are more usually employed as general subject teachers, but their interest in Geography serves them well. They must deal with the ceaseless barrage of questions and thirst for general knowledge which is so characteristic of this age-group.

(*b*) *Commerce and industry.* Below graduate level Geography is recognised as an essential part of the general education necessary for many occupations. A sample survey of the prospectuses of Colleges of Further Education in England revealed how widely the subject was included in such courses. Here is the list:

Diploma in Economics; Diploma in Commerce
G.C.E. Advanced level; G.C.E. Ordinary level
Civil Service Executive Grade and Civil Service Clerical Grade
Local Government Examination Board
Institute of Bankers; Institute of Export; Institute of Transport
Institute of Shipping and Forwarding Agents
National Certificate of Commerce Ordinary Level and Higher Level
Purchasing Officers' Association
Chartered Insurance Institute (Marine Branch)
Chamber of Shipping
Institute of Chartered Shipbrokers
National Certificate of Retail Distribution
Institute of Certificated Grocers
G.L.C. Major Establishment Grade
Royal Society of Arts Certificate
Certificate of London Chamber of Commerce
Certificate and Senior Certificate of the College of Preceptors
Institute of Meat
Police Promotion Examinations
Common Preliminary Examination of Engineering Institutions
Preliminary Examination of the Law Society
Institute of Cost and Works Accountants
Co-operative Union Examination
National Certificate in Textiles
Examination of the National Advisory Council for the Training and
  Education of Junior Journalists
Chartered Institute of Secretaries and Corporation of Secretaries
Retail Trades Junior Certificate

The fact of so many examining bodies recognising Geography shows that it is regarded as a valuable background subject for students undertaking vocational courses. As such, it is adapted by lecturers in Technical Colleges to suit the vocational interests of students, courses being given in the Geography of resources, industry, transport, etc. It is probable that the role of Geography in commercial or industrial education will be extended as it is concerned with the development of certain techniques which should have a useful application in these fields. Students trained in the plotting of distributions and their analysis should be able to help with the industrial and commercial problems to which such an approach is applicable. Again, geographical techniques should have an obvious application in problems connected with transport. At present it can be said that Geography is popular in the commercial departments of Technical and Comprehensive schools, and school leavers at 15–16 years with such interests are gravitating to posts with travel agencies, shipping firms and export firms.

(c) *Surveying and map-making.* There are also opportunities below graduate level in both surveying and map-making, for example with the Ordnance Survey and in the Hydrographic Department of the Admiralty. Surveyors in both these Departments are largely recruited from serving officers, but the Ordnance Survey offers employment to school leavers both as Cartographical Draughtsmen and occasionally as Surveyors. Selection is by interview. Draughtsmen are concerned with drawing maps from data provided by the Surveyors who work in the field. Surveyors move from place to place at frequent intervals and may be sent anywhere in Great Britain. For Cartographic Draughtsmen in the Hydrographic Department, the usual place of duty is at Cricklewood, London, N.W. 2. School leavers are also employed as Cartographical Draughtsmen with the Ministry of Housing and Local Government.

(d) *Civil service.* Here openings are in the Civil Service Executive Class, and Branch B of the Foreign Service, and the necessary information about these may be obtained from the relevant sources. Other non-graduate openings in the Civil Service include posts as Experimental Officer in the Meteorological Service for candidates who have passed Physics at Advanced level of the G.C.E., together with Geography.

(e) *Town and country planning.* Those interested in opportunities below graduate level in Town and Country Planning might consult their local planning office or their Youth Employment Officer, and obtain information from the Ministry of Land and Natural Resources or from one of the relevant professional bodies, such as the Institute of Town Planning. A number of diploma and certificate courses are offered in different towns, some for full-time students and others for day-release youths.

12

GEOGRAPHY TEACHING OVERSEAS

INTRODUCTION

The world is very large and its people differ widely in their attitude to the problems of everyday life. The Western idea of 'Culture' and 'Education' is very different from those held in Asia or Africa, whilst financial and scientific resources vary greatly from country to country. It is therefore not surprising that Geography teaching differs markedly both in content and in method. It is difficult for the people of Europe or the U.S.A., with all their wealth of building, visual aids, radio and television programmes, to visualise the conditions under which masters in some of the less developed countries are obliged to approach the Geography lesson. 'It is not realistic in this country to recommend any equipment depending on electrical power, since the vast majority of schools are without the necessary power connections'; so writes Mr C. Last, Director of the Medhare Alem School in Addis Ababa. 'Even such items as Globes and Wall maps are expensive and difficult to provide, and we must always bear in mind that there are many community schools which lack even blackboards and writing equipment, and where textbooks cannot be made available to individual pupils. Finally, the degree of qualification of teachers in many regions is not as high as it might be.' This is not an isolated example, for we find Professor I. M. Khaluf writing of Geography in Iraq: 'It should be conceded that the lack of necessary equipment, the untrained Geography teacher, the poorly written textbooks, the essay type of examinations, the unwieldly curriculum and the theoretical approach (dictation of notes and memorisation of facts) make the Geography instruction not only distant from usefulness but also dull and uninviting.'

It becomes apparent that there will be a wide variation in the range of amenities between different parts of the world, and that it is impossible in present circumstances to expect a uniform level of attainment. But it should also be realised that the actual content of material will vary from country to country. Geography is not just a collection of facts. Men look at their environments through different eyes and give them different perspectives. Nationalism, religion and

277

customs can markedly influence man's use of the land, and the result is different from what would be expected or, indeed, from what may be most economic or beneficial. We must expect to find therefore that the slant or bias of Geography teaching will vary according to the country, and for this reason alone a world syllabus would be impossible.

DIFFERENT APPROACHES

Social Studies and Geography

It is a matter of some concern that there are large areas in the world where Geography is not taught as a separate subject. It has lost its autonomy and has been integrated within the History and Sociology group, appearing under the name of 'Social Studies'. The main exponents of this approach are the people of Canada, India, Japan and the U.S.A. It is noteworthy, however, that the first two are starting to bring back more orthodox Geography teaching. The backbone of a Social Studies course lies in the teaching of such items as traditional custom, types of dress, rituals in marriage, religious taboos, folklore, social and economic problems and historical data about composers, artists, and literary figures in the countries concerned. 'How people live' takes precedence over 'where people live'. Physical Geography tends to be much less important than Human Geography and, as the late Professor Wooldridge has said, there is the danger that the 'Ge' may drop out of the teaching of Geography. There is also the grave danger that it will cease to hold its own as a subject, particularly as Physical Geography is taught in the General Science course in some countries and omitted from the Social Studies lessons.

Despite these dangers the teaching of Social Studies offers interesting possibilities and it is easy to see why it has found favour in so many parts of the world. It brings to the forefront that integration between subjects which the more traditional type of teaching has often neglected in the past. The division of subjects into watertight compartments is a natural misconception of most pupils, and they are slow to appreciate the connection between such subjects as History and Geography, Mathematics and Economics. Moreover, at the Primary school level, integrated teaching is particularly valuable and the curiosity of young children can be guided and their imagination focused on people and places both near and far, similar to and dissimilar from those with whom they are readily acquainted. Its successful application will depend very largely on the quality and training of the masters and it is perhaps again unfortunate that there are so many more trained in looking at the world through the eyes of a historian than through those of a geographer.

The teaching of Geography within the Social Studies group is also particularly advantageous when the method of teaching is by project. In many schools today, especially where younger or less able pupils are involved, a particular topic is studied in a variety of aspects and in its Geographical, Historical and Economic settings. Possible topics are suggested by the master and discussed with members of the class, who then divide themselves into groups in order to tackle different aspects of the project. There follows a hunt for information from books, documents and original sources, and the information is written up by one member of the group, who reads out the report to the whole class; often at the conclusion an exhibition is staged to which each member of the class makes some contribution. The project is completed by an objective test.

'Capes and Bays' Geography

In contrast with countries where Geography is not an autonomous subject there are still some areas where Geography is largely descriptive and heavily loaded with names of places and products. Place-names are learnt by heart and their positions inserted on outline maps, which have frequently been drawn from memory. The study of each country follows a stereotyped pattern; position, boundaries, chief rivers and mountains, climate and vegetation, positions of chief cities and lines of communication and a list of the chief products, imports and exports. The method of teaching is often by lecturing and the pupils are passively learning by heart instead of actively imbibing through finding out facts for themselves. This type of Geography teaching frequently results from a lack of textbooks and of audio-visual equipment or from the inadequate training of masters. It will most often be found in underdeveloped countries though this is not invariably the case.

Modern Geography

The third method of approach to the teaching of Geography is found in countries where the subject has gained full recognition for its own merits. Here ample resources are available both in the quality and quantity of manpower and in the adequate provision of the tools of the trade. It is not surprising therefore that the continent of Europe will figure largely in this category. Geography has become a core subject, set in space somewhere between the Humanities and the Sciences, an academic logical study of man in his relationship to his environment. Some countries, counties or even individual schools, may favour a scientific approach; others may swing towards the humanistic concept, but the subject has ceased to receive passive treatment. The Geography room has come to receive its rightful place in the school building. Within its confines are carried out laboratory experiments; its walls are covered with maps and pictures, graphs and diagrams; the pupils are taught by the assistance of visual aids, by lectures, by group work, by drawing, by writing, by listening, by reading. Attention is paid to verbal expression. Much emphasis is placed on field-work and direct contact with reality, and the pupils may spend part of their course with their teachers out of doors studying their own home region or even a region farther afield. In Germany, for instance, town schools often have access to a country building and whole classes of pupils visit it for one or two weeks at a time accompanied by one or more masters in order to pursue their studies in another area. Geography is thus being taught for its own sake, because it is thought that children should know about other countries as well as their own, understand the problems of other people and visualise their conditions of life. It is an exercise in deductive reasoning, like other scientific studies, and the content of its teaching advances according to the mental level of the pupils.

SYLLABUSES

Great Britain is one of the few countries where masters are free to choose the content and method of their teaching, though they are certainly guided by the requirements of public examinations. In the majority of countries it is the State Education Department which delineates the syllabus, and the teacher is required to follow it. In many cases, too, the master has no choice of textbook; these are also selected for him by the Education Authority. Too often in Britain we take freedom of choice for granted, but the lack of it is not necessarily resented in other countries. Some German schoolmasters, for instance, have asserted that they prefer to be relieved of the burden of choosing a syllabus for themselves. Many masters would in fact feel that it was the duty and purpose of the Education Authority to relieve them of what might be considered as an administrative responsibility. Furthermore, within such a syllabus, the position of the teaching of the mother country and in particular of the home region varies considerably. Generally speaking in most countries it occupies the central core of Geography teaching, from which the horizon is widened and the whole world comes into view in ever-increasing circles. The Germans, to give but one example, attach a very great importance to the teaching of 'Heimatkunde' and it occupies a central place in the curriculum. On the other hand, in Britain textbooks for young children may well concentrate on the theme of 'Children in other Lands', in order to stimulate the child's spirit and love of adventure and excite curiosity about the strange and unknown. Many countries, however, have taught little beyond the homeland before the age of twelve, though there is no doubt that the over-study of local environment is restrictive to an immature mind. Unless the master has a wide geographical culture it is difficult for the pupil to interpret local facts and study them with the necessary geographical understanding.

Geography teaching as such begins in most countries at the age of nine or ten. The Regional Geography of the world usually starts about the age of twelve. Very rarely in schools is the subject divided into separate elements such as 'Physical' and 'Human'. Systematic world Geography is, generally speaking, not taught except to the small proportion of the world's children who stay at school longer than eight years, and even then is less popular than the regional treatment. In most countries the use of the globe as a teaching aid begins about the age of ten and is followed a year later by the introduction of the atlas. This will depend, however, largely on the material wealth of the country concerned, and, as mentioned above, many of the underdeveloped countries of the world lack any form of geographical textbooks, let alone globe or atlas. Large-scale topographical maps are not normally introduced until the age of fourteen, except in some countries in Western Europe, where their use precedes that of the atlas. In many countries they do not exist at all.

THE POSITION OF GEOGRAPHY TEACHING IN INDIVIDUAL COUNTRIES: A REVIEW

The difficulty of collecting information about conditions in other countries is very considerable. While a country that deems itself advanced in methods of teaching is often eager to provide material, a less developed one may be somewhat reticent. In the circumstances it is only feasible to review the position of Geography in a limited number of countries. Even in these some of the information is possibly suspect, either because it represents the opinion of particular individuals, or has suffered through over-generalisation and dating. Subject to such reservations the committee is nevertheless of the opinion that a review is most instructive.

France

Rather more emphasis is placed on the physical aspect than in the schools of the United Kingdom, and Geography is having to compete with other subjects in a full curriculum. However, it is firmly established as a subject and is taught for at least one hour a week in the majority of schools. Serious attention is paid to field-work and new and up-to-date textbooks are plentiful. At least one series publishes coloured slides for use with the book. The production of *La Documentation Photographique* is an indication of the trend of thought in the use of visual aids, and great importance is attached to active methods of teaching. Teachers are well trained and specialisation is carried on through universities and professional courses.

Germany (*The Federal Republic*)

The syllabus is made by each of the *Länder*. Regional Geography predominates in the curriculum and General Geography is taught in the last three years only. Active methods, particularly by means of examples, are largely used. Textbooks and atlases are of high order and there is a wide collection of pictures, filmstrips and other visual aids. A large number of schools are equipped with special Geography rooms, and camps and excursions play a regular part in the curriculum. There is also a wide network of Youth Hostels which are used for field-work. Study of the Home Region is undertaken carefully and with meticulous detail, and the study of landscape plays an important role.

India

There are fifteen different States in India, each with its own Department of Education, and it is not surprising, therefore, that there are differences in the syllabus between these different states. Many of the States are unable to embrace compulsory education and few children receive more than five years of schooling. 'As a general rule it can be stated that throughout India Geography is neither taught not studied with that amount of zeal, interest or enthusiasm as it is in Western Europe or the United States' (Dr George Kuryan).

Until 1948 Geography was a separate subject of study in the

Secondary school classes, but since then there has been a change-over and Geography is a part of Social Studies. It is interesting to note, however, that in the two South Indian States of Andhora and Madras the pendulum has swung back and Geography is being taught as a separate subject. But in general the situation is that: 'Geography is losing its ground on the school front and consequently the number of periods allotted to the subject in the school time-table has been drastically reduced' (Shri G. T. Maidamwar).

In the majority of States, where Geography is taught within the Social Studies group, it receives approximately half the time allotted to the group as a whole. Moreover, the main concentration of studies is on India and the influence of geographical conditions in life, primarily in India and secondarily in the neighbouring countries of South-east Asia. There is also an emphasis on the human factor—how people live. Europe and North America are usually only studied as part of the world and not in detail. Where Europe is studied, there is a great concentration on Great Britain on account of her association with India over the past 200 years. There is really little conscious attempt made in the teaching of Geography in schools to interpret India to the West or the West to India. One of the main impediments is the lack of time. Most Indian students have to study two other languages in addition to their own mother tongue, and this detracts from the time and energy available for other subjects. Most schools, too, are ill-equipped, and there are few facilities available for audio-visual aids, weather stations or practical work. Moreover, only a handful of universities in India offer degrees in Geography (only six have professors of Geography), so that the teachers are ill-qualified and the Social Studies teacher will normally be a graduate in History, to the detriment of the Geography teaching.

The methods of teaching are often still outdated and akin to the 'Capes and Bays' Geography prevalent in the early part of the twentieth century. There is also too much reliance upon the assignment of material to be memorised, and in the treatment of Regional Geography there is an emphasis on the Human and Economic aspect. Textbooks are often completely absent, or are unsuitable. Teaching aids are still in short supply and separate Geography rooms practically unknown. On the other hand the value of excursions is appreciated, despite the enormous difficulties of finance and distance, and some schools are encouraging Field Work by classes. Refresher courses in Geography are too seldom organised to acquaint the conservative teacher with modern trends in the subject.

(Prof. R. L. Singh)

Japan

Secondary education begins at the age of twelve and is conducted in two stages:

(1) a 3-year compulsory course in Lower Secondary schools, followed by

(2) a 3-year full-time or a 4-year part-time course, neither of which is compulsory (Upper Secondary schools).

In the Lower Secondary school Geography is taught in the field of Social Studies, which comprises Geography, History and Civics. Between 4 and 6 hours per week are allotted to Social Studies, which varies between 12% and 20% of the time-table. In the Upper Secondary schools a credit system is in operation, under which Human Geography counts one-quarter of the Social Studies programme, which in turn would count for about one-fifth of the total amount of subjects studied for graduation. It will be noted that the Geography so taught is Human Geography, and only that amount of Physical Geography required to illustrate the Human Geography factors is included. Physical Geography as such has its place in the Natural Sciences and is termed 'Earth Science'.

Before the Second World War the content of Geography was often dull and uninteresting and the method of teaching was mainly formal, the pupil being a passive listener. Techniques of this kind may still be found amongst the less progressive and less qualified teachers, but big strides have been made since the war to improve the teaching technique in Social Studies. Subject-matter is now arranged into units of work.

The master will introduce the topics and guide the pupils in study, setting them the work in groups or individually, using original sources, books, newspaper cuttings, etc. There is then a class discussion to correlate the work of the groups, and finally the teacher evaluates the work by test or examination. But the problems of this method are manifold; most classes have fifty or more pupils in them, and few schools have special rooms set apart for Social Studies.

Most teachers of Social Studies in both Lower and Upper Secondary schools hold the requisite Teaching Certificate although only a small percentage hold University degrees in the subject. The standard of equipment is improving annually both in quality and in quantity. Of Lower Secondary schools 70% have projection equipment, 87% broadcasting receivers, 37% tape recorders, 79% large globes, 93% wall-maps of Japan, 92% wall-maps of the world and 80% wall-maps of each continent. In addition, maps on a scale of 1:50,000 are to be found in most schools. Practically every pupil has his own atlas.

In the Lower Secondary school the Geography is taught mainly in the first year and is centred on the homeland. Two-thirds of the time is devoted to the teaching of Japan and one-third to the teaching of regions of the world, but '...too much division into regions or sub-regions should be avoided' (*Established Teaching Guide*, Ministry of Education).

Stress is laid upon the importance of field-work, map reading (place-names should be memorised and blank maps used frequently), and the use of visual aids.

In the Upper Secondary school a comprehensive course of Systematic Geography is followed, with far more emphasis on the world and less on Japan. The bias is still strongly human, but there is an injunction in the official instructions not to neglect Regional Geography, either of Japan or of the world, and to emphasise the problems of Japan in the world.

Japan therefore presents a picture of vitality in its approach to Geography teaching within the Social Studies group. Some teachers make their own filmstrips, teaching aids are obtainable and are used, aerial photographs are studied. Radio and television broadcasts are devoted to Geography and although there is a scarcity of separate Geography rooms much is done to improve the amenities in the normal classrooms.

U.S.A.

Geography is usually integrated within Social Studies and its main purpose is to describe how people live. As such it tends to become ancillary to History, and many of the Social Studies teachers have qualifications in History rather than Geography. The content of the subject varies; there is no central syllabus as each state has charge of the educational programme within its orbit, but, generally speaking, in Primary schools and in the lower forms of Secondary schools it looms fairly large in the Social Studies syllabus. With the higher age-groups it becomes a separate subject, but is not widely taught except as Economic Geography. Of audio-visual aids, well-illustrated textbooks and well-equipped Social Studies laboratories there is no shortage. There is also a wealth of visual material available on loan or purchase and plenty of large-scale maps. The main concern is for the academic standing of the subject and a curriculum guide committee has been formed as a result of a resolution passed at the annual meeting of the National Council for Geographic Education in 1960 'to assist State and local school systems as well as individual teachers in the development of geographic learning in their curriculum'.

CONCLUSION

A great deal remains to be done to put the teaching of Geography in schools on to a healthy foundation. In Great Britain the position of the subject within the school curriculum has been acknowledged, and Geography masters are struggling for better surroundings and more numerous amenities rather than for the recognition of their subject. In comparison with the majority of other countries, however, we are in a privileged position. It appears as if the countries of Europe have accepted the subject for its own intrinsic worth and Geography is being well taught in the schools. But a large part of the rest of the world has not. The British Geography master is plaintive if he has to take the class to another room should he wish to show a filmstrip; a large number of the world's teachers have no access to a projector or filmstrips at all, and there would be no electric socket to provide the power if they could acquire them. We are almost alone in having freedom of choice in syllabus construction. We should therefore feel a measure of encouragement.

APPENDIX A: SPECIMEN SYLLABUSES

The following syllabuses give some guidance to possible methods of approach in various types of school.

SYLLABUS 1; THE REGIONAL APPROACH OF A WEST RIDING GRAMMAR SCHOOL

(First three years)

1. *Size.* 547 pupils, mixed. A full- and a part-time member of staff.
2. *Environment.* Village communities with industrial and market garden interests.
3. *Streaming.* Three forms each year, streamed on ability. Setting occurs in the fourth and fifth years, when some pupils drop Geography.
4. *Length and number of periods.* In the first three years either two or three 40-minute periods weekly. Fourth and fifth forms have two double periods.
5. *Principles guiding the syllabus.* A topic approach within a regional framework is adopted in the lower forms since there is neither time nor is it thought desirable to concentrate on Regional Geography *per se* at this stage. A 'world view' is gradually established. Since some pupils drop Geography at the end of their third year, the lower school syllabus acts both as a self-contained unit of study *and* a spring-board for G.C.E. work.

FIRST-YEAR GEOGRAPHY

Geographical techniques and the home district

1. Subject-matter and simple definition of Geography.
2. Maps. Plan of the school buildings and immediate locality. Explanation of scale, compass points, and simple drawing instructions.
3. Finding the position of the school district in an atlas.
4. Important lines of latitude and longitude in the world.
5. Sample Studies: Longthorpe Lane Farm, Newmarket Silkstone colliery, and dormitory function of the pupils' home villages. When possible, a visit is arranged to the farm.
6. Local weather: how it is recorded. Use of the school's Stevenson screen, and principles of graph construction.
7. Wool textile mills in the West Riding, illustrated by the use of the local 1 in. O.S. sheet.
8. Map summary: Industrial Yorkshire.
9. Location and principal activities of other industrial districts in Britain.
10. Life in the Western Highlands of Scotland, drawing a contrast with the intensively cultivated and industrialised home district.

Selected regions of the world

1. Life in a Norwegian fiord. Glacial troughs. Transhumance.
2. The life of an Italian farmer. Description of the Mediterranean climate.
3. Distribution map, and names of other Mediterranean lands.
4. A Saharan Oasis: Kufra.
5. Distribution map, and names of other hot desert lands.
6. Yam and Guinea corn growers in Northern Nigeria.
7. Distribution map, and names of Tropical Grasslands.
8. A rubber-growing plantation in Malaya—assignment work. (Pupils encouraged to do individual work.)
9. Distribution map of other Tropical Rain Forest areas.
10. Summary map: the world—a stencilled outline completed by the pupil. On it are marked the position of the topic studies, important lines of latitude and longitude, as well as the major natural regions which have been mentioned.

This map is pasted into the back of the pupil's notebook, and is for future reference purposes.

Ordnance Survey work

Work is mainly on local maps. Block diagram contoured sketches are used to introduce 'height'.

Selected topics: South America

1. Physical features.
2. Fold mountains and vulcanism.
3. Wild rubber collecting in the Amazon basin—contrasted with Malayan conditions.
4. Brazil—a coffee fazenda. An assignment.
5. The Pampas—wheat, sheep and beef cattle.
6. Chile—and its climatic divisions.
7. Peru and Bolivia: life of the plateau Indians. The Incas and the llama.
8. Venezuela: oil bearing rocks—an assignment. Some reference is also made to the Middle East in this connection.

SECOND-YEAR GEOGRAPHY

Selected topics: Africa

1. Major physical features, including a simple explanation of the Great African Rift Valley.
2. Climate and vegetation zones. This draws on first-year work, and also involves some comparison of Africa with South America. Convectional rainfall of Equatorial areas is explained.
3. Egypt. Methods of irrigation, including a study of the Aswan High Dam.
4. North-west Africa. A simple map summary.

5. The Sahara. Modern developments contrasted with the traditional way of life.

6. Cocoa growing in West Africa—an assignment.

7. Katanga and its mineral wealth.

8. East Africa: altitudinal zones, and wild life in the savannas. Emergent African countries.

9. Kariba. Economic and political development in Central Africa.

10. South Africa. Gold mining, a brief reference to other economic activities and apartheid.

Selected topics: Australasia

The work on *Australia* is done by means of a project. The following topics are studied:

1. Relief features.

2. Coral building. The Great Barrier Reef.

3. Climates and vegetation. Comparisons are made with Africa and South America.

4. Animal and plant life: 'Australia's living museum.'

5. The Aborigines.

6. The history of settlement. Brief references to Botany Bay and the influence of gold rushes.

7. Sample Study: A sheep station in the Outback.

8. Map of the sheep-rearing districts, and some reference to sheep/wheat economies.

9. Beef cattle rearing in Queensland, and the Great Artesian Basin.

10. Explanatory account: distribution of population, and the state capitals.

11. The White Australia Policy.

New Zealand is studied more formally. The major relief features are noted, and South Island's climate is compared with Britain's. Graph construction. Attention is concentrated on fat lamb farming in the Canterbury Plains. The main towns are also mentioned.

The southern continents: a summary

A stencil outline map is completed by the pupils and pasted into their notebooks.

Selected topics: Asia

1. The Monsoons, illustrated by reference to Bombay. Weather station figures are graphed and contrasted with those of the home area.

2. Rice growing. Sample Study of a peasant farmer's life in western Java, completed by a map of Asian rice-producing areas.

3. Plantation agriculture. Sample Study of a Ceylon tea garden. Assignment work. References to Malayan rubber.

4. Modern industrialisation in Asia: Bombay, Hongkong and Japan. Effects on British factories.

5. Entrepôts: Singapore, 'Cross-Roads of the Far East'.

6. Religions, and the political divisions of the Indian subcontinent.

7. China—Communist reorganisation of an age-old agricultural economy.

289

8. 'Asia's teeming millions.'
9. Completion of an stencil outline map of the continent. This is pasted into the pupil's notebook.

Ordnance Survey work

This continues in the second forms. Landscape description starts. Maps used are of Yorkshire landscapes within a 40-mile radius of the school.

THIRD-YEAR GEOGRAPHY

Selected topics: North America

1. Physical background. Major relief features and pattern of annual rainfall.
2. Wheat farming in the Prairies. A Sample Study. Assignment.
3. Lumbering in British Columbia.
4. Fruit growing in California. Assignment.
5. The great crop belts of the Mississippi Basin. Cotton and maize.
6. The Great Lakes—St Lawrence Seaway, and Lakeside industries.
7. Chicago, market and industrial centre.
8. New York. Its site and development. Assignment.
9. Completion of a stencil outline map, pasted into pupil's notebook.

Selected topics: Europe

Introduction

1. Climates—the coastlands of Western Europe, the continental interior, and the Mediterranean. Weather station graphs, and explanation of contrasts.
2. Natural vegetation, in broad terms a reflection of climate: tundra, conifer forest, deciduous woodland, and steppe.

Western Europe

Increasing emphasis to be placed on individual investigation.
3. Norwegian fiords—their influence on human life. H.E.P. development.
4. A Danish dairy farm. Co-operative farming.
5. Icelandic fishing, and international problems over territorial limits.
6. Map summary: The Nordic countries.
7. Polders in the Low Countries: 'Man's fight against the sea.'
8. Germany and its political divisions. Simple explanation of events leading to present situation.
9. France: diversity of relief and climate. Revision.
10. France: the Lille district. A comparison is made with the industrial West Riding. (The school plays an important part in the annual Yorkshire–Lille exchange.)
11. France: The Riviera and summer holidays. Brief references are also made to other South European resorts of increasing popularity.
12. Switzerland. Causes of economic specialisation.

The Mediterranean coastlands

13. Interrelationships: climate, vegetation and peasant life.
14. The Mediterranean lands: well-known products and places. Map work.

Soviet Russia and the Eastern bloc

15. Eastern Europe—mapped.
16. The U.S.S.R.—its vastness. Physical features and vegetation belts.
17. Wheat-growing in the Ukraine—a comparison made with the Prairies.
18. Collectivisation.
19. Planned industrial development: the Kuznetsk Basin.
20. The Trans-Siberian Railway, and waterways of European Russia.

Ordnance Survey work

This builds on the foundations laid in years 1 and 2. The 1 in. and $2\frac{1}{2}$ in. maps used are of parts of Northern England, Snowdonia and the Cotswolds. By this means it is hoped to stimulate pupils' interest in outdoor activities. A Geographical Society organises one-day field expeditions, and there is an annual Field Studies Camp, held successively at Conway, Whitby and Stratford.

CONSOLIDATION: LOWER SCHOOL WORK

A world outline stencil is now completed by the pupils—with a limited amount of detail. Class- and homework involves the use of atlases, and a simple knowledge of global relief, climates, vegetation, economic activities, countries and places.

To stress the importance attached to this aspect of the syllabus, *one* question on world patterns is set in every examination throughout the lower school.

NOTE: GEOGRAPHY IN THE MIDDLE SCHOOL

Pupils who opt to take Geography in G.C.E. follow a further two-year course. Systematic aspects of the subject are studied in greater detail, as well as the Regional Geography of one continent, and the British Isles. This meets examination board requirements.

Since an elementary knowledge of every continent can now be assumed, there is some flexibility of regional choice for Ordinary level purposes. This can be varied from set to set, or year to year.

SYLLABUS 2. THE SYSTEMATIC APPROACH IN A HERTFORDSHIRE GRAMMAR SCHOOL

(First five years)

1. *Size.* 940 pupils, mixed. Four full-time staff.
2. *Environment.* Suburbia.
3. *Streaming.* Setting begins in the fourths. About 70% of the pupils

continue with Geography, but the grouping is carried out very loosely, thus allowing many good pupils to remain in the lower streams. It is believed that this helps raise general standards.

4. *Length and number of periods.* In the first three years, either two or three per week. Fourth and fifth forms have four.

5. *Principles guiding the syllabus.* The essence of good Regional Geography is synthesis, but, before proceeding to the difficult task of achieving it, systematic aspects are studied. Thus one year is devoted to landscape, and another to climate. A more logical course is possible on these lines than in the piecemeal treatment typical of many Regional syllabuses. Under the scheme all continents are introduced at some time during each of the first four years. Thus, in year 2, though the subject-matter is only a part of Geography (landscape and man), examples are drawn from all over the globe. Year 4 is particularly important. In defending the systematic approach it can also be said to provide an easy transition to Advanced level work.

FIRST YEAR

Aims

1. To give the children some knowledge of the fundamental skills of the subject—particularly the drawing and use of maps of the topographical, atlas and sketch types.

2. To interest the children in peoples and places, particularly by giving them a wide range of descriptive material, thus setting the stage for the more analytical approach of later years.

3. To give the children an understanding of various geographical terms and ideas.

Course

The year's work will consist of a course in simple map reading and construction, together with a series of studies of people in different parts of the world.

Textbooks

Fundamental Geography, Book 1, *Many People in Many Lands*, by D. M. Forsaith.
Philips Elementary Atlas, Middlesex Edition.

Simple map reading

1. Drawing plans—the use of ruler, set squares and the idea of scale. Plans of classroom, house, journeys to school.
2. Measuring distance.
3. The need for symbols and keys—O.S. signs ($2\frac{1}{2}$ in. to 1 mile).
4. Direction—compass points and bearing (clockwise from 0°).
5. The problem of high and low ground. Layer-colouring—contour.
6. Section or profile drawing.
7. Simple land forms—plains, valleys, spurs, ridges, plateaux.
8. Description of a journey.
9. Drawing maps from description (using O.S. signs).

The course should first be worked through using the 2½ in. map TQO9 (Rickmansworth). The class should then be introduced to the 1 in. map (North London) and similar exercises should be done.

Local studies

Subjects covered should include rocks and soils, hills and valleys, weather, farming, industries, settlements and communications. The relationship to other parts of the British Isles should be brought out. Considerable use should be made of local maps, both Ordnance Survey and those on a smaller scale included in the Middlesex Edition of *Philips Elementary Atlas*. Outline maps should be used to give practice in map drawing (layer-colouring, printing, etc.).

Peoples at home and abroad

It is not essential that all of the studies in the list below should be covered. It is essential, however, that such studies as are attempted should be drawn from contrasting environments. A teacher's particular interest or the availability of good teaching material (slides, pictures or filmstrip) is a valid reason for bringing in other topics.

British Isles

1. London: capital city and port.
2. Farming in Britain: (*a*) A Dorset farm, (*b*) A crofting community (Lombain, Applecross).
3. Fishing by trawl and by drift net.
4. A coal miner in Fife.
5. Sheffield iron and steel.
6. Life in a mill town (cotton or wool).

Abroad

7. Eskimos of Baffin Land or the Lapps.
8. Newfoundland cod fishermen.
9. A corn belt farm.
10. A Swiss valley.
11. An Australian sheep farm or a Patagonian sheep farmer.
12. Moscow.
13. Provence—le pays des Primeurs; *or* Vinegrowers of Mildura.
14. Touggourt or the Hadhramaut—life in a hot desert.
15. The Bantu.
16. Yangtze River men.
17. The Semang or Sakai of Malaya.
18. An Assam tea garden.

Where appropriate, the work is to be based on the textbook. It is important to consolidate work by using the excellent series of exercises provided in this book. It is especially important at this stage to use ample illustrative material.

Course

The second year's work consists of a course in Geography based on land-scapes and the associated human response. Together with this will go a series of map studies developing the skills learned in the first year. This work will be upon maps of 2½, 1 and ½ in. scales. The emphasis will be mainly on description, though where the development processes are simple they will find a place. The human response must be brought out in all studies.

Textbooks

Fundamental Geography, Book 2, *The Earth in the Making*, by E. M. Coulthard.
Philips Modern School Atlas.

1. Rocks.

Chief types. A general classification into igneous, metamorphic and sedimentary. Their distribution in the British Isles. The types of scenery, vegetation and land use associated with them. Pictures of various types of scenery in the British Isles. With younger sedimentaries a simple study of the Wealden area using the filmstrip 'South-east England' will be employed.

Brief spells of map reading on O.S. sheets:
Granite—Bodmin and Launceston 1 in.
Gritstone and Mountain Limestone: Buxton and Matlock 1 in.
Weald: Bartholomew's ½ in. Kent; 2½ in. extract, the Mole Gap.

2. Volcanoes

Fissure and central vent eruptions—the products of an eruption, the land forms produced, the distribution of volcanoes.

3. Mountains

Folds and faults. The great fold mountains of the world. Rift valleys and block mountains. A mountain people—Switzerland.

4. Weathering and erosion

5. The work of the wind

Desert land forms and processes. Map study: Nairn and Cromarty 1 in. The distribution of deserts in the world. The Human Geography of a desert—Bushmen.

6. The work of ice

An outline of land forms and processes—highland and lowland. Map study: Ullapool 1 in. map or Argyll ½ in. map. Human study—Norway, a glaciated country.

7. *Rivers*

Land forms: young, mature and old rivers, including estuaries and deltas. Map study: Cardiff, Preston and Lincoln (R. Trent) sheets. Human Geography: (*a*) ancient civilisations—Nile, Tigris, Euphrates; (*b*) rivers as sources of cultivable land—Ganges; (*c*) rivers as highways—Rhine; (*d*) rivers as problems—Mississippi and Tennessee (TVA); (*e*) the growth of towns in river basins.

8. *The work of the sea*

Land forms and processes of: (*a*) erosion and deposition—cliffs, caves, inlets, headlands, stacks, spits, bars, lagoons; (*b*) uplifted and sunken coasts—fiords, rias, estuaries, Dalmatian-type, raised beaches. Map work upon Truro, Ullapool/Argyll, Bournemouth, Dorchester, Isle of Wight, 1 in. sheets, including man's activities. Great ports: study of the chief factors in their growth.

THIRD YEAR

Course

This will be centred on the environmental influence of climate. The factors of temperature, winds and rainfall will be considered in a simple manner leading to an understanding of the broad differences in climate throughout the world. The later part of the course will be devoted to a study of the effect of climate on man in different parts of the world, especially through simple activities such as hunting, collecting and farming. This will lead to an appreciation of the importance of the 'region' in Geography.

Textbooks

Fundamental Geography, Book 3, *Climate, Vegetation and Man*, by L. Hadlow.
Philips New School Atlas.

First term

1. *Position on the globe*

Latitude and longitude. Associated topic—Great Circle routes.

2. *Movements of the earth*

(*a*) Rotation (daily): (i) longitude and time, (ii) day and night.
(*b*) Revolution (seasonal): (i) time, (ii) the seasons, (iii) variations in length of day.

3. *Temperature*

(*a*) Major influences: (i) latitude, (ii) altitude, (iii) distance from the sea, (iv) ocean currents.
(*b*) Secondary influences: (i) aspect, (ii) local winds—Bora, Mistral, Sirocco, Harmattan, Chinook, Föhn.

4. *Pressure*

To be explained simply. The influences of rotation and temperature. The world's major pressure belts. The exceptions to the simple planetary scheme: (*a*) influence of continents, (*b*) swing of the overhead sun.

5. *Winds*

(*a*) The major system of Trades and Westerlies.

(*b*) The exceptions: (i) swing of wind belts, (ii) the monsoonal effect (introduced through land and sea breezes).

6. *Rainfall* (*condensation and dew point*)

(*a*) Relief rainfall.

(*b*) Clouds (dew and frost, types of cloud).

(*c*) Convectional rainfall.

(*d*) Cyclonic or frontal rainfall (*treated simply*).

7. *The weather map*

Simple examples of 'lows' and 'highs'.

Second and third terms

1. *The relationship between climate and vegetation*

2. *Climatic regions*

Each region should be studied in the following manner:

(i) A study of a particular country or area typical of the region. This will include a detailed study of the climate. Graphs are to be constructed and the features shown are to be analysed. The relationship between the principal activities and the climate is to be deduced.

(ii) Generalisations will be drawn and applied to similar areas in other parts of the globe.

Region:

1. Very cold belt—Eskimo and Lapp.
2. Cold belt—Canadian timber production.
3. Cool temperate margins—British Columbia—fish and timber.
4. Warm temperate Western margins—South-east Spain (huertas).
5. Warm temperate Eastern margins—The cotton belt of U.S.A.
6. Cool temperate interiors—Canadian prairies.
7. Warm temperate interiors—Corn belt Pampas.
8. Hot desert—The Atacama desert.
9. Tropical Monsoon—The Ganges basin.
10. Tropical maritime—The West Indies.
11. Savanna—West Africa.
12. Equatorial—West Africa

FOURTH YEAR
Course

The main course will be centred on various aspects of Human and Economic Geography. Parallel to this will run an intensive revision and extension of work on O.S. 1 and 2½ in. maps. During the second and third terms the map work will be largely on interpretation. Landforms will be given a more thorough treatment at this time and the map course will be correlated with this. During the third term, a fast revision course will be done on mathematical and climatic aspects and the year's work will be rounded off with an examination equivalent in scope and standard to an Ordinary level examination.

Textbooks

Fundamental Geography, Book 4. *Man's Work and Needs*, by R. Abbott. *Oxford School Atlas.*
Map Reading, by M. Wood.

A. *Map Reading*

1. *Grammar*

(*a*) Scales: (i) three methods of showing scale, (ii) transposition of one into the others, (iii) apply to 1 in., 2½ in. and continental maps available.

(*b*) Direction: (i) compass direction, (ii) bearings—to be taken as full bearings in a clockwise direction from North.

(*c*) Measurement of distance: (i) cotton, (ii) dividers, (iii) opisometer.

(*d*) Measurement of areas: (i) regular, (ii) irregular—using 1/10 in. graph paper for 1 in. map only.

(*e*) Representation of relief: (i) hachures, (ii) hill shading, (iii) layer-colouring, (iv) contours—use wide range of home and foreign topographical maps for comparisons of effect, e.g. French 1:200,000; British 1 and 2½ in.; Lake District Tourist; Irish 1 in.; 1:1m. International; Swiss 1:50,000. (v) Contour representation of simple relief features. These must include valleys, spurs, escarpments, cols or saddles, passes, plateaux, plains, undulating lowlands, cliffed and low coasts, even, concave and convex slopes.

(*f*) Section drawing: (i) full sections, (ii) sketch sections, (iii) inter-visibility.

(*g*) Gradients: determination as 1 in *x*.

(*h*) Map references: 4, 6 and 8 figure.

(*i*) Conventional signs of O.S. 1 in. (7th series) and 2½ in. sheets.

2. *Interpretation*

Use maps and exercises in textbook. These exercises need supplementing on the following lines:

(*a*) Ordered descriptions of: (i) landform areas—valleys, highlands, lowlands, coasts, (ii) an area seen from some particular viewpoint.

(*b*) Division of a map area into physical regions.

(*c*) Comparisons of photographs and maps.

3. *Map reading and Physical Geography*

Revision of chief topics of physical geography through use of topographical maps: chief rock types (limestones, granite, chalk, clays, young and old sandstones), rivers, glaciation, work of the wind, coastal erosion and deposition, coastal types.

Use textbook maps and exercises but these should be supplemented with full sheets or extracts.

Sections 2 and 3 should run concurrently.

B. *Human and Economic Geography*

The general theme is the distribution of world population through the consideration of man's work and needs.

1. Distribution of racial groups including the meaning of the term 'race'. A simple résumé of the influence of European emigration on the people of various continents.

2. *Ways of life*

(*a*) Primitive communities—three basic groups: (i) hunters, collectors and fishers, (ii) pastoralists, (iii) agriculturalists.

    (*b*) More advanced groups:
        (i) Agricultural:
            subsistence agriculture,
            cash crop agriculturalists,
            plantation farmers,
            market gardeners
        (ii) Extractive and Industrial:
            mining,
            manufacturing industry, e.g. Ruhr, Franco-Belgian.

3. *Production of chief commodities*

(a) Agricultural:
        (i) Chief cereals—wheat, maize, rice.
        (ii) Beverages—tea, coffee, cocoa.
        (iii) Sugar—beet and cane.
        (iv) Animals—beef and dairy products, mutton, pigs.
        (v) Textiles—cotton and wool.

In each case the following should be covered: (i) distribution of production, (ii) reasons for this distribution.

    (*b*) Industrial:
        (i) Fuel and power—coal, oil, H.E.P.
        (ii) Minerals—iron ore. If time permits, copper, gold, tin.
        (iii) Manufacturing industries:
            (*a*) Iron and steel—North-east U.S.A., Western Europe, Britain.
            (*b*) Textiles—cotton in Lancashire and U.S.A., woollen in Britain and U.S.A.

(c) Chemicals in Britain—Tees and Mersey.
(d) Associated industries, including shipbuilding. Emphasis here should be upon reasons for location.

4. *Settlements*

(a) Villages ⎫
(b) Towns ⎬ Analyse with O.S. 1 in. sheets.
(c) Ports ⎭

FIFTH YEAR

Course

The main course in this year is in Regional Geography. The aim is to make a synthesis using the knowledge gained in previous years of the various aspects of the subject. Concurrently, work should be continued on 'General Geography', i.e. material for paper 1 of the Ordinary level examination.

Textbooks

Fundamental Geography, Book 5, *The World*, by L. Brooks and E. M. Coulthard.
Modern Geography, Book 2, *The British Isles*, by D. Preece and H. Wood.
Physical Geography, by H. Dury.
Map Reading, by A. E. Meux.
Philips New School Atlas.

A. *Regional Geography*

1. Set areas for Ordinary level.
2. British Isles.
In each case the detailed regional work should be preceded by an account of the broad relief and climatic features.

B

1. Map work. O.S. extracts should be used together with the questions set in public examinations. With slower groups this stage may not be reached until the second term.[1]
2. Landforms.[1]
3. Climatic regions—their principal vegetational and human use characteristics.[1]
4. Mathematical Geography.[1]
5. Human and Economic Geography. In this section most work will be in the form of a quick revision followed by an examination question.[1]
6. Trade and transport. Use, advantages and disadvantages of each type of transport with localised examples—Suez, Panama, St Lawrence, Rhine.

Note on methods

1. Use statistics to construct
   (a) World map showing distribution of product: (i) dot distribution—

[1] Revision.

299

position of dots within country, (ii) shading method and comparison with dot method.

(*b*) Diagrams—graphs, circle diagrams.

2. Project method useful where information plentiful, e.g. oil.

C

Revision for summer examination:

1. Landforms—as under section A3 of year 4.
2. Mathematical Geography—as under first term of year 3.
3. Climates and vegetation.

SYLLABUS 3. THE REGIONAL APPROACH OF A LARGE COMPREHENSIVE SCHOOL IN THE LIVERPOOL AREA

1. *Size.* 1,850 pupils, mixed. Three full-time and two half-time members of staff.

2. *Environment.* New town housing overspill from Liverpool itself.

3. *Streaming and principles guiding the syllabus.* Since Geography studies 'aerial differentiation' the basis of the courses is Regional Geography, and it is within this framework that the various techniques and special grammar are introduced. Three courses are offered, each designed for three or more forms in the same ability range. Courses must allow, wherever possible, for the movement of children from one stream to another.

(Editorial note: Because of space, only the first-year courses are shown in detail, followed by a tabulated version of the second year.)

FIRST YEAR

Course A

(The first three streams)

This course deals with a few sample areas of the British Isles in particular and of the world in general, chosen not only for their intrinsic value, but also because they provide opportunity for practice in many of the basic geographical skills and help to emphasise both the diversity and unity of the world.

Ordnance Survey maps, sketch maps, diagrams, pictures, descriptions and other forms of geographical data should be included as material which the pupils have to study in order to answer problems.

Section 1. Sample areas of the British Isles

1. *Home Region*

In this study the following aspects may be covered:

(*a*) Map reading: plans, scales, direction, O.S. symbols, ways of representing scales, local sheets of O.S. maps, grid references.

(*b*) Techniques: use of tracing paper and mapping pens, use of colours in map work, use of thermometer, temperature scales, use of the rain gauge, basic ideas of barometric pressure, weather records (weather observations should form an integral part of the course).

(*c*) Physical basis—simple treatment of: weather and climate, different types of rock (visit quarry at Melling Mount).

(*d*) Economic and commercial basis: changes in the local area as seen from maps, information on historical aspects of Kirkby, list of ancient buildings in the area and features of interest, farming (perhaps visit arable farm—Knowsley—and/or market garden—Formby).

2. *Lancashire and Yorkshire industrial areas*

Additional ideas and skills which may be dealt with are:

(*a*) Map reading: ways of showing height, simple section drawing, elementary land forms.

(*b*) Techniques: the interpretation of geographical pictures, use of atlas and index, drawing of sketch maps, use of diagrams.

(*c*) Economic and commercial basis: sources of industrial power, coal mining, textile fibres, and some simple manufacturing processes, transport by land and sea, commercial ports (see below).

(*d*) A special study of Liverpool, including visits:

    (i) Mersey Estuary—tidal range, swift scour, sandbanks, harbour works, anchorages.

    (ii) Docks, e.g. Bootle, methods of handling cargoes.

    (iii) Shipping—types of ship, seamen, pilot service, Liverpool's hinterland, shipping firms.

    (iv) Industries—catering for the needs of the port, e.g. shipbuilding; dealing with imported raw materials, e.g. flour milling, sugar refining, cattle cake manufacture, soap making, serving needs of large population, others.

Presentation of material by maps, diagrams etc:

3. *South-east England*

Consolidation of previous work and special references to:

(*a*) Map reading: 1 in. and 6 in. maps, bench marks, spot heights, contours (contour interval), section drawing and landforms (escarpments), grid references.

(*b*) Techniques: use of maps for different purposes, sketch maps.

(*c*) Physical basis: latitude and longitude.

(*d*) Economic basis: Different types of farming, fruit growing.

4. *South-west England*

Points for special attention:

(*a*) Map reading: 2½ in. and 6 in. maps, relief features—river valleys, peninsulas, rias.

(*b*) Techniques: atlas work.

(*c*) Physical basis: types of rocks, vegetation.

(*d*) Economic basis: farming, fishing villages and holiday resorts, mining and quarrying.

5. *East Anglia*

(*a*) Map reading: if available, study 1 in. O.S. map of Yarmouth and ½ in. Bartholomew's map of Norfolk (layer-colouring).

(*b*) Technique: drawing climatic graphs, more atlas work and sketch maps.

(*c*) Physical basis: erosion, transport and deposition by rivers and sea. (Compare with local examples, e.g. Blundellsands shore—submerged forest, sand dunes, migration of River Alt. Use local 1 in. map.)

(*d*) Economic basis: arable farming, rotations (compare with farms near Kirkby), weather and agriculture (maps), fishing and activities of a fishing port (note fishing on East coast and Dogger Bank).

6. *Highlands of Scotland*

This study should afford more practice in map reading and in the use of geographical techniques, especially the interpretation of pictures, atlas work (e.g. areas in the world with fiord coasts), and the diagrammatic representation of climatic and other statistics.

In discussing farming, the contrasts between the highlands and East Anglia should be brought out and the problem of depopulation should also be discussed.

7. *A farm in Ireland*

Sketch maps and atlas work, the interpretation of pictures and the diagrammatic representation of facts should supplement this study.

8. *London*

The functions of London should be stressed:

(*a*) Capital city.

(*b*) Commercial town.

(*c*) Seaport.

(*d*) Industrial city.

(*e*) Shopping, cultural and amusement centre.

This should involve the study and interpretation of plans, pictures, trade statistics and the atlas.

Sketch maps should be used to show the space relations.

Section 2. Sample areas of the world

In these studies the following techniques should be developed and used:

(*a*) Atlas work—to find positions, distances, routes, and the physical characteristics of the areas etc.

(*b*) Study of photographs. From these much can be learnt of the physical background, the economic activities and the architecture in different areas.

(*c*) Sketch maps—on large and small scales.

The above should come into all studies. The following should be used where appropriate:

(*d*) Extracts from writings, e.g. travel memoirs.

(*e*) Diagrams, e.g. line and circular.

(*f*) Section drawing.

The human approach is the one to be borne in mind in studying these areas but in all cases various aspects of study will be dealt with, as listed below, though not necessarily in this order:

(*a*) Physical background, e.g. landscape, climate, natural vegetation.

(*b*) Land utilisation and occupations. Industry and fishing where appropriate.

(*c*) Architecture, e.g. characteristics of buildings, street plans, etc.

(*d*) Correlations with similar areas, i.e. use of world map; special attention should be paid to latitudes and position in relation to land masses.

(*e*) Comparisons with other areas, especially in the British Isles.

    (i)   A Norwegian fiord.

    (ii) Italian farmers—Mediterranean lands. Travel brochures may help in the discussion of distances and routes.

    (iii) An oasis in the Sahara—hot deserts.

    (iv) A village in Northern Nigeria—savanna lands.

    (v) Rubber from Malaya—equatorial forests.

    (vi) A Chinese village.

    (vii) Wool from Australia.

    (viii) Beef from Argentina.

    (ix) Cotton from U.S.A.

It is suggested that Section 1 should occupy most of the autumn and spring terms, the work until Christmas being mainly devoted to a study of the home district and the Lancashire and Yorkshire industrial areas.

Course B

(The fourth to the seventh streams)

How men live and how they make a living, in a wide variety of environments which the world has to offer, are the basic themes of this course. In order to bring such ideas home to the average Secondary school pupil in his first year, authentic descriptions of actual places and frequent comparison with conditions in Britain should be employed. No attempt need be made to be comprehensive; selectivity is the keynote. The pupil can extend his knowledge, however, by tackling exercises.

The ideas presented should be simple yet thought-provoking, so as to promote individual work by the pupil whenever possible. Illustrations have an equal part to play with the spoken word and the reading of the textbook, and should be incorporated in the work.

The plan involves intimate descriptions of selected, representative places or regions approached through topics which are available for study in the environment of the pupil.

Section 1. Sample Studies in the British Isles

1. *Geography in the home area*

(*a*) Plans of the neighbourhood. (Plans from Liverpool City Architects Dept. will be useful here.)

(*b*) Ideas of scale, direction, their representation on maps.

(*c*) O.S. maps on the district. Ordnance Survey symbols.

(*d*) The investigation of types of shops and the numbers of each type in the area can lead to a plan of the shopping areas and the diagrammatic representation of the results of the investigation. A comparison can then be made with other areas.

(*e*) Lists of foods produced at home and abroad. Use atlas to locate areas of production, and the areas can be shaded on outline maps.

2. *The baker and confectioner—flour and sugar—East Anglia*

(*a*) Atlas work to locate the region.

(*b*) Use a specific farm as an example, e.g. Flowerfield Farm in Suffolk.

(*c*) Further ideas of scale and area, e.g. compare size of farm with area of school grounds (which can be measured).

(*d*) Reasons for wheat growing.

(*e*) Rotation system.

(*f*) The farmer's life and work. The farmer's year. Compare with a farm in the Kirkby area.

3. *The dairyman—dairy farming—South-west England*

(*a*) Specific farm, e.g. Castle Farm in Cornwall, and make comparisons with the farm in East Anglia.

(*b*) Develop ideas of the relationship between climates and types of farming.

(*c*) The connection between the position of milk-producing area and the uses made of milk. Railway routes for transporting milk.

(*d*) Correlations between maps, e.g. map showing areas with many dairy cattle and a map of the actual counties.

4. *The butcher and the greengrocer—meat, vegetables and fruit*

(*a*) Beef—Midlands (use atlas to locate counties), e.g. River Farm in Leicestershire.

(*b*) Mutton and lamb. Consider sheep on farms previously studied, sheep rearing in Wales, e.g. Padam Farm in North Wales.

(*c*) Pork and bacon—relate to the milk-producing areas.

(*d*) Vegetables. Note particularly (i) production near towns, (ii) 'early' vegetables from the south-west of England, (iii) market gardening.

(*e*) Fruit. Map of the areas of fruit production; discuss the reasons for the distribution. Jam and tinned fruit labels can be collected.

(*f*) Atlas work very important.

(*g*) Charts are to be drawn to represent the rainfall at various places in the above areas.

5. *The fishmonger*

(*a*) Types of fish—chart for their relative importance in Britain.

(*b*) Drifting and trawling.

(*c*) Reasons for the good fishing grounds in West European seas.

(*d*) Note the main fishing ports and locate them on a sketch map.

6. *Fuel for cooking—coal, hydroelectric power, atomic energy*

(*a*) Coalfields (map). Special reference to Lancashire Coalfield. Open-cast, e.g. Billinge Hill, and concealed.

(*b*) How coal is obtained.

(*c*) Formation of coal and the different types—their uses.

(*d*) Hydroelectric power in North-west Scotland and North Wales.

(*e*) Development of atomic energy.

7. *The ironmonger—iron and steel industries, etc.*

(*a*) Things sold at the ironmonger's and where they are made.

(*b*) The making of iron—blast furnace.

(*c*) Map of areas producing iron ore and making iron and steel.

(*d*) Where different types of motor cars are made.

(*e*) Shipbuilding areas—especially Birkenhead. Processes of construction.

8. *Clothes for the winter and summer—woollen and cotton*

(*a*) West Riding woollen industry—processes and organisation.

(*b*) Reasons for the development: special aspects—(i) chart to show the origin of wool imports, (ii) routes from the ports to the West Riding, (iii) water—compare with Kirkby's water supplies, (iv) map essential.

(*c*) The Lancashire cotton industry. Map (main towns)—organisation—reasons for the development.

9. *The china shop—pottery and glass industries*

(*a*) The potteries—work in a factory—sources of raw materials, e.g. kaolin from Cornwall.

(*b*) Glass—St Helen's (use official guide), chemicals needed (Cheshire salt).

(*c*) At this stage it might be convenient to deal with the advantage Liverpool has as a port, although it would be discussed in the previous section. Atlases and guide books, etc., should be used to supplement the pupils' knowledge and the results may be expressed in diagrammatic form.

10. *Holidays*

(*a*) Reasons for the fact that it is warmer in summer than in winter. In connection with this topic a record of the length of a shadow of a post (net-ball or flagstaff) should be kept at the same time once a month for a year. A chart can be made to show the results. The shade temperature should be taken at the same time and then a comparison between temperatures and the lengths of the shadow can be made.

(*b*) Types of holidays and the reasons for going to different places. The pupils' own holiday experiences may serve this study admirably.

(*c*) The routes to the various places may be studied as well as the special features of the different places. Here is scope for individual work using guide books, brochures, atlases, etc. A form display may result from the study.

(*d*) Various principles may be dealt with in connection with this study: (i) factors governing routes and settlements; (ii) geographical terms, e.g. mountain, pass, gap, estuary, plain, plateau; (iii) a comparison of the relief with local area may be made, e.g. rivers, heights, etc.

11. *Transport and population*

(*a*) Pupils may make censuses of road transport (e.g. East Lancashire Road), rail transport (e.g. at Kirkby station) and canal transport (e.g. Leeds–Liverpool canal).

(*b*) The shortest railway route to London and the chief towns it passes through.

(*c*) Note the A and M class roads of the district and where they go. (The A.A. handbook will be useful.)

(*d*) Distribution of population (e.g. compare with distribution of main professional football teams). Reasons for the distribution. Chart to show the population of some important towns.

(*e*) Note the population of Kirkby, Liverpool and Lancashire.

12. *London*

Note the reasons for the growth of London as

(*a*) Capital city and centre of government.

(*b*) Centre of communications (note the stations used to reach various parts of the country).

(*c*) Centre of trade and industry (make a list of things at home and at school which have been made in some part of London).

Section 1 should occupy most of the autumn and spring terms and as much local work as possible should be done early in the course. Records, such as those mentioned in sub-paragraph 10, should start right at the beginning of the year.

Section 2. Aspects of North America

1. *Atlantic crossing—Southampton to Montreal*

(*a*) Southampton: description of docks—compare with other British ports, e.g. Liverpool and London.

(*b*) Atlantic crossing: fogs on the Grand Banks—St Lawrence estuary.

(*c*) Montreal: description—position (compare with London and Southampton).

In all sections atlas work is important.

2. *Wheat from the Prairies* (trace route to the Prairies from Montreal).

(*a*) Study of the specific farm (e.g. Popley). Compare with Flowerfold Farm in Suffolk in respect, especially, of the farmer's life and work in relation to the climate.

(*b*) Compare the temperature figures of, say, Winnipeg and London and draw charts to show these.

(*c*) Reasons why wheat grows well on the Prairies. Disadvantages of one-crop farming.

(*d*) Route by which wheat is sent from the Prairies to Britain (globe can be used).

3. *Paper and forest*

(*a*) Lumbering in Quebec.

(*b*) Lumbering in British Columbia. Compare with Quebec in respect of size of the trees and methods of lumbering.

(*c*) Other aspects of British Columbia, e.g. Kitimat Project.

4. *Meat and maize*

(*a*) Locate main cattle-rearing states.

(*b*) Study a specific farm, e.g. Long Lake Ranch in Western Wyoming—the work on a ranch.

(*c*) Fattening of cattle, e.g. Porter's Farm in Illinois. Buildings (photographs). Growing of maize and its uses, pigs, the farmer's calendar, the corn belt—compare with farm on the Prairies and with beef production in England.

(*d*) Chicago and its relations with the corn belt. Rail centre.

5. *Cotton and tobacco*

(*a*) The Mississippi—meanders, load, landscapes, delta. Compare with local streams. Sketch map of the Mississippi basin.

(*b*) Cotton states (locate on atlas map). Compare production with that of other cotton-producing countries (draw a chart to illustrate this).

(*c*) Cotton farming—farmer's calendar, conditions required for cotton growing, picking and processing, dangers, other crops, social system.

(*d*) Tobacco—main growing areas.

6. *Fruit, films and factories in California*

(*a*) Early history of California and its development. Lists can be made of things sold in the shops which come from California.

(*b*) Fruit—oranges, lemons, grapes, currants. Farm in San Bernardino valley—irrigation, truck farming.

(*c*) Film industry—reasons for growth and development.

(*d*) Holiday resorts—reasons. Compare with areas with a similar climate.

(*e*) Power supplies: (i) hydroelectric power, (ii) oil—method of production, compare production with other states in U.S.A. (map) and with other countries in the world (chart).

(*f*) Factories, e.g. airplanes. Advantages possessed by San Francisco and Los Angeles.

7. *Pittsburgh—the meeting of coal and iron*

(*a*) coal mining—advantages of this area, uses.

(*b*) Iron ore—transport facilities (e.g. Lake barges), sketch map of the industrial region, uses of steel.

(*c*) Pittsburgh—compare with, say, Middlesbrough.

307

8. *New York* (compare with London)

(*a*) Description—docks, streets, factories.

(*b*) Space relations—sketch map, introduce ideas of time zones in U.S.A. and the world.

(*c*) Collect cuttings about New York.

Course C

(The remaining four or more streams)

Many of the methods of approach mentioned in the previous courses will be useful in this course, but perhaps more emphasis can be put on visual methods. The children ought to be encouraged to collect pictures, etc., illustrating the topics discussed, and the illustrations should be fixed in the books. Excerpts from travel books or other literary works might occasionally be used to amplify certain points. In any case, a strict adherence to the textbook will probably be found to be neither wise nor practicable. Throughout the course stress should be placed on the making of clear, simple sketch maps.

The themes of this course are the Home region and the British Isles.

1. *Local study*

(*a*) Weather. Simple observations (e.g. wind direction, amount of cloud, approximate temperature, rainy days, length of a shadow) may be made and a weather diary or chart maintained.

(*b*) O.S. maps of the area should be used and the signs used on the 1 in. map learnt by heart. Note: direction and scale.

(*c*) Drawing of simple plans.

(*d*) Contours—gentle and steep slopes. Simple sections.

(*e*) From the above work certain terms should be gained, e.g. bay, confluence, delta, estuary, headland, peninsula, plain, plateau, spur, strait. Models (some made by the pupils) can help in the work and some of the terms might be used in discussing the course of the River Alt.

(*f*) Local farming. Pupils might find out where their meat and milk come from.

(*g*) A simple land utilisation map could be compiled showing many features, e.g. buildings, types of farm land, quarries.

(*h*) Liverpool—docks and goods handled. A traffic census could help here. Water supply.

2. *Cotton industry of Lancashire*

Reasons for its development, sources of raw cotton, Manchester Ship Canal. Towns and processes. This, together with the local study, will probably occupy most of the first term.

3. *West Riding woollen industry*

Sources of raw wool, towns, reasons for the rise of the industry.

4. *Coal mining in North-east England*

Coalfields (including concealed and opencast), work of the miner, uses of coal, shipment of coal.

5. *Shipbuilding in Central Scotland*

Reasons for the industry, towns.

6. *Highlands of Scotland*

Relief (including the results of faulting and glaciation). Climate (especially rainfall), farming (crofters). Hydroelectric power.

7. *Southern Uplands*

Woollen industry of the Tweed Basin. Compare with that of the West Riding.

8. *Lake District*

Compare with the Highlands of Scotland where practicable. Climate—relief, e.g. (i) lakes, their attractions and uses; (ii) The Fells (sheep), rocks (quarrying).

9. *East Anglia* (a lowland farming area).

Compare with farming in the highlands—area, climate. Farming (wheat, rotation system, sugar beet, the farmer's year). Other activities (note their relations with either agriculture or the sea).

10. *South-east England* (the growing of fruit and hops)

Relief (different types of land for different farming activities). Fruit and hop cultivation, towns (resorts, gap towns, ports).

11. *South-west England*

Climate, early vegetables, fruit (cider), holiday resorts and fishing. Kaolin.

12. *Wales* (note the contrasts between the south and the north)

(*a*) South Wales—coal mining (types of coal, mining valleys). Iron and steel and tin-plate industries.

(*b*) North Wales (compare with the Lake District)—relief and rocks (slate and granite), sheep, reservoirs, holiday resorts.

13. *Ireland* (another lowland farming area; compare with East Anglia)

Relief, climate, lakes and bogs (peat, rocks), farming, flax.

14. *General survey*

Relief (highlands and lowlands), climate (winds, rainfall, temperature).

15. *Fishing industry of Britain*

TABULATED SUMMARY: SECOND YEAR COURSES. GENERAL CONSIDERATIONS

During this year regional courses are developed. Opportunities occur to apply the basic principles and techniques of the first year. Side by side with regional studies go further map work and more Physical Geography.

Subdivision...	Course A	Course B	Course C
Remarks	The Regional Geography tackled will be comparative as well as descriptive	Factual content will be less than in course A, and ideas dealt with in simpler forms. 'From the particular to the general' is a maxim to be followed	The step this year takes the pupil overseas—to hot and cold lands, wet and dry areas, giving him a picture of human life lived under varying conditions. The emphasis should not be on place-names and statistics, but on how children elsewhere live, learn and play.
Syllabus	*Section 1. Africa* (details omitted) *Section 2. South America.* The Regional Geography of the Andes and the northern states. Argentina, Chile and Brazil. *Section 3. Australia and New Zealand.* (1) People in Australia. (2) The empty lands. (3) Murray–Darling Basin. (4) Swanland. (5) South and east coast areas. (6) Tasmania. (7) New Zealand. *Section 4. Linking up the southern continents.*	*Section 1. Africa* (details omitted) *Section 2. South America.* (1) Position, size, relief. (2) Climates. (3) Vegetation regions. (4) Life in the Amazon Basin. (5) Coffee growing in Brazil. (6) Cattle rearing on the Pampas. (7) Mineral-producing countries. (8) Chile. (9) Cocoa growing in Ecuador. *Section 3. Australia and New Zealand.* (1) Position and isolation and size. (2) Relief. (3) Climates and vegetation of Australia. (4) Exploration and settlement of Australia. (5) Production and trade of Australia. (6) New Zealand.	(1) Tundra peoples—Eskimos and Laplanders. (2) Life in coniferous forests—lumbering in Eastern Canada. (3) Temperate Grasslands—Prairie wheat, a Russian collective farm. (4) Highland peoples—Navajo Indians, Andean Indians. (5) West European peoples—Norwegians, Dutch and Danes. (6) Mediterranean lands—Spain; California and South Africa. (7) Desert peoples—Arabia and Egypt. (8) Savanna lands—West Africans. (9) Monsoon countries—Indian tea, Chinese rice growers. (10) Equatorial forests; Amazon rubber collectors; Ghana, cocoa. (11) Fishing people—Newfoundland cod and Alaskan salmon.

SYLLABUS 4. THE OUTLINE ARRANGEMENTS FOR A VERY LARGE, MIXED COMPREHENSIVE SCHOOL IN SUBURBAN LONDON

1. *Size.* Well over 2,000 mixed.
2. *Environment.* London suburban; a dormitory area of modest income, but little real poverty.
3. *Streaming.* Each school year is divided into three sections, on a basis of ability. Within each section there are five forms, or subject 'sets'.
4. *Principles guiding the syllabus.* One of the aims is to provide a common core of work for all pupils who are at the same stage in their school career. A topic approach set within Regional lines is thought most suitable, both on educational and administrative grounds.

(Editorial note: Because of space, only a small section of the syllabus follows this introduction. It is hoped, however, that it will be sufficient to demonstrate the major aim mentioned above.)

The full syllabus is prefaced by a statement of general aims and observations. Then the arrangement of work is explained as follows:

Work to be covered during each school year is given under six topic headings. Work on each topic should occupy about half a school term (i.e. about 6 weeks). It will be important to keep to this as closely as possible so that examinations common to all forms can be set as required. Some modifications may be agreed according to the length of terms, other social functions and the nature of the topics themselves (e.g. in year 2 a longer period might be spent upon rice than upon rubber).

The items to be studied under each topic heading are mainly such that work will be divided regionally as follows:

Year 1. Local area and the British Isles

Pupils should become familiar with the use of an atlas early in the year. Introduction to O.S. maps will be important.

Year 2. (a) Asia, (b) Africa, Australia, and New Zealand

These will be studied in reverse order by some forms in order to facilitate supply of textbooks.

Year 3. North and South America

An academic approach will be used increasingly for academic forms. Some of these forms may study regionally all parts of North America.

Year 4. Europe

Examination forms will study the continent regionally.

Year 5. Aspects of World Geography and more detailed study of the British Isles by regions

Examination forms will follow their own syllabus.
Items to be studied are classified as follows:

'E', Essential. It is expected that all pupils will study these items as fully as their capacity allows.

'D', Desirable. As many pupils as possible should also study these items, and certainly faster-working forms will do so.

'O', Optional. These items will be studied by a minority only.

In referring to map work it is pointed out that maps of many types will naturally be used in many ways at all stages of the course. In particular pupils should be encouraged to draw their own sketch maps and diagrams, adopting a clear bold style. Ordnance map study will be included in all years and should be related to appropriate topics and regions in Britain where possible.

This form of syllabus is given as an example in the appendix to *Geography in the Secondary School* by Briault and Shave, published by the Geographical Association. The school syllabus differs from that example not only in details of the topics selected but in the deliberate use of a Regional framework for the topics. The Regional framework was adopted partly to facilitate supply of textbooks, and partly so that a more formal Regional approach may be adopted with some classes if the teachers so desire.

OUTLINE OF THE SYLLABUS FOR YEAR I

Topics and items forming the basis of studies	Section A (Forms in Section B take items to an intermediate degree at discretion of staff)	Section C	Possible aids and devices appropriate to the the work
1. *Maps*			
Atlas and world. Continents and oceans	E	E	—
Latitude and longitude	E	D	—
Sea routes: North Atlantic and Britain to New Zealand	E	E	Ship adoption
Time differences	D	—	Time dials
O.S. maps			
Scale and symbols: local 2½ in.	E	E	—
Scale and symbols: local 1 in.	E	E	—
Use of National Grid	E	D	—
Use of maps in the field	D	D	Excursion
How to draw clearly			
(i) Simple sketch maps	E	—	—
(ii) Simple distribution diagrams	D	—	—
2. *London*			
Local area and London (cf. *Our World*, pp. 5–29, 48–53)	⎫	E	—
Port of London	⎬ Approach may be more regional than by topics ⎨	E	—
Water Supply	⎪	O	—
Weather: London and the school area	⎭	D	School records

Topics and items forming the basis of studies	Section A (Forms in Section B take items to an intermediate degree at discretion of staff)	Section C	Possible aids and devices appropriate to the work
3. Farming and Fishing			
Contrast Highland/Lowland Britain (Tees/Exe) in terms of structure etc.	Related to Physical Geography of Britain. Some regional work on East Anglia and South-west England	—	—
Wheat: simple soil study: East Anglian farm		E	Soil augers, soil pit on field. Sample Study (O.W. 1)
Dairy Farming: farm study		E	Farm visit: Sample Study (Association of Agriculture)
British fishing ports and fishing	D	D	—
4. Coal and Steel			
Locate South Wales, Yorkshire, Lancashire on map of Britain with two or three towns in each	E	E	—
Coal mining: Yorkshire, Derby, Notts. coalfield	E	E	—
Mine layout	E	E	Model
Steel industry	E	E	—
Other industries (except textiles)	O	—	—
South Wales:			
Coal	D	D	1 in. map extract
Steel	D	D	—
Tinplate	O	—	—
Main coalfields, iron ore areas, iron- and steel-producing areas of U.K.	E	—	—
5. Textiles			
West Riding wool	E	E	1 in. map (Britain and overseas), sample specimens
Lancashire: cotton	E	E	Sample specimens
Scottish highlands:			
Relief and climate	E	D	—
Crofts, sheep	E	E	Sample Study
Hydroelectric power	O	—	—
World wool production and trade	O	—	—
World cotton production and trade	O	—	—

Topics and items forming the basis of studies	Section A (Forms in Section B take items to an intermediate degree at discretion of staff)	Section C	Possible aids and devices appropriate to the work
6. The earth's crust			
Types of rock (especially British examples)	E	E	Sample specimens
South-east England:			
North Downs, escarpment	E	E	Model
Weald, transect	D	O	1 in. maps
Mountains and valleys:			
Fold, block and volcanic mountains	E	D	Sand tray, erosion tank and and models
V-shaped and U-shaped valleys:	O	—	
Simple land forms (*Intermediate Map Reading*, by T. Pickles)	D	O	
The Pennines:			
Cross-sections	O	—	—
Plateaux on grit (Peak)	E	—	—
Limestone features	D	—	1 in. maps

A similar pattern is used for years 2 and 3, but in years 4 and 5 many of the pupils follow more formal or systematic courses for examination purposes.

Backward pupils work under teachers catering specially for their needs but they do touch upon the same themes in Geography. As nearly all teaching is done by specialist geographers, detailed guidance upon teaching of each item is not given in the syllabus.

SYLLABUS 5: THE LEAST ABLE BOYS IN A CROYDON SECONDARY MODERN SCHOOL

1. *Size.* 600 boys. Four staff (teaching other subjects also).

2. *Environment.* Suburban, serving partly as a dormitory for London, although there are a number of light, local industries.

3. *Streaming.* Four streams, based upon ability.

4. *Number of periods.* In the first 3 years, three periods weekly, during year 4, there are five.

5. *Principles behind the fourth-stream syllabus.* These are outlined in the following paragraph.

(Editorial note: At this level of teaching, real flexibility of approach is essential. A detailed syllabus would cramp the initiative of the staff concerned.)

Major features which characterise many of the pupils of these forms are: limited ability, especially the ability of reasoning, of turning percepts into concepts, of forming accurate mental pictures from secondary experiences, and of retention; considerable apathy towards any form of mental effort in the fourth year; a slender cultural background, and little sense of social responsibility. Hence:

(i) The amount of material presented will be small. Because of the low powers of retention this material must be presented many times in different guises.

(ii) The material used will be largely descriptive—very little analytical work will be undertaken, especially with younger boys.

(iii) The material must be meaningful to the pupils—they must see a common-sense reason why they should learn it.

(iv) The material must be presented in such a way as to appeal to their limited academic interests—visual aids often have greater appeal than oral teaching.

(v) Experiences must be given which are as direct as possible. These pupils cannot readily transfer material. Films provide greater reality than textbooks; meeting people is more real than being told about them.

(vi) Since their cultural background is slight and they have little knowledge of current affairs, the pupils must be helped to make good these deficiencies—newspapers should be in frequent use in lessons.

(vii) Because of their lack of knowledge, the pupils cannot form true value judgements—they are easy prey to any form of propaganda.

(viii) Most of the boys are not anti-social. Rather they have a negative attitude towards social responsibilities—i.e. a-social. Most are more egocentric than boys of greater ability, and the attempt to create a sense of social responsibility towards a world community must thus be on a personal level—again it is hoped that visitors will help.

(ix) Because school work is often regarded as of little importance compared with the latest style in shoes, television advertisements or strip cartoon, there will be little effort to work unless the master creates interest.

(x) Apart from all this, he has to exert a benevolent type of discipline—firm, but friendly and reasonable.

YEAR I

Orientation and scales

Maps of desk top, the form room, part of the school locality. Study of the local 2½ and 6 in. maps. Orientation and scales. Exercises on local, British Isles and world maps. Considerable time should be spent on the local map to ensure that the pupils are thoroughly orientated within it, and to ensure that there is ample discussion of local factories, products and amenities as well as of local relief and drainage features.

Representation of relief

This is confined to coloured layers as used in the pupil's atlas although, when dealing with local O.S. maps, spot heights and trigonometrical points will be indicated and correlated with the boys' local knowledge. Only if the subject arises spontaneously will contour lines be discussed, and then not to any great depth.

Towards literacy

The rest of the year's work is closely bound up with the work of the English department. Since a large number of the form are barely literate,

315

the work is based upon easily read textbooks which describe journeys about the world. Reading and comprehension exercises largely follow the dictates of the English department at this stage, though atlases are also in constant need in order to ensure that the pupils obtain a fair idea of the shapes and relative sizes and positions of the continents and major countries. Though this stage can easily degenerate into merely 'reading round the class', there is no reason why it should not be useful from the points of view of both the English and the Geography department. The main aim is to assist the boys towards literacy; the subsidiary geographical aim is to give the pupils a sound idea of place, with perhaps some idea of the people who live in those places.

YEAR 2

In this year there is greater emphasis on truly geographic concepts. In the first term the form will follow a television series, e. g. 'People of many lands'. This should sustain interests—continuing Whitehead's stage of romance—and help to provide a basis of greater reality for the work of the following two terms. The series also affords an opportunity for continuing the practice of learning where places are—'Cape and Bays' Geography!

The television series should be followed by a comparison of the places seen in it with the home town. This should be used to remove the idea that 'different' means 'peculiar'. The remainder of the year is taken up with a study of the major geographic regions of the world, Sample Studies forming an integral part of the course. Use should be made of films, filmstrips and those tape-recordings which make use of dramatisation as an aid to reality of experience. Do not use photographs showing merely the unusual overseas—show those which depict coloured people doing the same sort of jobs which the pupils' fathers and brothers do. An industrial area should be included, e.g. North-east United States or the Ruhr.

YEAR 3

Though the effort to inculcate an accurate body of facts continues, there will be greater stress on values, social responsibilities and judgements. In the double period each week a cycle of lessons will be arranged as follows:

(i) An overseas visitor. He will not be expected to give a geography lesson, but merely to hold an informal conversation with the boys. The boys must be able to talk to their guest as well as he to them. Thus the boys will not be dependent only on newspapers for their impressions of other people.

(ii) A film. There are several which will give a vivid and accurate picture of various parts of the world, e.g. 'Major industries of India—agriculture'.

(iii) Either reading a story of geographical importance, but with a theme of exploration or adventure to sustain interest, or discussion and discovery of facts about an item of current but general interest, e.g. apartheid, agriculture versus wildlife in Africa, irrigation in India, the origin of the earth, the growth of population, the effect of industrialisation on underdeveloped countries, Britain as a trading nation.

The single period each week will be spent in following up the subject-matter of the double lesson, e.g. making a sketch of a visitor's home, preparing a written account of a discussion. The third term will be devoted to the Geography of the British Isles. This involves further study of local O.S. sheets.

YEAR 4

The attempt to inculcate knowledge and values will continue, but there will also be emphasis on applying what has been learnt in the previous years—Whitehead's stage of generalisation. Some boys leave in this year. Geography will now be combined with History, to deal with the major powers and more contentious parts of the world. These will largely be discussed in terms of current events, the Geography and recent history of the countries offering explanation. The Geography will be largely regional, but physical geography will enter to explain such matters as floods and earthquakes. In the main, the history taught will be restricted to that of the last sixty years. Constant use will be made of newspapers.

The regions dealt with will be:

> China
> Africa
> U.S.A.
> Europe and U.S.S.R.
> Britain and the idea of the Commonwealth

The Chinese section of the work is appended in greater detail, as an illustration of the intentions.

China (work to cover half a term)

(i) Position on globe and world map. Air routes from Britain.

(ii) Relief—mountain formation and how eroded material forms plains. Lack of stability of the earth's crust. Description of an earthquake (see article in *The Observer* in 1960) and film 'In the beginning'.

(iii) Size of population—bar graphs to compare with India, U.S.S.R., U.S.A., U.K. Distribution of population, tracing-paper map to superimpose on relief map.

(iv) Climate—the monsoons. Contrast climate graphs of Peking and London.

(v) Crops—effect of climate on crops of north and south.

(vi) Early civilisation and nineteenth-century weakness. Foreign incursions, e.g. the Opium war.

(vii) The Civil war and the Japanese war.

(viii) Communist victory in the Civil war. Changes under the Communists—advantages and disadvantages. Communes (Sample Study). Natural resources and industrialisation. The Korean war and Formosa problem. Chinese attitude to 'lost province'. Macao and Hongkong.

YEAR 5

In the last year, work is very closely linked with current affairs. Some topics are matters in the press headlines, whilst others range over more general issues. Much of the work is based on the television series *Spotlight* and from these programmes follow discussion, debate, sketching, map-drawing and written accounts; a relatively mature culmination of the study undertaken in the previous 4 years.

SYLLABUS 6: THE C.S.E. (MODE 3) COURSE OF A BI-LATERAL SCHOOL NEAR SHEFFIELD

1. SIZE. 1,150 pupils, mixed. Four full-time and one part-time Geography teachers.

2. STREAMING. Seven-form entry, streamed on ability after the first year. G.C.E., C.S.E. and non-examination courses are run in the fourths and fifths. The C.S.E. groups are mainly drawn from the D and E forms.

3. LENGTH AND NUMBER OF PERIODS. In the first three years, either two or three periods weekly, dependent on the form. Fourth-form C.S.E. groups have three single lessons a week, each of 40 minutes, while fifth formers have four lessons.

4. PRINCIPLES INFLUENCING THE SYLLABUS. Two criteria have been of particular importance in the selection of material.

(a) Subject-matter must be really relevant to the pupil's needs. It has to be meaningful to them, part of their preparation for adult life. Apart from emphasising local studies, attention is therefore given to some of the great issues of our time. Britain's dependence on imports is also brought out by considering several products in daily use.

(b) Selected material has to be such that it can be presented in an interesting and stimulating way. It has to catch the interest of average 15-year-olds.

The examination involves:

(i) The assessment of two projects, the first more closely guided than the second (20% of the marks); (ii) two written papers, each two hours in length (80% of the marks).

5. THE MATERIAL
Landscapes in South Yorkshire and elsewhere.

(i) Climbing in the Himalayas—the ascent of Everest.

(ii) Mapping—the major mountain ranges in the world (the opportunity is taken to revise other basic facts, including those about the oceans, seas and important islands).

(iii) Vesuvius—case study of a volcano in development and eruption.

(iv) Mapping—the volcanic and earthquake zones of the world.

(v) The landscape round the school. The origin of the coal measure rocks, their use and present-day scenery. Why it is hilly. The South Pennine anticline, and the cutting of youthful valleys.

(vi) Limestone scenery. Potholes and caves in North Derbyshire.

(vii) The work of the sea. Cliffs, headlands and beaches. Blackpool and the coast of Yorkshire.

(30 lessons)

318

Commercial products we use

(i) The oil industry: from drilling rig to petrol station. The Middle East and North Africa. (6 lessons.)

(ii) Timber, pulp and paper: lumbering and processing. Eastern Canada. (6 lessons.)

(iii) Palm oil and groundnuts: vegetable oils brought to Britain. West Africa. (6 lessons.)

Geographical background: some of the current trends and problems in the world

1. *Communism in action: life in the Soviet Union*

(a) Outline physical features and vegetation zones.

(b) Sample Study: 'The Fighter' collective farm near Moscow.

(c) The opening up of Siberia. Hydroelectric power at Bratsk, and young Communist volunteers.

(d) The Volga waterway: multi-functional regional planning.

2. *Race relations: apartheid in South Africa*

(a) The population of the Union, a bar graph.

(b) The case *for* apartheid or 'separate development'.

(c) The case *against* apartheid.

(d) Other countries with racial problems briefly mentioned.

(9 lessons)

3. *Freedom from hunger: life in an Indian village*

(a) Physical background, the Indian sub-continent.

(b) Sample Study: life in an Indian village.

(c) The work of relief teams and United Nations agencies.

(d) Other underdeveloped countries: the size of the problem.

(9 lessons)

Local studies and field-work

'The Peak District National Park'. Apart from any geographical merit, in the strict sense of the term, the opportunity is taken to discuss the country code, and the necessity of planned development of our resources.

The investigation includes field study and the analysis of various books and brochures, as well as map work. Much of the investigation is 'guided' but scope is left for individuality and originality in the work.

(15 lessons plus homework)

Britain: selected topics and areas

South Yorkshire Studies, and their relation to national patterns:

(a) The coalfield. Coal, its formation and occurrence (revision of lower school work). Contrasts between mining in exposed and concealed sections of the coalfield. Types of coal and by-products. Other coalfields in Britain.

(b) Textiles—the development of the Yorkshire wool textile industry, illustrated by reference to the Huddersfield district. Present-day specialisation in the woollen area.

(c) Steel—the making of iron and steel (revision of lower school work). Comparative studies: Scunthorpe, Middlesbrough and Stocksbridge (Sheffield).

(d) Water supplies—the local area, Sheffield, and Manchester. A problem of increasing proportions for the nation.

(e) Summer holidays.
> (i) Northern resorts and reasons for their growth. Major resorts elsewhere in Britain. The need to 'Save our coastline'. Caravans and commercialisation.
> (ii) Holidays abroad. Reasons for the popularity of such resorts. The main areas named.

Selected areas. N.B. The order of subject-matter allows contrasts to be drawn between successive areas.

(a) Life in the Highlands and the Isles.

(b) Shipbuilding on the Clyde.

(c) The Lake District: Sample Study of Stool End Farm, Great Langdale.

(d) The Industrial West Midlands: the motor-car belt, the motor-car as a product of the 'assembly' industry.

(e) Wales: accounting for the uneven distribution of population in the Principality.

(f) The Fens. Land reclamation and arable farming.

(g) Devon and Cornwall. Early flowers and vegetables. Holiday towns.

(h) East Anglia. Crop rotation systems.

(i) London and the pull of the south-east.

Pupils are required to submit a second project in this their final year. They choose a systematic or regional subject set within the British Isles. They are encouraged to specialise on topics of which they have first-hand knowledge or can investigate in the field.

6. THE POSITION OF MAP WORK IN THE SYLLABUS. O.S. maps are used in connection with the work on landscapes, the Peak Park, and Britain. The standard of map work is fairly elementary, and the emphasis, wherever possible, is on its practical use. A knowledge is expected of:

(a) Scales, six-figure grid references, compass points and orientation.

(b) Landscape description from particular points of view. This involves the recognition of simple landforms, patterns of vegetation, settlement and other signs of human activity.

(c) Route planning.

The majority of 'map extracts' are of districts adjoining the home area, or within a day's bus/car ride of it. Petrol company touring maps are sometimes used in conjunction with O.S. publications to illustrate British topics.

APPENDIX B: A BIBLIOGRAPHY
OF METHOD

This bibliography concerns only the method of teaching Geography. Most of the books and periodicals listed are available for loan through:
(1) The libraries of the various Institutions of Education.
(2) The library of the Geographical Association.
(3) Local public libraries via the Inter-Library lending service.

Abbreviations

Geog. Teacher	*Geographical Teacher*
Geog.	*Geography* (succeeded *Geog. Teacher* in 1927).
J. of G.	*Journal of Geography*
Vis. Ed.	*Visual Education*
O.P.	Out of Print
R.P.	Reprinted

Details of all the periodicals mentioned in the bibliography can be found in the section on References.

GENERAL AIMS AND PRINCIPLES

Balchin, W. G. V. 'Seventy years of geography: linking science and humanities', *Times Ed. Supp.* (4 Apr. 1958), p. 534.

Bowman, I. *Geography in Relation to the Social Sciences.* Charles Scribner's Sons Ltd., 1934. O.P.

Coleson, E. 'The application of educational theory to the teaching of geography', *J. of G.* LIII (Nov. 1954), 346–50.

Dawson, J. A. 'Teaching about U.N.O. The Geography teacher's contribution', *Geog.* XLIV (Jan. 1959), 34–7.

Fleure, H. J. 'Sixty years of geography and education', *J. of G.* LX (Dec. 1961), 422–7.

Geographical Association. 'Report on...the alleged overlap of the work in the sixth form and first year university courses in geography', *G.A. Supplementary Papers*, No. 1. 1962.

Geographical Association. 'Memorandum submitted to the Central Advisory Council of the M. of E. "to consider the education between the ages of 13 and 16 of pupils of average or less than average ability... following full-time courses..."', *Geog.* XLVII (Jan. 1962), 63–71.

Geographical Association. 'The place of geography in the education of boys and girls of 15 to 18 years', *Geog.* XLII (July 1957), 174–81.

Griffin, P. F. 'Secondary school geography and the needs of our times', *J. of G.* LII (Feb. 1953), 60–7.

High, J. 'Geography: co-ordinating element in secondary social studies', *J. of G.* LIX (Sept. 1960), 270–8.

Hill, W. 'New developments in geographical education', *J. of G.* LIX (May 1960), 234–8.

Honeybone, R. C. 'Balance in geography and education', *Geog.* XXXIX (Apr. 1954), 91–101.

Honeybone, R. C. 'Geography and international understanding', *Education Libraries Bull.* no. 13 (spring 1962), 9–12.

Kennamer, L. G. 'Beginnings in Geographic Education', *J. of G.* LII (Feb. 1953), 72–7.

Kimber, G. C. 'The place of geography in a general education programme', *J. of G.* XLVIII (Oct. 1949), 265–75.

Marchant, E. C. 'Geography in education in England and Wales', *Geog.* XLIX (July 1964), 175–86.

Marchant, E. C. and Heaton, P. R. 'Geography in 1962', *Education,* CXIX (26 Jan. 1962), 161–6.

Morris, J. A. 'Reality in geographical education', *Geog.* LI (Apr. 1966), 87–98.

Royal Geographical Society. 'Geography in education', *Geographical Journal,* CXXI (June 1955), 190–6.

Scarfe, N. V. 'Geographic education and teaching method', *J. of G.* LV (Feb. 1956), 57–67.

Scarfe, N. V. 'Geography across the curriculum', *J. of G.* LVIII (March 1959), 111–21.

Scarfe, N. V. 'Our educational environment and geography teaching', *J. of G.* LIX (March 1960), 103–12.

Shawkey, A. M. 'Contributions of high school geography to education for citizenship', *J. of G.* XLVI (Oct. 1947), 257–63.

Unesco. *Source Book for Geography Teaching.* Longmans, 1965.

University of London Institute of Education. 'Education for world understanding in secondary schools: a bibliography', *Education Libraries Bull.* no. 15 (autumn 1962), 15–23.

SYLLABUS

The Atlantic Treaty Organisation. *Transatlantic Understanding in the schools.* Atlantic Treaty Organisation, London, 1960. 2*s.*

British Association. 'Geology in schools', *The Advancement of Science* (Mar. 1957). Offprint available, 1*s.*

Becker, H. F. and Lichton, E. S. Preliminary report of the Curriculum Committee of the National Council of Geography Teachers. 1, *J. of G.* XLIV (Feb. 1945), 51–79; 2, *J. of G.* XLIV (Mar. 1945), 105–25.

Campbell, F. J. 'A report on the "A" level syllabus', *Geog.* XLIV (Nov. 1959), 262–3.

Geographical Association. 'Report on ...the alleged overlap of the work in the sixth form and first year university courses in geography', *G.A. Supplementary Papers,* no. 1 (1962).

Greensmith, J. T. 'The introduction of geology into the secondary modern school curriculum', *School Science Review,* 140 (Nov. 1958), 104–108.

Howarth, O. J. R. 'The Commonwealth in the geography syllabus', *Geog.* XXXIX (Jan. 1954), 5–12.

International Geographical Union. 'The teaching of geography and the adaptation of syllabuses to the mental level of pupils', preliminary report of the I.G.U. Commission on the teaching of geography. Montreal 1960. Printed by Dennoyer, Geppert Co., Chicago.

Jennings, J. H. 'The regional content of secondary school geography', *Geog.* XLVI (Nov. 1961), 338–42.

Jones, P. A. 'Meteorology in schools; a discussion of its value and practice', *Geog.* XXXIX (July 1954), 182–8.

Long, I. L. M. I, 'Geography in the Secondary Technical School'; II, 'Geography in the Secondary Grammar School', in *Handbook for Geography Teachers*, pp. 31–53. Methuen, 1964.

Lyons, H. R. 'Local geography and the five year course in a grammar school', *Geog.* XXXIV (Apr. 1949), 65–8.

Royal Geographical Society. 'Geography and social studies in schools', *Geographical Journal*, CXV (Oct.–Dec. 1950), 221–4.

Scarfe, N. V. 'Geography across the curriculum', *J. of G.* LVIII (Mar. 1959), 111–21.

Shave, D. W. *Geography in the Secondary Modern School*, pp. 25–31. Methuen, 1960. (Handbook for geography teachers.)

Swainson, B. M. 'An enquiry into the likes and dislikes of elementary school children in geography', *Geog.* XXIV (1939), 109–25.

UNESCO. *A comparative study of curricula in history, geography and social studies.* UNESCO, 1951.

UNESCO. *History, geography and social studies; a summary of school programmes in 53 countries.* UNESCO, 1953.

University of Birmingham. Report of an enquiry into the suitability of G.C.E. 'A' Level syllabuses in Science as a preparation for direct entry into First Degree Courses in the Faculty of Science. 1959 (includes sections on geography and geology).

Wilson, V. 'Teaching geology in schools', *Proc. Geologists' Ass.* LVIII (1947), 1–44.

Wilks, H. C. 'A scheme of field work throughout a school', I, *Geog.* XLI (Jan. 1956), 15–24; II, *Geog.* XLI (Apr. 1956), 108–13.

CLASS METHOD—GENERAL

Books and pamphlets

Barnard, H. C. *Principles and Practice of Geography Teaching.* U.T.P., 1949. O.P.

Bradford, E. J. G. *School Geography.* Benn, 1925. O.P.

Briault, E. W. H. and Shave, D. W. *Geography in and out of School: Suggestions for the Teaching of Geography in Secondary Schools.* Harrap, 1960.

B.O.A.C. Air Age Education Booklet, 1960.

Fairgrieve, J. *Geography in School.* 6th ed. U.L.P., 1949. O.P.

Ford, E. *Some Smaller Countries of the World: Suggestions for a Geography Project.* Evans, 1961.

Garnett, O. *Fundamentals in School Geography: a Book for Teachers and Students in Training.* 2nd ed. Harrap, 1949. R.P. 1960.

Gopsill, G. H. *The Teaching of Geography.* 2nd ed. Macmillan, 1961. R.P. 1962.

James, P. E. (ed.). *New Viewpoints in Geography.* 29th Yearbook of the National Council for the Social Studies. Washington D.C. 1959.

Kohn, C. F. *Geographic Approaches in Social Education.* 19th Yearbook of the National Council for the Social Studies. Washington D.C. 1948.

International Geographical Union. 17th International Geographical Congress. Report of the Commission on The Teaching of Geography. Washington, 1952.

I.G.U. 18th International Geographical Congress. Report of the Commission on The Teaching of Geography. New York, 1956.

I.G.U. 19th International Geographical Congress. Report of the Commission on The Teaching of Geography. Chicago, 1960.

I.G.U. 20th International Geographical Congress. Report of the Commission on the Teaching of Geography, London, 1964.

L.C.C. Education Committee. Report of a conference on the teaching of geography in London elementary schools. L.C.C. 1911.

Long, M. 'The teaching of Geography. A Review of recent British research and investigations', *Geog.* XLIX (July 1964), 192–205.

Long, M. (ed.). *Handbook for Geography Teachers.* 5th ed. Methuen, 1964.

Ministry of Education (G.B.). *Geography and Education.* H.M.S.O. 1960.

National Council of Geography Teachers. *Geography in the High School* (A compendium of selected articles from the *Journal of Geography*). McKnight and McKnight, Bloomington, Illinois, 1949.

Peattie, R. *The Teaching of Geography; a Dynamic Approach...*Appleton–Century–Crofts, New York, 1950.

Scarfe, N. V. *A Handbook of Suggestions on the Teaching of Geography.* UNESCO, Paris, 1958.

Scottish Education Department. *Geography in Secondary Schools.* H.M.S.O. Edinburgh, 1951. R.P. 1958.

Scottish Education Department. *Junior Secondary Education.* H.M.S.O. Edinburgh, 1955.

Scottish Education Department. *Teaching in Secondary Schools; Report on Geography.* H.M.S.O. Edinburgh, 1957.

Thomas, H. G. *Teaching Geography.* Ginn. Rev. ed. 1961.

Thralls, Z. A. *The Teaching of Geography.* Appleton–Century–Crofts, New York, 1958.

UNESCO. 'Some suggestions on the teaching of geography', *Towards World Understanding*, no. 7. UNESCO, Paris, 1951.

UNESCO. *Source book for Geography Teaching.* Longmans, UNESCO, 1965.

Walker, J. *Aspects of Teaching Geography in Schools.* Oliver and Boyd, 1953.

Wallis, B. C. *The Teaching of Geography.* 2nd ed. Cambridge University Press, 1939. O.P.

Whipple, G. M. (ed.). '*The Teaching of Geography*', *The 32nd Yearbook of the National Society for the Study of Education.* Chicago University Press, 1933. R.P. 1954.

Wood, G. A. *Geography in Schools.* Blackie, 1957.

Articles

Allen, H. C. 'Geography in the Secondary Modern School', *Times Ed. Supp.* (25 Apr. 1958), p. 642.

Becker, H. F. and Lichton, E. S. 'Preliminary report of the Curriculum Committee of the National Council of Geography Teachers', I, *J. of G.* XLIV (Feb. 1945), 51–79; II, *J. of G.* XLIV (Mar. 1945), 105–25.

Boscow, H. 'Geography in the secondary modern school', *Geog.* XXXII (Jan. 1947), 13–17.

Briault, E. W. H. 'Geography in the secondary modern school', *Journal of Education*, LXXXVII (Feb. 1955), 50–4.

Brocklebank, R. S. G. 'Pupil's approach to geography', *Geog.* XVII (Sept. 1932), 204–16.

Brooks, L. *et al.* 'Modern classroom technique', *Geog.* XXX (Jan. 1945), 20–7.

Brooks, L. 'Some thoughts on present day teaching of geography in schools', *Geog.* XXXVII (Apr. 1952), 63–71.

Fairgrieve, J. 'Can we teach geography better?', *Geog.* XXI (1936), 1–17.

Geographical Association. 'Memorandum on geography teaching', *Geog.* XLVII (Jan. 1962), 63–71.

Gardner, C. P. 'Geography in the secondary modern school', *Geog.* XXXII (Sept. 1947), 143.

Heamon, A. J. 'Geography teaching in a comprehensive school', *Geog.* XLII (Nov. 1957), 244–9.

Honeybone, R. C. 'Balance in geography and education', *Geog.* XXXIX (Apr. 1954), 91–101.

Jay, L. J. 'Textbooks for secondary schools: new titles and trends', *Geog.* XLIII (Jan. 1958), 47–50. Similar articles by Mr Jay have been published annually in *Geog.* since 1961. (1962 by F. J. Campbell.)

Jay, L. J. 'The training of geographers; report of a discussion', *Geog.* XLV (Jan.–Apr. 1960), 120–2.

Miller, J. G. 'Why geography?', *Bull. of the University of Nottingham Inst. of Ed.* (Jan. 1962), pp. 3–8.

Reswick, A. 'An inventory of motivating possibilities for the teaching of geography', *J. of G.* LVII (Sept. 1958), 306–8.

Sauvain, P. 'Lively geography', *Schoolmaster* (24 June, 1, 8, 15, 22, 29 July, 12, 19 Aug. 1960). A series of articles.

Scarfe, N. V. 'The teaching of geography in schools: a review of British research', *Geog.* XXXIV (June 1949), 57–65.

Shepherd, W. H. 'A one day conference on the teaching of geography; a report', *Geog.* XLV (Nov. 1960), 300–3.

Suggate, L. S. 'Aspects of geography teaching in the grammar school', *Geog.* XLI (Jan. 1956), 1–14.

Thralls, Z. A. 'The importance of developing geographic concepts', *J. of G.* LIX (Sept. 1960), 279–82.

Wooldridge, S. W. 'On taking the "GE-" out of geography', *Geog.* XXXIV (Jan. 1949), 9–18.

APPENDIX B

CLASS METHOD—PARTICULAR

Bailey, P. J. M. 'Teaching Regional Geography. The Synthetic Landscape Method', *Geog.* XLVIII (July 1963), 285–92.

Bramwell, R. D. 'Sample studies: a new method in geography', *Journal of Durham Inst. of Ed.* (Jan. 1962), pp. 87–90.

Brearley, D. 'The use of charter flights in the teaching of geography', *Geog.* LI (Jan. 1966), 42–9.

Van Burkalow, A. 'Teaching map projections in introductory geography courses', *J. of G.* LIV (Feb. 1955), pp. 82–8.

Coleson, E. 'Teaching locational geography on the elementary level', *J. of G.* LI (Apr. 1952), 147–51.

Conoyer, J. W. 'Why not a geographic exchange club?', *J. of G.* XLVIII (Nov. 1949), 337–40.

Course, E. A. 'Railway geography in the secondary modern school', *Geog.* XL (Jan. 1955), 40–6.

Cramer, R. E. 'Learning through international correspondence', *J. of G.* L (Oct. 1951), 288–94.

Crisler, R. M. 'Automobile licences as visual aid material in the teaching of geography', *J. of G.* XLVIII (Mar. 1949), 120–2.

Dean, L. 'A sixth grade travels in lands overseas', *J. of G.* LII (Sept. 1953), 239–48.

Dissanaike, A. W. 'A teaching note on the apparent movement of the sun', *Geog. Teacher*, XII (autumn 1924), 445–7.

Dury, G. H. 'Rivers in geographical teaching', *Geog.* XLVIII (Jan. 1963), 18–30.

Fisk, E. 'Exploration and geography', *Geog.* XVI (June 1931), 144–9.

Foster, R. J. 'Individual projects in grammar school geography', *Geog.* XXXV (Nov. 1950), 185–90.

Fuller, S. 'A teaching unit on the Polar Regions', *J. of G.* LVIII (Sept. 1959), 294–9.

Haddon, J. 'Newspapers in the geography class', *Geog.* XXXVI (Apr. 1951), 124–7.

Hall, G. S. 'Regional geography in the grammar school', *Geog.* XLIII (Nov. 1958), 259–63.

Hallworth, H. J. 'Group work in the teaching of geography', *Educational Review*, VII (Feb. 1955), 124–33.

Higgins, L. S. 'The Geographical Association and geography in the modern school', *Geog.* XXXII (1947), 17–20.

Hill, J. W. N. 'Film use in the lesson', *Geog.* XLV (1960), 90–7.

Hill, R. T. 'Postage stamps: a useful teaching aid', *J. of G.* LV (Mar. 1956), 144–9.

Howarth, O. J. R. 'The Commonwealth in the geography syllabus', *Geog.* XXXIX (Jan. 1954), 5–13.

James, L. B. 'The daily geographic news: a pupil newspaper', *J. of G.* LI (Apr. 1952), 151–6.

James, L. B. 'The mystery country—a lesson in the reading of graphs and statistics', *J. of G.* LI (Sept. 1952), 231–5.

326

Jay, L. J. 'Sketch maps and geography teaching: the emergence of a technique', *Researches and Studies*, xv (Jan. 1957), 53–61.

Jay, L. J. 'Experimental work in school geography', *Geog.* xLv (July 1960), 205–13.

Jennings, J. H. 'The regional content of secondary school geography', *Geog.* xLvi (Nov. 1961), 338–42.

Johnson, H. B. 'Geography from the grocery shelf', *J. of G.* LIII (Nov. 1954), 341–6.

Kapp, R. and Kapp, J. G. 'On teaching how the tides are produced', *School Science Review*, xLi (Mar. 1960), 281–90.

Lichton, E. S. 'Iron and Steel: a high school unit in world geography', *J. of G.* xLv (May 1946), 188–94.

Lichton, E. S. 'All the world makes dough: a teaching unit in intergroup relations through geography', *J. of G.* LIX (Oct. 1960), 317–21.

McIntosh, C. B. 'Geography in the grocery store (group work)', *J. of G.* LXIV (Mar. 1965), 123–6.

Naidu, R. D. 'Changing attitudes in the teaching of geography with special emphasis on the sample method', *J. of G.* LXII (Feb. 1963), 66–73.

Nicholson, J. E. 'A project on transport', *Geog.* xxix (Dec. 1944), 123–5.

Oliver, J. L. 'Directories and their use in Geographical enquiries', *Geog.* xLix (Nov. 1964), 400–9.

Phillips, M. V. 'Methods to improve skill in the use of a geography vocabulary at high school level', *J. of G.* Lv (Nov. 1956), 369–74.

Phillips, M. V. 'Making effective use of current events in a high school geography class', *J. of G.* Lvi (Feb. 1957), 70–4.

Proctor, N. 'Using block diagrams in teaching geography', *Geog.* xLviii (Nov. 1963), 393–8.

Proctor, N. 'Philately and geography teaching', *Geog.* L (Apr. 1965), 134–41.

Prudden, H. C. 'Classroom work on the daily weather report', *Geog.* xxxix (July 1954), 188–91.

Ray, J. B. 'A dramatized radio programme', *J. of G.* LIII (Oct. 1954), 307–9.

Rees, H. 'Lloyd's list as a source for port study in schools', *Geog.* xL (Nov. 1955), 249–54.

Robertson, B. S. and Long, M. 'Sample studies: the development of a method', *Geog.* xLi (Nov. 1956), 248–59.

Roberts, F. L. *History and Geography with Postage Stamps of the British Commonwealth*. Crowther, 1948.

Rutan, E. J. 'Learning the language of geography', *J. of G.* xLv (May 1946), 204–6.

Schauer, V. P. 'Teaching children to read the geography textbook', *J. of G.* xLiv (Oct. 1945), 279–87.

Shorter, A. H. 'An experiment in using accounts of voyages of cargo ships for the teaching of geography', *Geog.* xxi (Mar. 1936), 41–7.

Simons, M. 'Geography teaching without textbooks', *Journal of the University of Durham Inst. of Ed.* (Nov. 1961), pp. 48–9.

Skinner, C. J. 'Ship adoption in a Midlands school', *Geog.* xLix (Apr. 1964), pp. 123–6.

Small, R. J. 'Some criticisms of the teaching of geomorphology at "A" level', *Geog.* LI (Jan. 1966), 29–37.

Swainson, B. M. 'An enquiry into the likes and dislikes of elementary school children in geography', *Geog.* XXIV (June 1939), 109–25.

Symonds, C. 'A geography assignment and some of the results', *J. of G.* XLIX (Apr. 1950), 159–64.

Taylor, H. M. 'The use of problem solving groups in teaching geography', *J. of G.* LIX (Apr. 1960), pp. 187–9.

Tiller, S. W. 'An experiment in teaching geography to a class of backward children', *Geog.* XIX (March 1934), 132–9.

University of Southampton, Institute of Education Library. *Sample Studies: a Bibliography.* 1960. 1*s.*

Vent, H. 'The seminar and its modifications as teaching methods in geography', *J. of G.* LVII (Jan. 1958), 29–31.

White, J. T. 'The "Land Grant" as a lesson in map reading', *Geog.* XLVIII (Apr. 1963), 181–3.

Wood, H. R. 'A teaching note on the relations of sun and earth'. *Geog. Teacher,* XIII (autumn 1925), 225–6.

PRACTICAL GEOGRAPHY

Anderzhon, M. L. 'Observing the position of the sun through a systematic recording of shadows', *J. of G.* XLIV (Dec. 1945), 355–8.

Ahern, J. H. *Miniature Landscape Modelling.* Rev. ed. Percival Marshall, 1955. R.P. 1962.

Atkins, K. G. 'Making a school tellurion', *Vis. Ed.* (Mar. 1958), pp. 22–3.

Balchin, W. G. V. 'Local climatic studies for schools', *Geog.* XXXIII (Sept. 1948), 128–36.

Balchin, W. G. V. and Richards, A. W. *Practical and Experimental Geography.* Methuen, 1952. O.P.

Barker, E. J. *Modelling Geography.* Ginn, 1954, R.P. 1963 (a pamphlet).

Barton, T. F. 'Teaching soil in the lower grades', *J. of G.* XLV (Nov. 1946), 309–16.

Barton, T. F. 'Collecting and visualizing precipitation data in schools', *J. of G.* LI (Jan. 1952), 23–30.

Birch, T. W. 'Constructive and creative work in geography', *Geog.* XXVIII (Jan. 1943), 19–25.

Carr-Gregg, R. H. C. 'Meteorology and climatology in schools. The Lea Valley Climatological Survey', *Geog.* XLVI (Nov. 1961), 307–14.

Dan Mal Mathur. 'Construction of a simple model for teaching interpretations of contour lines', *J. of G.* LI (Sept. 1952), 245–7.

Dixon, L. and Browning, B. R. *Cardboard modelling.* Vol. 1. *History and Geography,* Pitman. R.P. 1950.

Eves, J. *Model Making in Schools.* Batsford, 1961.

Flierl, H. H. 'A movable date line chart', *J. of G.* LXII (Apr. 1963), 175–7.

Gerlach, A. C. 'Soil profile section', *J. of G.* XLVIII (Nov. 1949), 344–9.

Gopsill, G. H. and Beesley, F. *Practical Geography.* Macmillan.

Harder, C. H. *et al.* 'Prelude to the long summer; a study of weather in the Vale of Mowbray', *School Science Review*, XLI (June 1960), 401–7.

Hess, M. 'Recipe for a papier mâché relief map', *J. of G*. LVIII (Dec. 1959), 457.

Higgins, A. L. *Elementary Surveying*. Longmans, 1943. R.P. 1960.

James, L. B. 'How to prepare and evaluate materials for students' exhibits', *J. of G*. LVIII (May 1959), 251–5.

Jones, P. A. 'Meteorology in schools', *Geog*. XXXIX (July 1954), 182–8.

Kennamer, L. 'Visualisation of latitude and longitude', *J. of G*. LXI (Jan. 1962), 9–11.

Kramer, F. L. 'A teaching aid for the International Date Line', *J. of G*. LI (Nov. 1952), 337–8.

Kuester, S. 'Starch and detergent relief models', *J. of G*. LVIII (Jan. 1959), 44.

Lebon, J. G. H. 'Notes on the construction of simple meteorological instruments', *Geog*. XXIV (1939), 187–9.

Lismer, W. and Playle, M. *Handicraft and Physical Geography*. Pitman, 1934. O.P.

McMichael, J. A. 'A cyclic experiment in teaching astronomical geography', *Geog. Teacher*, VI (spring 1911), 49–52.

Miller, E. E. and Burnham, R. C. 'A simple rain gauge', *J. of G*. XLIX (March 1950), 121–2.

Pedgley, D. E. 'Running a school weather station', *Weather*, XVII (Feb. 1962), 41–53.

Proctor, N. 'Philately and Geography teaching', *Geog*. LXV, 134–41.

Prudden, H. C. 'Classroom work on the daily weather report', *Geog*. XXXIX (July 1954), 188–91.

Sanders, E. M. 'Use and construction of models and block diagrams', *Geog. Teacher*, X (autumn 1919), 107–12.

Schon, A. *The Construction and Drawing of Block Diagrams*. Nelson, 1962. 5s.

Sewell, G. K. 'Model making in school', I, *Vis. Ed*. (Dec. 1960), 2–10; II, *Vis. Ed*. (Jan. 1961), 2–11; III, *Vis. Ed*. (Feb. 1961), 7–15.

Smith, J. and Jones, T. F. *Handwork Methods in the Teaching of Geography*. Wheston, 1941. O.P.

Spary, V. C. 'Weather records in the concrete', *Geog. Teacher*, XI (autumn 1921), 149–50.

Stevens, G. and Bell, R. 'Construction and operation of a low cost scientifically sound weather station for the 5th and 6th grades', *J. of G*. LII (Nov. 1953), 324–30.

Sylvester, D. 'A method of panorama construction from contoured maps', *Geog*. XXVIII (Jan. 1943), 12–18.

Taylor, G. *The Geographical Laboratory*. Toronto University Press, 1942. O.P.

Taylor, J. A. 'The geographic method', *Weather*, XIII (Sept. 1958), 303–7.

Thomson, W. E. 'Construction of a simple cyclone storm model', *J. of G*. LIII (May 1954), 208–11.

White, J. T. 'The uses of Manila Card in the Classroom', *Geog.* (Apr. 1965), 142–4.

Wills, B. L. 'Coffee can aneroid barometer', *J. of G.* LIX (Dec. 1960), 421–3.

Young, E. 'Value of surveying in teaching geography', *Geog. Teacher*, VIII (spring 1915), 45–53.

MAP WORK

Asa, J. 'Maps and slow learners', *J. of G.* L (Apr. 1951), 155–149.

Bacon, H. P. 'Making a pace map—an activity for the 5th and 6th grades', *J. of G.* LIII (May 1954), 203–8.

Bathurst, L. H. Developing map reading skills', *J. of G.* LX (Jan. 1961), 26–32.

Boucher, B. P. 'Urban land-use maps, their role in the social studies programme', *J. of G.* LIII (Mar. 1954), 106–11.

Cobb, R. T. 'Topographical maps for use in the classroom', *Geog.* XLI (July 1956), 178–82.

David, E. 'The teaching of contours', *Geog.* XXIX (June 1944), 57–61.

Geographical Association. 'An investigation into children's ability to interpret contour lines', *Geog.* XXVI (Sept. 1941), 131–40.

Geographical Association. 'Ordnance Survey maps in secondary schools; report of a discussion', *Geog.* XLIV (Nov. 1959), 262–5.

Goodman, M. C. 'Recent maps of interest to teachers of geography', I, *J. of G.* LI (Jan 1952), 13–20; II, *J. of G.* LII (March 1953), 116–24; III, *J. of G.* LIII (Dec. 1954), 384–92; IV, *J. of G.* LV (May 1956), 227–35.

Illingworth, A. 'Approach to map reading', *Geog.* XXXI (June 1946), 53–8.

James, L. B. 'The teaching of hypothetical maps', *J. of G.* L (Dec. 1951), 361–6.

Johnson, H. M. 'The place of maps in the teaching of geography', *Bull. of the University of Nottingham Inst. of Ed.* (May 1959), pp. 8–13.

Mathur, D. M. 'Construction of a simple model for teaching interpretations of contour lines', *J. of G.* LI (Sept. 1952), 245–7.

Rodyenko, R. 'A three dimensional model illustration reading relief by contour lines', *J. of G.* LVII (Feb. 1958), 78–83.

EXAMINATIONS AND TESTING

Daniels, J. C. 'Methods of testing geography at the "O" level of the G.C.E.', *Bull. of the University of Nottingham Inst. of Ed.* (Sept. 1953), pp. 11–12.

Daniels, J. C. 'Testing geography at the "O" level of the G.C.E.', *British Journal of Educational Psychology*, XXIV (Nov. 1954), 180–9.

Dunn, S. S. 'Critical note on "testing geography at the 'O' level of the G.C.E." [above]', *British Journal of Educational Psychology*, XXV (Nov. 1955), 204–5.

King, W. J. *General Certificate of Education. Model Answers; Geography (Ordinary level).* The Artemis Press, 1959. 5s. 6d.

Moncrieff, J. I. 'The Blank map test in geography examinations', *British Journal of Educational Psychology*, XXI (Feb. 1951), 71–5.

Owen, E. E. 'Geography in school. Test of basic knowledge', *New Zealand Geographer*, XVII (Oct. 1961), 19–30.

Renner, G. T. 'Learning readiness in elementary geography', *J. of G.* L (Feb. 1951), 65–74.

Scarfe, N. V. 'Testing geography objectively', *J. of G.* LII (Oct. 1953), 275–8.

Scarfe, N. V. 'Testing geographical interest by a visual method', *J. of G.* LIV (Nov. 1955), 377–87.

Schools Council. *Examinations Bulletin No. 1. The C.S.E. Examination: some suggestions for teachers and examiners.* H.M.S.O. 1963.

Schools Council. *Examinations Bulletin No. 3. The C.S.E. Examination: An introduction to some techniques of examining.* H.M.S.O. 1964.

Schools Council. *Examinations Bulletin No. 4. The C.S.E. Examination: An introduction to objective-type examinations.* H.M.S.O. 1964.

Schools Council. *Examinations Bulletin No. 5. The C.S.E. Examination: School based examinations.* H.M.S.O. 1965.

Scottish Education Department. *Teaching of Geography in Secondary Schools.* Edinburgh, H.M.S.O. 1958.

University of Cambridge. *Local Examinations Syndicate, G.C.E. 'O' Level, Examiners' reports.* Cambridge University Press, 1958. 2s.

Unstead, J. F. 'The place of map tests in examinations', *Geog. Teacher*, VIII (summer 1915), 102–12.

GEOGRAPHY ROOMS

Bonham, J. A. 'A modern geography department in a secondary school', *J. of G.* LIV (Feb. 1955), 60–3.

Morris, J. A. and Cole, R. 'Geography Room Survey 1957', *Geog.* XLII (Nov. 1957), 238–43.

Giffard, E. O. *Geography Rooms: their Construction and Equipment.* Philip, 1961. 1s. 6d.

Heaton, P. R. *The Geography Room in a Secondary School.* Geographical Association, 1954. 2s. 6d.

Vincent, A. 'Classroom display material: aids to preparation, display and storage', *Vis. Ed.* (Nov. 1958), pp. 8–28. (Reprinted as a booklet published by the National Committee for Visual Aids in Education, 1959, 1s. 6d.)

AUDIO-VISUAL AIDS

Allison, R. 'The film in Geography teaching in the Secondary School', *Vis. Ed.* (Aug./Sept. 1963), pp. 43–46.

Bailey, P. J. M. 'Blackboard and camera: some combined uses in the teaching of geography', *Geog.* XLVI (July 1961), 232–7.

Barton, T. F. 'Are we adequately utilizing the geographic film strip?', *J. of G.* LIII (Apr. 1954), 171–8.

British Film Institute. *Geography teaching films.* B.F.I. 1948.

Carson, J. R. 'Human geography: an experiment in teaching by films', *Vis. Ed.* (Nov. 1957), pp. 2–4.

Christensen, D. E. 'Experimenting with Geography teaching by television', *J. of G.* LXIV (Feb. 1965), 59–64.

Cons, G. J. *Geography and Visual Education*. Royal Geog. Soc., 1947. O.P.

Cons, G. J. 'The geographic film in education', *Geographical Magazine*, XXXI (Jan. 1959), 456–66.

Coppen, H. 'Wall sheets', *Vis. Ed.* (Oct. 1957), 11–24.

Crichton, J. S. and Rae, G. *Blackboard Drawing for Geography*. Nelson, 1958. R.P. 1962. 4s.

Devereux, E. J. P. *An Introduction to Visual Aids*. The Visual Aids Centre (Matthews, Drew and Shelbourne Ltd., 78 High Holborn, London), 1962. 25s.

Danklefsen, J. 'Televising geography', *J. of G.* LII (Sept. 1953), 253–7.

Educational Foundation for Visual Aids. *Visual Aids: Films and filmstrips (A comprehensive catalogue)*, Part III, *General, Physical and Economic Geography;* Part IV, *Regional Geography;* Part VII, *Agricultural, Science, Industrial Processes and Crafts*. New editions every two years. 2s. 6d. each.

Fairgrieve, J. 'The use of films in teaching geography', *Geog.* XVII (June 1932), 129–40.

Gilbert, W. L. 'The raw material film', *Geog.* XXIV (Dec. 1939), 250–3.

Goodall, G. *The Globe and its Uses*. Philip, 1948. O.P.

Gopshill, G. H. 'T.V. broadcasts in geography', *Geog.* XLIV (July 1959), 186–94.

Harrison, K. M. 'Large pictures for class teaching', *Vis. Ed.* (Nov. 1963), pp. 2–5.

Haupert, J. S. 'Televising political geography', *J. of G.* LIX (March 1960), 127–31.

Heaton, P. R. 'Air photography as a visual aid,' *Vis. Ed.* (Dec. 1954), pp. 6–8.

Heimonen, H. S. 'A laboratory exercise in aerial photo interpretation', *J. of G.* LVI (Sept. 1957), 286–90.

Hill, J. W. N. 'Film use in the lesson: an analysis', *Geog.* XLV (Jan.–Apr. 1960), 90–7.

Hill, R. T. 'Maps for television use', *J. of G.* LXI (May 1962), 204–8.

Hills, T. L. 'Visual Aids in the teaching of geography', *Canadian Ass. of Geographers. Ed. Comm. Bull.* no. 2. Montreal, 1961.

Linton, D. L. 'The interpretation of air photographs', *Geog.* XXXI (Sept. 1946), 89–97.

Linton, D. L. 'The use of air photographs in the teaching of geography', *Geog.* XXXI (Dec. 1946), 129–34.

Phillips, M. V. 'The effective use of filmstrips in teaching geography at the high school level', *J. of G.* LVII (Feb. 1958), 70–5.

Long, M. 'Children's reactions to geography pictures', *Geog.* XXXVIII (1953), 100–7.

Long, M. 'Research in picture study. The reactions of grammar school pupils to geographical pictures', *Geog.* XLVI (Nov. 1961), 322–37.

Long, M. 'Looking at geographical pictures', *Vis. Ed.* (Nov. 1953), pp. 2–3.

Money, D. C. 'The interpretation of photographic prints in the classroom', *Vis. Ed.* (Oct. 1959), pp. 2–4.

National Committee for Visual Aids in Education. *The Making of Geography Teaching Films*, 1956.

N.C.F.V.A.E. *Yearbook*, July 1962.

School Broadcasting Council for the U.K. *Geography and School Broadcasting*. B.B.C. 1953.

Sheppard, B. W. T. 'The integration of visual aids in classroom teaching', *Vis. Ed.* (Nov. 1959), pp. 13–15.

Teske, A. E. 'Geography field trips via coloured slides', *J. of G.* LVIII (Oct. 1959), 334–40.

Thomas, A. K. and Raup, H. F. 'Photography for the geography teacher', *J. of G.* LV (May 1956), 243–7.

Vincent, A. 'Wall charts in the classroom', I, *Vis. Ed.* (Feb. 1958), pp. 2–3; II, *Vis. Ed.* (Apr. 1958), pp. 10–12, III, *Vis. Ed.* (May 1958), pp. 24–6.

Vincent, A. 'Classroom display material, aids to preparation, display and storage', *Vis. Ed.* (Nov. 1958), pp. 8–28. (Available in pamphlet form, N.C.F.V.A.E. 1959.)

Vincent, A. 'Design for teaching; daylight and blackout', *Vis. Ed.* (June 1961), pp. 2–4.

Watkins, W. J. H. and Watkins, H. S. L. *How to look at Geographical Pictures*. Macmillan. Series I, 4th ed. 1958; series II, 3rd ed. 1962.

Wrathall, J. E. 'The overhead projector', *Geog.* LI (Jan. 1966), 38–41.

FIELD-WORK AND LOCAL STUDIES

Books and pamphlets

Armstrong, J. M. and Hopkins, P. G. H. *Local studies*. Workers' Educational Association and Workers' Educational Trade Union Committee, 1955.

Barnard, H. C. *Observational Geography and Regional Survey*. Le Play House, 1935.

Bell, G. E. 'Yorkshire field studies', *University of Leeds Inst. of Ed. Occasional Papers*, no. 3. 1961.

Bracey, H. E. *Village Survey* ('Get to know series'). 2nd ed. Methuen, 1957.

Bracey, H. E. *Country Town Survey* ('Get to know series'). 2nd ed. Methuen, 1961.

Branford, S. and Farquarson, A. *An Introduction to Regional Surveys*. Le Play House Press, 1947.

Clark, G. R. *A study of Soil in the Field*. Oxford University Press, 1957.

Coleman, A. and Maggs, K. R. *Land Use Survey handbook*. Isle of Thanet G.A. 1962.

Dempster, D. *Docks and Harbours* ('Get to know series'). Methuen, 1951. R.P. 1959.

Evans, F., Searson, V. R. and Williams, G. H. *Local Studies for Schools*, 4th ed. Philip, 1962.

Fagg, G. and Hutchings, G. E. *An Introduction to Regional Surveying*. Cambridge University Press, 1930. O.P.

Finberg, J. *Exploring Villages*. Routledge and Kegan Paul, 1958.

Fry, L. *A Record of Local Geography*. Wheston. O.P.

Fry, L. *Bridges*. ('Get to know series'). Methuen, 1951. R.P. 1959.

Geographical Association. Local studies; schemes of work...G.A. Rev. ed. 1949.

Hoskins, W. G. *Local History in England.* Longmans, 1959.

Hutchings, G. E. *Landscape Drawing.* Methuen, 1960.

Layton, E. and White, J. B. *The School Looks Around: a Book for Teachers about Local Surveys.* Longmans, 1948. O.P.

Le Play Society. *Exploration: Regional Survey.* Le Play House.

Ministry of Education (Great Britain). *Local Studies.* H.M.S.O. 1948.

Ministry of Education (Great Britain). *Schools and the Countryside.* H.M.S.O. 1958. R.P. 1961.

Nunneley, F. W. *A Port* ('How to explore series'). Educational Supply Ass. 1957. 2nd ed. 1959.

Russell, J. *Lessons on Soil.* Cambridge University Press, 1911. 2nd ed. 1950.

Shillito, G. H. *A Village* ('How to explore series'). Educational Supply Ass.

Simpson, C. A. *The Study of Local Geography; a Handbook for Teachers.* 2nd. ed. Methuen, 1950. O.P.

Simpson, C. A. *Making Local Surveys, an Eye for Country.* Pitman, 1951.

Tansley, A. G. and Evans, E. P. *Plant Ecology and the School.* Allen and Unwin, 1947. O.P.

Tomalin, M. *Water Supply* ('Get to know series'). Methuen, 1953. R.P. 1960.

Thornhill, P. *Houses and Flats* ('Get to know series'). Methuen, 1953. R.P. 1961.

Thornhill, P. *Inland Waterways* ('Get to know series'). Methuen, 3rd ed., 1959.

Thornhill, P. *The Parish Church* ('Get to know series'). 3rd ed. Methuen, 1960.

Thornhill, P. *Roads and Streets* ('Get to know series'). Methuen, 1951. R.P. 1959.

Voysey, A. *Farms* ('Get to know series'). Methuen, 1955. R.P. 1960.

Young, I. V. *Farm Studies and the Teaching of Geography.* (Based on the farm study scheme of the Assoc. of Agriculture.) University of London, Institute of Education, 1959.

Articles

Allen, K. G. 'Local studies and the secondary modern school', *Bull. of the University of Nottingham Inst. of Ed.* (Jan. 1955), pp. 10–13.

Anderzhon, M. L. 'Geographic field work in community study for junior high level (a study of a local postal service)', *J. of G.* LI (Nov. 1952), 325–32.

Baker, J. 'The local region as an introduction and basis for the teaching of geography in the grammar school', *Studies in Education* (June 1951), pp. 118–24.

Beaver, S. H. 'The Le Play Society and field work', *Geog.* XLVII (July 1962), 225–40.

Briault, E. W. H. 'The study of local geography as an integral part of the school course', *Geog.* XXXVIII (Jan. 1953), 29–32.

Bull, G. B. G. 'Field work in towns', *Geog.* XLIX (July 1964), 206–21.

Clark, B. M. 'Field geography', *Vis. Ed.* (March 1960), pp. 8–11.

Clark, L. 'Farm studies in a secondary school', *Geog.* XLIV (Apr. 1959), 111–17.

Frost, M. J. 'Field study from a narrow boat', *Geog.* XLVI (Jan. 1961), 50–5.

Gerlach, A. C. 'Soil profile sections', *J. of G.* XLVIII (Nov. 1949), 344–9.

Harder, C. H. *et al.* 'Prelude to a long summer; a study of weather in the Vale of Mowbray', *School Science Review*, XLI (June 1960), 401–7.

Hart, P. J. 'A pilot project on rivers', *Vis. Ed.* (Sept. 1961), pp. 11–15.

Hunt, A. J. and Moisley, H. A. 'Population mapping in urban areas', *Geog.* XLV (Jan.–Apr. 1960), 79–89.

Hutchings, G. E. 'Geographical field teaching', *Geog.* XLVII (Jan. 1962), 1–14.

Jay, L. J. 'Significant place names in geography', *Geog.* XXXIX (Jan. 1964), 28–32.

Lambert, A. M. 'Early maps and local studies', *Geog.* XLI (July 1956), 167–77.

Lawson, C. 'Tapping the interests of senior school leavers: a project in geography and biology', *Slow Learning Child*, IX (July 1962).

Long, M. 'The status of field work', *Geog.* XLVII (Jan. 1962), 72–84.

Lyons, H. R. 'Local geography and the five year course in a grammar school', *Geog.* XXXIV (Apr. 1949), 65–8.

Reynolds, L. M. 'Geography in the open air', *Geog. Teacher*, III (spring 1906), 152–9.

Simpson, C. A. 'A venture in field geography', *Geog.* XXX (June 1945).

Sinker, C. A. 'Vegetation and the teaching of Geography in the Field', *Geog.* XLIX (Apr. 1964), 105–10.

Taylor, J. A. 'Methods of Soil Study', *Geog.* XLV (Jan.–Apr. 1960), 52–67.

Taylor, J. W. 'The air field trip', *J. of G.* LIX (May 1960), 225–9.

Teske, A. E. 'Geography field trips via coloured slides', *J. of G.* LVIII (Oct. 1959), 334–40.

Toulson, S. 'Field studies', *Vis. Ed.* (Feb. 1960), pp. 8–10.

Tubbs, A. E. 'Local surveys', *Educational Review* (Oct. 1948), pp. 3–18.

Tubbs, A. E. 'Local studies', *Educational Review* (Feb. 1952), pp. 117–44.

Tubbs, A. E. *et al.* 'Local studies in practice: (1) a small all-age rural school; (2) a large secondary modern school; (3) an urban secondary modern school', *Educational Review*, VI (Nov. 1953), 25–42.

Wilks, H. C. 'A scheme of field work throughout a school', I, *Geog.* XLI (Jan. 1956), 15–14; II, *Geog.* XLI (Apr. 1956), 108–13.

Wood, L. R. 'A town survey by school children', *Geog.* XX (June 1935), 125–9.

Wooldridge, S. W. 'Field studies for secondary modern schools', *Education*, CIX (19 Apr. 1957), 683–4.

Young, I. V. *Farm Studies and the Teaching of Geography*. Ass. of Agric. 1959.

CORRELATION

The Atlantic Treaty Association. *Transatlantic Understanding in the Schools*. Atlantic Treaty Association, London, 1960.

Balchin, W. G. V. 'Seventy years of geography: linking science and humanities', *Times Ed. Supp.* (4 Apr. 1958), p. 534.

23-2

Bennett, W. J. 'Teaching geography in Malaya: in a British Army secondary school', *Geog.* XLIII (Apr. 1958), 114–17.

Bowman, I. *Geography in Relation to the Social Sciences.* Scribner's Sons, 1934. O.P.

British Association. 'Geology in schools', *The Advancement of Science*, no. 52 (March 1957). Offprint available.

Courtenay, P. P. 'Teaching geography in Malaya: in a Federation secondary school', *Geog.* XLIII (Apr. 1958), 118–25.

Dawson, G. A. 'Teaching about U.N.O. The geography teacher's contribution', *Geog.* XLIV (Jan. 1959), 34–7.

Fisk, E. 'Exploration and geography', *Geog.* XVI (June 1931), 144–9.

Fermor, J. 'Geography teaching in Bulgaria', *Geog.* XLVII (Apr. 1962), 175–8.

Geographical Association. Recent geographical articles. Published twice a year in the April and July issues of *Geography*: the section on teaching includes articles appearing in foreign periodicals.

Clegg, J. M. 'The teaching of geography in Norwegian Grammar schools', *Geog.* XXXV (Dec. 1950), 209–14.

Greensmith, J. T. 'The introduction of geology into the secondary modern school curriculum', *School Science Review*, CXL (Nov. 1958), 104–8.

Higgins, A. L. *Elementary Surveying.* Longmans, 1943. R.P. 1960.

High, J. 'Geography: co-ordinating element in secondary social studies', *J. of G.* LIX (Sept. 1960), 270–3.

Hodgson, H. B. 'The use of folk tales in teaching geography', *Geog.* (25 Jan. 1940), pp. 29–33.

Honeybone, R. C. 'Geography and international understanding', *Education Libraries Bulletin* (spring 1962), pp. 9–12.

Hoskins, W. G. *Local History in England.* Longmans, 1959.

Hutson, R. E. 'Geography in Nautical Education', *Geog.* L (April, 1965) 130–3.

Jay, L. J. 'The teaching of geography in the secondary schools of France', *Geog.* XLIII (July 1958), 200–5.

Jones, P. A. 'Meteorology in schools: a discussion of its value and practice', *Geog.* XXXIX (July 1954), 182–8.

Keinard, M. 'Using music to enrich geography', *J. of G.* LII (May 1953), 189–91.

Kohn, C. F. 'Geographic approaches in social education', *19th Yearbook of the National Council for The Social Studies.* Washington D.C. 1948.

Lawson, C. 'Tapping the interests of senior school leavers: a project in geography and biology', *Slow Learning Child*, IX (July 1962).

Mallinson, G. G. 'The relationship between the work of elementary science and geography teachers', *J. of G.* XLIX (May 1950), 206–10.

Parker, G. 'Human geography in the technical college', *Geog.* XLVII (July 1962), 278–84.

Phillips, M. V. 'Making effective use of current events in a high school geography class', *J. of G.* LVI (Feb. 1957), 70–4.

Quinn-Young, C. T. and White, J. E. H. *Handbook for Geography Teachers in West Africa.* Evans Brothers, 1960.

Roberts, F. L. *History and Geography with Postage Stamps of the British Commonwealth.* Crowther, 1948.

Royal Geographical Society. 'Geography and "social studies" in schools', *Geographical Journal,* cxv (Oct.–Dec. 1950), 221–4.

R.G.S. and The Geographical Association. 'Geography and technical education', *Geographical Journal,* cxxiv (June 1958), 232–4.

Schärer, G. 'Geography in an African girls' school in Tanganyika', *Geog.* xlvii (Apr. 1962), 170–4.

Shawkey, A. M. 'Contributions of high school geography to education for citizenship', *J. of G.* xlvi (Oct. 1947), 257–63.

Smith, N. 'Geography in Business Education', *Geog.* li (Apr. 1966), 130–2.

Stimson, C. D. J. 'The use of literature in teaching geography', *Education,* lxxvii (Sept. 1956), 24–9.

Tansley, A. G. and Evans, E. P. *Plant Ecology and the School.* Allen and Unwin, 1947. O.P.

Thomson, J. A. 'How to teach the geographical distribution of animals', *Geog. Teacher,* iii (autumn 1905), 116–19.

UNESCO. *Geography Teaching for International Understanding.* Paris, 1951.

UNESCO. *History, Geography and Social Studies: a Summary of School programmes in 53 Countries.* Paris, 1953.

Wagner, E. 'Geography in German education', *Geog.* l (Apr. 1965), 120–9.

Welch, L. M. 'Music and geography', *Music in Education,* xx (Sept./Oct. 1956), 121–2.

Wilson, V. 'Teaching geology in schools', *Proc. Geologists' Ass.* lviii (1947), 1–44.

Wise, M. J. 'The role of geography in technical education', *Geog.* xlvi, (Nov. 1961), 342–8.

REFERENCES

Bibliography

The following publications also contain bibliography on the teaching of geography.

American Geographical Society. Current geographical publications. Ten issues per year.

Long, M. (ed.). *Handbook for Geography Teachers.* 5th ed. Methuen, 1964.

Geographical Association. Recent geographical articles. Published in the April and July issues of *Geography.* Includes articles on the teaching of Geography published in foreign journals.

Royal Geographical Society. New geographical literature and maps. Published in June and December of each year.

Saxelby, C. H. *A Geographer's Reference Book.* Geographical Association, 1955.

The Librarians of the Institutes of Education. *British Education Index.* The Library Ass. Published three times a year.

UNESCO. 'Geography teaching (a select bibliography of books and articles on the teaching of geography in countries)', *Education Abstracts,* xiii, no. 1 (Paris, 1961).

University of Southampton Institute of Education Library. *The Teaching of Geography and History and Related Local Studies: a Select Bibliography*. 2nd ed. Dec. 1957.

Periodicals

Articles on various aspects of the teaching of Geography appear from time to time in the following periodicals.

British Journal of Educational Studies. May and November.

Bulletin of the University of Cambridge Institute of Education. July and December. Free (limited circulation).

Journal of the University of Durham Institute of Education. September, November, January, March, May.

The Durham Research Review. Research publication of the University of Durham Institute of Education. Annually.

Education. Weekly.

Educational Abstracts. Bulletin of the University of Nottingham Institute of Education. Annually.

Education Libraries Bulletin. Published by the University of London Institute of Education. Three times a year, spring, summer, autumn.

Educational Review. Journal of the University of Birmingham Institute of of Education. November, February and June.

Educational Research. Published by The National Foundation for Educational Research in England and Wales. November, February and June.

Geography. The quarterly journal of The Geographical Association. January, April, July and November.

Geographical Journal. Quarterly Journal of Royal Geographical Society. March, June, September, and December.

Journal of Geography. Published by The National Council of Geography Teachers (U.S.A.). Monthly, except for June, July and August.

Researches and Studies. Published by the University of Leeds Institute.

The School Science Review. Published by The Association for Science Education (formerly The Science Masters' Association). March, June and November.

Studies in Education. Published by the University of Hull Institute of Education. Annually.

Teachers' World (*Secondary Education*). Weekly.

Times Educational Supplement. Weekly.

Visual Education. Magazine of The National Committee for Visual Aids in Education. Monthly. Also a useful Yearbook published as the July issue.

Weather. Published by the Royal Meteorological. Society Monthly. Includes a supplement for schools.

APPENDIX C: SOURCES OF TEACHING MATERIAL

NOTES

1. Although these lists have been checked for reliability, please ascertain the latest position with regard to particular items.

2. Pupils should *not* be encouraged to write for material of their own accord unless prior permission has been granted. This is a provision increasingly being made by commercial organisations.

3. *Index and key to the lists*

Projected Visual Aids	p. 339
Non-Projected Visual Material	p. 354
Outside Speakers	p. 374
Weather Study Material	p. 379

S = Sale, H = Hire, FL = Free loan, F = Free distribution

PROJECTED VISUAL AIDS

1. *Sources of film* (16 mm. unless otherwise stated)

The catalogues of the Educational Foundation for Visual Aids (E.F.V.A.) are extremely useful in this connection. Part 3 is devoted to films of 'Physical and Economic Geography', and Part 4 to 'Regional Geography'. Both of these sectional lists (but *not* the actual films) can be obtained from 33 Queen Anne Street, W. 1. There is a small charge.

Here it is as well to repeat the warning given earlier in the memorandum. Viewing before class use is essential. Note, too, that films should be booked well ahead of the proposed date of screening.

FILM LIBRARIES

Address	Comment	Conditions
Aims of Industry Ltd., 78 Victoria Road, Surbiton, Surrey	These films are sponsored by industrial organisations, and a number of them include geographical considerations	FL
Associated Rediffusion Ltd., Television House, Kingsway, W.C. 2	A limited amount of screened educational film is available. This includes some 20 min. geographical documentaries	FL
Boulton-Hawker Films Ltd., Hadleigh, Ipswich, Suffolk	Films covering systematic and regional aspects of the subject. Most of them are in colour	H and S

Address	Comment	Conditions
Central Office of Information Library, Government Buildings, Bromyard Avenue, W. 3 *and* The Central Film Library of Wales, 42 Park Place, Cardiff	Documentaries on a wide range of subjects including farming, industry, various Commonwealth countries in Africa, Asia, etc., foreign lands, and town and country planning	Mainly H but some FL
Columbia Pictures Corporation Ltd., 16 mm. Division, Film House, 142 Wardour Street, W. 1.	Offer a number of colour shorts in the series: 'This Wonderful World.' There are also 16 mm. versions of some longer films	H
Educational Foundation for Visual Aids, Film Library, Brooklands House, Weybridge	Most of the available material is documented in the catalogues—see introductory note. The Foundation operates a special hire scheme whereby L.E.A.s and schools may borrow a number of films per year at a moderate charge	H
Educational and Television Films Ltd., 164 Shaftesbury Avenue, W.C. 2	A library of Soviet, East European and Chinese films. There is a 35 mm. list	H
Ford Film Library, Dept. R. 5, 135–147 Cheapside, E.C. 2	Mainly of Technical and advertising interest. Some of the films concentrate on British farming and industry, as well as overseas topics	FL
Gateway Film Productions Ltd., 470 Green Lane, Palmers Green, N. 13	A limited number of good geographical teaching films are available	H and S
John King Ltd., Film House, East Street, Brighton	Over seven hundred titles in stock, including a limited number on travel. Discount given on school hiring	H
Local Education Authorities (various)	The majority of L.E.A.s maintain film libraries for class purposes. Some stocks are small (only 50 reels), but others large (up to 10,000!)	FL

Address	Comment	Conditions
The Public Relations Department, P. and O. Orient Lines, 122 Leadenhall Street, E.C. 3	Films dealing with ships of the company's fleet, and the routes served by P. and O. There is 35 mm. stock	FL
Petroleum Films Bureau 1. England, Wales and Northern Ireland, 4 Brook Street, W. 1 2. Scotland, The Scottish Films Office, 16–17 Woodside Terrace, Charing Cross, Glasgow, C. 3	A variety of films, both on 16 and 35 mm. reels. Some, but by no means all, of them deal with the oil industry. The bureau acts as the distributing centre of the films made by many of the independent petroleum companies	F
Plymouth Films Ltd., Stoke Plymouth, Plymouth	Cinepacs (i.e. 4 min., 8 mm. films) are available. Some of them deal with travel	H
Rank Film Library, 1 Aintree Road, Perivale, Greenford, Middlesex	Maintains a very wide range of films	FL, H and S
Sabena, Belgian World Airlines, 36–37 Piccadilly, W. 1	Films of those parts of the world served by the airline	FL
Sound Services Ltd., Wilton Crescent, S.W. 19	A considerable number of educational and general interest films. The catalogue is very useful	FL (majority)
Information Division, Unilever Film Library, Unilever House, Blackfriars, E.C. 4	Offer films on vegetable oils and fishing, as well as parts of Africa in which the company has interests	FL
The United Nations and its specialised agencies	Details of film material, some of which is 35 mm. stock, obtainable from the United Nations Information Centre, 14/15 Stratford Place, W. 1	FL
Wallace Heaton Ltd., 127 New Bond Street, W. 1	Details of a school library service will be given on request	H
West of England Film Unit, 50 Broad Street, Bristol 1	A limited number of special geographical films	H

341

FILMS OF INDIVIDUAL PRODUCTS

Subject	Address of supplier	Conditions
Bananas, their growth and marketing	Elders and Fyffes Ltd., 15 Stratton Street, Piccadilly, W. 1	FL
Bauxite mining	The Aluminium Development Association, 33 Grosvenor Street, W. 1	FL
Coal industry	Film Library, National Coal Board, 2 Grosvenor Place, S.W. 1	FL
Cocoa and chocolate	Cadbury Bros. Ltd., Schools Dept., Bournville, Birmingham 30	FL
Coffee	The Coffee Information Bureau, Williams House, Eastbourne Terrace, W. 2	FL
Copper	Copper Development Association, 55 South Audley Street, W. 1	FL
Cotton and the textile industry	The Textile Council, Education Dept., 3 Alberton Street, Manchester 3	FL
Dairy produce	National Dairy Council and English Country Cheese Council, Melbourne House, Aldwych, W.C. 2	FL
	United Dairies Film Library, 34 Palace Court, W. 2	FL
Iron and steel	The British Iron and Steel Federation, Film Library, Steel House, Tothill Street, S.W. 1	FL
	Publicity Manager, English Steel Corporation, Deon Works, Sheffield 9	FL

Subject	Address of supplier	Conditions
	United Steel Co. Ltd., The Mount, Broomhill, Sheffield 10	FL
	The Welfare Officer, Parkgate Iron and Steel Co. Ltd., Park Gate Works, Rotherham	FL
Nickel mining	The Publicity Dept., International Nickel Company (Mond) Ltd. 20 Albert Embankment, S.E. 1	FL
Oil industry	Esso Petroleum Co. Ltd., Public Relations Dept., Victoria Street, S.W. 1	FL
	Petroleum Films Bureau, see entry under 'Film Libraries'	—
	Shell International Petroleum Co. Ltd., Films Department, Shell Centre, S.E. 1	FL
Pulp and paper	Bowater Paper Corporation Ltd., Public Relations Dept., Knightsbridge, S.W. 7	FL
	Reed Paper Group, Educational Services Dept., 82 Baker Street, W. 1	H
Rubber	Dunlop Rubber Co., Education Section, 10/12 King Street, St James's, S.W. 1	FL
	Information Officer, Natural Rubber Bureau, 19 Buckingham Street, W.C. 2	FL
Silk	The Silk Centre, 13 Portman Square, W. 1	H
Sugar	Tate and Lyle Ltd., 21 Mincing Lane, E.C. 3	FL
Tea	Brooke Bond Tea Ltd., Education Dept., 35 and 37 Cannon Street, E.C. 4	FL

Subject	Address of supplier	Conditions
Tea (*continued*)	Ceylon Tea Centre 22 Regent Street, S.W. 1	FL
Timber	The Timber Research and Development Corporation, St John's Road, Tylers Greens, High Wycombe, Bucks.	FL
Vegetable oils	Unilever Ltd., Information Division, Unilever House, Blackfriars, E.C. 4	FL
Wool	The International Wool Secretariat, Department of Education, Dorland House, 18–20 Regent Street, S.W. 1	FL

FILMS OF INDIVIDUAL COUNTRIES

Country concerned	Address of supplier	Conditions
Argentina	The Argentine Embassy, 9 Wilton Crescent, S.W. 1	FL
Australia	Australian News and Information Bureau, Australia House, Strand, W.C. 2	H
Belgium	Sabena, Belgian World Airlines, 36–37 Piccadilly, W. 1	FL
Brazil	The Brazilian Embassy, Commercial and Information Service, 157/161 Regent Street, W. 1	FL
Britain	Associated Rediffusion Ltd., Television House, Kingsway, W.C. 2	FL
	British Transport Films, Melbury House, Melbury Terrace, N.W. 1	FL
	The Central Film Library, Government Buildings, Bromyard Avenue, Acton, W. 3	H or S

Country concerned	Address of supplier	Conditions
Britain (*continued*)	or 42 Park Place, Cardiff	
	The Publicity Officer, London Transport, 55 Broadway, S.W. 1	FL
	The Manchester Ship Canal Company, Ship Canal House, King Street, Manchester	FL
	The Scottish Central Film Library, 16/17 Woodside Terrace, Charing Cross, Glasgow, C. 3	H or S
	Youth Hostels Association, Publicity Dept., Trevelyan House, St Albans, Herts.	H
Canada	Canadian National Railways, Cunard Building, Pier Head, Liverpool 3	FL
	Canadian Pacific Railway Company, 62 Trafalgar Square, W.C. 2	FL
	The National Film Board of Canada, 1 Grosvenor Square, W. 1	S or H
Ceylon	Office of the High Commissioner for Ceylon, Press and Information Attaché, 13 Hyde Park Gardens, W. 2	FL
China	Britain–China Friendship Association, 228 Gray's Inn Road, W.C. 1	FL or H
	Chinese Government Information Office, 51 Cavendish Street, W. 1	FL
Eire	The Irish Tourist Office, 71 Regent Street, W. 1	FL

APPENDIX C

Country concerned	Address of supplier	Conditions
European countries	British European Airways, 103 Wigmore Street, W. 1	FL
Finland	Finland Travel Information Centre, Finland House, 56 Haymarket, S.W. 1	FL
	Films supplied by: Sound Services Ltd., Wilton Crescent, S.W. 19	
France	French Institute, Queensbury Place, S.W. 2	H
	French Railways Ltd., Publicity Dept., 170 Piccadilly, W. 1 (but order via Sound Services Ltd.)	FL
Ghana	Office of the High Commissioner for Ghana, 13 Belgrave Square, S.W. 1	FL
India (Republic of)	A 35 or 16 mm. version of 'The Peaceful Revolution' is available from A.E.I. Film Library (CT3), Crown House, Aldwych, W.C. 2	FL
	Information Service of India, India House, Aldwych, W.C. 2	FL
Israel	Israel Government Tourist Office, 59 St James' Street, S.W. 1	H
Italy	The Assistant Director, Italian Institute of Culture, 39 Belgrave Square, S.W. 1	FL
	Italian State Tourist Office, 201 Regent Street, W. 1	FL
Japan	Embassy of Japan, The Press and Cultural Section, 46 Grosvenor Street, W. 1	FL
Malaya	The Librarian, Malaya House, 57 Trafalgar Square, W.C. 2	FL
Netherlands	Netherlands National Tourist Office, 38 Hyde Park Gate, S.W. 7	H

Country concerned	Address of supplier	Conditions
New Zealand	New Zealand Film Library 415 Strand, W.C. 2	F, H or S
Northern Ireland	Information Officer, Government of Northern Ireland, 13 Lower Regent Street, S.W. 1	FL
Norway	Bergen Line, 21–24 Cockspur Street, S.W. 1	
	Counsellor for Press and Information, Royal Norwegian Embassy, 25 Belgrave Square, S.W. 1	FL
Pakistan	Press Attaché, High Commissioner for Pakistan, 35 Lowndes Square, S.W. 1	FL
Republic of South Africa	Obtainable from: Sound Services Ltd., Wilton Crescent, S.W. 19	FL
Rhodesia	Information Officer, Rhodesia House, 429 Strand, W.C. 2	FL
Sweden	The Swedish Institute for Cultural Relations, 49 Egerton Crescent, S.W. 3	H
Switzerland	Swiss National Tourist Office, and Swiss Railways, 458 Strand, Trafalgar Square, W.C. 2	H
Turkey	Turkish Embassy, Press Attaché, 43 Belgrave Square, S.W. 1	FL
United Nations Organisation, and its Specialised Agencies	Catalogue and further information from: U.N. Information Centre, 14/15 Stratford Place, W. 1 (some 35 mm. stock kept)	FL
United States	The film service of the American Embassy (U.S.I.S.) has been discontinued. Its stock is now obtainable from the E.F.V.A. and British Film Institute, 81 Dean Street, W. 1	H

347

Country concerned	Address of supplier	Condi-tions
U.S.S.R.	The Society for Cultural Relations with the U.S.S.R. 14 Kensington Square, W. 8	FL
Western Australia	West Australian Government Office, Savoy House, 115 Strand, W.C. 2	FL
Western Germany	Curzon Publicity Ltd., 31 St James' Place, S.W. 1 (who are advertising consultants of the German Embassy)	FL
Yugoslavia	The Yugoslav National Tourist Office, 143 Regent Street, W. 1	FL

SOURCES OF FILMSTRIPS

The sectional catalogue of the Educational Foundation (E.F.V.A.) is equally suitable for filmstrips—refer to the introductory note under the film heading. Details are given below of the more important *specialist* producers and distributors. Commercial firms and private organisations who sponsor strips are not included, but such material can often be obtained through the Foundation.

Name and address of source	Comment	Condi-tions
Amalgamated Filmstrip Distributors, 34 Middle Street, Brighton 1	Deal with Tartan strips and those of a number of overseas firms. Their geographical section is of a general nature, although there are some more specialised economic and regional strips	S
The Central Office of Information, (Strips obtainable from the Central Film Library, Bromyard Avenue, Acton, W. 3	A variety of subject matter is covered by the strips. See the comment under Film Sources	FL and S
Cheshire Films, Rendell and Wilson, 176A, Ashley Road, Hale, Cheshire	Three strips, dealing with the weather, natural vegetation zones, and the City of Sheffield	S
Common Ground (1951) Ltd., 44 Fulham Road, S.W. 3	Offer a very wide range of topics, both in black-and-white, and colour. Preview facilities on a sale or return basis	S

348

Name and address of source	Comment	Conditions
Filmstrip Department, The Commonwealth Institute, Kensington High Street, W. 8	A library of Institute-sponsored, commercially produced strips dealing with the Colonies and self-governing members of the Commonwealth. Ask for leaflet 7, a catalogue of material arranged under continental headings	FL and S
Daily Mail Filmstrips (distributed by E.F.V.A.)	Enquiries to: E.F.V.A., 33 Queen Anne Street, W. 1. Most of the strips are of a travel nature	S
Diana Wyllie Ltd., 3 Park Road, Baker Street, N.W. 1	Market a number of filmstrips some of which are concerned with weather phenomena	
The Educational Foundation for Visual Aids, 33 Queen Anne Street, W. 1	Their catalogues (part 3, Physical and Economic Geography, and part 4, Regional), together with interim supplements in the journal *Visual Education*, act as reference lists for most material	FL, H and S
Educational Productions Ltd., East Ardsley, Wakefield, Yorks.	A wide range of subject-matter is covered, both in black-and-white and colours. It is mainly on a regional basis. Preview facilities exist	S
Encyclopaedia Britannica Ltd., 18/20 Regent Street, S.W. 1	Sections in the catalogue include 'Geography—Physical; Economic; and Regional.'	S
Filmstrip and Slide Distributors Ltd., 6 Portman Mews South, W. 1	A miscellaneous collection, mainly regional in character	S
Hulton Educational Productions Ltd., 55/59 Saffron Hill, E.C. 1	An extensive range of strips—on a sale or return basis. The frames in some strips are individually titled	S
Local Education Authority Filmstrip Libraries	Many of them offer a wider selection of material than can be stocked in school, and thus provide a means of pre-purchase viewing and occasional use	FL
Marian Ray, 36 Villiers Avenue, Surbiton, Surrey	Offers a set of strips on soil and one as an introduction to the study of fossils	S

Name and address of source	Comment	Condi-tions
The Rank Film Library, Aintree Road, Perivale, Greenford, Middlesex	Formerly the G.B. Film Library. It distributes filmstrips produced by other companies. There are preview facilities	S
Stripslides Ltd., 93 Cheyneys Avenue, Canons Park, Edgware, Middlesex	Strips on physical geography. The firm was formerly known as 'Dance-Kaufmann Ltd.'	S
Unicorn Head Visual Aids Ltd., 42 Westminster Palace Gardens, S.W. 1	Have produced a number of systematic and regional strips for various age-groups	S
Visual Information Service, 12 Bridge Street, Hungerford, Berks.	The main emphasis in a considerable range of strips is on Regional Geography, although systematic aspects are also covered	S
Visual Publications Ltd., 197 Kensington High Street, W. 8	Offer a number of strips on various aspects of climate, the weather, and ocean currents	S

Postscript

Your own picture material will be assembled in filmstrip form by:
1. Carwal Ltd., 85 Manor Road, Wallington, Surrey.
2. Common Ground Ltd., 44 Fulham Road, S.W. 3.
3. Charles Rimmer, 168A, Battersea Bridge Road, S.W. 11
4. Kay Film-Strip Studio, 3 Greek Street, W. 1.
5. The Dawn Trust, Aylesbury, England.
6. Unicorn Head Visual Aids Ltd., 42 Westminster Palace Gardens, S.W. 1.

SOURCES OF SLIDES

(2 in. × 2 in. unless otherwise stated)

General collections

The Photographic Officer, Photographic Section, B.O.A.C., Stratton House, Piccadilly, W. 1	A colourslide Library of countries and cities to which B.O.A.C. fly. Sets could be made up, depending on subject-matter required. The Section is gradually going over to 2¼ in. slides	FL

Name and address of source	Comment	Conditions
The Education Officer, Commonwealth Institute, Kensington High Street, W. 8	Sets of slides covering various parts of the Commonwealth. There are also some 3¼ in. slides	FL
The Geographical Magazine, Slide Service, 17 Broderick Road, S.W. 17	Some of the colour photographs used in the *Geographical Magazine*, as well as others, are available in slide form. The subject-matter of the sets ranges from the Great Victoria Desert to Corsica and the Geography of Britain	S
Grant Colour Slides, The Grant Educational Co. Ltd., 91–93 Union Street, Glasgow, C. 1	Optical glass-protected colour slides of different parts of the world. They are available in sets, or can be individually purchased. There are preview facilities	S
Diapositives: L'Institut Pédagogique National, Paris. The sole English agents: Parker and Son Ltd., Broad Street, Oxford	The Geographical Section of the catalogue (F) lists slides on a regional basis, one country or area per set. Subject-matter from various parts of the world is on offer, but the most extensive coverage is of European countries	S
John King (Films) Ltd., Film House, East Street, Brighton	Colour slides (in sets of five) of the British Isles, and various parts of the world. The subject-matter is mainly of a tourist nature, e.g. famous views, buildings, and churches	S
Philips Geography Colour Slides; orders dealt with by Film Strip and Slide Distributors Ltd., 6 Portman Mews South, W. 1	The first series is devoted to Physical Geography. Topics covered in different sets include weathering, glaciated landforms, and types of relief	S
The Rickitt Encyclopaedia of Slides, 14 Seamill Park Crescent, Worthing, Sussex	Lists are available of topographical and geographical subjects	S
The Royal Geographical Society, Kensington Gate, S.W. 7	A large, unclassified collection, some of which are very old. Nevertheless personal selection of very useful material is possible. The majority are 3¼ in. slides.	H

Specialised collections

Name and address of source	Comment	Conditions
(a) Geological and physical aspects		
Flatters and Garnett Ltd., Mikrops House, Bradnor Road, Manchester 22	Fossil Botany and geological subjects.	H and S
The Director, Geological Survey, Exhibition Road, South Kensington, S.W. 7	Slides can be made to order from the library of prints, but a limited number of transparencies are on general offer. They illustrate various landforms	S
Diana Wyllie Ltd., 3 Park Road, Baker Street, N.W. 1	Slides of optical phenomena and storms	S
(b) Commercial products		
The Aluminium Development Association, 33 Grosvenor Street, W. 1	$3\frac{1}{4}$ in. $\times$ $3\frac{1}{4}$ in. as well as 2 in. $\times$ 2 in. slides. They are mainly of technical interest, but some are of geographical use. The latter are connected with bauxite mining	FL
The Petroleum Information Bureau, 29 New Bond Street, W. 1	A set of thirty-six colour transparencies. The general title is 'An outline story of oil'	FL
Shell International Petroleum Co. Ltd., Trade Relations Division, Shell Centre, S.E. 1	A set of fourteen colour transparencies, based on the series of wall charts: 'What is oil?'	FL or S
(c) Individual countries		
Austria		
Austrian State Tourist Department, and Austrian Federal Railways, 219 Regent Street, W. 1	Lantern slides in colour	FL
Finland		
The Finnish Embassy, 66 Chester Square, S.W. 1	The colour slides cover a wide variety of subjects, e.g. landscapes, agriculture, architecture, villages and towns	FL

SOURCES OF TEACHING MATERIAL

Name and address of source	Comment	Condi-tions
France		
The French Embassy, Cultural Services, 22 Wilton Crescent, S.W. 1	Colour transparencies of French châteaux, towns and different parts of the country. Ask for list	FL
Israel		
Israel Government Tourist Office, 59 St James's Street, S.W. 1	A limited number of colour slides, mainly of a tourist nature. The office could help with request for special scenes	FL
Netherlands		
Netherlands National Tourist Office, 38 Hyde Park Gate, S.W. 7	Various topics	FL
Norway		
The Royal Norwegian Embassy, Press and Information Office, 25 Belgrave Square, S.W. 1	Thirty-five different sets (six slides in each) are available. Topics include 'Oslo', 'Bergen', 'The western fiords', and 'Mountain Norway'	FL
Spain		
The Institute of Spain, 102 Eaton Square, S.W. 1	Slides to illustrate the towns and art of Spain. There is a small charge for packing	FL
Sweden		
The Swedish Institute for Cultural Relations, 49 Egerton Crescent, S.W. 3	Various topics are covered with an emphasis on buildings and towns	H
Western Australia		
The Agent General for Western Australia Savoy House, 115 The Strand, W.C. 2	An extensive colour transparency library is maintained. It covers many geographical aspects	FL
Yugoslavia		
Yugoslav National Tourist Office, 143 Regent Street, W. 1	Slides—but mainly of tourist resorts and scenery	FL

NON-PROJECTED VISUAL MATERIAL

PICTURES, POSTERS, PHOTOGRAPHS AND WALL CHARTS

General sources of material

Name and address of source	*Comment*	*Conditions*
Aerofilms and Aero Pictorial Ltd., 4 Albemarle Street, W. 1	Maintain a library of oblique and vertical air photographs of Britain and many other lands. The catalogue itself is a collection of various shots	S
B.O.A.C. The Reference Officer, Stratton Street, Piccadilly, W. 1	Twenty thousand negatives are stocked. Photographic prints to order. Topics covered include views of countries and towns on routes operated by the company	S
Central Office of Information, Hercules Road, Westminster Bridge Road, S.E. 1	Supply picture sets (i.e. a map, verbal description and up to six 15 in. × 12 in. photographs). Like the 30 in. × 40 in. photo posters they cover various aspects of life in Britain and her dependencies	S
Commonwealth Institute, Kensington High Street, W. 8	The institute acts as a central agency for the distribution of wall charts, photo posters, and photographic picture sets. Ask for leaflet no. 5. The special 'Study Kits' are also very useful.	S and H
Council for Education in World Citizenship, 93 Albert Embankment, S.E. 1	Photographic exhibitions on free loan to affiliated schools. A variety of topics is covered, e.g. Freedom from Hunger. These are changed as circumstances demand	FL
Educational Foundation for Visual Aids, 33 Queen Anne Street, W. 1	A comprehensive catalogue of wall charts is obtainable	S
Educational Products Ltd., East Ardsley, Wakefield	Maintain a wide range of charts, dealing with systematic and regional aspects of Geography	S
Evans Bros. Ltd., Montague House, Russell Square, W.C. 1	Publish *Pictorial Education*, monthly and quarterly. It is designed for children in the 8–16 age-group, and includes well-illustrated geographical articles	S

354

Name and address of source	*Comment*	*Conditions*
The Geographical Magazine, 91 St Martin's Lane, W.C. 2	Its photographically illustrated articles cover many different parts of the world. From time to time there are map-inserts. A monthly publication	S
National Geographic Magazine, Enrolment and dues: Barclay's Bank Ltd., Chief Foreign Branch, 168 Fenchurch Street, E.C. 3	A lavishly illustrated monthly magazine, popular in type. A wide range of colour illustrations and map inserts is characteristic	S
Pictorial Charts Educational Trust, 181 Uxbridge Road, W. 7	A comprehensive series of 40 in. × 30 in. colour charts. Mainly a regional approach	S
The Times Publishing Co. Ltd., Photographic Sales Dept., Printing House Square, E.C. 4	Photographic prints can be ordered from a large library	S
United Nations Information Centre, 14/15 Stratford Place, W. 1	Wall sheets, poster sets, and photographs on all aspects of the work of the United Nations throughout the world. Stocks change	F

Material on specialised topics

(a) Physical aspects

The landscape

Geological Survey and Museum, Exhibition Road, S.W. 7	Photographic prints, monochrome and coloured picture postcards. The views are to illustrate the geology and physical geography of Britain	S

The sea

The Seven Worlds of the Sea, Exhibits Office, U.S. Information Service, W. 1	A set of nineteen posters. Three of them are devoted to tides, currents, and waves	FL

Name and address of source	Comment	Conditions
(b) Economic aspects		

Bauxite

| The Aluminium Development Association, 33 Grosvenor Street, W. 1 | A wall chart (30 in. × 40 in.) illustrating the extraction of virgin metal from bauxite. Also fully annotated photographs of the production, fabrication and applications of the metal in many fields | S and H |
| Alcan (U.K.) Ltd., Aluminium Canada House, 30 Berkeley Square, W. 1 | Offer sketch-map-illustrated accounts of 'Alcan's Kitimat and Saguenay projects', as well as others on Jamaica and Guyana | F |

Bananas

| Elders and Fyffes Ltd., 15 Stratton Street, W. 1 | A photographically illustrated pamphlet called 'The banana story' | |

Butter

| The National Milk Publicity Council, Melbourne House, Aldwych, W.C. 1 | A wall chart showing how butter is made. Notes and ten postcard-size illustrations are also available | S |

Coal

| Public Relations Dept., The National Coal Board, Grosvenor Place, S.W. 1 | Offer a number of interesting wall charts including 'How a coal mine works', and 'The search for new coal seams' | F |

Cocoa

| The Schools Dept., Cadbury Bros. Ltd., Bournville, Birmingham | Six charts illustrating stages in cocoa growing, the life of the grower, and transport of the crop. Other charts are available, but mainly designed for junior work. Write for the catalogue: 'Visual aids for education' | F |

Coffee

| The Coffee Promotion Council Ltd., 10, Eastcheap, E.C. 3. | Wall chart and booklet 'Know about Coffee' | F |
| The Nestlé Company Ltd., St George's House, Wood Street, E.C. 2 | A wall chart (20 in. × 30 in.) illustrating the production of Nescafé, from the coffee bean to the finished product | S |

Name and address of source	Comment	Condi-tions
Cotton		
The Textile Council 3 Alberton Street, Manchester 3	Wall charts of (1) the Cotton Growing Countries, and (2) the Principal Cotton Textile districts	S
Fishing		
British Trawlers Federation Ltd., Publications Dept., F. C. Peichard, Wood and Partners Ltd., 25 Sarde Road, W. 1	A colour chart showing the principal North-west European fishing grounds, and the types of catch	F
The Public Relations Officer, White Fish Authority, 2/3 Cursitor Street, E.C. 4	Offer an illustrated booklet and colour chart of Britain's fishing grounds. On the latter are also shown the different vessels in use, and kind of fish caught. (There is an accompanying filmstrip)	F and S
Iron and steel		
Training Department, The British Iron and Steel Federation, Steel House, Tothill Street, S.W. 1	Their wall charts (30 in. × 40 in.) deal with topics like the Blast Furnace, From Iron into Steel, Sources of Imported Ore, and Home Supplies. They are very useful	F
Leather		
The Leather Institute, 17–19 Barter Street, W.C. 1	Market two wall charts	S
Linen		
The Irish Linen Guild, Leather Trade House, 17–19 Barter Street, W.C. 1	Some wall charts are available. 'From Flax to Irish Linen' (19 in. × 24 in.) is the most useful. Others are 'Linen in History', and 'Know your Irish Linen'	F
Oil		
The Petroleum Information Bureau, 4 Brook Street, Hanover Square, W. 1	The bureau distributes wall charts, as well as 'A brief photographic story of oil'. The latter consists of 51 mounted photographs (11 in. × 9 in.). In addition, a Folding Display Cabinet can be borrowed	F, FL and S

Name and address of source	Comment	Condi-tions
Oil (cont.)		
Shell Aids for Teachers, Shell International Petroleum Co. (TRS/211), Shell Centre, S.E. 1	A series of wall charts on the oil industry	F
Rubber		
The Educational Section, Dunlop Rubber Co. Ltd., 10/12 King Street, S.W. 1	The company have supplied Photo-sets of a Malayan Rubber Estate, also sponsor coloured wall charts (30 in. × 20 in.) of the industry. The latter are obtainable from Educational Productions Ltd.	F and S
Silk		
The Silk Centre, 13 Portman Square, W. 1	A set of fourteen photographs taken at Lullingstone Silk Farm, illustrating the rearing of silk-worms and reeling of raw silk	FL
Sugar		
The British Sugar Corpora-tion, 134 Piccadilly, W. 1	Several charts on sugar beet growing and refining	F
Tate and Lyle Ltd., Educational Aids Bureau, 21 Mincing Lane, E.C. 3	A display card, illustrating stages in processing and eventual products	F
Tea		
The Education Officer, The Tea Centre, 22 Regent Street, S.W. 1	A fine selection of posters, charts, and maps. Catalogue available	S
Vegetable oils and fats		
Unilever Ltd., Information Division, Blackfriars, E.C. 4	The Education Catalogue gives details of wall charts, educational booklets (and filmstrips). Subjects include vegetable and essential oils, as well as fishing	F
Messrs Van den Berghs Ltd., Bridgewater House, Great Suffolk Street, S.E. 1	Charts illustrating the sources of vegetable oils, and picture friezes of the native production of palm oil, groundnuts and copra	F

Name and address of source	Comment	Conditions
Wool		
The International Wool Secretariat, Dorland House, 18–20 Regent Street, S.W. 1	A United Kingdom wall-map of wool growing and manufacturing industries, as well as pastoral wall sheets of sheep country in various areas of the world	S
Wool (and Allied) Textile Employers' Council, 55 Well Street, Bradford 1	A series of photographs depicting processes within the industry. Material is free of charge or on free loan to schools in Yorkshire	S

Material connected with individual countries

Australia		
The Press Officer, Australia News and Information Bureau, Australia House, The Strand, W.C. 2	The bureau produces a number of useful pictures, but supplies fluctuate. Note, too, that material can be obtained from the Agent-General of each state	F
Britain		
The Area Publicity Representative, British Railways, 64 Cardington Street, N.W. 1	Dispatch poster maps of various counties in Britain	S
The Secretary, National Parks Commission, 1 Cambridge Gate, Regent's Park, N.W. 1	Offer interesting pictorial maps of some of our National Parks (20 in. × 30 in.), as well as Country Code posters (13 in. × 20 in.)	F
The National Trust, 42 Queen Anne's Gate, S.W. 1	Exhibition pictures of National Trust properties can be made available.	FL
The Chief Information Officer, Port of London Authority, Trinity Square, E.C. 3	Twelve photographic enlargements (13½ in. × 10 in.) of the handling of ships and goods. In addition, there is a map of the Port of London	S
Canada		
The Information Officer, Office of the High Commissioner for Canada, Canada House, S.W. 1	'Facts on Canada', their map-illustrated account, is very good. The office also offers wall sheets devoted to natural resources, as well as tourist posters. The Agents-General of Provincial Governments are other possible sources of material	F

359

Name and address of source	Comment	Conditions
China		
The Britain–China Friendship Association, 228 Gray's Inn Road, W.C. 1	Illustrated journals, art prints and photographs	FL and H
Denmark		
The Assistant Attaché, The Royal Danish Embassy, 29 Pont Street, S.W. 1	Masters can obtain an illustrated gazetteer. In addition, there are a number of brochures and booklets	F
Finland		
Press Attaché, Finnish Embassy, 66 Chester Square, S.W. 1	Posters, photographs and maps are available	FL and F
France		
Exhibitions Section, Cultural Services, French Embassy, 22 Wilton Crescent, S.W. 1	Offer travelling exhibitions, consisting of photographs and colour reproductions (26 in. × 40 in.)	FL
French Government Tourist Office, 66 Haymarket, S.W. 1	Various monochrome and colour posters of a tourist nature	F
French Railways Ltd., 179 Piccadilly, W. 1	Some railway posters. A charge is made for packing and posting. Apply on school notepaper	F
Ghana		
The High Commissioner for Ghana, 13 Belgrave Square, S.W. 1	Posters and maps illustrating the economic, social and human aspects of development in Ghana	F and FL
India		
Information Services, India House, Aldwych, W.C. 2	Supplies of material fluctuate. Write to India House to ascertain position	F
Japan		
Press and Cultural Section, Embassy of Japan, 46 Grosvenor Street, W. 1	Photographs and posters are available, on request. Also a colour-illustrated booklet.	H
The Netherlands		
Dept. for Press and Cultural Affairs, Royal Netherlands Embassy, 38 Hyde Park Gate, S.W. 7	Posters, maps and photographs. In addition, there are exhibition cases of items devoted to reclamation, agriculture and Dutch life	H and F

Name and address of source	Comment	Conditions
New Zealand		
Press Sections, Public Relations Branch, New Zealand Government Offices, 415 Strand, W.C. 2	A poster map of the Dominion, as well as photogravure posters of sheep rearing, butter production, etc.	F
Northern Ireland		
Information Officer, Northern Ireland Government Office, 13 Regent Street, S.W. 1	A lending library of photographs depicting many aspects of life in Northern Ireland, and a specially prepared set of twelve pictures for display purposes	FL
Norway		
Press and Information Officer, Royal Norwegian Embassy, 25 Belgrave Square, S.W. 1	Posters and photographic library facilities are available	FL
Poland		
The Polish Cultural Institute, 16 Devonshire Street, W. 1	Offer illustrative photographs, maps and pamphlets, as well as Exhibitions	F and FL
Sweden		
The Swedish Institute for Cultural Relations, 49 Egerton Crescent, S.W. 2	Photographically illustrated brochures of Sweden, the land, its people, natural resources, and economy. Mention the age of the pupils, for there is a possibility of supplying more material	F
Republic of South Africa		
South African Embassy, Trafalgar Square, S.W. 2	A number of photographically illustrated brochures, and a general map of the Republic are available. Some illustrative material is sold by Educational Productions Ltd.	F
United States		
The Exhibits Officer, Cultural Services (U.S.I.S.), American Embassy, Grosvenor Square, W. 1	Descriptive details of material will be sent by the Exhibits Officer. The Embassy circulates displays which cover a wide variety of subjects	FL

Name and address of source	*Comment*	*Conditions*

U.S.S.R.

Visual Aids Dept.,
The Society for Cultural
  Relations with the U.S.S.R.,
14 Kensington Square, W. 8

A large selection of photographs on
most aspects of life in the Soviet
Union (9 in. × 6 in.) to (12 in. × 16 in.)
There are sets on agriculture,
forestry, industry, and education.
No fee is charged, but a donation
is welcome.

FL

Venezuela

The Venezuelan Embassy,
3 Hans Crescent, S.W. 1

Illustrated booklets, tourist brochures and similar types of
material

F

Western Germany

The German Tourist
  Information Bureau,
61 Conduit Street, W. 1

Posters may be available during
the last four months of the year

F

Sources of maps

(a) *Outline map for pupils' use*

Publisher	*Comment*

Block and Anderson,
Banda House,
Cambridge Grove, W. 6

By means of 'Bandatrace' accurate
coloured maps can be provided. Pre-
drawn master outlines of the world and
continents are available.

Creteway Press,
Potters Green,
Buxted, near Uckfield,
Sussex

Supply a 15 in. × 10 in. map outline of the
World on Mollweide's Projection. There
is space for note making

Dennoyer-Geppert,
(Distributed by Sifton,
  Praed & Co. Ltd.,
67 St James's Street, W. 1)

Offer maps of various states and regions of
the U.S.A. as well as of other countries,
and the continents. Three sizes are available, 11 in. × 8½ in., 11 in. × 16 in. and
16 in. × 22 in.

Gestetner Duplicators Ltd.,
210 Euston Road, N.W. 1

Duroprint stencils and pre-cut map outlines can be purchased

The Grant Educational Co.
  Ltd.,
91–93 Union Street,
Glasgow, C. 1

Good-quality paper-printed maps. There
are outlines on both sides (size
10 in. × 8½ in.)

Johnson and Bacon Ltd.,
30 Museum Street, W.C. 1

Maps of many different parts of the world
(size 10 in. × 7½ in.)

Publisher	*Comment*
The Mapograph Co. Ltd., 440 High Road, Chiswick, W. 4	Rubber rollers with ink pad for the insertion of maps in pupils' notebooks. Specimen outlines are available and rollers can be made to personal specification. Standard size—$7\frac{1}{4}$ in. × $5\frac{1}{4}$ in.—but there are also foolscap maps
The Meteorological Office, (obtainable through H.M.S.O.)	Outlines for plotting weather in the British Isles and North-west Europe. Forms 2214 (North-west Europe), 2216 (British Isles), and 2217 (British Isles and North-west Europe)
Philip and Tacey Ltd., 69 Fulham High Street, S.W. 6	Outlines available of the continents and most countries (sizes 10 in. × $7\frac{1}{2}$ in. and 13 in. × 11 in.)
Roneo Ltd., Machines and Supplies Division, Southampton Row, W.C. 1	Standard pre-cut outline maps. Details can be easily added with a Roneo drawing pen

(b) Three-dimensional, model maps

Map reliefs

Map Reliefs, Ltd. 33 Hillcrest Road, Goff's Oak, Herts.	Offer plastic relief models, including a series corresponding to some of the $\frac{1}{4}$ in. O.S. maps of England. There is also a local model service

Oxford plastic relief maps

Education Department, Oxford University Press, Oxford	Series 1 (24 in. × 16 in.)—an outline edition of parts of Great Britain and the continents. Series 2—fully coloured models

Philip's plastic relief model maps

George Philip and Son, 30–32 Fleet Street, E.C. 4	Coloured models of the World (57 in. × 42 in.) and British Isles (12 in. × $8\frac{3}{4}$ in.). Also some which depict regions within Britain. Models can be made to personal specification

(c) Coloured and printed wall-maps

Dennoyer-Geppert maps

Distributed by: Sifton, Praed and Co., 67 St James's Street, W. 1	Visual Relief Maps of different parts of the U.S.A., the continents, and the world. Different sizes available.

Publisher	*Comment*

Haak's series of wall-maps

Distributed by
    Sifton, Praed and Co.,
    67 St James's Street, W. 1

First-class maps—of the continents, and various parts of Europe. Approximate size 80 in. × 60 in.

Johnston

Johnston and Bacon Ltd.,
30 Museum Street, W.C. 1

A political series, as well as Physical–Political maps. Various sizes, but particularly 52 in. × 38 in.

Ordnance Survey publications

Conversions undertaken by many firms, including George Philip and Son Ltd.

Can be converted into district and regional maps, using ½ in., 1 in., 2½ in. or 6 in. sheets.

Oxford wall-maps

Education Dept.,
Oxford University Press,
Oxford

Printed in full colour on stout paper (41 in. × 28 in.). The maps are enlarged editions of those in Oxford atlases.

Philips wall-maps

George Philip and Son Ltd.,
Victoria Road, N.W. 10

A wide range available, including wall-maps of individual countries, particular areas, the continents, and the world. See catalogues.

Westermann

Distributed by:
    The House of Grant Ltd.,
    Glasgow, C. 1

World-famed maps. Many of them are now available with place-names in English. Supplied on stout linen

Washable and reversible outline wall-maps

The House of Grant Ltd.,
91–95 Union Street,
Glasgow, C. 1

White outlines on black, plastic-coated material (54 in. × 42 in. approximately). There are maps on both sides. Surface can be wiped clean of chalk with a damp cloth

Demonstration outline maps

Johnston and Bacon,
30 Museum Street, W.C. 1

Yellow outlines on blackboard paper (45 in. × 35 in.), but a number of other types are also available

Philips outline wall-maps, and map-building sheets

George Philip and Son Ltd.,
Victoria Road, N.W. 10

Map-building sheets—yellow outlines on black. In other types black is used for coastlines. Latter series, of the major parts of the world, measure 41 in. × 32½ in.

Publisher	*Comment*

Cellograph maps

Philip and Tacey Ltd., 69–79 Fulham High Street, S.W. 6	Outline maps with a special plastic surface (30 in. × 40 in.). After using coloured wax pencils they can be wiped clean with a dry duster

(e) **Sheet maps**

Topographical

John Bartholomew and Son Ltd., 12 Duncan Street, Edinburgh 9	A layer-coloured $\frac{1}{2}$ in. series, covering the British Isles in sixty-two sheets. Each sheet is 23 in. × 33 in.

Postal orders: 1. The Ordnance Survey, P.O. Box No. 5F, Leatherhead Road, Chessington, Surrey 2. Edward Stanford Ltd., 12–14 Long Acre, W.C. 2 and other O.S. agents through the country)	Produce a standard $\frac{1}{4}$ in., 1 and $2\frac{1}{2}$ in. contoured series. For the position about $\frac{1}{2}$ in. maps, and 6 and 25 in. plans write directly to the Ordnance Survey. There are also special 10 miles to 1 in. maps. A current list of old examination paper stocks is kept at Chessington, and the Survey gives an educational discount on normal maps purchased *directly* from them (ask for form O.S. 318)

Geological

The Geological Survey, Exhibition Road, South Kensington, S.W. 7 (*Catalogues* are available from the above address, but *orders* must go through the Ordnance Survey Dept. or Edward Stanford Ltd.)	Stocks were destroyed during the Second World War. Reprinting and New Editions are well in hand. Since issues occur at frequent intervals write for the current catalogue. Note that the 1 in. map is issued both in Solid and Drift editions. There are also a limited number of 6 in. sheets

Soil survey

The Ordnance Survey Department distributes the flat sheet maps	Surveying is in progress. To date the coverage is small, although some memoirs (with enclosed maps) and sheets have been published

Land use

Miss A. Coleman M.A., Kings College, Strand, W.C. 2 *or* Edward Stanford Ltd.	An increasing number of the second Land Utilisation Survey Sheets are now available

| *Publisher* | *Comment* |

(f) Sheet maps of other parts of the world

British overseas territories

| The catalogue of maps issued by the Directorate of Overseas Surveys is obtainable from Messrs Edward Stanford Ltd. | There are maps on all scales. Map extracts prepared for overseas school certificate examinations can be purchased from the Directorate itself: Kingston Road, Tolworth, Surbiton, Surrey. Write for the current list |

Official Foreign Maps

| British Agents are:
 (a) Sifton, Praed and Co.,
 67 St James's Street, W. 1
 (b) Edward Stanford Ltd.,
 12–14 Long Acre, W.C. 2 | Catalogues are available |

Geographical section, general staff maps

| The Agents—as above | Catalogues are available |

French topographic map extracts

| Institut Géographie National,
 107 Rue la Boétie,
 Paris VIIIe | Collection of 16 maps (25 cm. × 35 cm.) at scales of 1:50,000 and 1:200,000. Plastic relief models and notes of same areas also supplied |

United States topographical maps (for teaching purposes)

| U.S. Geological Survey, Washington Distribution Centre, Acorn Building, Eastern Avenue and Newell Street, Silver Spring, Maryland, U.S.A. | Sets (either of 25 or of 100) of maps illustrating specific physiographic features. Write for more information and discount details |

(g) Marine charts

The Agent is J. D. Potter, 145 Minories, E.C. 3.

(h) Edge-binding machines

(1) The 'Speedguide'	Ofrex Ltd., 93 Talbot Street, Nottingham
(2) The 'Admel' machine	Lawes Rabjohns Ltd., Victoria Street, Westminster, S.W. 1
(3) The 'Mormil' machine	A. West and Partners Ltd., 684 Mitcham Road, Croydon, Surrey

Sources of aerial photographs

Obliques

(*a*) Aerofilms and Aero Pictorial Ltd., 4 Albemarle Street, W. 1. This firm offers a preview and inspection service.

(*b*) Dr K. St Joseph, Dept. of Aerial Photography, University of Cambridge.

(*c*) C. H. Wood (Bradford) Ltd., 82 Manningham Lane, Bradford 8.

Verticals

(*a*) *Government department*

England and Wales

The Air Photographs Officer,
Ministry of Housing and Local Government,
Whitehall, S.W. 1

Scotland

Department of Health for Scotland,
Air-photo Library,
Room 016A, York Buildings,
Queen Street,
Edinburgh 2

Northern Ireland

Deputy Keeper of Public Records,
Public Records Office for Northern Ireland,
Law Courts Building,
May Street,
Belfast,
Northern Ireland.

State whether full stereo coverage or simple mosaic lay-down coverage.

The order must be accompanied by a tracing from the 1 in. O.S. map, showing a latitude and longitude intersection and sufficient major detail to permit positive identification.

N.B. A National Grid Reference is *not* acceptable.

(*b*) *Other sources*

(i) The Director General,
Ordnance Survey,
Air Photo Cover Section,
Leatherhead Road,
Chessington, Surrey

The Ordnance Survey are building up a record collection of air photographs taken within the U.K. for survey and map revision purposes. Enquire about the extent of the cover, providing a tracing from the 1 in. sheet in which you are interested. It should be keyed to the National Grid.

(ii) Fairey Surveys Ltd.,
24 Bruton Street, W.1

(iii) Meridian Air Maps,
Shoreham Airport, Sussex

367

Sources of atlases

Examples of the better-known atlases in each publisher's
range have been singled out in the following list.

Publisher	*Comment*
Blackie and Son Ltd., 16/18 William IV Street, W.C. 2	Publish *The Palaeographical Atlas*, which deals with the geological evolution of Britain, and *How to Use an Atlas*. This book contains eighty-two sets of exercises
Collins-Longmans Atlases, 144 Cathedral Street, Glasgow, C. 4	Publish a series of very useful atlas-textbooks, e.g. *The British Isles—Where, How and Why*. The maps are clear, colourful and simple. They also market a family of atlases, designed with different ages, abilities and interests in mind.
Faber and Faber Ltd., 24 Russell Square, W.C. 1	Offer the *Faber Atlas*, originally produced by Verlag E. Hotzel of Vienna. It was designed for geography students, and is consciously presented for the British Market. Recently, Faber's *New School Atlas* has been added to the series
The House of Grant, The Grant Educational Co. Ltd., 91–93 Union Street, Glasgow, C. 1	Distribute a number of German atlases in this country, including *The Diercke World Atlas*. This has fifty double-page maps, and is useful for reference purposes. It has, however, a German text
Johnston and Bacon Ltd., 30 Museum Street, W.C. 1	Market *The Modern School Atlas*, designed for the first three years of Secondary school courses, and *The Advanced Modern School Atlas*
George Harrap & Co. Ltd., 182 High Holborn, W.C. 1	Offer Harrap's *3 D Junior Atlas*, and distribute *L'Atlas Général Larousse*. In the latter work of reference thirty-five pages are devoted to World Economy, fifty-five to Historical Development, and seventy-two to regional considerations. It has a French text.
H.M.S.O.—for the Meteorological Office, Atlantic House, Holborn Viaduct, E.C. 1	Sells a *Climatological Atlas of the British Isles* with sections devoted to seasonal and annual amounts of sunshine, frost, rain, snow etc. It is illustrated by means of maps, diagrams and tables.

Publisher	*Comment*
Longmans, Green and Co. Ltd., 48 Grosvenor Street, W. 1	Linked with Collins in atlas production. *The Study Atlas* includes not only maps but also photographs and accompanying exercises.
Methuen and Co. Ltd., 36 Essex Street, The Strand, W.C. 2	Market two sketch map books in which maps and accompanying text illuminate the main centres of current interest: (1) *An Atlas of World Affairs* (2) *An Atlas of African Affairs*
John Murray, 50 Albemarle Street, W. 1	Publish *Atlas of Western Europe* by Jean Dollfuss, dealing with distributional material on a European basis. Each map is accompanied by a commentary
The National Geographic Society, Washington 6, D.C.	Offer the *National Geographic Atlas of the World*
Thos. Nelson and Sons Ltd., 36 Park Street, Park Lane, W. 1	*Nelson's School Atlas* was designed as a teaching atlas, providing maps that are clear, and appropriately simple. Also offered is *Nelson's Concise World Atlas*, edited by J. Wreford Watson.
Oliver and Boyd Ltd., Tweeddale Court, 14 High Street, Edinburgh 1	Publish *The Advanced Atlas of Modern Geography* by Bartholomew, and *The Comparative Atlas*. The latter has coloured maps, and thirty-two pages of text with black and white diagrams
Oxford University Press, Amen House, Warwick Square, E.C. 4	Their range includes the *Oxford Economic Atlases* and the *Oxford School Atlas*. The national *Atlas of Britain and Northern Ireland* maps our material resources on a monumental scale. Note, too, *The Oxford Atlas*
George Philip and Son Ltd., 98 Victoria Road, N.W. 10	*The University Atlas* is very useful for sixth-form work. Among their junior-level products is the *Elementary Atlas*, now past its hundredth edition and popular for first- and second-form work
The Reader's Digest, 7 Old Bailey, London, E.C. 4	Their *Great World Atlas* includes Origin of Life, Systematic, and Regional maps. More recently they have produced a *Complete Atlas of the British Isles*. The unabridged educational edition is marketed by Collins-Longmans

369

Publisher	*Comment*
The Times Publishing Co. Ltd., Printing House Square, London, E.C. 4	Is responsible for a standard British work of reference: *The Times Atlas of the World.* The Mid-Century edition is in five volumes: (1) The World, Australasia and East Asia; (2) India, the Middle East and Russia; (3) Northern Europe; (4) The Mediterranean and Africa; (5) The Americas
The University of Wales Press, Cardiff	Offer *Wales in Maps*, by Dr Margaret Davies. It includes both maps and text

General note

(1) Some firms (e.g. Oxford University Press, Philips and Longmans) publish *overseas editions* of their atlases.

(2) *Local supplement maps* are also available in a number of cases.

Sources of globes

Maker	*Comment*
Dennoyer-Geppert Services, (Distributed by Sifton, Praed and Co. Ltd., 67 St James's Street, W. 1	An American firm. They market a wide range of all types of globes, including slate-surfaced and tactual relief ones. Poster paints can be applied to the latter type
Diana Wyllie Ltd., 3 Park Road, Baker Street, N.W. 1	Sell 12 in. diameter 'Raised Relief' globes. They can be marked in crayon or ink and then wiped clean
George Philip and Son Ltd., 30–32 Fleet Street, E.C. 4	Maintain a comprehensive range of orthodox-type globes: from 6 in. to 6 ft. in diameter, and in varying styles, i.e. slate-surface, physical or political. A rubberised inflatable globe is also marketed
Johnston and Bacon Ltd., 30 Museum Street, W.C. 1	Offer three 12 in. diameter globes: politically coloured, physically coloured and blackboard surfaced (for chalk use)
The National Geographic Magazine, European Office, 161–166 Fleet Street, E.C. 4	12 in. and 16 in. models are available. They show political divisions and towns. One version of the smaller scale globe can be illuminated

Sources of samples

Name and material, and address of the source	Comment	Conditions
Geological specimens		
The Geological Laboratories, 168 Moss Lane East, Manchester 15	Catalogues obtainable on request	S
The Director, The Geological Survey and Museum, Exhibition Road, South Kensington, S.W 7	Small quantities of rock, fossil, and mineral specimens are available from time to time. To put them to the best use schools should state how far Geology is taught and what specimens are required	F
Gregory, Bottley and Co., 30 Old Church Street, Chelsea, S.W. 3	Samples of British, foreign and Commonwealth minerals and rocks. Comprehensive catalogues are available. There are showrooms in London	S
Aluminium		
The Aluminium Development Association, 33 Grosvenor Street, W. 1	Specimen boxes: small samples of the raw materials used in obtaining aluminium, and the semi-finished forms of the metal	F
Cocoa		
Schools Dept., Messrs Cadbury Bros. Ltd., Bourneville	Life-size plastic model of a cocoa pod, a paper section showing the size and position of the beans, box of specimens, and wall chart	F
Cocoa and coffee		
The Nestlé Co. Ltd. (Educational Aids), Great Castle Street, W. 1	(i) A project box and wall chart on chocolate making	S
	(ii) A box containing samples of coffee beans	F
Cotton		
The Textile Council 3 Alberton Street, Manchester 3	A box of cotton samples 'from cotton boll to woven fabric'	S
Flax (linen)		
The Flaxspinners' Association of Great Britain, Public Relations Office, 4 Chamber of Commerce Buildings, Dundee	A visual aid box containing flax seed, straw scutched flax, grey and bleached yarns, and samples of finished articles	S

371

Name and material, and Address of the source	Comment	Conditions

Flax (cont.)

| The Irish Linen Guild, Citation House, 91–101 Oxford Street, W. 1 | Educational Box: includes different types of linen and weaves, as well as a filmstrip | S |

Iron and steel

| The British Iron and Steel Federation, Training Dept., Steel House, Tothill Street, S.W. 1 | A box of samples including six iron ores, sintered ore, coke, limestone, pig iron, blast furnace iron, slag and mild steel | S |

Jute and hessian

| The British Jute Trade Federal Council, Royal Exchange, Dundee | A visual aid box, containing samples of raw and processed jute, along with teachers' notes | F |

Leather

| The Boot and Shoe Manufacturing Industry, 35 College Street, Northampton | A display case | |

Nickel

| The Mond Nickel Company Ltd., Education Section, Thames House, Millbank, S.W. 1 | Two specimens of sulphide ore: nickeliferous and cupriferous iron sulphide | F |

Oats

| Quaker Oats Ltd., Trade Promotion Dept., Southall, Middlesex | Small plastic-box samples of: (a) prepared oats, (b) groats | F |

Oil

| The Petroleum Information Bureau, 29 New Bond Street, W. 1 | Samples and display cabinet. Included is a small rock core from Eakring, and some Scottish oil shale | FL |

| Trade Relations Division, Shell International Petroleum Co. Ltd., Shell Centre, S.E. 1 | A geological sample box. In it there are igneous, metamorphic and sedimentary rocks, an oil-well core, and working model to show how oil is contained in the sand | FL |

Name and material and Address of the source	Comment	Conditions
Oilseeds		
Unilever Ltd., Information Serivce, Unilever House, Blackfriars, E.C. 4	A box of samples to accompany their filmstrips and wall charts.	S
Pulp and paper		
The Reed Paper Group, Education Services Dept., 82 Baker Street, W. 1	A paper sample set: this contains sixteen samples of different types of pulp, paper and board. One set per class is supplied	F
Rubber		
Publications Dept., British Rubber Development Board, Market Buildings, Market Lane, E.C. 3	The kit includes samples of latex and rubber in various stages of manufacture, with a variety of finished rubber products	S
Information Officer, Dunlop Rubber Co. Ltd., 10/12 King Street, St James's, S.W. 1	A sample box containing a tube of liquid latex and pieces of smoked sheet rubber	F and FL
Silk		
The Silk Centre, 13 Portman Square, W. 1	Cocoons, thrown silk and patches of finished cloth are available. They are supplied together with photographs and leaflets. The small charge covers postage	S
Lullingstone Silk Farm Ltd., Ayot House, Ayot St Lawrence, Herts.	A students box, silkworm eggs, live silkworms, etc.	S
Sewing Silks Ltd., Perivale Mills, Greenford, Middlesex	Sample boxes and cocoons	S
Sugar		
Tate and Lyle Ltd., Educational Aids Bureau, 21 Mincing Lane, E.C. 3	Samples of raw and refined sugar on a display board, illustrating factory processing	F
Timber		
Education Dept., Timber Development Assoc. Ltd., 21 College Hill, E.C. 4	Fifty-four specimens available—e.g. Greenheart, Douglas Fir, Teak and African Walnut. They can be bought separately	S

Name and material, and Address of the source	Comment	Conditions
Timber (cont.)		
The Agent-General for Western Australia, 115 The Strand, W.C. 2	Twelve specimens, including jarrah and karri	S
Wheat and flour		
The Flour Advisory Bureau Ltd., 21 Arlington Street, S.W. 1	A display board on which are pinned samples of the milling process (from wheat to flour)	F
Rank's Hovis McDougall Ltd., Public Relations Division, (J. Walter Thompson Co. Ltd.) 40 Berkeley Square, W. 1	A colour folder which shows the processes of flour milling and contains samples at different stages	F
Wool		
The International Wool Secretariat, Dept. of Education and Training, Wool House, Carlton Gardens, S.W. 1	A set of raw wool, yarn and cloth samples on a display board	S

Special Note: Commonwealth products

The Commonwealth Institute, Kensington High Street, W. 8, offers samples of many different products, both of agricultural and of mineral origin. There are small charges. In a number of cases explanatory leaflets can also be purchased.

Write to the Publications Dept., and ask for the detailed list, i.e. leaflet no. 9.

Sample boxes

Transparent, moulded plastic display boxes are obtainable from Map Reliefs Ltd., 33 Hillcrest Road, Goffs Oak, Herts.

SOURCES OF OUTSIDE SPEAKERS

One way of developing a lively interest in geographical matters is to make use of outside speakers. While some lecturers are sponsored by interested bodies, others act purely out of good will. Local people will often help schools in this regard, and the following list of addresses is intended merely to suggest ways in which the range might be extended. Always give the age-group of the pupils concerned, as well as the approximate number who will be in the audience.

A. *Speakers on particular topics*

Coal and the mining industry

H.Q. The National Coal Board, Hobart House, 2 Grosvenor Place, S.W. 1.

Depending on the location of the school, write to the Public Relations Officer:

Northern (N. and C.) Division,
Whitley Road,
Longbenton,
Newcastle upon Tyne 12

Durham Division,
Team Valley Trading Estate,
Gateshead 11

North-west Division,
(i.e. Lancs, Cheshire and North Wales)
40 Portland Street,
Manchester 1

Yorkshire Division,
[N.B. The Secretary],
The Lodge,
South Parade,
Doncaster

West Midlands Division,
Himley Hall,
near Dudley, Worcs.

East Midlands Division,
Sherwood Lodge, Arnold,
near Nottingham

South-west Division,
(i.e. South Wales, Somerset, etc.)
Ty Glas Avenue,
Llanishen, Cardiff

Southern England
(including the London area),
Room 55 (Speakers Panel),
Hobart House,
Grosvenor Place, S.W. 1

Subjects of talks range from the history of coal mining to developments in recent years, and future prospects. No fees or travelling expenses are incurred.

The iron and steel industry

The British Iron and Steel Federation, Training Department, Steel House, Tothill Street, S.W. 1.

The Federation will arrange visits by men from the iron and steel companies, or independent lecturers.

Oil

The Esso Petroleum Co. Ltd., Public Relations Manager, Victoria Street, S.W. 1

There are no full-time lecturers, but help will be given, if possible. Requests throughout the country will be considered, and representatives speak on the production, transport and uses of oil, particularly in connection with Britain.

Silk

The Silk Centre, Dorland House, 18–20 Regent Street, W. 1.

Write to make arrangements.

375

B. *Speakers on individual countries*

Australia

The Chief Migration Officer, Office of the High Commissioner, Australia House, W.C. 2.

There are no official lecturers on the staff. They deliver L.E.A. and privately arranged addresses all over the U.K. Apply at least six months beforehand.

Brazil

The Anglo-Brazilian Society, 1 Hamilton Place, W. 1.

Lectures can be colour-slide illustrated. Appointments are confined to an area within a radius of thirty miles of London.

Britain

1. *The physical background*

The Museum Lecturer, Geological Survey and Museum, Exhibition Road, South Kensington, S.W. 7.

There are opportunities for talks and demonstrations to be given to visiting parties.

2. *The Ordnance Survey*

Leatherhead Road, Chessington, Surrey.

The Survey will consider requests and these should be sent to the Director-General. Lecturers speak on general or particular aspects of the work of the Ordnance Survey. Fees and/or travelling expenses may be required.

3. *National Trust*

42 Queen Anne's Gate, S.W. 1.

Slide-illustrated lectures of the work and properties of the Trust are voluntarily undertaken by members.

British waterways

H.Q. Melbury House, Melbury Terrace, N.W. 1.

Requests should be made to the Divisional Manager:

North-western Division,
Lime Street Chambers,
Lime Street,
Liverpool 1

North-east Division,
P.O. Box 9,
1 Dock Street,
Leeds 1

South-west Division,
Dock Office,
Gloucester

South-east Division,
Willow Grange,
Church Road,
Watford, Herts

Representatives speak on the commercial or amenity aspects of British Waterways. There are no fees or travelling expenses.

France

The French Embassy, Cultural Services, 22 Wilton Crescent, S.W. 1.

Japan

The Embassy of Japan, Press and Cultural Section, 46 Grosvenor Street, W. 1.

At present invitations can only be accepted in London and adjacent districts. There is a shortage of suitable speakers.

Netherlands

The Royal Netherlands Embassy, 38 Hyde Park Gate, S.W. 7.

Fees and travelling expenses are paid by the school. Visits throughout Britain are possible, but it is easier to arrange speakers in the London area.

Northern Ireland

Government Information Service, Stormont Castle, Belfast 4, *or* The Agent in Great Britain, Government of Northern Ireland, 13 Regent Street, S.W. 1.

Lecturers are not concerned with party politics. They speak about Northern Ireland in general, or on more specific aspects. The service is restricted to Grammar school senior pupils.

Spain and Spanish culture

The Institute of Spain, 102 Eaton Square, S.W. 1.

Requests should be submitted well in advance.

Sweden

The Secretary, The Swedish Institute, 49 Egerton Crescent, S.W. 3.

A panel of speakers reside in various (but not all) parts of Britain. They are mainly British teachers who have taught in Sweden. Travelling expenses and a small fee are payable.

The U.S.A.

The Speakers Bureau, Cultural Section. U.S.I.S., American Embassy, Grosvenor Square, W. 1.

Lectures on various aspects of American life and policy are arranged. Travelling expenses are normally expected.

The U.S.S.R.

The Society for Cultural Relations with the U.S.S.R., 118 Tottenham Court Road, W. 1.

The Society (not to be confused with the Soviet Embassy) can provide speakers in various parts of the country. Travelling expenses are expected, but every effort is made not to involve schools in heavy expenditure.

Western Germany

Apply to the Public Relation Consultants of the West German Embassy: Curzon Publicity Ltd., 31 St James's Place, S.W. 1.

C. *Speakers on a wider range of topics and countries*

The Commonwealth Institute, Kensington High Street, W. 8

Lecture tours in the provinces are arranged through L.E.A.s, and take place two or three times a year. Inter-school conferences on specific topics are also organised.

The English Speaking Union, 37 Charles Street, Berkeley Square, W. 1

The Speakers Bureau will help to find speakers on Commonwealth or American affairs. There is, however, only a small staff, and no regular lecturing panel. Fees are not expected, but reimbursement of travelling and out-of-pocket expenses is normal.

The Kodak School Lecture Service, Kodak Ltd., Kingsway, W.C. 2

Offer a series of seven illustrated talks under the general title 'Other People, Other Lands', e.g. 'Desert Journey—across the Sahara in a Land Rover'. Kodak provide the lecturer and necessary projection equipment. The talks are free, but demand is heavy.

The Royal Commonwealth Society, 18 Northumberland Avenue, W.C. 2

The School of Oriental and African Studies, London University, W.C. 1

The school distributes a leaflet on the lectures which they offer.

The United Nations and its specialised agencies

The Meetings Secretary, Council for Education in World Citizenship, 93 Albert Embankment, S.E. 1.

Speakers are sent to all parts of England and Wales, affiliated schools meeting their travelling expenses. Conferences are also frequently arranged. Various topics are offered, e.g. 'The Freedom from Hunger Campaign', and 'The U.S.S.R.' Ask for the current list, and membership pamphlet.

The University Institutes of Education

The following Institutes (or, in some cases, Departments) have expressed their willingness to co-operate with schools in providing overseas student speakers. The people concerned are generally post-graduates or experienced teachers in their own right. Whether or not anyone is available naturally depends on a number of factors, including the student enrolment, existing commitments, individual self-confidence and fluency in English. However, experience has shown that occasional visits of this nature are well worth the effort involved, for they are enjoyable and also mutually beneficial. Write to the Institute, unless it is otherwise stated: Aberystwyth (Faculty of Education), Bangor, Birmingham, Bristol, Cambridge, Cardiff (The Department), Exeter, Keele (The Lecturer in Geography Method at the Department), Leeds, Leicester (The School of Education), Liverpool, London (apply through the Adviser to Overseas Students), Manchester (The Department), Newcastle upon Tyne, Nottingham, Oxford, Reading, Sheffield, Southampton, Swansea (The Professor of Education), and Queen's, Belfast.

TEACHING MATERIAL IN CONNECTION WITH WEATHER STUDY

A. *Establishing a Weather Station*

Sources of information:

1. *Outline of the observational routine at rainfall stations and climatological stations*: Meteorological Publication 1110.

2. *Making weather observation*: M.O. 5.

3. *Observers' Handbook*: M.O. 554.

4. *Instructions for making Thermometer Screens of the Stevenson type*: M.O. 63.

5. *Memorandum on the Requirements of a Climatological Station*: M.O. 3003.

6. *Running a School Weather Station* by D. E. Pedgley. The reprint of an article in the February 1962 issue of *Weather*. Obtainable from the Royal Meteorological Society, 49 Cromwell Road, S.W. 7.

7. *Colour filmstrips*
  (i) Instruments and Observations (Ref. F41)
  (ii) Field and Laboratory experiments (Ref. F42)
  (iii) A screen colour ⎫ Part A. Convection clouds; clouds of a cyclone;
  and guide to ⎬ warm and cold fronts (Ref. F52). Part B.
  (iv) clouds ⎭ Waves and billows; Ice Clouds; Contrails; Optical Phenomena; Stratus; Fog (Ref. F53)
    The third and fourth items are annotated in a book *A Colour Guide to Clouds*, published by the Pergamon Press.
  (v) Unstable Weather (Ref. F30)
  (vi) Stable Weather (Ref. F31)
These filmstrips are issued by Diana Wyllie Ltd., 3 Park Road, Baker Street, N.W. 1.

8. The nearest R.A.F. Meteorological Station—for advice, and possible visit.

B. *Instrument makers*

These include:

C. F. Casella and Co. Ltd., Regent House, Britannia Walk, N. 1.

F. Darton and Co. Ltd., Watford Fields, Watford, Herts.

Heath, Hicks and Perken (Thermometers) Ltd., New Eltham, S.E. 9.

Negretti and Zambra Ltd., 122 Regent Street, W. 1.

George Philip and Co. Ltd., Education Dept., Victoria Road, N.W. 10.

Short and Mason Ltd., 280 Wood Street, Walthamstow, E. 17.

C. *The daily weather report*

(i) Orders for copies, and any correspondence: The Meteorological Office, London Road, Bracknell, Berks.

(ii) Outline maps for plotting purposes: M.O. Form 2216 (British Isles) and M.O. Form 2217 (British Isles and North-west Europe).

(iii) Information:
  (*a*) *Instructions for the Preparation of Weather Maps*: M.O. Publication 515.

(b) *Your own Weather Map*—being a reprint from the magazine *Weather* for August/October 1964.

(iv) Film material:

(a) *Interpreting the Weather Map.* Colour. E.F.V.A. (315 D41).

(b) *The Weather Map.* No 14L/5473. B/W. Useful for 'O' and 'A' level work. Hire charge £4. The R.A.F. Cinema Corps, Africa House, Kingsway, W.C. 2.

(c) *The World Meteorological Organisation.* B/W. V605. The Central Film Library, Bromyard Avenue, Acton, W. 3.

D. *Publications of the Meteorological Office*

These are obtainable from: H.M. Stationery Office, York House, Kingsway, London, W.C. 2.

M.O. Publication No. 225: *The Weather Map*
M.O. Publication No. 554: *Observer's Handbook*
M.O. Publication No. 630: *Handbook of Aviation Meteorology*

Note that there is also a manual entitled *A Course in Elementary Meteorology.*

E. *Other useful addresses*

A photographic, slide and filmstrip library:

The Meteorological Office,
London Road,
Bracknell, Berks.

Enquiries about the journal *Weather*, the library of slides (on loan), and other activities in connection with weather study:

The Royal Meteorological Society,
49 Cromwell Road, S.W. 7

APPENDIX D: ORGANISING FIELD-WORK

SOURCES OF INFORMATION
A. *In book form*
Field-work: techniques and worked examples

1. *Handbook of Geographical Fieldwork*, produced by the Surrey Fieldwork Society 1963.
2. *The Purpose and Organisation of Field Studies* (part 1), edited by Margaret S. Dilke. Rivingtons. (With extensive bibliography.)
3. *A Geographical Field Study Companion*, by P. Sauvain. Hulton.
4. *London's Countryside*, by S. W. Woolridge and W. S. Golding. Collins. New Naturalist series.
5. *The Geography of Greater London*, general editor, R. Clayton. George Philip and Son Ltd.
6. *Yorkshire Field Studies*, edited by G. E. Bell. University of Leeds Institute of Education.
7. *Field Excursions in North-west England* (part 2), edited by Margaret S. Dilke. Rivingtons.
8. *Field Studies in the British Isles*, edited by J. A. Steers. Nelson, 1964.

Regional information: general background sources

1. *British Landscapes through Maps*, edited by Prof. K. C. Edwards. The Geographical Association. E.g. 'Snowdonia', 'The Chilterns' and 'Merseyside'.
2. *Great Britain: Geographical Essays*, editor Jean B. Mitchell. Cambridge University Press.
3. The Regional Monographs of Collins New Naturalist series. e.g. *Dartmoor* and *The Broads*.
4. Regions of the British Isles—A Nelson series, e.g. *North England*, and *The Highlands and Isles*.
5. The County Reports of the First Land Utilisation Survey. General Editor, L. D. Stamp.
6. The National Park and Forest Guides (H.M.S.O.), e.g. *The Peak District*.
7. The Victoria County Histories of England.
8. Methuen's Little County Guides.

Regional Information: The Physical Background

1. The Geologists' Association Guides, i.e. the geology of the districts round university towns, and elsewhere in Britain, e.g. Snowdonia. Each booklet gives detailed itineraries. Information and copies are obtainable from Benham and Co., Sheepen Road, Colchester.

2. The Handbooks of British Regional Geology. Published by the Stationery Office for the Geological Survey, e.g. The Bristol and Gloucester District.

3. Sheet Memoirs, each describing a 1 in. Geological Map. Published by H.M.S.O. for the Survey. Many of them are out of print, but others have been revised. Ascertain the position from the Geological Survey.

4. The Geological Survey's Memoirs on Special Topics, e.g. water supply and mineral resources.

5. *The Climatological Atlas of the British Isles*, compiled by the Meteorological Office.

6. *Climate and the British Scene*, by Professor G. Manley. Collins New Naturalist Series.

7. *The British Islands and their Vegetation*, 2 vols., by A. G. Tansley. Cambridge University Press.

Regional information: the human response

1. The Buildings of England—a county series of illustrated books, edited by Dr N. Pevsner. Penguin Books.

2. County Development Reports, prepared by Town and Country Planning Departments.

3. English Place Names, a county series. The English Place Name Society. Cambridge University Press.

4. Regional Archaeologies, e.g. *The Severn Basin* and *Yorkshire*. Cory, Adams and Mackay.

B. *In statistical form*

1. *Averages of bright sunshine, temperature, humidity and snowfall of official weather stations* are available for purchase as separate items. Ask H.M.S.O. for details. Also consider the detailed records in *British Rainfall*, an annual publication. Information about the weather is also kept by Water Boards, Museums, and Surveyor's Offices, who are often willing to help.

2. *Parish crop and land use returns.* Those for the period 1866–1917 are available for inspection at the Public Record Office, Chancery Lane, W.C. 1. Extracts from the period since 1917 can be supplied, on prepayment of a fee to cover the work, from the Agricultural and Sampling Branch, Ministry of Agriculture, Fisheries and Food, Epsom Road, Guildford, Surrey.

3. *National Census of Population Returns*, taken at ten-yearly intervals, starting 1801. From public reference libraries.

FIELD-WORK ACCOMMODATION

(a) *The C.H.A.* Headquarters: Birch Heys, Cromwell Range, Manchester 14.

Parties are welcomed at the following houses, except in peak periods, leaflets available on request: Borrowdale, Ambleside, Bassenthwaite, Eskdale, Llanfairfechan, Llangollen, Rhu, Cove, Whitby, Peel, Dawlish, Shanklin, Hope and Hindhead.

(b) *The Field Studies Council.* Headquarters: 9 Devereux Court, The Strand, W.C. 2.

General enquiries about the Council and its field centres, as well as details of future programmes, are obtainable from the Publicity Secretary, F.S.C., Ravensmead, Keston, Kent.

Addresses of individual centres:

(i) Dale Fort Field Centre, Haverfordwest, Pemb.
(ii) Flatford Mill F.C., East Bergholt, near Colchester.
(iii) Juniper Hall F.C., Dorking.
(iv) Malham Tarn F.C., near Settle, Yorks.
(v) Orielton F.C., Pembroke, Pemb.
(vi) Preston Montford F.C., near Shrewsbury, Salop.
(vii) Rhyd-y-Creuau, F.C. near Betws-y-Coed, Caern.
(viii) Slapton Ley F.C., Slapton, Kingsbridge, Devon.
(ix) Nettlecombe Court F.C., near Williton, Somerset (Opening 1968.)

Programmes for the forthcoming year are sent out to paid-up members some time in November, and places allotted soon afterwards. The latter can be booked by individuals or on behalf of parties. Schools can either undertake their own field teaching or take advantage of instruction by centre staff.

(c) *The Holiday Fellowship Ltd.* Youth Dept., 142 Great North Way, Hendon, N.W. 4.

Camps are maintained at Devils Bridge (near Aberystwyth), Kessingland, (near Lowestoft), Langdale (Westmorland), Malhamdale, Minard (Argyll), Newlands (Keswick), Nant Gwynant (Snowdonia), and Staithes (north-east coast).

Subject to availability, accommodation can also be offered at the normal guest houses.

(d) *The Scottish Field Studies Association (of S.F.S.A.).* Headquarters: 141 Bath Street, Glasgow, C. 2.

The permanent Field Centre of the Association is at Kindrogan, 8 miles east of Pitlochry, Perthshire. School party bookings are accepted here as well as at various Holiday Fellowship houses where S.F.S.A. courses are run.

(e) *The Young Men's Christian Association.* The General Secretary, Y.M.C.A., 112 Great Russell Street, W.C. 1.

Ask for Association's brochure, and enquire about the possibilities of using their hostels which have sleeping accommodation.

(f) *The Youth Hostels Association.* Headquarters: (1) Trevelyan House, 8 St Stephen's Hill, St Albans, Herts.; (2) Scottish Y.H.A., 7 Bruntsfield Crescent, Edinburgh 10.

Apply (large S.A.E.) for the illustrated booklets *Youth Hostels for Field Studies* and *Youth Hostels for School Journey Parties.* The following Youth Hostels are specially equipped for field study in various subjects:

Northumberland coast: Rock Hall, Rock, Alnwick, Northumberland.
North Yorkshire coast: Boggle Hole, Fyling Thorpe, Whitby, Yorkshire.
Lake District: Hawkshead, Esthwaite Lodge, Ambleside, Westmorland; High Close, Loughrigg, Ambleside, Westmorland.

Yorkshire Pennines: Grinton Lodge, Richmond, Yorkshire.
Peak District: Leam Hall, Grindleford, via Sheffield.
Norfolk coast: Sheringham, Norfolk.
Oxfordshire Cotswolds: Charlbury, Oxfordshire.
Gloucestershire Cotswolds: Duntisbourne Abbots, Cirencester, Glos.
North Downs and Kentish Weald: Kemsing, Sevenoaks, Kent.
Dorset coast: Swanage, Dorset.
Quantock Hills: Crowscombe, Taunton, Somerset.
North Devon coast: Instow, Bideford, Devon.
Snowdonia: Bryn Gwynant, Nant Gwynant, Caernarvonshire; Lledr House, Dolwyddelan, Caernarvonshire.
Isle of Man: Bradda Head, Port Erin, Isle of Man.

At each hostel there is a workroom, blackboard, and reference collection of books and maps. By arrangement, workrooms can be used during the period 10 a.m. to 5 p.m. when the hostel is normally closed.

(g) *The Geographical Association.* 343 Fulwood Road, Sheffield 10.

The Association maintains a list of camp sites and addresses of possible accommodation for field-work.

EQUIPMENT FOR FIELD-WORK

Maps

Copies of relevant 1, 2½ and 6 in. O.S. sheets, as well as Geological Maps, are obtainable from the Ordnance Survey. See the map section of this appendix.

Soil testing

Augers are on sale at J. H. Steward Ltd., Scientific and Precision Instruments, 406 The Strand, W.C. 2, and can be made to specification by Cornelius Whitehouse and Son Ltd., Cannock Edge Tool Works, Cannock, Staffs.

B.D.H. Universal soil testing indicator is supplied by British Drug Houses Ltd., and can be obtained from most chemists.

Geological hammers

Write to Gregory, Bottley and Co., 30 Old Church Street, Chelsea, S.W. 3; J. H. Steward Ltd. (address above); The Geological Laboratories, 168 Moss Lane East, Manchester 15; or Charles Frank Ltd. (address in the following paragraph). Also many local suppliers, e.g. Scout shops.

Surveying instruments

Ask for the catalogues of:

A. Clarkson and Co. Ltd., 338 High Holborn, W.C. 1 (levels, theodolites, etc., may be *hired*).

Charles Frank Ltd., 145 Queen Street, Glasgow, C. 1.

George Philip and Son Ltd., Educational Department, Victoria Road, N.W. 10.

J. H. Steward Ltd., 406 The Strand, W.C. 2.

RESEARCH PROJECTS AND EXPEDITIONS

Bio-probe, 7 Kingsgate, Red Lion Square, W.C. 1.

'Bio-probe' is a charitable organisation which aims to provide facilities for education and training in the field sciences, as well as advice, help with or the actual sponsorship of research expeditions both in Britain and overseas. These facilities are intended for use by Universities, colleges, learned societies and schools. Camping gear, trucks, and various items of field equipment are available for hire. Among the early projects backed by Bio-Probe was a sixth-form geographical, ethnological and sociological survey of a Moroccan oasis.

Apply to the General Secretary for more detailed information.

APPENDIX E: MAKING ARRANGE-
MENTS FOR FOREIGN TRAVEL

1. *Advisory services*

(a) *The Central Bureau for Educational Visits and Exchanges.* 55 A Duke Street, Grosvenor Square, W. 1.

This is an educational advisory service maintained by grants from the Ministry of Education which will help with advice and suggest contacts. Members are strongly advised to consult the Central Bureau about individual Travel Agencies.

(b) *The Joint Four International Sub-Committee.* Gordon House, 29 Gordon Square, W.C. 1.

Through the World Confederation of Organisations of the Teaching Profession (W.C.O.T.P.) and the Fédération Internationale des Professeurs de L'Enseignement Secondaire Officiel (F.I.P.E.S.O.). The Sub-Committee works closely with Teachers' Organisations abroad and can thus help with advice and suggest contacts. Ask for N.U.T./Joint Four pamphlet 'School Journeys Abroad'.

2. *School Journey Insurance*

This should include indemnity against accident and illness expenses, and liability at law.

The A.M.A. has a special School Journey Insurance Scheme with the Commercial Union Insurance Group, Teachers' Department, P.O. Box 323, 40 City Road, E.C. 1. A suggested indemnification form which parents might be asked to sign is contained in the Association leaflet 'Accident to Pupils'.

3. *Travel bookings*

(a) *By railway*

Enquiries regarding reduced fares for group travel to the continent via London should be made to: The Continental Superintendent's Office, Special Traffic Section, British Rail (Southern Region), Victoria Station, S.W. 1.

British Railways and most European companies offer reductions, but masters should realise that concessions may not be available at week-ends during peak travelling periods.

For travel through other ports in England and Wales contact the Local Passenger Traffic Superintendent, British Railways.

(b) *For sea passages*

Booking Offices:

1. *Cross-Channel.* Dover, Folkestone, Newhaven and Southampton. For address see above under 3 (a). For Harwich write to the Continental Traffic Manager, Harwich House, Bishopsgate E. C. 2.

386

2. *North Sea routes* (via Hull, Goole, Newcastle and Harwich, as well as London). The Bergen Line, 21–24 Cockspur Street, S.W. 1; Ellerman's Wilson Line, Commercial Road, Hull; Fred Olsen Line, 33 Bury Street, E.C. 3, and Main Square, Central Station, Newcastle upon Tyne; Swedish Lloyd, c/o The Swedish Travel Bureau, 7–8 Conduit Street, Regent Street, W. 1.

3. *The Highlands and Western Isles.* David Macbrayne Ltd., Clyde House, 44 Robertson Street, Glasgow, C. 2.

4. *Irish Sea Routes* (Stranraer, Heysham, Liverpool, Holyhead and Fishguard). The British Rail Booking Offices.

4. *Other useful addresses*

An Oige (Irish Youth Hostel Association), 39 Mountjoy Square South, Dublin.

Austrian State Tourist Department, and Austrian Federal Railway, 219 Regent Street, W. 1.

Belgian State Marine Railway and Tourist Offices, 167 Regent Street, W. 1.

Bergen Line, 21–24 Cockspur Street, S.W. 1.

The British Travel and Holidays Association, 64–65 St James's Street, S.W. 1.

Czechoslovakia: c/o Czechoslovak Embassy, 6 Kensington Place Gardens, W. 2.

Danish National Travel Association, 2/3 Conduit Street, W. 1.

Danish Embassy, Press and Cultural Dept., 29 Pont Street, S.W. 1. Will supply a booklet entitled *Life in Denmark—the Land and People*.

Danish Tourist Bureau, Denmark House, 71 Piccadilly, W. 1.

Finnish Embassy, 66 Chester Square, S.W. 1.

France, Comité d'Acceuil des Elèves des Ecoles Publiques en Voyagées d'Etudes, Ministre de L'Education Nationale, 110 Rue de Grenelle, Paris VIIᵉ.

French Government Tourist Office, 66 Haymarket, S.W. 1. *and* 178 Piccadilly, W. 1.

French Railways, Ltd., 179 Piccadilly, W. 1.

Italian State Tourist Office, 201 Regent Street, W. 1.

Netherlands National Tourist Office, 38 Hyde Park Gate, S.W. 7.

Norwegian National Tourist Office, 20 Pall Mall, S.W. 1.

Portugal, Casa de Portugal, 20 Regent Street, W. 1.

Scottish Youth Hostels Association, 7 Bruntsfield Crescent, Edinburgh 10.

Spanish Tourist Office, 70 Jermyn Street, S.W. 1.

Swedish Travel Bureau, 7–8 Conduit Street, W. 1.

Swedish National Travel Association, 52 Conduit Street, W. 1.

Swiss National Tourist Office and Railways, 458 Strand, Trafalgar Square, W.C. 2.

West German Tourist Information Bureau, 61 Conduit Street, W. 1.

Youth Hostel Association of Northern Ireland, 28 Bedford Street, Belfast.

Y.H.A. Travel Services, 29 John Adam Street, W.C. 2—for information on hostelling in continental countries.

Yugoslav National Tourist Office, 143 Regent Street, W. 1.

APPENDIX F: ORGANISATIONS OF
INTEREST TO THE GEOGRAPHY
MASTER

1. *Major societies*

Royal Geographical Society

Kensington Gore, S.W. 7.

Publishes *The Geographical Journal*, free to members. Facilities include the use of the library, map room and museum at headquarters, as well as the loan of slides and expedition equipment.

Geographical Association

343 Fulwood Road, Sheffield 10.

Publications include the quarterly journal *Geography*, and a considerable number of booklets. Members are eligible to attend various conferences and summer schools, as well as making use of the library (by post or in person). Standing and Section committees deal with enquiries, give advice, and are responsible for specialised aspects of the subject. There are also local branches of the Association. For details, apply to the Assistant Secretary.

Institute of British Geographers

Hon. Sec. Prof. A. E. Smailes, Queen Mary College, Mile End Road, E.1.

The objects are the study, discussion and advancement of Geography. Proceedings are published.

Royal Scottish Geographical Society

Synod Hall, Castle Terrace, Edinburgh 1.

The Scottish Geographical Magazine is sent to members, and there is a large lending library.

The Geographical Society of Ireland

19 Dawson Street, Dublin.

2. *Allied organisations*

Association of Agriculture

36 Victoria Street, S.W. 1.

Offers the farm study scheme to schools, advice on agriculture in education, and residential courses.

British Association for Advancement of Science

18 Adam Street, Adelphi, W.C. 2.

The main function is the annual meeting (early September). Section E is devoted to papers read by geographers.

British Society for International Understanding

Benjamin Franklin House, 36 Craven Street, W.C. 2.

Issues surveys devoted to different parts of the world and international topics. There is also a lecture service.

British Ship Adoption Society

H.Q.S. Wellington, Victoria Embankment, W.C. 2.

The Society will link schools with ships sailing to different parts of the world. A news sheet is sent to member organisations.

Central Office of Information (C.O.I.)

Hercules Road, Westminster Bridge Road, S.E. 1.

A government department which maintains a library of photographs and other illustrative material of Britain, the British way of life, and U.K. dependencies. Prints are for purchase. Photo-posters and picture sets of the same material are available on loan from the Circulation Section of the Central Office, or its branches in Cardiff, Bristol, Birmingham, Nottingham, Manchester, Leeds and Newcastle upon Tyne.

Commonwealth Institute

Kensington High Street, W. 8.

Offer a variety of services (set out in leaflet no. 1) to assist the classroom study of the Commonwealth. These include the provision of study kits, publications, projected material of all kinds, lectures, conferences and a permanent schools advice desk. In the newly built Institute there are Exhibition Galleries and a cinema.

Council for Education in World Citizenship

The Secretary, C.E.W.C., 93 Albert Embankment, S.E. 1.

C.E.W.C. is a national organisation of the United Nations Association. Among its services to schools is the provision of material on current problems, use of a library of photographic exhibits, and participation in conferences and lectures.

Field Studies Council

The Publicity Secretary, Ravensmead, Keston, Kent.

The council publishes an annual journal *Field Studies*, and maintains nine residential field centres. General enquiries should be sent to the above address.

Geologists' Association

The General Secretary: F. H. Moore, Esq., 278 Fir Tree Road, Epsom Downs, Surrey.

Publishes its proceedings and monthly circulars. Local groups are affiliated to the Association. Activities include field meetings.

Geological Society of London

Burlington House, Piccadilly, W. 1.
Among its scientific publications is the quarterly journal. There is also a large library.

International African Institute

St Dunstan's Chambers, 10–11 Fetter Lane, W.C. 4.
Two quarterly publications: *Africa* and *African Abstracts*.

Royal Anthropological Institute

21 Bedford Square, W.C. 1.
Issues a journal, and a monthly illustrated record called *Man*. There is also a large postal library.

Royal Commonwealth Society

Northumberland Avenue, W.C. 2.
At the headquarters of the Society there is an extensive library and Information Bureau. There are also a number of local branches.

Royal Institute of International Affairs

Chatham House, 10 St James's Square, S.W. 1.
The Institute publishes monthly, quarterly, and annual reviews.

Royal Meteorological Society

49 Cromwell Road, S.W. 7.
Issues the magazine *Weather* and a quarterly journal. There is a postal library, and collections of photographs and slides. Vacation courses are organised in conjunction with the Field Studies Council.

The United Nations Association

25 Charles Street, W. 1.

APPENDIX G: ADDRESSES OF BOOK PUBLISHERS

Allen and Unwin, 40 Museum Street, W.C. 1.
Allman and Son, 50 Grafton Way, W. 1.
Arnold, Edward, 41 Maddox Street, W. 1.
Athlone Press, 2 Gower Street, W.C. 1.
Bartholomew and Son, 12 Duncan Street, Edinburgh 9.
Batchworth Press, Drury House, Russell Street, W.C. 2.
Batsford, 4 Fitzhardinge Street, Portman Square, W. 1.
Bell and Sons, 6 Portugal Street, W.C. 2.
Benn, Ernest, 154 Fleet Street, E.C. 4.
Black, A. and C., 4 Soho Square, W. 1.
Blackie, Bishopbriggs, Glasgow.
Blackwell, Basil, 49 Broad Street, Oxford.
Bodley Head, 10 Earlham Street, Cambridge Circus, W.C. 2.
Butterworth, 88 Kingsway, W.C. 2.
Cambridge University Press, 200 Euston Road, N.W. 1.
Cape, Jonathan, 30 Bedford Square, W.C. 1.
Cassell and Co., 35 Red Lion Square, W.C. 1.
Chambers, W. and R., 11 Thistle Street, Edinburgh.
Chapman and Hall, 11 New Fetter Lane, E.C. 4.
Chatto and Windus, 40 William IV Street, W.C. 2.
Cleaver-Hume, 4 Little Essex Street, W.C. 2.
Collins, 144 Cathedral Street, Glasgow, C. 4.
Constable and Co., 12 Orange Street, W.C. 2.
Cory, Adams and Mackay, 39 Sloane Street, S.W. 1.
Cresset Press, 11 Fitzroy Square, W. 1.
Dalesman Publications, Clapham, via Lancaster.
Dent, J. M., 10 Bedford Street, W.C. 2.
Duckworth and Co., 3 Henrietta Street, W.C. 2.
Educational Supply Association, Publishing Division, 233 Shaftesbury Avenue, W.C. 2.
Elek Books, 14 Great James Street, W.C. 1.
English Universities Press, St Paul's House, Warwick Lane, E.C. 4.
Evans Bros., Montague House, Russell Square, W.C. 1.
Eyre and Spottiswoode, 167 Fleet Street, E.C. 4.
Faber and Faber, 24 Russell Square, W.C. 1.
Gill, George, 67 Chandos Place, W.C. 2.
Ginn and Co., 18 Bedford Row, W.C. 1.
Gollancz, Victor, 14 Henrietta Street, W.C. 2.
Hachette, 127 Regent Street, W. 1.
Hale, Robert, 63 Old Brompton Road, S.W. 7.
Harrap, George, 182 High Holborn, W.C. 1.
Heinemann, William, 15–16 Queen Street, Mayfair, W. 1.

Her Majesty's Stationery Office, Atlantic House, Holborn Viaduct, E.C. 1.
Hodder and Stoughton, St Paul's House, Warwick Square, E.C. 4.
Hollis and Carter, 10 Earlham Street, W.C. 2.
Hulton Educational, 55/59 Saffron Hill, E.C. 1.
Hutchinson, 178–202 Great Portland Street, W. 1.
Johnston, W. and A. K., and Bacon, G. W., Edina Works, Easter Road, Edinburgh 7.
Liverpool University Press, 123 Grove Street, Liverpool 7.
Longmans, Green and Co. Ltd., 48 Grosvenor Street, W. 1.
Lutterworth Press, 4 Bouverie Street, E.C. 4.
Macdonald and Evans, 8 John Street, W.C. 1.
Macmillan and Co., 4 Little Essex Street, W.C. 2.
McGraw Hill, 3 Choppenhangers Road, Maidenhead, Berks.
Meiklejohn and Son, *see* Oliver and Boyd.
Methuen, 11 New Fetter Lane, E.C. 4.
Muller, Frederick, 110 Fleet Street, E.C. 4.
Murray, John, 50 Albemarle Street, W. 1.
Nelson, Thomas, 36 Park Street, W. 1.
Odhams Press, 93 Long Acre, W.C. 2.
Oldbourne Press, 1–5 Portpool Lane, Grays Inn Road, E.C. 1.
Oliver and Boyd, 14 High Street, Edinburgh 1.
Oxford University Press, Ely House, 37 Dover Street, W. 1.
Parrish, 1–5 Portpool Lane, E.C. 1.
Penguin Books, Harmondsworth, Middlesex.
Pergamon Press, Headington Hill Hall, Oxford.
Philip, George, and Son, 98 Victoria Road, N.W. 10.
Phoenix House, 10–13 Bedford Street, Strand, W.C. 2.
Pitman, Sir Isaac, 39–41 Parker Street, W.C. 2.
Prentice-Hall, 28 Welbeck Street, W. 1.
Rivingtons, Montague House, Russell Square, W.C. 1.
Routledge and Kegan Paul, 68–74 Carter Lane, E.C. 4.
Schofield and Sims, 35 St Johns Road, Huddersfield.
Secker and Warburg, 14 Carlisle Street, W. 1.
Staples Press, 9 Grape Street, W.C. 2.
Thames and Hudson, 30 Bloomsbury Street, W.C. 1.
University of London Press, St Paul's House, Warwick Square, E.C. 4.
University Tutorial Press, 7 Queen Anne Terrace, Cambridge.
Van Nostrand, 358 Kensington High Street, W. 14.
Ward Lock, 116 Baker Street, W. 1.
Warne, Frederick, 1 Bedford Court, Bedford Street, W.C. 2.
Watts and Co., 39 Parker Street, W.C. 2.
Weidenfeld and Nicholson, 20 New Bond Street, W. 1.
Wheaton, A., and Co., 143 Fore Street, Exeter.
Williams and Norgate, Bouverie House, Fleet Street, E.C. 4.

INDEX

393